EVALUATING FAMI...

MODERN APPLICATIONS OF SOCIAL WORK

An Aldine de Gruyter Series of Texts and Monographs

SERIES EDITOR

James K. Whittaker

Paul Adams and Kristine E. Nelson (eds.), **Reinventing Human Services: Community and Family Centered Practice**

Ralph E. Anderson and Irl Carter, **Human Behavior in the Social Environment: A Social Systems Approach** (fourth edition)

Richard P. Barth, Mark Courtney, Jill Duerr Berrick, and Vicky Albert, **From Child Abuse to Permanency Planning: Child Welfare Services Pathways and Placements**

Kathleen Ell and Helen Northen, **Families and Health Care: Psychosocial Practice**

Marian Fatout, **Models for Change in Social Group Work**

Mark W. Fraser, Peter J. Pecora, and David A. Haapala, **Families in Crisis: The Impact of Intensive Family Preservation Services**

James Garbarino, **Children and Families in the Social Environment** (second edition)

James Garbarino, and Associates, **Special Children—Special Risks: The Maltreatment of Children with Disabilities**

James Garbarino, and Associates, **Troubled Youth, Troubled Families: Understanding Families At-Risk for Adolescent Maltreatment**

Roberta R. Greene, **Social Work with the Aged and Their Families**

Roberta R. Greene, **Human Behavior Theory: A Diversity Framework**

Roberta R. Greene and Paul H. Ephross, **Human Behavior Theory and Social Work Practice**

André Ivanoff, Betty J. Blythe, and Tony Tripodi, **Involuntary Clients in Social Work Practice: A Research-Based Approach**

Paul K. H. Kim (ed.), **Serving the Elderly: Skills for Practice**

Jill Kinney, David A. Haapala, and Charlotte Booth, **Keeping Families Together: The Homebuilders Model**

Robert M. Moroney, **Social Policy and Social Work: Critical Essays on the Welfare State**

Peter J. Pecora, Mark W. Fraser, Kristine Nelson, Jacqueline McCroskey, and William Meezan, **Evaluating Family-Based Services**

Peter J. Pecora, James K. Whittaker, Anthony N. Maluccio, Richard P. Barth, and Robert D. Plotnick, **The Child Welfare Challenge: Policy, Practice, and Research**

John R. Schuerman, Tina L. Rzepnicki, and Julia H. Littell, **Putting Families First: An Experiment in Family Preservation**

Madeline R. Stoner, **The Civil Rights of Homeless People: Law, Social Policy, and Social Work Practice**

Albert E. Trieschman, James K. Whittaker, and Larry K. Brendtro, **The Other 23 Hours: Child-Care Work with Emotionally Disturbed Children in a Therapeutic Milieu**

Harry H. Vorrath and Larry K. Brendtro, **Positive Peer Culture (Second Edition)**

Betsy S. Vourlekis and Roberta R. Greene (eds). **Social Work Case Management**

James K. Whittaker, and Associates, **Reaching High-Risk Families: Intensive Family Preservation in Human Services**

EVALUATING FAMILY-BASED SERVICES

Peter J. Pecora, Mark W. Fraser,
Kristine E. Nelson, Jacquelyn McCroskey,
and William Meezan

ALDINE DE GRUYTER
New York

About the Authors

Peter J. Pecora is Manager of Research, The Casey Family Program, and Associate Professor, School of Social Work, University of Washington.

Mark W. Fraser is John A. Tate Professor for Children in Need, School of Social Work, University of North Carolina at Chapel Hill.

Kristine E. Nelson is Professor, Graduate School of Social Work, Portland State University.

Jacquelyn McCroskey is Associate Professor and Chair of the Family and Children's Concentration, School of Social Work, University of Southern California.

William Meezan is Professor, School of Social Work, and Director of the Doctoral Program, University of Southern California.

Copyright © 1995 Walter de Gruyter, Inc., New York

ALDINE DE GRUYTER
A division of Walter de Gruyter, Inc.
200 Saw Mill River Road
Hawthorne, New York 10532

This publication is printed on acid-free paper ∞

Library of Congress Cataloging-in-Publication Data

Evaluating family-based services / Peter J. Pecora . . . [et al.].
    p.   cm. — (Modern applications of social work)
   Includes bibliographical references and index.
   ISBN 0-202-36093-8 (cloth : acid-free paper). — ISBN 0-202-36094-6
(paper : acid-free paper)
    1. Family services—United States—Evaluation. 2. Family social work—
United States—Evaluation. I. Pecora, Peter J. II. Series.
HV699.E84   1995
362.82'8'0684—dc20   94-49161
                                                               CIP

Manufactured in the United States of America

10 9 8 7 6 5 4 3 2 1

Contents

Preface   *ix*
Acknowledgments   *xi*
Introduction   *xiii*

1   EVALUATING FAMILY-BASED SERVICES:
    CHALLENGES AND TASKS   1

        Critical FBS Implementation Challenges   7
        Program Evaluation Challenges and Tasks:
            An Overview   9
        Conclusion   15
        Notes   16

    Appendix to Chapter 1

    EVALUATING CHANGES IN SYSTEMS
        Charles L. Usher   17

2   DESIGNING FAMILY-BASED SERVICE
    PROGRAM EVALUATIONS   23

        Evaluation Designs   30
        Conclusion: Control and Variation   41
        Notes   42

3   SAMPLING CHILDREN AND FAMILIES   45

        Targeting FBS   46
        Sampling   51
        Sample Size   54
        Protections in the Research Process   57
        Conclusion   64
        Note   64

4   ASSESSING SERVICES AND INTERVENTIONS   65

    Approaches to Studying Interventions   66
    Quality Assurance and Quality Improvement   81
    Assessing Worker Performance   84
    Conclusion   85

5   ASSESSING FAMILY FUNCTIONING   91

    Outcome Measurement   92
    Building Family Assessments to Meet Both
        Clinical and Evaluation Purposes   94
    Assessment for Evaluating Purposes   96
    Domains of Family Functioning   98
    Selected Instruments   99
    Conclusion   113
    Notes   114

6   ASSESSING CHILD FUNCTIONING   117

    Assessment for Service Planning
        and Evaluation   119
    Domains of Child Assessment   130
    Conclusion   136

7   ASSESSING PARENT FUNCTIONING AND
    SOCIAL SUPPORT   139

    Parenting Instruments   145
    Parent Social Support   152
    Selected Measures of Social Support   155
    Conclusion   161
    Notes   162

8   PLACEMENT PREVENTION   163

    Issues in Using Child or Family
        Placement Rates   163
    Ways of Using Placement Rates   174
    Conclusion   177
    Notes   177

9   MEASURING PROGRAM EFFICIENCY   179

        Cost-Effectiveness Measurement   181
        Benefit-Cost Analysis   181
        Conclusion   190
        Notes   190

10 CONSTRUCTIVIST RESEARCH:
    A QUALITATIVE APPROACH
        Mary K. Rodwell   191

        Expectations for the Constructivist
            Inquiry Process   195
        Principles of Constructivist Evaluation   200
        When and Where to Undertake Alternative
            Forms of Evaluation   201
        Overview of Phases of an Emergent
            Evaluation Method   202
        Researcher as Instrument   203
        Data Collection Techniques   204
        Data Management   205
        Special Challenges of Qualitative and
            Constructivist Research   211
        Conclusion   213
        Notes   213

11 THE MANAGEMENT AND IMPACT OF
    FAMILY-BASED SERVICES EVALUATIONS:
    DOING RESEARCH IN THE REAL WORLD   215

        Implementation Issues   216
        Impact of Research   229
        Conditions Necessary for Successful
            Implementation   232

    Appendix to Chapter 11

    A SAMPLE RESEARCH PROPOSAL   235

12   ANALYZING FINDINGS AND
     WRITING REPORTS   241

        The Data Analysis Plan   242
        Analyzing the Data   247
        The Research Report   254
        Conclusion   258

13   SOCIAL POLICY AND EVALUATION:
     AN EVOLVING SYMBIOSIS
        Charles Gershenson   261

        Evaluation and Policy   261
        Policy Process and Evaluation   265
        Limitations in the Evaluation Approach
           for Policy   266
        Are Evaluation Findings Meaningful?   269
        Framing Evaluation Recommendations   270
        Time Frames and Lags   271
        Evaluation and Child Welfare Legislation   273
        Conclusion   274

     AFTERWORD   277

     REFERENCES   279

     INDEX   308

Preface

The development of hundreds of family-based service (FBS) programs across the country at a time of increasingly scarce human service resources makes evaluation imperative. The purpose of this book is to help administrators, practitioners, and evaluators balance clarity, precision, rigor, usefulness, and sensitivity to client needs and diversity in evaluating FBS programs.

This book assumes a basic familiarity with research methods and program evaluation in order to devote attention to the challenges encountered in conducting research in this program area. Many basic research and evaluation concepts, therefore, will not be addressed in detail. Readers are instead referred to a number of additional resources for more information. However, the major steps and issues that are central to conducting a successful FBS evaluation are described. Our goal is to provide a practical, realistic discussion of the difficult issues that must be addressed in the evaluation of FBS programs.

Reviewers of an early draft of this book emphasized that while there are many similarities in population characteristics among child welfare, juvenile justice, mental health, and other areas that employ FBS, there are also important differences. The service delivery context for each of these systems varies. Thus, while some examples from different systems are cited, the major context for the book is public and voluntary child welfare services.

All clients deserve the best services possible. Well-designed evaluation studies can help FBS agencies refine intervention technology, making it more effective. Anyone who attempts evaluation in this area must recognize that the families being served by FBS programs, while vulnerable to many social problems, have strengths and resources upon which to draw. With this in mind, the fact that the families being served are the ultimate beneficiaries of the research effort provides extra incentive to conduct rigorous evaluation studies.

Peter J. Pecora, Mark W. Fraser,
Kristine E. Nelson, Jacquelyn McCroskey,
and William Meezan

Acknowledgments

In completing this book we are deeply grateful for helpful comments and suggestions from our colleagues who are in the midst of evaluating family-based services programs. In particular Marianne Berry, Sally Davis, Dean Fixen, Ray Kirk, Robert Plotnick, Sonya Schoenwald, Lynn Usher, Kathleen Wells and James Whittaker each reviewed selected chapters. Teresa Patterson, Merrily Wolf, and Lila Hurwitz helped edit and format numerous drafts.

Two of the senior editors at Aldine, Richard Koffler, executive editor, and Arlene Perazzini, managing editor, deserve special recognition for their consultation and patience. We appreciate the support of our deans and agency administrators: Frank Baskind, Dick Edwards, Nancy Hooyman, Ruth Massinga, Rino Patti, James Traglia, and James Ward. This book is dedicated to the families who use family-based services, to the staff members who work with them, and to our own families who provide us with encouragement and support in our work.

Introduction

Reform of the policies and systems that provide services to families and children is underway throughout the nation. Public agencies, not-for-profit agencies, and grass roots organizations are developing new service approaches, integrating services across traditionally separate domains, and collaborating with new partners to demonstrate the potential of reform and to better serve families. While the terminology differs by area—in education the watchword is "restructuring," in health and mental health care "managed care," in social services "family based services"—the underlying themes of these reform efforts are remarkably similar: meeting changing family needs, maximizing limited resources, and increasing effectiveness. This book focuses on the third theme: demonstrating the effectiveness of service reform efforts across a broad array of family-based services.

A variety of social services that focus on strengthening families to prevent out-of-home placement of children have emerged in the fields of child welfare, mental health, and juvenile justice. In the 1950s and 1960s, early forerunners of these services were developed as programs to treat the "multi-problem family."[1] Since that time, these placement prevention services have been described as "family-based services," "home-based services," "services to children in their own homes," and "family preservation services." While program design and specific interventions differ, most of the programs fitting the broader name of family-based services share some or all of the following characteristics:

- A primary worker or case manager establishes and maintains a supportive, empowering relationship with the family.
- A wide variety of helping options are used (e.g., "concrete" forms of supportive services such as food and transportation may be provided along with clinical services).
- Caseloads of two to twelve families are maintained.
- One or more associates serve as team members or provide backup for the primary worker.
- Workers (or their backup person) are available twenty-four hours a day for crisis calls or emergencies.

- The home is the primary service setting, and maximum utilization is made of natural helping resources, including the family, the extended family, the neighborhood, and the community.
- The parents remain in charge of and responsible for their family as the primary caregivers, nurturers, and educators.
- Services are time-limited, usually one to four months (Bryce & Lloyd, 1981).

RATIONALE FOR FAMILY-BASED SERVICES

Historical Overview

Family-based services arose in various service systems for somewhat different reasons. The fields of child mental health, juvenile justice, and child welfare were criticized during the 1960s and 1970s from a number of perspectives. In child welfare, FBS emerged out of concern that traditional services were not meeting the needs of children and their families in the United States. In mental health there was concern that services to some children were not adequate to meet their needs and that use of restrictive treatment systems might not actually be necessary. In juvenile justice there has been a continuous emphasis on community-based treatment despite the use of "just desserts" models in some states. Across all three service areas, it was thought that some children were placed in foster care, juvenile justice facilities, or residential treatment centers who could have remained at home or in less restrictive settings. Children in substitute care usually lacked clearly specified case plans. In foster care this resulted in unnecessarily long placements, "drift" from one place to another, and no sense of permanence for many children (Gruber, 1973; Maas & Engler, 1959).

Parental involvement and visitation were not encouraged (Fanshel & Shinn, 1978). The child welfare settings, termination procedures, and adoption practices constrained the use of adoption as a realistic case goal. Furthermore, federal funding policies encouraged maintenance of foster care placements and did not adequately fund preventive or restorative family services. Finally, most state agencies did not have adequate management information systems in place; consequently program administrators did not know how many children were currently placed in substitute care, the average lengths of placement, or other essential planning information (see Knitzer, Allen, & McGowan, 1978; National Commission on Children, 1991).

Exposés of the shortcomings of child welfare services, and of foster care in particular, were written and widely publicized by both child welfare experts and investigative reporters.[2] In addition, the growing incidence and costs of out-of-home care, concern about possible harmful effects of substitute care, the discovery of "foster care drift," and the trend toward deinstitutionalization prompted the development of a variety of foster care preventive programs (Compher, 1983; Magazino, 1983; Jones, 1985).

One of the principal assumptions underlying foster care prevention and permanency planning efforts is that, in most cases, a child's development and emotional well-being are best ensured through efforts to maintain the child in the home of her or his biological parents or extended family (providing that at least minimal standards of parenting are maintained). Most practitioners and researchers agree with this assumption, but realize that child placement in some situations may be the more beneficial and necessary option.

A number of policy and program innovations have been instituted by federal, state, and local authorities to address critiques of the child welfare system. Most notable among these was the Adoption Assistance and Child Welfare Act of 1980 (P.L. 96–272). This federal law established permanency planning as a guiding philosophy and mandated that a series of reforms be implemented in state child welfare agencies in order to qualify for special supplemental Title IV-B federal appropriations under the Social Security Act. P.L. 96–272 also requires that states implement a variety of placement prevention services as part of their strategy to ensure that "reasonable efforts" have been made to strengthen and preserve the family before a child is placed in substitute care (Pine, 1986).

Permanency planning refers, first, to efforts to prevent unnecessary child placement and, second, to efforts to return children from foster care to their biological families or to some other form of permanent placement such as an adoptive home or long-term foster care family with guardianship. This emphasis took hold in child welfare agencies in the late 1970s and 1980s with the leadership of the Oregon Permanency Planning Project and other training efforts (Emlen, Lahti, Downs, McKay, & Downs, 1978). Permanency planning has been helpful in reducing the numbers of children lingering in family foster care (as of 1985, 26% of the children who left substitute care had been there for four months or less; 46% of the children were in placement less than six months (Maximus, 1985, p. III-37)). There is, however, growing concern about a lack of program alternatives for family reunification, foster care reentry, and, more importantly, placement prevention through improving child and family functioning.

Criticism of the child welfare service delivery system has been brought to public attention by the numerous class action suits filed by the American Civil Liberties Union and other advocacy groups. In fact, many would argue that the focus on permanency planning, creating service alternatives, and child stability has not been supported through staff training, supervision, and provision of the necessary resources (Fanshel, 1992). Although the child population in substitute care had fallen from 502,000 in 1977 to 276,000 in 1985, by the end of 1992 it had again risen to 442,000, considered to be a very conservative estimate (Tatara, 1992, p. 1; Tatara, 1993, p. 1). Foster care placements are projected by Gershenson to reach 553,600 by the mid-1990s (850,000 if mental health and juvenile justice placements are included), unless something is done to address the increased flow of children into substitute care and the backlog of children who could benefit from more systematically defined and delivered reunification services (Select Committee on Children, Youth, and Families, 1990, p. 15).

Some of this increase in placements is no doubt due to increased substance abuse among parents. A number of studies have found that various forms of child maltreatment are associated with abuse of alcohol or other drugs (Murphy et al., 1991). There have been large increases in the number of drug-exposed infants coming into foster care. In addition, a volatile economy, increasing rates of teen parenthood, a rise in never-married parents, AIDS, urban poverty, a growing shortage of affordable housing, and significant rates of unemployment have all contributed to the rise in child placement rates (e.g., Testa, 1992).

Some experts believe that state agencies are already better at reducing the number of unnecessary placements. While in many states the percentage of children placed in relation to the number of child protective service cases being reported appears to have decreased (Wald, 1988, p. 34), this may be due to a lack of emergency placement resources. Child advocates, therefore, remain concerned that essential preventive services are not being provided. These advocates maintain that it is possible to identify families with a sufficiently high risk of maltreatment or harm to justify an intensive intervention to prevent further family deterioration or child placement. But these services are not being provided, in part due to ineffectual enforcement of P.L. 96–272, a general lack of funding for preventive services (Forsythe, 1992), and continuing problems of targeting and screening of families most in need of the service. Consequently, many children have been placed outside their homes not once but multiple times in different family, group home, residential treatment, juvenile justice, and psychiatric hospital settings (Fanshel & Shinn, 1978; Rzepnicki, 1987).

New Program Reforms

In response to the rising number of child placements, some juvenile court judges are ordering local departments of social services to provide housing assistance or FBS under the "reasonable efforts" mandate of P.L. 96–272 (personal communication, Judge Richard Fitzgerald, 1991). Furthermore, some states have continued to fund previously developed placement prevention efforts such as homemaker, emergency day care, parent aide, and crisis nursery services. These services have been supplemented recently by a new array of family-based programs that are designed to help families remain together safely. The program reforms promoted by P.L. 96–272, increasing placement rates, and a search for "revenue-neutral" service innovations have all combined to produce an environment supportive of the development of FBS programs. These programs have different names and program characteristics,[3] but provide a viable alternative to out-of-home placement for some children, and help to improve family functioning in specific areas.

According to Farrow (1991), Nelson (1991), Whittaker (1991) and others, family-based services and support programs represent a significant departure from the more traditional categorical services that embrace a child rescue philosophy, that place treatment within a narrowly "person-centered" perspective, and that give little attention to addressing the family's needs in a holistic manner. According to Whittaker (1991, pp. 295–296), these new ideas represent alternative conceptions of human services toward:

1. *Establishing a service continuum*—from preclusive prevention to secure treatment—with expanded capacity for individualized case planning through *flexible* funding and service eligibility.

2. *Promoting competence and meeting basic developmental needs of children and families in "normalized" settings by teaching practical life skills and by providing environmental supports as opposed to uncovering and treating underlying pathology.* Evidence for this trend is apparent in the explosion of educational or life skills approaches (Danish, D'Angell, & Hauer, 1980); by the move away from presumptive labeling and toward more developmentally focused, competence-oriented assessment; and by the move in many fields toward "normalization" of both the location and focus of treatment (Wolfensberger, 1972).

3. *Considering services as family supportive and family strengthening, not as "child saving."* The rapid expansion of crisis-oriented family-support services (Whittaker, Kinney, Tracy, & Booth (1990), the family support movement (Zigler & Black, 1989), and the renewed emphasis on family

involvement in child placement services (Jenson & Whittaker, 1987) all
offer partial evidence of the strength of this idea.

4.   *Reestablishing a person-in-environment perspective in theory, empirical
research, and clinical practice as a foundation for intervention design.* Bronfenbrenner's (1979) ecology of human development, the empirical work
of Garbarino, Schellenbach, Sebes, & Associates (1986) on the environmental correlates of child maltreatment, and the rapid growth of
preventive-remedial intervention designed to enhance social support
(Gottlieb, 1988; Biegel, Farkas, Abell, Goodin, & Friedman, 1988) indicate a return to traditional social work paradigms (Whittaker & Tracy,
1989; Brieland, 1987).

FAMILY-BASED SERVICES PROGRAM MODELS

Overview

Within the broad framework of family-based services, there is wide
variation across the nation in the kind of interventions, duration of
services, size of caseloads, and components of service that characterize
family-centered programs.[4] Perhaps this is inherent in all program innovations, but it is one reason why research findings on FBS programs
have been confusing. Despite a growing body of literature, it is not clear
what these services are and who benefits from them.

There is enormous variation in the service characteristics of these new
programs. The programs themselves are often described using more
specific terms such as *intensive family preservation services, intensive family
services, family support, family-centered, home-based,* and *placement prevention services.* In all of these services the family is not seen as deficient but
as having many strengths and resources (Kagan, Powell, Weissbourd, &
Zigler, 1987). The term *family support* has been used as an umbrella under
which clusters a broad range of family-strengthening programs. While
family-based and family preservation services have both been cited as
family support programs, these programs are distinct from primary prevention and child development–oriented family support programs such
as prenatal care, home-visiting, early childhood education, parent education, home-school-community linkage, child care, and other family-
focused services that tend to provide one type of service (e.g., education, housing, financial assistance, or counseling); work with clients
exclusively in an office, community setting, or classroom; provide service over a long period of time (one year or more); or plan/monitor client
services delivered by other agencies.[5]

Recently, the Child Welfare League of America proposed a trichoto-mized typology of family-centered programs:

1. *Family resource, support, and education services.* These community-based services assist and support adults in their role as parents. Services are available to all families with children and do not impose criteria for participation that might separate or stigmatize certain parents (Child Welfare League of America, 1989, p. 13). We will refer to these as "family support services." Examples are the school- or community-based family resource centers being implemented in states such as Connecticut, Maryland, Kentucky, Minnesota, and Missouri (Farrow, 1991; Kagan & Weissbourd, 1994).

2. *Family-centered services (i.e., family-based services).* These services encompass a range of activities such as case management, counseling/therapy, education, skill building, advocacy, and/or provision of concrete services for families with problems that threaten their stability. As mentioned earlier, the philosophy of these programs differs from the more traditional child welfare services in the role of parents, use of concrete and clinical services, and other areas (Child Welfare League of America, 1989, p. 29).

The more common term is family-based services (FBS), although in some states programs are referred to as "family preservation" services. The majority are currently found in child welfare agencies, although a number have been initiated by mental health centers. FBS programs have recently been started in a number of new service arenas, including juvenile justice, developmental disability, adoption, and foster care re-unification programs. An example of a FBS program with a broad public health and family-centered focus is Hawaii's Healthy Start program, which provides a comprehensive array of health care, counseling, and concrete services to families judged to be at moderate to high risk of child maltreatment (Breakey & Pratt, 1991).[6]

3. *Intensive family-centered crisis services.* These services are designed for families "in crisis," at a time when removal of a child is perceived as imminent, or the return of a child from out-of-home care is being consid-ered. Yet the reality is that this service model is also being applied to chronic family situations, involving child neglect or abuse, that do not involve crisis. These programs often share the same philosophical orien-tation and characteristics as family-centered services, but are delivered with more intensity (including shorter time frames and smaller case-loads), so they are often referred to as *intensive family preservation service* or IFPS programs. Caseloads generally vary between two and six fami-lies per worker. Families are typically seen between six and ten hours

per week, and the time period of intervention is generally between four and twelve weeks.

The emphasis of these services is upon providing intensive counseling, education, skills training, and supportive services to families, with the goal of protecting the child, strengthening and preserving the family, and preventing an unnecessary placement of children (Whittaker, Kinney, Tracy, & Booth, 1990). In some cases, however, the primary case goal is to reunite children with their families (Child Welfare League of America, 1989, pp. 46–47). We will refer to these programs as IFPS—intensive family preservation services, and they include programs such as HOMEBUILDERS™ in Washington, Intensive Family Services in Maryland, and certain types of Families First programs in various states.[7] While these programs may share core features, much diversity in treatment models exists among them.

Target Population for FBS and IFPS

Most often, the target population for both FBS and IFPS programs is families in serious trouble, including families no longer able to cope with problems that threaten family stability, families in which a decision has been made by an authorized public social service agency to place a child outside the home, and families whose children are in temporary out-of-home care. Although a "crisis orientation" may be emphasized by some programs, it must be recognized that many families who are served by these agencies are not in crisis and have been trying to cope with an abusive or neglectful family member, child mental illness, juvenile delinquency, or other problem for some time. Thus, these services may be appropriate for families seen by the child welfare, juvenile justice, or mental health systems, as well as for adoptive or foster families facing potential disruption.[8]

The distinction between the various program categories is not definitive, but the taxonomy does help to clarify some distinguishing features of the three types of programs and to suggest some of the program design questions facing practitioners and administrators in the field. (See Figure I.1 for a sample of programs of each type.) Throughout the remainder of this book, when reviewing the general literature on family-based or family-centered services we will use the term *family-based services* (FBS). When referring specifically to programs that deliver both concrete and clinical services primarily in the home on an intensive basis, we will use the term *intensive family preservation services* (IFPS).

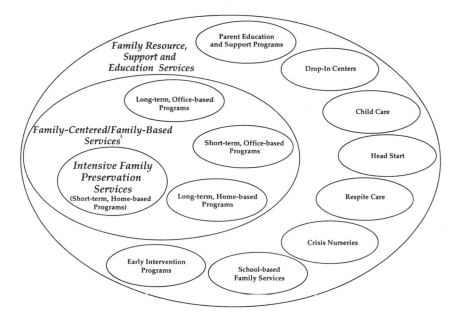

Figure I.1.   A typology of family-centered service programs.

PROGRAM LIMITATIONS AND POLICY PITFALLS NEED TO BE RECOGNIZED

While family-based services represent a significant step in the evolution of social services, and some program results have been positive, FBS programs can not replace other types of child and family services or substitute for broader societal and service system reforms (Halpern, 1990). While a number of case situations can be addressed by FBS programs alone, some families will always be in need of one or more other child welfare services such as day treatment, family foster care, residential treatment, or adoption; and most will need other preventive or supportive services such as income support, child care, parent education, substance abuse treatment, or job training. (See Figure I.2.)

Studies of FBS and other programs have repeatedly shown that many families need assistance with housing, food, medical care, employment, and basic financial support. Most of the families served by public systems live in communities with few resources to help parents or support healthy child development. In addition, many families experience other problems, such as ineffective communication among family members,

Figure I.2. An array of child and family supports.

poor self-esteem, serious mental illness, lack of social support, and pronounced deficits in parenting or basic social skills. Many of these derive from larger societal problems and/or significant psychological or social impairment (Polansky et al., 1981; Polansky, Gaudin, & Kilpatrick, 1992). As with other social service interventions such as home-visiting (Weiss, 1993), there is a danger that FBS will be oversold as a cure-all for families because of its emphasis upon family strengthening and early reports of cost-effectiveness.

Therein lies one of the major challenges of the family preservation and support movement—to assure that public assistance, housing, health care, and other services that are essential to child and family well-being are not cut to fund FBS, and that they are available to FBS consumers. While significant foster care and residential treatment program savings may be realized for some children, FBS programs are just one of an array of services that must be available to support families throughout the life cycle. Without a broader network of family supports available in the larger society and local community, families may not be able to maintain the gains made during FBS, and children may be vulnerable to continued abuse or neglect. (Some recent critiques of FBS have overlooked the role that concrete services in the form of income assistance, food, and housing provision have played in many FBS programs from their inception.) Some families, however, need services on a long-term basis and are not well served by a short period of intensive work (Maluccio, 1991). Other families need high-quality foster care to help them through a difficult period or until the child reaches adulthood (Fanshel, Finch, & Grundy, 1990).

It is incumbent upon evaluators as well as program staff to locate FBS programs within the larger network of services, and to emphasize to policymakers that both the short- and long-term success of these programs is dependent upon the family's ability to access a range of community services and other societal supports. More immediately, an evaluator must consider how the availability of these services will affect the success of the program. While some families may need just FBS, for many families maintenance of gains made in FBS is affected significantly by the availability of continuing services in the community.

CHAPTER OUTLINES

The major purpose of this book is to summarize current knowledge about evaluating FBS programs, while highlighting some of the more useful research strategies and reviewing research instruments that can be used to measure changes in child and family functioning. Many of the chapters will be talking simultaneously about evaluation efforts designed to influence policy and those devoted to determining the *success* of the policy. This book is therefore written for FBS practitioners, administrators, and policymakers, as well as for evaluators. Increasingly, however, the diverse program models in the family support field are being recognized as being closely aligned with FBS. Many of the evaluation issues in this book are germane to both fields and we hope that the material complements the work of Weiss and Jacobs (1988a); Olds, Henderson, Chamberlin, and Tatelbaum (1986); and other evaluation pioneers in family support.

For maximum benefit, readers should have a basic knowledge of research methods and program evaluation. More complex conceptual, methodological, and statistical concepts are summarized in end notes. We are indebted to FBS administrators, therapists, earlier researchers, and evaluation methodologists who have identified many of the challenges and solutions discussed in this volume. Their writings are recognized throughout this book.[9]

In light of the complexity of assessing the impact of FBS, what knowledge and skills does the evaluator need to have besides skills in research? We believe that the primary evaluator must have a substantive background in the program area in addition to technical skills. In other words he or she must understand the program. Otherwise, much staff time will need to be devoted to educating the "evaluation expert" about the fundamental intervention issues, agency environmental complexities, and the particular challenges associated with measuring program outcomes. In Chapter 1 a number of issues and tasks related to evaluating FBS are presented.

Funding and consumer groups want programs to achieve *results*, not merely provide services. However, determining if the program is "successful" poses a number of challenges to evaluators, including one of the most important: selecting an appropriate research design. Some of the most practical, yet rigorous quantitative designs for the evaluation of family-based programs are described in Chapter 2. This chapter also discusses matching evaluation designs to stages of program development; matching evaluation questions and measures to program structure and treatment models; and the importance of interviewing consumers, follow-up procedures, and other design issues.

Sampling is a critical component of the evaluation design because it determines how families and children are selected for participation in evaluation studies. Selection criteria, sampling procedures, and power analysis are discussed in Chapter 3, along with the concept of "risk of imminent placement." Human subjects protection and common institutional requirements, including a sample Informed Consent Form, are also covered.

Because of the plethora of FBS models, one unique aspect of the evaluation of these programs is the assessment of the impact of key elements of service. Some FBS programs emphasize the provision of concrete assistance to families, such as transportation and child care, while others emphasize the reorganization of family systems or structures. In Chapter 4, we discuss methods of partitioning services into their key elements and assessing their impact. Quality assurance and families' use of services before, during, and after receiving FBS are also discussed. These issues are addressed not only because of the fundamental need to understand the intervention, but because the contingencies under which FBS programs operate will likely remain stringent and programs will be required to justify all elements of the service.

In addition to the challenges of developing research designs and sampling approaches, measuring change in ways that are appropriate for different ethnic groups is a developing science. Family-level measures, as distinct from measures of individual parent or child functioning, are defined and described in Chapter 5. A broad range of instruments organized by domains of functioning is examined for their utility in FBS research. In Chapter 6, the assessment of child functioning in the home, school, and community is outlined. The use of multiple perspectives including child, parent, and teacher reports is emphasized.

While it is critical to measure the family and child outcomes, poor parenting practices—contributing to child neglect and abuse—are a major reason that children are removed from their homes. The assessment of a variety of domains of parent functioning including parenting skills, social support, and parent-related problems such as alcohol or drug abuse is summarized in Chapter 7. Some of the scales may be used by FBS workers to assess parental capacities and conditions, and others, completed by parents themselves, may be useful in assessing the impact of services on their attitudes and behaviors.

Across the nation, the primary benchmark for success in most FBS programs has been the prevention of out-of-home placement. Recent studies, including those conducted by each of the authors, have indicated that assessing placement prevention is a complex undertaking. Differing definitions and sources of information about placement (workers, parents, children, and management information systems), the social desirability of placement, and ways of calculating placement prevention rates (depending on data sources and population characteristics) are discussed in Chapter 8. In Chapter 9 two approaches to measuring program efficiency are presented: cost-effectiveness and benefit-cost analysis.

Qualitative research designs offer rich and viable alternative methods for some types of evaluation studies. Very few rigorous ethnographic, grounded theory, or other types of qualitative studies have been conducted on FBS; yet many questions about the various FBS interventions and their effects remain to be addressed. In Chapter 10, Mary K. Rodwell describes ways of using "constructivist" qualitative methods in the evaluation of FBS.

A number of different implementation issues have been problematic for FBS evaluations. These problems and limitations must be resolved in order to produce valid and reliable findings. These include developing procedures for training interviewers, establishing working partnerships with referring and FBS case workers, establishing rapport with families, tracking children after the conclusion of FBS services, and managing the flow of case data. In Chapter 11, we take a frank look at the realities of managing FBS evaluation studies and suggest some strategies for project refinement.

Data analysis and reporting are generally the last and most under-developed aspects of an evaluation project. In Chapter 12, we provide a conceptual framework for data reduction, analysis, and presentation. Report formats are described, along with methods for interpreting the data. Finally, the test of any evaluation study is how the results are used to affect policy, program design, and practice. The concluding chapter, authored by noted child welfare scholar Charles Gershenson, discusses how FBS research data can be used to affect policy development and legislation on the local, state, and federal levels.

NOTES

1.   See Brown (1968), Geismar and Ayers (1958), Geismar and Krisberg (1966), Levine (1964), Overton (1953).

2.   See, for example, Fanshel and Shinn (1978), Gruber (1973), Knitzer et al. (1978), Maas and Engler (1959), Mnookin (1973), Wooden (1976).

3.   See, for example, Bryce and Lloyd (1981), Compher (1983), Kinney, Haapala and Booth (1991), Maybanks and Bryce (1979), Nelson and Landsman (1992).

4.   Portions of this section are adapted from Pecora, Haapala, and Fraser (1991).

5.   For examples of these types of family support programs, see Jones (1985, pp. 27–34), Gomby, Larson, Lewit, & Behrman (1993), Kagan, Powell, Weissbourd, & Zigler (1987), Levine and Beck (1988a, 1988b), Olds et al. (1986), Yale Bush Center in Child Development and Social Policy, and Family Resource Coalition (1983), and Weiss and Jacobs (1988).

6.   For studies of program characteristics and effectiveness of FBS programs see, for example, AuClaire and Schwartz (1986, 1987), Berry (1994), Cabral and Callard (1982), Heying (1985), Hinckley and Ellis (1985), Jones (1985), Jones, Newman, and Shyne (1976), Nelson and Landsman (1992), and Szykula and Fleischman (1985).

7.   For studies of IFPS program dimensions and effectiveness see Feldman (1991b), Haapala and Kinney (1988), Haapala, McDade, and Johnston (1988), Henggeler, Melton, & Smith (1992), Kinney, Haapala, and Booth (1991), Kinney and Haapala (1984), Kinney, Madsen, Fleming, and Haapala (1977), and Yuan, McDonald, Wheeler, Struckman-Johnson, and Rivest (1990).

8.   See Barth (1991), Buchard and Clarke (1990), Dore (1991b), Haapala, McDade, and Johnston (1988b), Hodges, Guterman, Blythe, and Bronson (1989), Walton, Fraser, Lewis, Pecora, & Walton (1993), Whittaker and Maluccio (1988).

9.   The literature applicable to evaluating social service programs, while less developed than the physical sciences, is vast. Important topics not addressed by

this book include the ethical issues encountered in conducting evaluation studies (Chambers, Wedel, & Rodwell, 1992, Schinke, 1981), how program evaluation research can be part of an agency approach to quality improvement (Gabor & Grinnell, 1993, Walton, 1986), survey schedule construction and data collection (Dillman, 1978), interviewing techniques (Dillman, 1978, Frey, 1983), approaches to coding research data, statistical analysis, and a variety of other more specialized topics.

Chapter 1

Evaluating Family-Based Services: Challenges and Tasks

Legislators and agency administrators increasingly require FBS to gather data on program costs and to document the outcomes of services. These requirements reflect increasing emphasis on service accountability and monitoring the utilization of governmental and charitable funds, as well as growing concern about troubled families and their children. While some preliminary studies of FBS are positive, the research findings, particularly those based on more rigorous designs, are mixed. The information gathered thus far by early studies, together with reports from consumers and practitioners, has created a controversial body of evidence about the effectiveness of these service approaches.

Equivocal Evaluation Findings

As illustrated by Tables 1.1 and 1.2, the first program evaluation results, while promising in regard to some outcomes, do not show dramatic differences between control and treatment groups in terms of placement prevention. However, early studies have been challenged by a number of implementation and evaluation problems. Problems in program implementation have included referral, staff training, and lack of community resources. Evaluation problems have included the use of nonexperimental designs, small samples, poor case targeting, and inappropriate assessment measures.[1] More recent studies, designed to address many of these problems, are already under way and initial findings about the potential for FBS programs to improve some aspects of family and child functioning are promising (e.g., Henggeler & Borduin, 1990; McCroskey & Meezan, in press).

Recent meta-analyses of laboratory and clinic-based studies of psychotherapy have also found a lack of dramatic differences between control

1

Table 1.1. Placement Prevention Rates of Selected FBS Evaluation Studies Using Experimental or Quasi-Experimental Designs[a]

Site and source	Service intensity[b] (hours per month)	Placement prevention rates (%)[c]	
		Experimental group	Control or comparison group
California	High[d]	82[d]	83[d]
Unit of analysis: children (Yuan et al., 1990)	(26.8)	(n = 356)	(n = 357)
Families First (Wood et al., 1988)	(not available)	74 (n = 26)	45** (n = 24)
Hennepin County, MN	Low	49	47
Unit of analysis: families (Hennepin County, 1980)[d]	(3.3)	(n = 66)	(n = 72)
children (Nelson, 1984)	Low (3–6)	77 (n = 34)	55 (n = 40)
Illinois (Schuerman et al., 1993, pp. 94, 113)	High overall but with large site variation (median = 23.2)	Probability of placement: .06	Probability of placement: .07
12-month follow-up		.28	.20
Michigan	High (2–3 cases served over a 4– 6 week period)		
Unit of analysis: children (Bergquist, Szwejda, & Pope, 1992)			
3-month follow-up:		92.9	87.6
12-month follow-up:		73.4	64.9**
(Used a matched sample comparison group for the 3-, 6-, and 12-month follow-up study of placement prevention)		(n = 225)	(n = 225)
Nebraska	Medium[e]	96	89
Unit of analysis: families (Rosenberg et al., 1982)	(4–8)	(n = 80)	(n = 73)
New Jersey	Low[f]	76	82
Unit of analysis: families (Willems & DeRubeis, 1981)	(2.1)	(n = 45)	(n = 45)
New Jersey	High	94	83.5*
Unit of analysis: children (Feldman, 1991a)	(27.2 face-to-face hours)	(n = 117)	(n = 97)
6-month follow-up		73.5	50.5**
12-month follow-up		57.3	43.3*

(continued)

Table 1.1. *(Continued)*

Site and source	Service intensity[b] (hours per month)	Placement prevention rates (%)[c]	
		Experimental group	Control or comparison group
New York	Low[g]	72	61***
Unit of analysis: children (Jones et al., 1976)	(6.8 contacts)	(*n* = 662)	(*n* = 329)
5–6-month follow-up		78	60**
5-year follow-up[h]		66	54*
		(*n* = 175)	(*n* = 68)
New York City	Low[i]	96	83***
Unit of analysis: children (Halper & Jones, 1981)	(3–6 hours)	(*n* = 156)	(*n* = 130)
Oregon	Medium (15–25 hours per case)		
Unit of analysis: children (Szykula & Fleischman, 1985)			
Less difficult cases:		92	62**
		(*n* = 13)	(*n* = 13)
More difficult cases		36	55
		(*n* = 11)	(*n* = 11)
South Carolina	Medium	*Arrest rates (no. of Arrests)*	
Unit of analysis: children (Henggeler et al., in press; Henggeler et al., 1992)	(33 hours in 13.4 weeks)	42% (.87)	62% (1.52)*
59 weeks postreferral more difficult cases		*Incarceration rates (no. of weeks)*	
		20% (5.8)	68% (16.2)**
		Rearrest Prevention Rate at 2.4 years postreferral	
		39%	20%
		(*n* = 43)	(*n* = 41)
Utah	High	55.6	14.8[j]
Placement prevention Unit of analysis: children (Fraser et al., 1991)	(18.4)	(*n* = 27)	(*n* = 27)
Family reunification	High	*Family reunification rates at 6 months[k]*	
Unit of analysis: children (Walton et al., 1993)	(3 visits per week)	70.2%	41.5%**
		Reunification rates at 12 months[k]	
		75.4%	49%**
		(*n* = 62)	(*n* = 58)

(continued)

Table 1.1. (*Continued*)

Site and source	Service intensity[b] (hours per month)	Placement prevention rates (%)[c]	
		Experimental group	Control or comparison group
Washington	High	76%	0%[l]
Unit of analysis: children (Kinney & Haapala, 1984; Kinney et al., 1991, p. 54)	(36.8 hours)	(*n* = 25)	(*n* = 5)

$^*p \leq 0.05.$ $^{**}p \leq .01.$ $^{***}p \leq .001.$

[a] *Source:* Adapted from P. J. Pecora (1991a). Family preservation and home-based services: A select literature review. Pp. 23–24 in *Families in crisis: Findings from the family-based intensive treatment project*, edited by M. W. Fraser, P. J. Pecora, and D. A. Haapala. Hawthorne, NY: Aldine de Gruyter.

[b] Service intensity is defined by the number of hours of in-person and telephone/client contact per month: low, 1–7 hours per month; medium, 8–12 hours per month; high, 13 or more hours per month.

[c] The unit of analysis and sample size (*n*) used for calculating placement prevention rates is noted for each study. Data were collected at the point of case termination unless noted in the table or separately.

[d] Placement rates based on an 18-month follow-up.

[e] First-year criteria excluded families with prior foster care placement or prior CPS referrals. Families received, on average, 4 contacts per month, with some families receiving much more service. Placement rates are underestimated due to a variety of factors, including difficulties in system monitoring and no tracking of relative and other privately funded placements (see Rosenberg et al., 1982, Appendix A, pp. 9–11).

[f] The client contact statistic does not include the services provided by the therapists as part of a variety of group activities that were offered (see Magura & DeRubeis, 1980, pp. 41–42). For example, the adolescent group met weekly for approximately 2 hours (Willems & DeRubeis, 1981, pp. 12–13). Thus, for those families participating in one or more group activities, client contact was at least at the medium level and possibly higher.

[g] The client contact figure was calculated using unduplicated family statistics (see Jones et al., 1976, pp. 54–56). Sample included children living at home and in placement at time of intake. Children living with friends or in an adoptive home were counted as being "at home" (Jones et al., 1976, p. 81).

[h] Original sample was reduced from 549 families to 142 families (243 children) by including only those families in the New York sites with at least one "at-risk" child who was at home at the start of the study (Jones, 1985, pp. 46–47).

[i] Families were seen by workers, on average, 2.9 times per month, with 43% of the contacts lasting over one hour (see Halper & Jones, 1981, pp. 97–100).

[j] Children in the comparison group formed through a case overflow design were matched on a variety of characteristics with children from the IFPS treatment group. Follow-up period is 12 months past intake (Pecora, Bartlomé, Magana, & Sperry, 1991, pp. 20–24).

[k] Children were randomly assigned to either the treatment or control group.

[l] A case overflow comparison group was formed for this study, which was designed to prevent psychiatric hospitalization of children.

Table 1.2. Additional FBS Outcome Criteria and Findings from Selected Studies*a*

Days in Placement and Case Closure

• Children in the IFPS treatment group spent significantly fewer days in placement than comparison group children (e.g., AuClaire & Schwartz, 1986, pp. 39–40*b*; Nelson, 1984*b*; Yuan et al., 1990, p. v*b*).

• The likelihood of case closing for the FBS cases was 46% greater than for the control group cases (Littell & Fong, 1992; as cited in Rzepnicki, Schuerman, Littell, Chak, & Lopez, 1994, p. 61*b*).

• There is some evidence that FBS may shorten the placement time of those children served by the program. In one study in Connecticut, more than half of the children placed were home within 12 months compared to the statewide average placement duration of 31 months (Wheeler, Reuter, Struckman-Johnson, & Yuan, 1992, p. 5.10).

Changes in Placement Rate

• In Michigan counties where IFPS programs were established using a "staging approach" where some counties who did not yet have the service were used as comparison sites, out-of-home placement rates grew more slowly in the counties with IFPS than those in nonserved counties. In those counties where IFPS programs were implemented later, placement rates also appeared to slow as a consequence of the service. Considerable costs were saved by the governmental agencies in those counties as a result of the placement trend decrease (Visser, 1991, as cited in Bath and Haapala, 1994).

Restrictiveness of Placement

• Treatment group used a larger proportion of shelter care days compared to other forms of placement (e.g., Yuan et al., 1990*b*)

• Children in the FBS treatment group used "less restrictive" placement options (e.g., Kinney & Haapala, 1984*b*; Willems & DeRubeis, 1981, pp. 16–25*b*).

Further Reports of Child Maltreatment

• Treatment group children (*n*=52) from chronically neglecting families had fewer subsequent reports of child maltreatment compared to control group children (*n*=19) (Littell, Kim, Fong, & Jones, 1992, pp. 8, 16*b*).

Improving Child, Parent, and Family Functioning

• Improvements in child and family functioning were found, with the treatment group being rated as better in several areas compared to the control group (Feldman, 1991a, pp. 30–33*b*). In some studies the differences in improvement found at about 7 months after FBS services began, however, did lessen over time, with few differences reported by parents at a 16-month follow-up (Rzepnicki et al., 1994, pp. 67–68*b*).

• In a quasi-experimental study, ratings by workers and clients indicated improvement in caretaker parenting skills, verbal discipline, knowledge of child care, child's school adjustment, child oppositional or delinquent behavior, and child's oppositional behavior in the home (Spaid et al., 1991, pp. 139–56).

• In the Los Angeles study of two IFPS programs, there were improvements in the following areas of family functioning: parent-child interactions, living conditions of the families, financial conditions of the families, supports available to families and developmental stimulation of children (personal communication, J. McCroskey and W. Meezan, January 4, 1994*b*).

• Parental use of new skills at 6-month follow-up was higher in a recent family reunification study using an experimental design (E=62, C=58) (Walton, 1991, pp. 113–14; Walton et al., 1993*b*).

(continued)

Table 1.2. *(Continued)*

Family Reunification
- Stein, Gambrill, and Wiltse (1978b) emphasized behaviorally specific case planning to achieve more permanent plans for children in family foster care. They found that more experimental group cases were closed (50%) than comparison group cases (29%), and a greater number of experimental group children were returned to their birth families.
- Lahti (1982, p. 558b) found that 66% of the treatment group children either returned home or were adopted, as compared to 45% of the comparison group children, when special efforts were made to provide services to birth families.
- A recent experimental study of IFPS focused on serving children who were in foster care for more than 30 days and who were randomly assigned to receive a 3-month IFPS intervention. These children were reunited more quickly, in higher numbers, and remained in the home for a greater number of days during a 12-month follow-up period than the control group youth (Walton et al., 1993).

Consumer Satisfaction
- Primary caretakers have reported relatively high satisfaction levels with most aspects of the FBS service (e.g., Hayes & Joseph, 1985; Magura & Moses, 1984, p. 103), including studies that involved comparison of the FBS-served parent ratings with those of parents receiving traditional child welfare services (McCroskey & Meezan, 1993b, p. 6, 1993a; Rzepnicki et al., 1994, p. 77b).
- Primary caretakers mentioned as positive the ability of the worker to establish a good rapport with them, as well as the teaching of communication, problem-solving, and chore chart/reward systems (Pecora, Fraser, Bennett, & Haapala, 1991).
- In a recent family reunification study using an experimental design ($E=62$, $C=258$) consumer satisfaction ratings in a number of areas were significantly higher for the experimental group families (Walton, 1991, pp. 106–9b). (Also see Walton et al., 1993.)

Juvenile Delinquency Reduction
- In a quasi-experimental study of a home-based service program, based on Alexander's behavioral systems family therapy (Alexander & Parsons, 1982), the FBS treatment group participants were assigned based on the need to prevent placement or reunify, and high likelihood of recommitting a delinquent offense within one year. Recidivism in juvenile delinquency differed between the FBS and comparison groups (11.1% treatment, 66.7% comparison group**). When the recidivism rates were adjusted for different follow-up periods, the differences were maintained (5%, 25%). (See Gordon et al., 1988, p. 250b.)
- A home-based FBS program using the Multi-Systemic Treatment (MST) model was used as the treatment for 43 youths (an additional 41 youths were in the control group) to reduce rates of institutionalizing young juvenile offenders. At 59 weeks postreferral, youths who received MST had statistically significant lower arrest rates, had an average 73 fewer days of incarceration, and had less self-reported delinquency (Henggeler et al., 1992b).

* $p \leq 0.05$.   ** $p \leq .01$.   *** $p \leq .001$.
[a] Source: Adapted from P. J. Pecora (in press). Assessing the impact of family-based services. In *Research on the child welfare system*, edited by B. Galaway and J. Hudson. Toronto: Thompson Educational Publishing.
[b] An experimental or case overflow research design was used in these studies.

and experimental groups (Weisz, Weiss, & Donenberg, 1992). Across many different fields, evaluation studies appear to suggest that we cannot expect single services to produce large changes in complex social problems, especially when we focus measurement on a narrow set of outcomes. Furthermore, the statistics in Tables 1.1 and 1.2 report only a fraction of the research data generated by this selected group of major studies. The full reports must be read to understand the particular objectives, findings, and limitations of each study since intake criteria, treatment model, program maturity, services, and even definitions of terms such as *placement* differ.

CRITICAL FBS IMPLEMENTATION CHALLENGES

Theory Building

Despite the work of a number of program developers and researchers (e.g., Adnopoz & Nagler, 1993; Barth, 1991; Bryce & Lloyd, 1981, Jones, 1985; Kinney et al., 1991; Soulé, Massarene, & Abate, 1993), the theories that guide FBS have not been fully delineated. And yet, ideally, high-quality evaluations use theory as a way of guiding the choice of dependent and independent variables, as well as the research design and measures. Perhaps qualitative research approaches can be used to supplement quantitative research, particularly in areas where the theory base is underdeveloped or ambiguous (Wells & Freer, 1994).

Case Targeting

Targeting services to cases at imminent risk of placement, if placement prevention is the primary purpose of the program, remains a serious challenge. Targeting will be discussed in more detail (see Chapters 3 and 8), but readers should be aware that many of the largest FBS studies with placement prevention objectives were unable to target services to children truly at risk of imminent placement, as evidenced by the fact that few children in control groups were placed within 30 days of referral to the study.

If imminent risk of placement is to be used as one of the criteria for service eligibility, efforts will be needed to refine referral criteria, implement interdepartmental screening committees, involve juvenile court personnel, better manage the politics of implementation, and address staff concerns about child safety in order to improve case targeting and screening. Even if the field moves to a broader definition of eligibility criteria, there is still a great deal of work that needs to be done on defining and implementing specific referral criteria. Only when we better understand which families do and do not get referred to family preservation services can we make informed comparisons between populations and services.

Program Implementation

Another serious issue that has been inadequately addressed by many FBS initiatives to date is the need to achieve program consistency and rigor with respect to model specification, staff selection, staff training, program funding, quality control, staff turnover, and maintaining *planned* program refinement in contrast to model "drift" (Pecora, Haapala, & Fraser, 1991). For example, during the third year of implementation, when control groups were being formed, a major California FBS evaluation encountered staff turnover and decreased state administrative support. Other recent statewide evaluation studies have also faced considerable methodological and implementation challenges(e.g., Gershenson, 1993; Schuerman, Rzepnicki, & Littell, 1991, 1994).

One of the most comprehensive studies thus far, conducted in Illinois, found no significant differences in child placement rates between the experimental and comparison sites. Given, however, that only 7% of the comparison group cases were placed within 30 days and 16% at six months, there was a relatively small pool of cases for comparison (Schuerman, Rzepnicki, Littell, & Chak, 1993, p. 104). Despite some innovative approaches to random assignment and careful measurement strategies, a number of complications arose in the Illinois study that should be guarded against in subsequent studies: (1) substantial differences between the experimental sites in the risks of subsequent maltreatment, placement, and case closing; (2) patterns of case openings and closings that differed across sites; and (3) significant variation across sites in the amounts, types, and duration of services provided to experimental and control group cases (Schuerman et al., 1993, p. 118). As illustrated by the Illinois and other evaluations of FBS, the program implementation process, worker training, variation in services, and other implementation factors are critical in interpreting study findings and in developing research designs.

To date, the field lacks conclusive evidence that FBS prevent child placement and about which types of FBS programs are most effective with different client subpopulations including those involved in physical abuse, neglect, parent-child conflict, delinquency, or other areas. We also need a better understanding of effectiveness with different age groups of children and of program components that contribute to success with different families (e.g., in-home services, active listening, client goal setting, concrete services). Studies are beginning to look at subpopulations and to estimate the value of different intervention components.[2] These are all important evaluation goals, along with the fundamental need for FBS programs to assess effectiveness, to refine interventions, and to be accountable to funding agencies. Because the programs reported in these tables varied significantly in target group, model consistency, program maturity, and services provided, it is premature to draw any firm conclusions about the effectiveness of any particular type of FBS program.

Building Cultural Competence

Families of color comprise the majority of the FBS service population, and yet, as with other social service programs, most FBS staff members lack special training in assessment, interviewing, case planning, and treatment with different ethnic groups. While the values of FBS, range of services, and in-home orientation contribute directly to success with many families of color, intervention model-building and specialized staff training are still needed.

These are just a few of the program implementation challenges that remain to be fully addressed. And problems in any one of these areas can complicate or compromise aspects of the evaluation effort.

PROGRAM EVALUATION CHALLENGES AND TASKS: AN OVERVIEW

Depending upon the research design, evaluation studies must address a number of challenges and complete certain research tasks (see Table 1.3 for a summary). While subsequent chapters will address many of these issues and tasks in more detail, a few will be highlighted in the next sections.

Maintaining a Clear Definition of the Program Model

First, clear program goals and objectives must be developed. These establish the foundation for intake criteria, service philosophy, service delivery methods, and outcome criteria (see Chapter 9; Austin et al., 1982; Kettner, Moroney, & Martin, 1990). Given variability in both program definitions and stability, it is extremely important to monitor vari-

Table 1.3.   Selected FBS Program Evaluation Challenges and Tasks

Specifying the Program Model
- Setting clear goals and objectives for the program
- Developing the program model and services in ways that enable clear definition and measurement of intervention components
- Establishing specific intake criteria for families and children
- Promoting and assessing program stability

Determining the Purpose and Scope of the Evaluation
- Determining the purpose and primary audience of the evaluation
- Identifying major research questions and hypotheses
- Defining the independent (service) and dependent (outcome) variables

Research Design
- Developing a design that addresses the research questions in a valid manner while minimizing alternative explanations for outcomes
- Specifying outcomes to be achieved
- Selecting assessment instruments and strategies for measuring outcomes
- Determining the sampling approach to be used
- Developing incentives for client and worker participation
- Recognizing and accounting for client diversity in the sample and plan for analysis
- Designing data collection procedures that maximize reliability and validity of the information

Implementing the Evaluation
- Organizing an evaluation team
- Training FBS staff members and research assistants
- Implementing a data collection monitoring system

Data Analysis
- Coding the data, including categorizing responses to open-ended questions
- Developing a plan for statistical analysis
- Fitting statistical models to the data, being observant of the assumptions for the statistical tests being used

Report Writing
- Summarizing the data in clear language and with appropriate graphics
- Disseminating the information in varied ways to inform practitioners, administrators, policymakers and other researchers

ous aspects of the implementation process. New FBS programs may be volatile, with the service delivery model varying across program sites or staff members. Without adequate time for program stabilization and consistent efforts to ensure program consistency and quality, there may be *several* "models" under study, with a concomitant reduction in sample size due to the necessity of analyzing each separately. Evaluators in a number of related service areas have noted the importance of specifying and measuring the implementation of specific program components to help identify such problems, as well as fitting evaluation strategies to stages of program maturity.[3] For example, the particular stage of program development and purpose of the evaluation will limit the range of valid research approaches. Jacobs (1988) developed an excellent framework for addressing many of these issues (see Table 1.4).

Purpose and Scope of the Evaluation

What is the purpose of the evaluation to be undertaken? Is it to monitor program implementation, measure client outcomes, track child placement rates over time, determine differential effects among certain client groups, gather cost-effectiveness data, or some other purpose? Who is your primary audience—practitioners, program administrators, policy analysts, or legislators? While the evaluative data can to some degree be reported in a variety of ways to address the needs of different groups, the primary focus and audience for the evaluation must be addressed in the design, data collection, and report writing phases.

In terms of scope, the logistics and cost of the study must be considered early in the planning process. What type of research design at what cost is necessary and feasible at this point in time? The Jacobs (1988) framework illustrated in Table 1.4 is helpful for determining some design issues, but the cost of the project also guides planning, as available time and resources may prohibit certain types of studies.

Research Design

Program outcomes need to be agreed upon by the various stakeholders, carefully designated, and measured. One challenge is to balance what practitioners see as important outcomes with what current best practice indicates are important and realistic case outcomes. Client diversity also needs to be considered. Programs may work with families experiencing different types of child maltreatment or parent-adolescent conflict. Treatment approaches and success rates tend to differ among these subtypes and they should be analyzed separately (Bath, Richey, & Haapala, 1992; Nelson & Landsman, 1992; Pecora, Haapala, & Fraser, 1991). It is also important, when possible, to include sufficient numbers of ethnically diverse families to assess program effectiveness with different groups.

Another fundamental question is the array of indicators that should be used to determine effectiveness (e.g., differences in placement rates, improvement in child or parent functioning, and/or reduced child maltreatment). Put another way, how much difference in specific areas should be expected between the group of families served by FBS and families served by other programs? Further complicating this question are the complexities inherent in developing consensus about "significant

Table 1.4. Summary of Five-Tiered Approach to Program Evaluation[a]

Evaluation level	Title of evaluation tier	Purpose of evaluation	Audiences
Level 1	Preimplementation	1. To document the need for particular program within community 2. To demonstrate the fit between community needs and proposed program 3. To provide "data groundwork"	1. Potential funders 2. Community/ citizen groups

Level 2	Accountability	1. To document program's
		  a. utilization
		  b. entrenchment
		  c. penetration into target population
		2. To justify current expenditures
		3. To increase expenditures
		4. To build a constituency
			1. Funders, donors
			2. Community leaders, media

Level 3	Program clarification	1. To provide information to program staff to improve the program	1. Program staff 2. Program participants
Level 4	Progress toward objectives	1. To provide information to staff to improve program 2. To document program effectiveness	1. Staff members 2. Program participants 3. Funders 4. Other programs

Tasks	Types of data to collected/analyzed
1. Detail basic characteristics of proposed program 2. Conduct community needs assessment to support establishment of such program 3. Revise proposed program coordinated to assessed needs	1. Locally generated statistics that describe populations and needs for service (including public/personal costs of not providing the program) 2. Interviews with community leaders on seriousness of problem 3. Interviews or survey data from prospective participants

1. Describe accurately program participants and services provided
2. Provide accurate cost information per unit of service
	1. Client-specific monitoring data
	2. Service-specific monitoring data
	3. Case material
	  a. Data from interviews with clients indicating clients—needs and responses
	  b. Community (nonuser) reactions to program

1. Question basic program assumptions: what kinds of services for whom and by whom? 2. Clarify and restate program's mission, goals, objectives, and strategies	1. Content of staff meetings, supervision sessions, interviews with staff 2. Observation by staff of program activities and staff process 3. Previously collected staff and service data 4. Interview data from parents on desired benefits to program 5. Client satisfaction information
1. Examine outcome (short-term) objectives 2. Derive measurable indicators of success for a majority of the outcome objectives 3. Decide on data analysis procedures 4. Assess differential effectiveness among individual clients 5. Assess community awareness among individual clients	1. Interview material regarding individual client's progress toward objectives 2. Standardized test scores for clients, where applicable 3. Client-specific information from criterion-referenced instruments 4. Client satisfaction data 5. Evidence of support/resistance to program in community

(*continued*)

Table 1.4.   (Continued)

Evaluation level	Title of evaluation tier	Purpose of evaluation	Audiences
Level 5	Program impact	1. To contribute to knowledge development in the substantive fields of child development, family process, organizational theory, and/or to the refinement of evaluation practices 2. To produce evidence of differential effectiveness among alternative program approaches 3. To suggest program models worthy of replication	1. Academic and research communities 2. Policymakers at federal, state, and local levels 3. General public, through the media 4. Potential program directors and funders

differences" from a consumer, clinical, administrative, policymaking, benefit-cost, and other perspectives. What may be statistically significant may not be viewed as clinically significant, and vice versa (see, for example, Kendall & Grove, 1988). Various forms of power analysis and calculation of expected "effect sizes" are critical in order to address these concerns (see Chapters 3 and 11 in this volume; Bickman, 1990). With large samples expected minimum differences should be established at the start of the study because even small differences may be statistically significant (Gershenson, 1993, p. 10).

In smaller studies, however, evaluators should be careful that sample sizes are large enough to detect expected differences. This is especially important because in control group studies two different types of service are being compared—FBS and "regular" services—and it is not usually possible to find out how families would fare if they received no service (see Chapters 2 and 3; Jones, 1991). Finally, conditions that would provide an alternative explanation for client change threaten the validity and generalizability of the findings must be prevented or minimized, if at all possible (Cook & Campbell, 1979). Possible implementation problems should be carefully considered before initiating the study and carefully monitored during the research process.

Tasks	Types of data to collected/analyzed
1. Delineate specific impact objectives that are to be achieved, presumably through the accretion of short-term objectives—success 2. Identify measure(s) that can assess enduring and/or lifestyle changes among participants 3. Develop evaluation plan that reflects common understandings among evaluator(s), program personnel, contractor (if different from program)	1. Quantifiable client-specific data, including standardized test results collected over time (longitudinal client data) 2. Control group data or comparison group standards 3. Qualitative client data, including record reviews, client interviews, etc. 4. Cost-effectiveness information, necessary for planning program replication

[a] *Source*: F. H. Jacobs (1988). The five-tiered approach to evaluation: Context and implementation Pp. 52–55 in *Evaluating family programs*, edited by H. B. Weiss and F. H. Jacobs. Hawthorne, NY: Aldine de Gruyter, reprinted with permission.

Developing a Systems Perspective

One of the most difficult aspects of evaluating the impact of FBS is that there are so many possible factors that potentially affect and are affected by these services. A broader "systems" perspective is useful for conceptualizing both the program and evaluation efforts. For example, it is important to understand the intervention itself ("program management and structure" and "program operations") before moving to assess other major evaluation domains such as program impact on youth and families, and public policy. The interrelationship of these domains can be addressed by systems evaluation efforts, which are described by noted evaluation expert, Lynn Usher, in Appendix A.

CONCLUSION

Evaluating FBS programs is a challenging and exciting process. These services represent a new approach to working with families, but their promise is yet to be fully realized. Evaluation data can help to further refine FBS and guide service reform efforts. We hope that the following chapters will provide you with a practical set of principles and strategies for improving your FBS programs and assessing their impact on the families being served.

NOTES

1.   For critical reviews of selected evaluation studies of family-based services or the research as a whole, see Bath and Haapala (1994), Blythe, Salley, & Jayaratne (1994), Frankel (1988), Jones (1985), Magura (1981), Rossi (1992a, 1992c), Stein (1985), and Wells and Biegel (1991). For an incisive discussion of similar challenges with home-visiting program research see Olds and Kitzman (1993).

2.   See Bath et al. (1992), Feldman (1991b), Fraser, Pecora, & Haapala (1991), Lewis (1991), Haapala (1983), Nelson, Emlen, Landsman, and Hutchinson (1988).

3.   Maintaining program implementation and fitting the evaluation design to program stage are underemphasized areas. For more information, see Basch, Sliepcevich, Gold, Duncan, & Kolbe (1985), Bielawski and Epstein (1984), Doueck, Bronson, and Levine (1992), King, Morris, & Fitz-Gibbon (1987), and Scanlon, Horst, Nay, Schmidt, & Waller (1977).

Appendix to Chapter 1

Evaluating Changes in Systems[1]

CHARLES L. USHER

Most efforts to develop FBS recognize that such services represent but one element of a broader system of highly interdependent components. For example, while many families of children now in foster care could be served more effectively by home-based family preservation programs, family foster care is likely to remain the most appropriate service for *some* children. It is thus necessary to strengthen and maintain family foster care, but simultaneously to refine assessment procedures and develop home-based alternatives so that the needs of children who require foster care can be met effectively and efficiently. Depending on the values and principles that prevail at the national, state, and local levels, however, such a continuum of care may not exist and the matching of services to families' and children's needs and strengths may not be appropriate. Therefore, even if efforts are made to expand FBS, inappropriate targeting may undermine their effectiveness or result in their inefficient use of them (for example, see Schuerman, Rzepnicki, Littell & Budde, 1992b).

From this perspective, any given program or service is but one component of the *system* each community develops—consciously or unconsciously—to respond to the needs of its families and children. Therefore, in evaluating FBS and assessing their impact as part of a systemic reform effort that transcends individual programs and services, we must understand the policy, programmatic, and organizational context within which these services fit. This broad perspective is crucial to designing and implementing effective program and service enhancements and evaluations that can determine whether a community's reform objectives are being met.

The Policy and Program Context of FBS:
Systems Evaluation

Family-based services exist within a complex, multilevel system. To change the way in which any single service is delivered and ultimately to improve outcomes for families receiving those services requires changes at many points in the system. In order to measure those changes and to understand fully why they do or do not take place, the evaluation strategy must capture relevant information from throughout the system. Figure A.1 depicts the context in which FBS exist as a set of four planning and evaluation *domains*:

- The *public policy context* includes the values and principles held among policymakers (elected officials, administrators, and judges), as well as the budgets, regulations, and legislation that translate attitudes and opinion into policies and programs. The resource allocations and operating policies that define FBS are determined within this domain.
- *Program management and structure* defines the way in which specific services are organized into programs, the channels through which funds are allocated, and the ways in which staff and other resources are organized to provide services. Decisions made within this domain determine the range of services that are available and ways in which they interact.
- The *program operations* domain encompasses the volume and mix of services and the patterns of assessments that channel families toward one form of service rather than another. Also within this domain are ancillary programs, such as staff training and resource development, that affect the quality and availability of services. Basic management and staff capabilities also are critical factors in program operations.
- The last domain is *program impact*, including outcomes for individual families and children, and the cumulative impact on neighborhoods and communities. This concerns the experience of children and families served by the system as measured by conventional permanency outcomes such as the frequency and duration of out-of-home placements, patterns of family preservation and reunification, and the emergence of service needs over the longer term (for example, reentry into foster care for children who have been reunited with their birth families). It also includes the more challenging areas of changes in family functioning and the health and development of children served. On a broader level, program im-

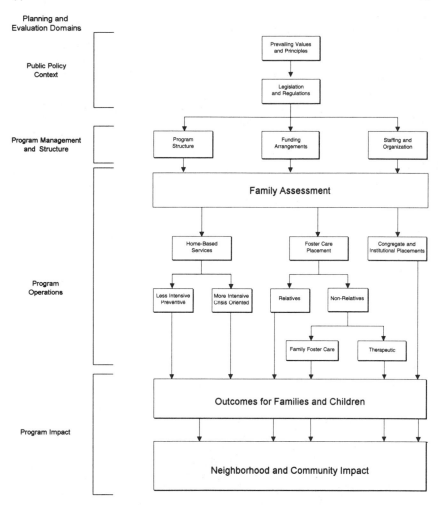

Figure A.1. The policy and program context of FBS systems.

pact involves aggregate effects such as changes in the quality of life in communities and in how communities respond to the needs of families and children. While some indicators change slowly, such as the rate of adolescent pregnancies in a neighborhood or community, it is important to put into place the reporting mechanisms by which they can be monitored. Other indicators, such as the proportion of children entering out-of-home care who are placed in their own neighborhood, may point to growing strength of a community to meet the needs of its residents.

Although improvements in family conditions and functioning are the ultimate goals of attempts to improve service delivery, measuring outcomes for individual families and children provides only part of the picture of the effects of systemic changes. Reforming a system requires changes within *each* of the domains described above, and changes in one domain often cannot occur until constraints in another domain have been eased. Therefore, a systems-level evaluation strategy examines changes at each level in order to present a comprehensive picture of *how* changes in outcomes were produced. Similarly, since changes in one part of a system can be expected to produce secondary effects (such as the availability of funds that can be redirected because fewer institutional beds are needed), information is often collected across the full continuum of care in order to measure the full extent of a broad reform effort. This is systems-oriented evaluation.

Measuring Changes in Systems

The primary thrust of many efforts to reform family and children's services is to move community systems away from the tendency to serve *children* outside their homes and communities, toward an emphasis on serving *families* in their own homes and communities. Determining whether this shift takes place requires time series data that can provide an historical perspective on changing patterns of service delivery.

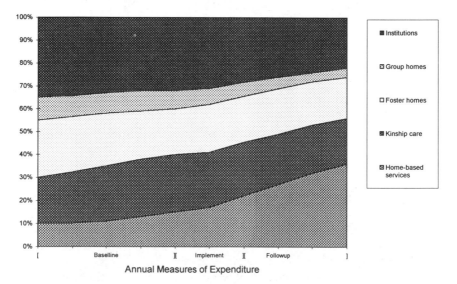

Figure A.2.   Allocation of resources in a community.

Such data can be used to determine how a community tends to allocate financial and other resources to out-of-home placements compared to home-based services to families and children. Similarly, how does the allocation of resources in one community compare to the allocation in similar communities in a state, both in level and pattern? Using hypothetical data, Figure A.2 illustrates a change in resource allocation that entails a shift from congregate care to home-based services over a ten-year period that encompasses a baseline period, a period during which reforms were implemented, and a brief follow-up period.

Similar time series could be developed for measures of outcomes for individual families and children. For example, using data that track the experience of families and children coming into care, it would be possible to show improvements in the frequency and duration of different types of out-of-home placements, and to describe changes in the characteristics of families needing services. By phasing in the implementation of changes on a neighborhood basis, communities could determine whether the desired objectives were being achieved before expanding the reform effort to other areas. In this deliberate fashion, a community could pursue reform in a way that would build in both historical and geographic comparisons for "self-evaluation" (see Usher, 1993).

Systems evaluations require that agencies and organizations in a community share information about who they are serving, the form and cost of services they are providing, and the impact of those services. In many communities, an objective of reform efforts is to create a collaborative planning or governing entity that provides a forum for sharing such information and for making decisions about how to invest existing and new resources to serve families more effectively (for example, see National Alliance for Restructuring Education, 1993, pp. 20–27). The ability of such bodies to plan hinges on their obtaining valid and reliable information of the type outlined her. Similarly, their ability over the longer term to assess the efficiency and effectiveness of services to families and children depends on their receiving up-to-date information about the delivery and impact of services across the entire system

NOTES

1. This Appendix is adapted from Charles L. Usher, Deborah A. Gibbs, & Judith B. Wildfire (forthcoming). A framework for planning, implementing, and evaluating child welfare reforms. *Child Welfare*. Reprinted with permission.

Chapter 2

Designing Family-Based Service
Program Evaluations

Evaluating family-based programs is similar to other forms of program evaluation. Whether a quantitative or more qualitative design is used, the data collected should inform the work of program managers, practitioners, court officials, legislators, funding agencies, skeptics, and others. Moreover, the design should produce conclusions that will withstand critical analysis. Like researchers in delinquency, child abuse, and substance abuse, FBS evaluators deal with difficult family problems about which parents and children are often reluctant to talk, so special sensitivity to family and cultural differences is needed.

Conducting evaluations of FBS is different from other kinds of program evaluation in two ways. First, the field of FBS is so new that evaluators have relatively little theory to guide them in designing evaluation projects. While we are not entirely in the dark about FBS programs and the things that make them work, we lack the rich history of research that exists in some fields and the agreement on guiding theoretical orientations present in others.[1] Second, when families are studied, knotty methodological problems often arise in measurement and data analysis. If a goal of FBS is to strengthen families, one must ask: What constitutes "strengthening" families? In whose view? Parents? Children? Workers? How can we determine whether changes in families are due to the effects of a program rather than the effects of normal development, other services being delivered concurrently with FBS, intervention by extended family members, or other events? Such questions go to the heart of practice and evaluation strategies. In answering them, evaluators work collaboratively with workers, administrators, consumers, and other stakeholders.

Designing an Evaluation

In evaluation, the term *design* refers to the sampling, measurement, and data collection strategies that are used to assess a service or program. The design is the way that evaluators go about seeking answers to a question such as, Is the program effective?

In this chapter, we will consider two elements of an evaluation design: (1) defining the problem, and (2) selecting a specific research design strategy. The design is based on the definition of the problem and the relative maturity of the service model and/or program. As suggested in the previous chapter, there is a time and place for all kinds of designs. The corollary of this is also true: there are times when certain kinds of designs should not be used.

Designing an evaluation begins with defining a problem and setting forth a research question to guide the study. A typical research question might be, Compared to younger children, do teens and their families have significantly different outcomes in FBS programs? In FBS, there is no shortage of questions. Evaluators must choose a focus in order to guide and limit the scope of data collection.

Studies are rarely definitive. No single study will be able to prove that FBS works (or does not work). It is only in the long run, across many studies, that one may begin to develop a sense of what works and what does not. Therefore, the problem selected should be a limited one. It should be based on the joint concerns of local stakeholders—the FBS staff, the agency, legislators, and consumers—and on an analysis of the FBS literature. With help from stakeholders and the literature, evaluators identify questions that lead to specific kinds of research designs.

Types of Evaluation Questions

There are four major types of evaluation questions: (1) questions that focus on the needs of clients (*needs assessment*); (2) questions that focus on program processes (*process or systems evaluation*); (3) questions that focus on program outcomes (*outcome evaluation*); and (4) questions that focus on program efficiency or costs (*cost-effectiveness and benefit-cost evaluation*; Rossi & Freeman, 1993). As shown in Table 2.1, each question leads to somewhat different evaluation strategies. For example, a question on the needs of FBS families might lead, logically, to a survey of caregivers at the start of treatment. Such a survey might focus on the habitability of children's homes or some other aspect of particular importance in the design of services.

Table 2.1. Types of Evaluation with Exemplary Research Questions, Evaluation Designs, and Data Sources

Type of evaluation	Potential research questions	Evaluation designs	Sample data sources
Needs assessment	What are the health and housing needs of families at intake?	Survey	Children Parents Neighbors
Process assessment	Is service crisis oriented and intensive?	Secondary data analysis	Case records
Outcome assessment	Are the behaviors of children and parents improving? Are placement rates different for FBS versus other kinds of child welfare services?	Experiment Quasi-experiment	Children Parents Teachers Management information systems
Cost assessment	Is FBS cheaper than foster family care or other forms of substitute care?	Cost comparison of secondary data	Purchase of service records

Process questions are directed toward the nature of service. They focus on the amount and characteristics of services that are provided to clients over time. Many FBS programs attempt to replicate existing FBS programs and a process evaluation may be focused on the relative success in meeting programmatic goals. Given a particular service model, is the service effort sufficient? How many hours of service do families receive? What kinds of services do families receive? Are the operations associated with service working as planned? Process evaluation assesses the fit between the intended service model and actual service model as delivered in practice. It often includes elements of quality assurance and quality improvement.

Outcome studies focus on the immediate and long-term results of service. At the individual, family, program, and systems levels, they attempt to assess the net impact of the service after controlling for other possible explanations. Lacking control, dramatic findings can be observed but they may be spurious—due to events that are not at all related to family-based treatment. Alternatively, significant outcomes may be marked as extraneous factors. To increase control and to eliminate competing explanations for the postservice behaviors of parents and children, outcome studies often employ designs with random assignment, matching, or other techniques to create comparison groups. If the groups are equivalent, this tends to eliminate alternative explanations for positive (or negative) findings, and it increases the evaluator's ability to make a strong argument that an FBS program is effective. Without control groups, or elaborate longitudinal studies, this is extremely difficult.

At the systems level, outcome studies focus on changes in patterns of service delivery that result from the introduction of a policy innovation (see Appendix A of Chapter 1). In FBS, systems-level evaluation is used to examine changes in the use of foster care and other child welfare resources as a result of the introduction of family preservation programs. Systems-level evaluation is usually longitudinal in nature. Information is collected over many months and changes are plotted on graphs and maps. Counties, districts, or even states may be matched on certain characteristics (e.g., foster care placement rate) and compared as service innovations are implemented.

Finally, efficiency assessment is focused on the costs of FBS relative to alternative services. Cost evaluation requires the calculation of service utilization for families that receive FBS and equivalent families that do not receive FBS. Because FBS clients make use of many different kinds of services and because referral criteria are not perfect (i.e., some families are referred and served but are not truly in need of services), benefit-cost and cost-effectiveness analyses require assumptions about service utilization that almost always place results at risk. Doing a convincing cost assessment is challenging, and various strategies for assessing program efficiency through benefit-cost and cost effectiveness analyses are discussed in Chapter 9.

Quantitative and Qualitative Evaluation

All four kinds of evaluation questions may be addressed quantitatively and/or qualitatively. Qualitative approaches tend to produce rich and descriptive findings. Well-designed qualitative research uses methods that are rigorous and time-consuming (see, e.g., Denzin & Lincoln, 1994). In the best qualitative research, the evaluator joins with clients in an empathic and intensive experience that leads to detailed narrative and systematic analysis of themes, underlying ideas or latent constructs, and theory. In Chapter 10, we describe the qualitative research methods that have emerged from one branch of qualitative methodology, constructivist inquiry. In the current chapter, we will focus on quantitative research methods. It is our view—held strongly—that a mix of both approaches (not necessarily in the same study) produces the strongest information for documenting program development and effectiveness.

Defining the Problem

Our guess is that you might not have picked up this book if you did not already have in mind a need, process, outcome, or cost question related to families or family-oriented services. Questions often arise in the course of developing and delivering a service. Clinicians need information that systematically compares some families to other families. Program managers want information about the delivery of service. Legislators want information about placement prevention. Having a question in mind— even if it is not fully refined and polished—and describing the problem related to the question are excellent beginning places. Most research starts with the analysis of program (or process) data and the identification of some problem. Program data, for example, may indicate that placement rates are high for certain kinds of families or that service is not being delivered equally well across program sites.

Collecting Data. The first step in defining a problem is to collect data. Data gathering can include both qualitative information, such as impressions from consumers, and service-level information, such as the percentage of children placed subsequent to service. Depending on the issue, sources of information may include service records, worker-based assessments, information from follow-up phone calls with parents or children, and data from the FBS literature. It is useful to identify sources of information that will help to define the specific problem of concern.

Searching the Literature. One important source of information is the literature. In the past, accessing the FBS literature was difficult. Few FBS studies were published. Many of the journals were difficult to find in local libraries. But new bibliographic search procedures at many libraries make the FBS literature much more available. In particular, CD/ROM searches offer flexible and inexpensive ways to search the literature for information on FBS programs.

CD/ROM searches permit the user to print out the entire abstract from an article. In a recent search, the keywords AGGRESSION and CHILDREN were entered. The search produced close to 30 articles on aggressive children. By reading the abstracts as they appear on the screen of a computer, you can determine which to keep (or print) and which to pass by. CD/ROM searches access a number of databases, including PsycLIT (psychological and some social work abstracts), Sociofile (sociological and some social work abstracts), ERIC (educational abstracts), Social Work (articles written by social workers), and Medline (medical, psychiatric, and health-related social work abstracts). At most university libraries and some public libraries, these searches are free.

Table 2.2. Organizing Information into Child, Parent, and Environmental Categories by Factors Associated with Service Delivery

Category	Antecedent factors	Service factors	Proximal outcomes	Distal outcomes
Child	Age Gender Prior service Ethnicity Presenting problems School attendance	Availability of special services Amount and nature of service	Changes in presenting problems Changes in skills	Desirability of current living situation Subsequent delinquency substance abuse, or truancy
Parent(s)	Age Income Employment status Prior service Ethnicity Presenting problems Attachment to children	Amount and nature of service	Changes in presenting problems Changes in skills and attitudes Changes in employment	Subsequent child abuse or neglect Skill in caring for children
Environment	Community attitudes Community resources Court attitudes and practices	Service resources Worker training Worker attitudes, skills, and behaviors	Changes in community attitudes Changes in court attitudes or practices	Changes in resources allocation Changes in community rates of child maltreatment

Organizing Information into Categories. Once preliminary data are collected and a literature review completed, it may be helpful to consolidate information in a table. By collapsing information into categories, it is sometimes possible to make sense of a confusing mass of findings from related studies, input from practitioners, data from client needs surveys, anecdotal reports, and so on. Often this helps to narrow and sharpen the primary questions of a study. In the case illustrated in Table 2.2, child, parent, and environmental information categories are constructed. In the leftmost column are factors that are antecedent to FBS. These include child, parent, and environmental conditions that define the start of service and influence the constellation of services provided. In the next column are service-related characteristics or factors. These factors describe the elements of service—intensity, duration, kinds of treatment techniques, and so on. In the next column are immediate or proximal service outcomes such as changes in parents' child management skills. Finally, in the rightmost column are distal outcomes such as family preservation or child placement.

Environmental characteristics affect both the kinds of problems that families present to FBS programs and the resources that workers have available to solve these problems. At the community level, successful FBS programs may have important effects on the attitudes of judges and legislators. In the long run, these effects can produce systemic outcomes—changes in public attitudes toward child placement and changes in the allocation of resources within the child welfare system. Such changes are rarely measured in FBS evaluations, but they are important.

Defining the Service Model

To be evaluable, a service must be stable. In the Introduction and Chapter 1, we discussed various program models and we introduced the idea of "program drift." Over time, programs change in character and content. Without systematic staff training and strong clinical supervision, treatment models drift. From an evaluation perspective, maintaining control over a service is critical. A service that is changing significantly in unplanned or uncontrolled ways is not evaluable. There are several simple steps that help to define and stabilize a service.

Step 1. The first step in program development is needs assessments. Services should be designed to meet the needs of families, children, and other stakeholders, and so needs should be systematically identified through a formal needs assessment process.

Step 2. After a needs assessment has been conducted, the next step in stabilizing and tailoring a service is to conduct process evaluations to ensure that the service is being delivered as planned. This involves comparing program goals, needs assessment information, and process evaluation data to look for inconsistencies. This is a repeated process that may take up to three years. In fact, many long-standing programs continuously check service characteristics against client profiles.

Step 3. Once a service has been defined and data have been collected to show that the service is delivered as intended, outcomes can be examined. *Prior to the refinement of a FBS model and the gathering of data that demonstrate program integrity, we do not recommend conducting an outcome evaluation.* Even if outcome data are collected on a developing service, one does not know what was evaluated. If a service is stable, it may then be appropriate to assess its outcomes, and the next step in such an undertaking is the selection of an evaluation design.

EVALUATION DESIGNS

In the next few pages, common evaluation designs are discussed. Because it involves widely known survey methods (see, e.g., Rubin & Babbie, 1993), we will not discuss needs assessment. Process evaluation is described in Chapter 4, and cost analysis methods are described in Chapter 9. Here, we focus on basic evaluation strategies for assessing outcomes. Starting with simple single-system designs and working up to more complex group designs, these are approaches that may be used to answer questions such as, Is an FBS program having an impact on family functioning? Are out-of-home placements prevented?

Single-System Designs

Single-System Designs. Single-family or single-system studies provide data over time on a particular case. Although there are some exceptions, single-system designs (SSD) often require that data be collected on a daily or weekly basis well before the start of service and well after the conclusion of service (Bloom & Fischer, 1982). There are many different kinds of single-systems designs. Some involve the collection of data on multiple aspects of family functioning (multiple-baseline studies); others focus on the responses of individual parents or children to different kinds of treatment techniques (multiple-element studies); and others focus on responses to the termination and reintroduction of services (withdrawal studies).

To show that changes occur, most SSD require that families demonstrate a stable baseline of functioning before the introduction of service. This limits the utility of SSD in FBS evaluation, because referral criteria for many FBS require that a family be "at risk of imminent placement." If a family is at risk of placement, behaviors that one might wish to target in intervention are probably not stable. Lack of stability is, in a sense, a reason for referral to FBS, and thus evaluation designs that require stability are compromised. Moreover, the mere requirement that baseline data be collected *prior* to the delivery of service renders many SSDs ill fitted to FBS practice, where emphasis is placed on immediate responses to family problems.

Reconstructed or Retrospective Baseline Single-System Design. As an alternative to the prospective baseline, baseline data can sometimes be reconstructed from school records (as in the case of truancy), court records (as in the case of police contacts), and family reports (as in the case where several family members agree on the frequency of some particular problem). This approach suffers from the well-known limitations of public record keeping and client recall. But for variables for which information may be reliably recorded—e.g., school attendance—or for events that are confirmed by multiple family members, a retrospective, reconstructed baseline may be used in place of the traditional prospective baseline (Reid, 1993).

Signed-Cause Single-System Designs. When the effect of an intervention is immediate, clearly observed, predicted by theory, and unlikely to have resulted from any other factor, the effect is said to be the "signature" of treatment (Cook & Campbell, 1979). In signed-cause SSD, data on an intervention and its expected result are collected. This design may be used only when effects are large, immediate, and logically unconfounded (Reid, 1993). If an FBS worker resolves to locate a truant child every time that the child's school reports her/him to be tardy and to then take the child directly to school, the effect of the intervention on truancy should be immediate, large, and logically unconfounded. Under such a circumstance, a signed-cause SSD might be used.

Single-System Time-Series Design. One important extension of single-system studies is the single-system time-series design. In this design, data are collected daily or weekly on a small number of variables for as long as the client is in a program. The evaluation design does not affect the course of treatment and findings are based on observation of changes over many months (Corcoran, 1993). The Alaska Youth Initiative used such a design, selecting nine daily performance indicators to track children on placement, medications compliance, school attendance, drug/alcohol use, and various behavioral problems (Burchard & Clarke, 1990). Over time, such data provide a record of improvement or lack of improvement in various settings and programs. Even when a small number of variables are selected, however, these designs require careful data collection and analysis efforts. But when children or parents can be tracked over long periods of time, single-system time-series designs provide rich information.

Group Designs: The Basics

Group evaluation designs are more common than single-case designs for a reason. Single-case methods are vulnerable to two kinds of criticisms. First, with the less complex SSDs, observed changes may be due to events other than the FBS. Critics may argue, for example, that the changes are due to the inherent creativity of families in crisis: that fami-

lies in crisis often make adjustments that lead them out of crisis. Thus
the skeptic would say that service had no effect and that, if left alone,
most families would recover to a stable state. To counter such arguments, some sort of comparison to families who were similar at the point
of referral but did not receive FBS is necessary. Second, critics can argue
that a single family is unique, that the case observed was not representative of the target population, and thus that the findings cannot be generalized to the broader population of FBS families. While the argument
that a group of families may also be unrepresentative of the target population is heard occasionally, it is not convincing when some form of
probability sampling is used. This criticism leads, then, to the use of
more than one case, and some method of selecting cases so that they are
representative of a target population.

The essential elements of group designs include:

- systematic sampling of families or cases
- assignment to experimental and control or comparison groups
- measurement after treatment
- comparison of differences between experimental and control
  groups
- follow-up.

A group design is only as good as the sample. If a study involves only
those families that are court referred or only those families that have
younger children, it is not possible to generalize findings to a broader
population of FBS program participants (of course, this situation is fine if
that client group is the population of interest). Some form of probability
sampling is always necessary in group designs.

Random sampling is one type of probability sampling. There are
many sampling approaches that produce representative samples. The
class of sampling procedures known as probability sampling techniques
have a unique and important characteristic. When probability sampling
is used, the likelihood that a case in the target population will be selected is known. In a purely mathematical sense, then, it is possible to
generalize the findings from a small group to the population of interest.
No matter what design is chosen, the sampling procedure should be
specified as a part of the larger research design. Sampling and random
assignment to experimental and control groups are discussed in detail in
Chapter 3.

Types of Group Designs

There are many types of group research designs, each of which em-
ploys different design elements. The most common designs useful for

FBS are described below. The following symbols are used to represent service provision, data collection, random assignment, and other aspects of a research design:

X—provision of FBS
A—provision of alternative or routine services
O—data collection or observation
R—random assignment
M—matching

Pretest-Posttest Single-Group Design. The pretest-posttest single-group design is the most commonly used and weakest group design. As shown in Figure 2.1, it compares a group of families at two points in time, once before treatment and once afterwards. It does not control for changes in the environment, such as new laws that might affect placement resources and rates. Nor does it control for naturally occurring changes in family functioning over time. Many families enter treatment in a state of crisis, and make some sort of accommodation on their own. Their accommodation may be poor (or it may be good) but it is likely to reduce the stress that family members feel. From a systems perspective, families tend to regress toward less stressful functioning; they move out of crisis even in the absence of treatment. In this design, there is no way to distinguish such natural changes from the effects of treatment.

This design is not strong for a variety of other reasons. Shown in Table 2.3, there are seven alternative explanations for an observed treatment effect. Each represents an explanation other than service effectiveness for findings from pretest-posttest designs. The forces of history (environmental effects), regression, maturation, testing, instrumentation, selection, and attrition can produce significant pre- to posttest differences, *even when there are no differences resulting from family-based treatment.* With the pretest-posttest design, one never knows whether treatment was effective or whether one of these other factors was at play.

Time-Series Single-Group Design. Like the pretest-posttest design, the time-series single-group design uses a "reflexive" control (Rossi & Freeman, 1993). Group members' behavior and attitudes before treatment are compared to group members' behavior and attitudes after treatment. Although it has this reflexive characteristic, the time-series design is stronger than the pretest-posttest design, because trends over time are portrayed. Shown in Figure 2.2, multiple pre- and posttests are used.

O	X	O
Pretest	FBS	Posttest
	Treatment	

Figure 2.1. Pretest/posttest design.

Table 2.3. Seven Alternative Explanations (See Cook & Campbell, 1979)

HISTORY: History refers to specific events other than FBS treatment that occur between the first measurement at pretest and the second measurement at post-test. These events occur during the course of treatment and pose rival explanations for an observed pretest-posttest difference. The longer the time between the start and termination of service, the greater the likelihood that historical events will covary with treatment and confound the effect of treatment.

REGRESSION: Regression refers to the statistical artifact that, with repeated testing, extreme scores tend to become less extreme. Groups of scores that fall into extreme ranges tend to have more measurement error in them. Because they contain a larger amount of error (than more moderate scores), extreme score "regress" toward the mean upon repeated application of the same test. They tend to become less extreme because the repeated occurrence of large random errors in measurement decreases over time.

MATURATION: Maturation refers to changes that occur in organizations, families, parents, and children as a result of the mere passage of time. When a treatment program is long, some subjects—especially children—tend to change as a result of social, cognitive, and physical development. Programs also mature. They go through stages of development. Pretest-posttest differences in studies of children exposed to a brand-new FBS program could be due to developmental changes in the children or the program, rather than to the effect of treatment per se.

SELECTION: Selection refers to the use of a group assignment procedure that results in experimental and control conditions that are not equivalent. Random assignment usually eliminates selection biases.

TESTING: Testing refers to the effect of taking the pretest. Pretest-posttest differences may be due to the effect of subjects remembering pretest items and being sensitive to them. Suppose, for example, parents were asked to score their children's temper tantrums at pretest. During the treatment period, parents might have heightened concern for tantrums. They might read and be influenced by material on tantrums that is not associated with FBS treatment. [*Note:* Fortunately, research indicates that the effect of a pretest on posttest scores is usually insignificant. See Bingham & Felbinger, 1990.]

INSTRUMENTATION: Instrumentation refers to changes in the data collection instrument or data collection procedures over time. Sometimes interviewers become jaded and their effectiveness wanes across the course of a study. Occasionally, instruments are actually changed in the middle of a study. Instrumentation effects can be controlled by careful, ongoing training of interviewers and by avoiding changes in data collection procedures during the course of a study.

EXPERIMENTAL ATTRITION: Attrition, also known as "mortality," refers to dropout rates that differ between experimental and control conditions. Differential dropout can produce incommensurability, even when random assignment has been used to create groups. Whenever attrition occurs, subjects who drop out must be compared against subjects who remain. When significant differences are found, attrition is called "biased." When it differs between experimental and control groups, it is called "biased experimental attrition."

Figure 2.2. Time-series single-group design.

Sometimes this design is called the *interrupted time-series* design because treatment interrupts the measurement of a particular behavior over time. Changes in behavior (or other outcomes) are interpreted as resulting from family-based treatment. Time-series designs can be used when daily or weekly measures of an outcome measure are available before and after FBS. Like single-subject designs, this design can be interpreted only when baseline data are stable.

Pretest-Posttest Control Group Design with Random Assignment. The pretest-posttest control group design with random assignment is the classic experimental design. It controls all of the alternative explanations in Table 2.3, so long as attrition in the treatment group is equivalent to attrition in the control group. This can be tested post hoc and, if attrition is found to be "biased," statistical adjustments usually can be employed to make the groups equivalent for comparison on posttest measures.

Shown in Figure 2.3, the classic experiment relies on random assignment of individuals or families to treatment and control groups. In theory, the control group is not supposed to receive services. But in most FBS research this is unethical and control group families receive routine services, while experimental families receive an innovative family-based program. Technically, there are no limits on the number of control and experimental conditions that can be used. For practical reasons, how-

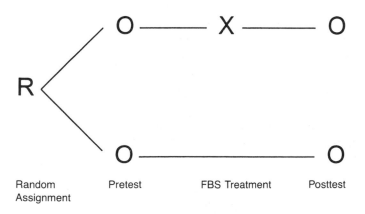

Figure 2.3. Classical experiment with no-treatment control group.

Table 2.4. Steps in Random Assignment Using a Table of Random Numbers

1. Assign a unique number to each family in the study. If you expect to assign 130 families to an experimental or control group, the first unique case number should be 001, the second should be 002, and so on through the last case number (130).
2. Using a table of random numbers (found in the appendices of many statistics texts), select a starting point with the same number of digits as the highest case number. If 130 families are to be assigned, for example, start with a three-digit number.
3. Beginning with this three-digit number, go down the three-digit column until a real case number between 001 and 130 is encountered. Assign this case to the experimental group. If 65 families are needed in the experimental group, continue using the same procedure to select 64 additional case numbers. If you come to the bottom of a column, proceed to the top of the next column. The remaining case numbers—families not selected—will constitute the control group.

ever, most experimental research uses just one experimental and one control group.

Random assignment is done in a variety of different ways. Often a table of random numbers is used to assign families to experimental and control groups. The steps for randomly assigning a known group of families are described in Table 2.4. As long as the group sizes are large (usually 50 or more), random assignment is assumed to produce equivalent groups. However, it is a probabilistic procedure, and thus there is always a chance that random assignment will not result in comparable conditions. It is good practice to double-check the equivalence of groups by comparing group means on pretest variables.

After randomization in the pretest-posttest experiment, subjects are compared using difference scores. For each group, pretest scores are subtracted from posttest scores. This produces a mean difference for each group. If the treatment was effective, the difference score of the treatment group should be significantly larger (or smaller) than the difference score of the control group.

Posttest-Only Control Group Design with Random Assignment. The posttest-only control group design is a twist on the classic experiment. Shown in Figure 2.4, this design is exactly the same as the pretest-posttest design with randomization except that no pretest is used. Families are randomly assigned to experimental and control groups. The impact of treatment is estimated by comparing posttest scores only.

This design relies upon random assignment to create equivalent and comparable groups. As we mentioned, random assignment is usually reliable. However, it is a probabilistic procedure, and there is always the chance—a fairly large chance when the sample size is small—that it will

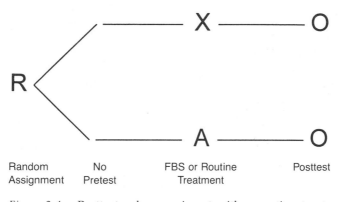

| Random | No | FBS or Routine | Posttest |
| Assignment | Pretest | Treatment | |

Figure 2.4. Posttest-only experiment with a routine treatment control group.

not work. When that happens, the evaluator who uses a posttest-only design has little recourse for salvaging the study.[2]

Notice that in this design an alternative treatment, A, is introduced by assigning control families to routine services. In FBS evaluation, this is nearly always a desirable practice. The classic experiment with a no-treatment control group is practically, ethically, and legally objectionable. Families referred for child welfare, mental health, and court services are entitled to professional services. There can rarely be such a thing as a "no-treatment" control group.

When no-treatment control groups are replaced with alternative-treatment control groups, the treatment effect is usually smaller. In most cases, the effect of an alternative treatment will be larger than the effect of no treatment. Thus the differences between experimental- and alternative- (routine) treatment conditions will be smaller than if the control group received no services at all. Although there are several ways to compensate for this problem (e.g., employing measures of outcome that are more precise), ultimately this design has a greater risk of finding no significant difference. In the view of many, however, this risk is counterbalanced by the fact that all participants receive an ethically acceptable service.

Matched-Pairs Comparison Group Design. The term *experiment* is usually reserved for designs that employ random assignment, whereas the term *quasi-experiment* is usually applied to designs that do not employ random assignment. Quasi-experiments rely on comparison rather than control groups. The distinction is an important one. Control groups are created by random assignment, and comparison groups are created by matching or some other procedure. While random assignment is broad-

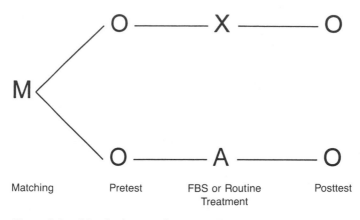

Figure 2.5. Matched-pairs design with routine-treatment con-
    trol group.

ly recognized as creating equivalence in all areas between treatment and
control conditions, matching designs create equivalence only on the
matched variables.

Shown in Figure 2.5, a common matching design involves pairing
individuals who are similar on several variables. In matched-pairs designs, the evaluator chooses variables that are likely to influence the
outcome measure and then matches individuals on these variables. In a
family-based program for ungovernable children, for example, you
might match children on truancy, drug use, gender, ethnicity, and age.
After matching, one member of a pair is assigned to the comparison
group and the other to the treatment group. Matching is usually done
prospectively. But, occasionally, when a large number of families who
receive FBS or an alternative treatment are available, it may be done after
the fact (see, e.g., Fraser et al., 1991). In principle, matching produces
equivalence between the treatment and comparison groups on key
variables—those variables that are conceptually important.

Matched-pairs designs are analyzed by computing and summing the
differences across pairs. If a family-based intervention were successful in
reducing ungovernable behavior, the results of a study where matching
took place on truancy and drug use might be reported as follows:

> Matched for truancy and drug use at the start of service, children in the
> experimental family-based treatment condition were significantly more
> compliant in home, school, and . . .

Matching designs can provide persuasive findings that all but eliminate the seven alternative explanations in Table 2.3. To pair subjects so
that they are truly equivalent, however, requires matching on a number

of variables, and herein lies a problem. People are different, and it is hard to match subjects on more than a few variables. Some children or families may simply not be "matchable" and must be eliminated from study. Aside from reducing the representativeness of the sample, this tends to reduce variability. In the hands-on world of pair making, there is a practical upper limit to the number of variables on which subjects can be matched. Moreover, the evaluator is faced with a conundrum: The more variables on which one tries to match, the more likely matching will fail. The fewer the variables on which matching is successful, the weaker the design.

Case-Overflow Comparison Group Design without Random Assignment. Sometimes naturally occurring events produce opportunities to conduct evaluations that approximate the strength of the classic experiment. One such design is called the case overflow design. This design is based on the idea that caseload openings occur randomly. That is, when a FBS program is small and cannot take every referral, families who are referred but turned away (and usually referred to other programs) constitute an equivalent control group that does not receive FBS. By tracking what happens to these referred-but-not-served cases, an evaluator can generate information on what should be an equivalent comparison condition.

The linchpin of case overflow designs is the referral and case screening process. If referrals are similar throughout the study period, and if it is possible to identify families that otherwise would be eligible for FBS but were turned away for administrative reasons, then the referred—but not served—families should be quite similar to the referred-and-served families.

Case overflow designs may be compromised when there is a systematic bias in the referring process such that families that are referred-but-not-served are different from those that are referred and served. This can happen when referring agencies become aware that caseloads are full. They may refer only extreme cases in the hope that the urgency of the case will compel the FBS agency to serve a family in dire circumstances. Or, alternatively, they may refer families with relatively minor needs, preferring to divert families in crisis to agencies that they know will be able to respond immediately. Either way, this can bias the findings from case overflow designs.

Dismantling or Factorial Designs. In long-standing programs, resources may be such that caseloads are rarely full and, therefore, a FBS agency cannot consider a case overflow design. But agencies can still do rigorous research by testing innovative aspects of FBS programs against the basic FBS program. Dismantling or factorial designs are used for this purpose.

Dismantling designs get their name from the idea that service can be dismantled or partitioned into discrete components. Many FBS programs make use of different kinds of skills training in combination with concrete services. If one wanted to test a new kind of skills training, for example, some families might be randomly assigned to a FBS unit using a new skills training component, while others would receive the standard treatment.

If a program serves a large number of families, more complex dismantling designs may be developed. For example, if you wished to test the relative impact of concrete services and a new skills training package with a classic pretest-posttest design, a 2×2×2 factorial design could be used. Each factor would have two values: design (pretest, posttest), skills training (routine, new), and concrete services (yes—provided, no—not provided). In such a study, families would be randomly assigned to one of four separate treatment conditions: (1) routine skills training with concrete services; (2) routine skills training without concrete services; (3) new skills training with concrete services; and (4) new skills training without concrete services. Data would be collected before and after services. Pretest-posttest differences would allow the evaluator to estimate the relative impact of concrete service alone, the new skills training package alone, and the combination of concrete service plus the new skills package.

Dismantling designs have an important limitation. They do not permit drawing an inference about whether the service is effective compared to other non-FBS programs. They are more useful in developing new elements of service that respond to specific client problems or developments in interventive technology. Because dismantling designs lack a no-treatment or routine treatment control, the differences between groups are apt to be small. And when differences are small, it is hard to detect them. Thus the expected effects of the aspect of treatment that is partitioned should be precisely measured and all stakeholders should understand that no-effect findings do not imply that an FBS program is ineffective, just that the particular service being tested does not, by itself, have significant impact on outcomes.

Guidelines for Selecting a Design

Whether simple or complex, FBS evaluations are often based on a common set of strategies. These strategies may help to tailor a design to regional or local needs.

- *Think in terms of a series of evaluation studies.*   For developing programs, needs assessment followed by process evaluations are first steps. Process evaluations focus on difficulties in delivering a service as planned. As services become more refined, work from smaller studies to larger ones. Resist pressure to start with a classic experiment.

- *Match the evaluation design to the problem, treatment model, level of program development, and stakeholders' needs.* Practice knowledge tends to spiral upward as a result of a variety of knowledge-building enterprises. These include, but are not limited to, evaluation. One's own introspection, observations from workers, and the sometimes stinging words of skeptics help to formulate FBS "theory." Be prepared to experiment with the service model.
- *Use the literature.* Workers, administrators, and evaluators are not alone. Often local concerns are shared by others across the nation. The literature can suggest solutions to service delivery and evaluation design problems.
- *When assessing the impact of service, minimize the alternative explanations by using as strong a design as possible, including follow-up.* Designs with random assignment control for maturation, regression, selection, and other alternative explanations. Although our figures do not show follow-up observation, posttreatment measurement should occur multiple times. It is a common evaluation practice to examine outcome measures at the close of FBS and 6 and 12 months after service.
- *Reduce attrition.* Attrition occurs when families or family members discontinue participation in a study. When this happens, the sample size and statistical power are reduced. Attrition can produce bias. Use incentives to maintain participation. Allocate resources to pay family members for participation in data collection. Obtain permission to contact neighbors and relatives in order to locate participants who may have moved during the study.
- *Use multiple sources of information.* If a variable is important for pairing subjects in a matched-pairs design, measure it several different ways. Take advantage of existing tests and instruments. If out-of-home placements are important, avoid reliance on a single source of information. In addition, make use of parent, child, worker, and perhaps even teacher reports.

CONCLUSION: CONTROL AND VARIATION

In FBS evaluation, control and variation counterbalance one another. *Control* is important in several different ways. A service must be controlled or stable during an evaluation. If it is fluctuating (because of worker turnover, because of inadequate in-service training, because of poor leadership, etc.), a mix of qualitative and quantitative approaches might be used to identify the sources of variation and to develop a knowledge base from which to stabilize the FBS program. Control is important because there are many alternative explanations for an observed difference between pretest and posttest scores. Lacking a comparison or control group, one cannot argue that an FBS program is effective on the basis of pretest/posttest changes in the behaviors of children or parents who received FBS. Used this way, the word *control* means that variability due to alternative explanations has been reduced by the design. No design does this perfectly, but some designs are better than others.

Variation is important in several different ways. On balance, evaluators like big differences. An FBS should be genuinely different from the routine treatment received by a control or comparison group. Big differences in the nature of services between the experimental and control groups are more likely to produce large posttest differences. It makes little sense to spend a great deal of time testing a weak intervention. The experimental FBS should be potent. It should be quite different from the control or comparison service.

In a similar sense, differences across important variables should be maximized. Say, for instance, that younger children and teens are expected to have different outcomes. There should be enough variation in the sample to conduct separate analyses of differences by age groupings. One way to insure that there is sufficient variation on important variables is to use stratified probability sampling (see Chapter 3).

Variation and control are sought simultaneously, and it is this fact that makes evaluation design exhausting. While seeking variation, evaluators also want control. Only with a rigorous sampling strategy and a rigorous group assignment mechanism is it possible to maximize variation without sacrificing control.

Whether conducting qualitative or quantitative research, the themes of control and variation influence design selection, choice of measures, and sampling or subject assignment strategies. In qualitative research designs, control and variation affect strategies for collecting, coding, and analyzing information. In quantitative research designs, they affect the selection of samples and procedures for measurement. These, in turn affect the statistical tools and analytic strategies available to the evaluator. In the chapters that follow, we provide a practical review of sampling, measurement, and data analysis.

NOTES

1.   For example, see the use of theory in FBS, Fraser et al. (1991), Henggeler and Borduin (1990), Henggeler et al. (1992), Henggeler, Melton, Smith, Schoen-

wald, and Hanley (1993), Henggeler and Schoenwald (1993), Meezan and Mc-Croskey (1993), Nelson and Landsman (1992), Schuerman et al. (1993), University Associates (1992).

2. Sometimes where random assignment has failed it is possible to rescue posttest-only studies by increasing the sample sizes, by adjusting groups using covariance analysis, or by matching families on known variables. The latter two approaches will produce tacit equivalence, but the evaluator can never have confidence that the groups are equivalent on unknown variables. Only random assignment does this, and no amount of statistical adjustment or matching can produce the equivalence that comes from randomization.

Chapter 3

Sampling Children and Families

Once the decision has been made to conduct an evaluation, you must decide who you will study or observe. While the answer seems obvious—the clients of the program—the question remains: Which clients? Although the decision as to whether to study parents, children, agency personnel, other program participants, and/or observers of the program is determined by the program goals and the research questions that the evaluation poses, you still need to decide which members of these groups will be included. Sampling is the process through which you decide *specifically* who you will collect data from or about, and thus it is critical to the evaluation process.

Evaluating FBS involves a number of issues regarding the group of families, parents, children, and agency personnel to be included in the evaluation. Some of these issues, such as the target population of the program, are decisions that are made prior to beginning the program and its evaluation. Preferably, the evaluator should be involved in making decisions about targeting, since they affect both the way in which the evaluation will be designed and how the data will be analyzed.

Other sampling decisions are made when the program is stable and an outcome evaluation is being planned. These include the sampling procedures to be followed, the number of program participants to be studied, and the ways in which the rights of participants in the research will be protected. Each of these decisions has consequences for the evaluation, for they determine the specific program participants who will be included in the evaluation, whether the findings from this program can be generalized to other similar programs, the possibility that changes observed in the program participants will be judged to be statistically significant (see Chapter 12), and whether the research will appropriately protect the participants and be carried out in an ethical manner. This chapter covers these important issues, and the choices you have to make in these areas. It begins with the targeting of home-based services: to whom should services be provided? It then discusses approaches to sampling recipients or observers and the critical issue of how many program participants to include in the evaluation. The chapter ends with a discussion of how to protect the rights of clients or other participants in the research process.

TARGETING FBS

Prior to actually choosing a sample, it is important to decide the target of intervention. Defining a target service population enables the programs to set eligibility requirements. In FBS, the target population is usually defined by the agency's catchment area and by the range of issues that program personnel believe can be alleviated by the service.

Target problems and target populations are defined in a political context. Different stakeholders (program personnel, program administrators, policymakers, clients, evaluators, etc.) may have different views of who should be served by the program and what its goals should be (Rossi & Freeman, 1993). It is therefore important to take these varying perspectives into account in making decisions about targeting. If they are not, the program and the results of the evaluation may be dismissed as "irrelevant" or "unimportant."

In defining a target population, agencies need to consider how inclusive or exclusive to be. The more inclusive, the less specific you are likely to be, and therefore you are more likely to serve clients who may not need this intervention. In contrast, more restrictive and exacting targeting is likely to eliminate potential clients who could benefit from the service. This might lead to an underinclusion of families who could benefit from services and a smaller sample for testing evaluation questions.

Thus, in making targeting decisions, you need to have both *sensitivity* (correct identification of families who should be included in the program) and *specificity* (correctly excluding from the program families who do not have a condition that the program can help to ameliorate).

Both overinclusion and underinclusion in defining the target population can have significant consequences for both the program and its evaluation. As Rossi and Freeman (1993) discuss, overinclusion decreases the probability that positive program effects will be demonstrated, since services will be targeted to those who do not need them or cannot benefit from them. On the other hand, strictly adhering to specific targeting criteria can be expensive and time-consuming, since great effort must be taken to ensure that only those who meet specific criteria get the service. Further, underinclusion may raise ethical issues regarding exclusion of potential recipients from service, and thus alienate the community that the program was intended to serve.

Criteria for Program Inclusion in FBS

Many FBS programs exclude certain types of families from their services on programmatic grounds or on the assumption that excluded families would not benefit from the program. Among the exclusionary criteria reported in the literature are (1) substance abuse, serious mental illness, or severe cognitive impairment of the primary caregiver(s); (2) homelessness; (3) history of previous placements; (4) rejection of services, lack of caregiver motivation to use services, or inability to engage in service; (5) absence of children from home; (6) receipt of intensive services in the past; (7) court involvement; (8) inability to ensure a child's safety; and (9) inability to ensure worker safety (Feldman, 1990a; Rossi, 1992b; Schuerman, Rzepnicki, Littell, & Budde, 1992a; Tracy, 1991).

Application of some exclusionary criteria can present problems both for an evaluation and for the credibility of a service. First, by excluding families based on one or more of these criteria, agencies can be accused of "creaming" families for their programs. That is, it can be charged that "easier" families are screened into the program, while families with seemingly more difficult problems are excluded.

Second, application of certain exclusionary criteria may mean that the service will not be evaluated on the full range of families for whom they may be appropriate. If you target only families with particular problems for service, then you can only assess the effectiveness of service with these families. Nothing can be inferred about the effect on other types of families who did not receive services.

Third, you must question which if any of these criteria are appropriate. There is little to suggest that some families currently excluded from service could not benefit from them. For example, initial evidence indicates that parents who are substance abusing, mentally ill, or cognitively impaired can benefit from FBS if the services are structured and presented appropriately (McCroskey & Meezan, 1993). In addition, it may not be legitimate to assume that families who are court involved, have had a previous placement, or have received these services in the past cannot currently benefit from services.

Fourth, FBS do not necessarily have to take place in the home (Nelson, Landsman, & Deutelbaum, 1990). Thus, while office-based services may not be appropriate for all family situations, some families such as those who are homeless, who live in extremely dangerous neighborhoods, or who are very motivated to receive services can be seen in alternative settings. Finally, it should be remembered that exclusionary criteria such as "lack of parental motivation" are based on personal judgments that may not be reliable or applied consistently.

These concerns have led a number of child advocates and scholars to question exclusionary criteria outside "substantiated concern for the child's immediate safety" or "unwillingness to meet with staff after a number of attempts" (Rossi, 1992b). Limiting exclusionary criteria allows for studies to more comprehensively address which types of families, living under what circumstance, are more likely to benefit from FBS, especially if sample sizes are large (Tracy, 1991).

The Question of Placement Risk

While exclusionary criteria present thorny questions for both program personnel and evaluators, the greatest challenge currently facing the field is the criterion used by many programs that the family must have a child at *risk of imminent placement*. Some have argued that intensive FBS, developed to prevent out-of-home placement, are only cost-effective when they reach such families, and that fiscal savings disappear when these services are extended to families that do not yet have a child at risk of imminent placement (Nelson, 1989, 1991; Tracy, 1991).

While establishing imminence of placement may be useful in screening families referred for service, it has proven to be difficult to operationalize for research purposes, since (1) there are no indicators of imminent placement that are uniformly present at the point of referral to FBS; (2) placement decisions and therefore the risk of placement are not fully determined by case characteristics—systems issues, including the policies and intentions of the child protective service system and the availability of foster homes, may determine whether a child is placed; (3) imminence of risk may be assessed without a thorough knowledge of the family; (4) family circumstances can change dramatically during a crisis, which will affect risk; (5) determination of risk is often based on the worker's intuition, judgment, values, biases, ideology, and/or clinical impressions; (6) there has been little consistency in the time frame used to define imminence; and (7) there is no valid and reliable assessment tool to determine whether placement is imminent (Feldman, 1990a; Rossi, 1992a, 1992b; Schuerman, Rzepnicki, Littell, & Budde, 1992; Tracy, 1991).

The difficulty encountered in operationalizing imminence has been evident in the research conducted in this field. Early studies, which used simple pretest/posttest designs, assumed that all the children in the programs would have experienced out-of-home care without this service, and claimed success rates of 70–90 percent. Cost savings were calculated based on the cost of placements avoided for these children versus the cost of FBS.

Nelson (1991), however, recognizes the potential flaws in this argument when he states that "the findings we have regarding 'percentages of placements avoided' lack a desirable standard of precision. More control group studies . . . would certainly offer a more accurate and unassailable estimate of family preservation's real potential effectiveness rate" (pp. 210–211). It was exactly such control group studies that demonstrated the difficulty of operationalizing placement risk and therefore of substantiating these early claims of success.

In child welfare, at least five controlled evaluations of family-based programs employing risk of imminent placement criteria have been conducted (AuClaire & Schwartz, 1986; Feldman, 1990b; Fraser et al., 1991; Schuerman, Rzepnicki, Littell, & Budde, 1992b; Yuan et al., 1990). Three of these studies used randomized control groups, while two used case overflow designs. Three studies relied solely on worker judgment that a child was at imminent risk, while two had an external review or control. In all five studies, substantial numbers of control group children remained at home, and therefore were not at risk of imminent placement. If they had been, most would have been placed. More importantly, in the randomized studies in which the determination of imminent risk was left solely to worker judgment, more than 80% of the control samples remained at home.

There have been a number of solutions proposed to the problem of operationalizing imminence of risk. Some researchers have successfully trained workers to make more accurate judgments regarding whether a child is at imminent risk and provided them with a supportive context in which to make such assessments (Wells & Whittington, 1993). Before this proposed solution is adopted, however, it needs further testing, and the type of training provided to workers needs to be specified.

Others have suggested developing and refining screening tools that would increase the likelihood that those at greatest risk would be reached (Feldman, 1990a), and that such screening tools include multiple parent, child, and family factors considered within the ecological system of the family. They stress the need for multiple measures, since risk of placement is not a unitary concept but is composed of multiple, interacting variables.

It should be remembered, however, that the ability to predict other, more frequently occurring events in child welfare has not been all that successful, particularly when the prediction is based on a complex system of variables that interact with each other in unknown or unpredictable ways. Even with a significant investment of energy, time, and money, efforts to assess the risk of repeated child maltreatment have not proven particularly successful (Pecora, 1991b; Wald & Woolverton, 1990). While a few studies have shown that worker judgments about factors contributing to the potential for abuse tend to be consistent and reliable (Nasuti & Pecora, 1993), they have not yet been demonstrated to be valid predictors of current maltreatment, child placement, re-referral to child protective services, or future reports of child maltreatment.

A strategy that has been employed to better screen for risk of placement has been the "certification process." That is, it is first certified, either by an expert panel or by the court, that families referred to FBS will have children placed if services are not provided. Compared to other studies, in the two studies that have used this procedure (Au-Claire & Schwartz, 1986; Feldman, 1990b) much smaller percentages of control group children remained at home. However, even with this strategy, a sizable proportion of children in the control group did not enter care.

Another strategy has been to use family-based interventions to reunify families whose children are already in placement (Walton, Fraser, Lewis, Pecora, & Walton, 1993). While this is a promising use of this technology and eliminates the need for judging risk of placement, it redefines the service: placement prevention is no longer the goal.

A final strategy that has been suggested is to drop risk of imminent placement from consideration when choosing families for FBS (Rossi, 1992b). A number of programs are already using this "relaxed" criterion. There may be advantages to this idea even though it might result in providing services to some families for whom they were not initially intended, and in breaking the "contract" with policymakers around potential reductions in out-of-home care and the attendant cost savings. First, the operational imprecision present in the concept of risk of imminent placement, which has plagued evaluations to date, would be eliminated. Second, programs would serve families with more varied needs and characteristics and therefore would be able to determine success rates with different types of families and the impact of services on families with different presenting problems (assuming a large enough sample; variability in family characteristics, problems, and services might suppress program effects if only a small sample were studied). Finally, eliminating the criterion of imminent placement would address the criticisms that FBS is provided only when a family is facing dissolution and does not serve the large number of families who could benefit from earlier intervention (Fein & Maluccio, 1992; McGowan, 1989).

SAMPLING

Once the target population has been identified, you need to decide whether all families served by the program should be studied. If not, do you want the sample of families studied to be representative of all families served by the program, or do you want to select certain families for study? Answers to these questions (as well as others) will determine the sampling plan for the evaluation.

In programs serving relatively few clients, it is best to study all of the families and thus guarantee the largest possible sample. The families studied will be *representative* of the families served by the program, since you have studied the entire population. Your sample will not be *biased* in any way, and the need for a more complex sampling strategy will be avoided.

However, when the program serves a large number of clients, perhaps at multiple sites, it is often costly to study all program participants, particularly if you are collecting large amounts of data. In such situations, it is almost as effective, and far less costly, to study a sample of families. In choosing a sample there are two general approaches, *probability* and *nonprobability sampling*, and you must decide which is appropriate for your study given the evaluation questions.

Probability Sampling Methods

Probability sampling helps to guarantee that the families chosen for study will be *representative* of (i.e., accurately reflect) the population of families served by the program. Probability sampling ensures that each family served by the program has an equal chance of being chosen for study. Three types of probability samples are most likely to be used in an evaluation of FBS: simple random samples, systematic samples, and proportional stratified samples.

In *simple random samples*, each family served during the evaluation period is identified and given a number. Then families are chosen using a table of random numbers available in most statistics books, or a list of random numbers generated by a computer. Choose a starting point at random and select families sequentially until you have the required number.

Systematic sampling is perhaps the simplest method of drawing a probability sample. If, for example, you wanted to study 200 out of 600 families who participated in the program, you would calculate that your sampling ratio as 1:3 (200/600). From the first three families on the list, you would choose one at random; let us say family number 2. You would then choose every third family on the list starting with number 2 (5, 8, 11, etc.) to be in your sample.

Systematic random sampling is effective if one precaution is heeded. You must make sure that the list of families is not biased or cyclical in any way. For example, if every third person on the list had a worker in the same unit within the agency you would be evaluating the effectiveness of a single unit rather than the entire program.

The third method of choosing a probability sample is through *proportional stratified sampling*. This type of sample is drawn when two or more distinct groups are present in the population, and you wish to ensure that these groups (called strata) are represented in the sample in *exactly* the same proportion as they are present in population. For example, suppose you have three service units and wish to have an exact representation of families from each of the three units in your sample. You would first divide the families into three groups, depending on the unit that provided service to them, and then choose the same number of families from each group using either systematic or simple random sampling procedures. While the other forms of probability sampling would yield approximately this result, it would be unlikely that they would provide exact proportions on the variable stratified, since all probability samples contain some error.

Two other types of probability samples may be useful in the evaluation of large FBS programs. These are *disproportional stratified samples* and *cluster samples*. Each is used under special conditions (e.g., when certain groups are underrepresented in the population and you want to have sufficient numbers to do statistical analysis, when a full listing of those served by the program is not readily available or easily accessible, when families are spread over a wide geographic area). When these conditions exist, it is wise to consult a sampling expert, because these sampling methods will require either special statistical procedures or create greater error in the sample (it will be less representative than other types of samples)(Grinnell, 1993; Rubin & Babbie, 1993).

Despite care in choosing and carrying out a sampling method, three factors can diminish the representativeness of a sample. These are incomplete lists of program participants, refusal to participate or nonresponse by members of the sample, and attrition during the course of the study. If these circumstances affect more than a small percentage of the families in your sample, you must be careful when interpreting your data, since the representativeness gained by choosing a probability sample might have been compromised. For example, if some families do not appear on the list of program participants, or their records are missing when such a list is compiled, they have no chance of being chosen for the sample. If this is true for a large number of families, the sample may be biased—if there are differences (such as degree of program participation) between those whose names were on the participant list and those whose names were not. Similarly, if a significant proportion of the sample refuses to participate in the research, or participates at pretest but not at posttest, then bias may occur if those who participated were systematically different from those who did not.

Nonprobability Sampling Methods

In nonprobability sampling, one cannot assume that the families chosen for study will be representative of the families who participated in the program; each family does not have the same chance of being chosen for study. This type of sampling is usually regarded as inferior to probability sampling, and useful only when a list of the population (in this case the program participants) cannot be assembled.

There are occasions, however, when such a sample can be appropriate in evaluating FBS. For example, at the beginning of the evaluation process, when you are trying to decide on the appropriate outcome measures, you may wish to study a group of families with whom workers believe they have been particularly successful. These families might be able to provide information about the ways in which they think they have changed as a result of the program. They may also be able to identify the program inputs that they think were valuable. Similarly, when pretesting instruments to see if they are understandable to program participants, the sampling method may be unimportant as long as it includes a broad cross section of families.

Selecting a small nonprobability sample may also enhance your understanding of the data once they are collected, since selected program participants may have particular insight into the meaning of the data and the reasons certain results were obtained. Further, in some forms of evaluation, nonprobability samples may be preferred. In qualitative research, for example, nonprobability methods are sometimes used to capture the experiences of "extreme" cases (both successes and failures) to add to the thick description (Geertz, 1973) that is desired (See Chapter 10; Guba & Lincoln, 1989; Patton, 1990).

There are basically four types of nonprobability sampling techniques that can be useful in evaluating family-based programs: convenience sampling, purposive sampling, quota sampling, and snowball sampling.

In *convenience sampling*, also referred to as *availability or accidental sampling*, the researcher chooses to study the most readily available program participants. Thus, a mother who is at the agency when the researcher is present might be asked to help in pre-testing an instrument.

Purposive sampling, also known as *judgmental sampling*, occurs when the evaluator or program personnel identify a participant who is particularly knowledgeable about a question of concern. For example, a participant in the program, who has been identified as being particularly engaged with the program, might be able to provide the researcher with a useful interpretation of an unanticipated finding. Similarly, an African-American or Latina mother will be able to tell a researcher whether an instrument is relevant and understandable in her cultural context.

Quota sampling occurs when critical population characteristics are identified. The researcher establishes the occurrence of these characteristics in the population and selects, usually through convenience sampling, participants in each category until a "quota" for each group is filled. While this may appear to be analogous to stratified sampling, it differs in that each quota is filled based on convenience. For example, a researcher may wish to test, early in the research process, a group of children who represent the population on the variables of age and gender. Results of an early analysis performed on these data may give some clues as to whether an instrument, which is supposed to be sensitive to age and gender considerations, does differentiate these groups.

The final type of nonprobability sampling is known as a *snowball sampling*. Snowball sampling occurs when a member of the population is identified based on some characteristic and is asked to identify other members of the population who are similar on the same characteristic. For example, suppose a program concentrates its efforts in a particular neighborhood. A researcher is interested in knowing why families discontinued service and the ways in which dropout families differ from families who completed service. While the researcher may know the names of all of the families who discontinued (and therefore, theoretically, could choose a probability sample to interview), such families are often difficult to locate. In a snowball sample, a family who has discontinued might be able to help the researcher locate other similar families in the neighborhood (who might also be able to help the researcher locate still others, etc.). This process can increase the numbers of non-completers available to the researcher for study. While it cannot be said with any certainty that the final sample of noncompleters is representative of the population, larger samples tend to be more representative than smaller samples.

SAMPLE SIZE

In some programs, the sample size is determined by the number of families who participated in the program. That is, the entire population of families is studied. If, however, you are choosing a sample of families to study, or can prolong the evaluation period until a desired sample size is reached, you should consider the amount of error in the sample (how confident you can be that the sample truly represents the population) and whether you will be able to detect differences between program (experimental) and nonprogram (control) families in the statistical analysis of the data.

Determining Sample Size to Diminish Sampling Error

Any sample drawn from a larger population is only one of an infinite number of samples that might have been drawn from that population. Some of these samples will approximate the characteristics of the population better than others. When a *probability* sample of a particular size has been drawn from a population, it is possible to estimate how well the sample reflects the true characteristics of the population. While this involves statistical calculations that are beyond the scope of this chapter [for more information, see Grinnell (1993, pp. 165–169) or Rubin & Babbi (1993, pp. 226–236)], two general principles should guide your decision regarding sample size. The first is that *the more people in your sample, the more likely it is to reflect the population*. The second is that there is *"a point of diminishing return"* (Smith, 1990, p. 102), a point beyond which the cost of increasing your sample size is not worth the increased precision. An example, taken from Smith (1990), illustrates these principles:

> A program serves 1,000 people. If we interview 100 people, we might have a sampling error rate of plus or minus 10%. This could mean that if 60% of those in our sample liked the program, the percent of those in the population who like the program could range from 50% to 70%. . . . If you select a sample of 280, your error rate might be reduced to only plus or minus 5%. In other words, by interviewing 180 more people, we cut our error rate in half. If 60% of those 280 interviewed like the program, the population figure for all 1,000 people in the program might be 55% or 65% who liked the program. . . . So what if you wanted to reduce the error rate by another 3% to plus or minus 2%. Well, you would have to increase the size of your sample from 280 to 715, an increase of 435 more people who you must interview . . . In this example, 280 was the point of diminishing returns, and increasing the sample beyond 280 was not likely worth the extra effort and expense. (p. 102)

When you are able to draw a probability sample from a large population of program participants, decisions regarding how much error you should tolerate within the sample, and therefore the sample size, should be made in consultation with a statistician. Sampling principles are based on complex rules involving statistical inference, and sampling

Table 3.1.   Appropriate Sizes of Simple
Random Samples with a 5% Margin
of Error and 95% Confidence Level
Assuming a Population Proportion of
50%[a]

Population size	Sample size
25	24
50	44
75	63
100	80
150	108
200	132
250	152
300	169
400	196
500	217
750	254
1000	278
2000	322
4000	351
5000	357

[a] Source: D. Royse (1992). Program evaluation:
An introduction. Chicago: Nelson Hall, p. 160.
Reprinted with permission.

error is affected by factors other than sample size. As a general guide, however, Table 3.1 shows sample sizes for simple random samples with a ±5% margin of error under specified statistical assumptions.

Enhancing the Ability to Detect Program Effects
Through Sample Size

When you study a small number of families, the potential for detecting statistically significant program effects is diminished. This can create problems for your evaluation if the program serves only a small number of families at a given time, if the project period is short, if complex analyses are planned, or if a complex design has been chosen. One must remember the following basic statistical principles:

(1) More subjects are needed if one sets the significance level at $p=.01$ or $p=.05$ rather than $p=.10$. The more stringent the significance level (alpha) is, the larger the necessary sample size.

(2) If one is only testing whether, for example, the experimental group improved more than the control group and does not wish to test concomitantly for the possibility that the control group improved signifi-

cantly more than the experimental group, fewer subjects are needed; testing nondirectional hypotheses requires larger sample sizes.

(3) Subtle effects are more difficult to detect than gross effects, and thus the smaller the critical effect size one wishes to detect, the larger the necessary sample.

(4) Greater protection from failing to show effects of a program requires more subjects. The larger the power required, the larger the necessary sample size (Kraemer & Thiemann, 1987).

The chances that the effectiveness of your program will be captured by your study are affected by the significance level you choose, whether you will be testing directional or nondirectional hypotheses, the size of the effect you want to detect, which statistical tests you will be using, and how sure you want to be to show an effect. Having made these decisions, you can then determine the sample size you need through the use of a *power analysis*. (You can also determine how much power an analysis had to show effects after the fact, but you cannot then make corrections.) These decisions, and the power analysis, should be made in consultation with someone knowledgeable about statistics and this procedure. For the sake of illustration, Figure 3.1 shows this decision-making process and the resulting sample size in one study of FBS.[1]

PROTECTIONS IN THE RESEARCH PROCESS

Because research in FBS involves collecting data from or about persons participating in service, and may involve withholding or withdrawing a "preferred" service, most practitioners and researchers in the field believe that it is important to follow procedures that protect clients in the research process. Such "human subjects" protections are required when the research is sponsored by a governmental entity and/or undertaken within a university setting. They are clearly consistent with professional values and ethics since they protect client confidentiality and help to ensure that clients are not exposed to unnecessary risks.

Some have argued that such procedures are unnecessary in agency-based services research, except under unusual circumstances (e.g., Thyer, 1993). While some situations may need to be handled differently, we believe that researchers have a responsibility of protecting clients or other subjects (e.g., workers, teachers) of FBS research, particularly when the research is not conducted by agency staff. While we hope that eventually the evaluation of interventions will become a routine part of professional practice, this is currently the exception rather than the rule.

The power analysis performed for this study, is based upon an alpha level of .05, a moderate effect size (the magnitude of the relationship to be detected; $d = .5$ for t-tests), and power of .80 (the probability that a moderate effect will be detected as significant).

Necessary sample sizes for commonly used bi-variate statistical tests would be:

Test		Sample size required
t-test (2 tailed)		64 per group
t-test (1 tailed)		50 per group
F-test (2 tailed)		3 groups, 52 per group
		4 groups, 45 per group
chi-square	df = 1	87 for 2 × 2 table
	df = 2	107 for 3 × 2 table
	df = 4	133 for 3 × 3 or 2 × 5 table

Based on the figures above, a desirable final sample size, after attrition, would be 256 families—128 families randomly assigned to both experimental and comparison groups assuming a two-tailed t-test would be used. From the above table it can be seen that moderate effect can be detected with a 2-tailed t-test for as few as 64 families in each group, and therefore a sample size of 128 subjects per group will provide more than sufficient power. This sample size will not allow "small" effects (<.2) to be detected, but will identify intermediate effects ($.3 < d < .5$ for t-test) (Cohen, 1988).

While this size sample is adequate, it is not ideal. Much of the research in the field has demonstrated that only small effects can be expected from programs such as this, evaluated through similar designs. However, for small effects to be detected, the sample size would have to be larger than the capacity of the programs under study. For example, for a 1-tailed t-test using the sample alpha and power level as above, each group would have to contain 310 subjects to detect small effects (not shown in the above table); larger groups would be needed if one wished to test 2-tailed hypotheses.

Figure 3.1. An example of a power analysis. [*Source:* Adapted from W. Meezan and J. McCroskey (1989). An evaluation of the home-based services programs of Children's Bureau of Los Angeles and Hathaway Children's Services: A proposal submitted to the Stuart Foundations, University of Southern California, School of Social Work, Los Angeles.]

We believe that as long as evaluations are conducted primarily by people outside the agency, clients and other research subjects must be as fully protected as possible in the research enterprise. We further believe that all subjects of research should be informed about research procedures and have the right to refuse them, even if the choice not to comply has negative consequences for them. And, while obtaining informed consent often presents logistical difficulties, we believe that training in these procedures and compliance with them are necessary if researchers are to fulfill their ethical responsibilities.

Given this position, three questions need to be addressed: (1) Who should determine whether the proposed research will protect the subject? (2) On what criteria should such a determination be made? (3) What constitutes informed consent on the part of the client? These questions will be addressed in the following sections.

The Human Subjects Committee or Institutional Review Board

Research conducted in a social agency, either by a member of the staff or an outside evaluator, should be reviewed by the agency, even if human subjects clearance has already been gained through an institutional review board at a university or other research organization. In this way, the agency maintains control over access to data, clients, and other research subjects, and can help to ensure that professional ethics in the conduct of research are adhered to fully.

While an agency may have a "research" committee that evaluates the merits of research proposals, human subjects review, when logistically possible, should be a separate process conducted by a separate body. In this way, the human subjects committee is uncontaminated by any political pressures that might be present; the sole purpose of this committee is to ensure (as much as possible) that the client population is protected from harm during the research.

The human subjects committee or research committee should judge a number of elements in any proposal that comes before it. These include that (1) the research methods (design, sampling, instrumentation and methods of data collection) are appropriate given the objectives of the research, (2) the research methods and data gathering techniques pose no unnecessary risk, (3) any risks to the subjects are justified in terms of the related benefits, both to the subjects and society, (4) the subjects' privacy is protected, (5) to the fullest extent possible, subjects participate willingly and knowingly, and (6) research activities are monitored for compliance to procedures to protect subjects' rights. In order to approve

Table 3.2. Information Provided by the Researcher to the Human Subjects Committee

(1) The major objectives of the research.
(2) Research plan and procedures.
(3) A description of where the subjects will be drawn from, and how they will be obtained and selected. Renumeration to subjects, if any, should be disclosed and should not be so large as to be considered coercive.
(4) Whether the sample will include particularly vulnerable subjects (children, the mentally disabled, etc.) and, if so, how their rights will be protected.
(5) A statement of how informed consent will be obtained, including conditions where consent will have to be obtained from a surrogate.
(6) An explanation of what research procedures will be involved, including interview protocols and sample questionnaires.
(7) An explanation of what is to be done with the collected data.
(8) A risk/benefit analysis that consists of an explanation of what risks are involved in the research, how subjects are to be protected, and whether the risks to the subjects are reasonable in relation to the anticipated benefits and the importance of the knowledge to be gained.
(9) Measures to be taken to minimize risks to the subject, including the availability of alternative procedures.
(10) A description of the researcher's qualifications.

a research study, the agency's human subjects committee needs the information regarding the proposed research, which is outlined in Table 3.2. (Also see American Psychological Association, 1982.)

Informed Consent

As part of its procedure, the human subjects committee should review the steps taken to ensure that the research is conducted only with the informed consent of the participant. Informed consent is consent freely given by a participant, based upon as full a disclosure as possible of what the individual will be exposed to, and any risks, dangers, or other expected or possible consequences. The human subjects committee should have written evidence concerning such procedures and should approve the consent form that the investigator is planning to use. Both the subject and the investigator should retain a copy of the informed consent document after it is signed.

There are a number of general requirements for obtaining informed consent. These include that (1) no research should involve human subjects without the informed consent of the subject or the subject's legal guardian, (2) the subject be allowed the opportunity to consider whether or not to participate in the research without coercion, (3) information be

Figure 3.2. Model informed consent form for a family-based research project. [*Source:* Adapted from W. Meezan and J. McCroskey (1989). An evaluation of the home-based services programs of Children's Bureau of Los Angeles and Hathaway Children's Services: A proposal submitted to the Stuart Foundations, University of Southern California, School of Social Work, Los Angeles.]

You and your family are invited to participate in a study of the services provided by child welfare agencies in   (location of study) . If you agree to participate, you and your children will become part of a group of   (number of participants)   families taking part in this project. The knowledge obtained through this study will be helpful to people planning family and children's services so that they can better serve families in need.

If you decide to participate, an interviewer will meet with you and your child(ren) for about two hours and ask you to answer some questions. Interviewers will come back in about four months and about a year after that to find out how you and your child(ren) are doing.

A major benefit of your participation in this study will be that you will be able to talk about yourself, your family, and your experiences together. In addition, your responses could help in shaping the delivery of social services to families with children.

There are no known risks to those who participate in the study, but some of the questions that you are asked may touch on sensitive areas. You should also be aware that state law requires that we report any evidence of child abuse or neglect in your family to the   (name of child protective service agency) .

You may refuse to answer any question, and may stop the interview at any time. Your decision to participate or not to participate in the research will in no way affect the services or benefits you receive from any of the agencies with whom you are involved.

In addition to the interview, signing this consent to participate in the research will allow the researchers to collect information from your case records at   (agency name)   and from your child(ren)'s teacher(s), if he or she is in school. Any information obtained in connection with the study will remain fully confidential and will only be available to the research team. All information collected will be kept in locked files, and your name will not appear on any research form.

If you have any questions about the research, you should feel free to ask you interviewer at any time. You may also contact the researcher(s) conducting the study: (name)   or   (name)   at   (name of institution)   at   (phone number) . If at any point you have questions regarding the way the research is being conducted, you may contact   (human subjects committee chair)   at   (phone number)   who is in charge of research protocols at   (name of agency or university) .

In recognition of the important contribution you are making by participating in the research, and compensation for your time, you will be given a $25 gift certificate at the end of each interview—one now, one four months from now, and one a year from now.

Your signature below indicates that you understand your rights in the research and are participating in this study freely.

(continued)

presented in language that is understood by the subject or his/her representative including translation if necessary, (4) there be no waiver of legal rights of the subject, nor release of the researcher from liability, and (5) if deception is necessary, there be a prompt and complete debriefing of the subject during which withdrawal from the research is permitted.

Documentation of informed consent should include a statement that the intervention involves research, an explanation of the purposes of the research, the expected duration of the subject's participation, a description of the research procedures to be followed, and the identification of any procedures that can be considered experimental. The consent form should include a description of any reasonable, foreseeable risks or discomforts to the subject as well as a description of any benefits that might accrue to the subject or to others.

Further, in order to protect subjects, the consent form should contain a statement describing how confidentiality of records and other information gathered will be maintained, an explanation of any compensation for participation in the research, and a description of any treatment that is available if injury or distress results from participation in the research. Subjects should also be given information regarding who to contact for answers to questions regarding the research and the rights of the participants regarding the research.

Finally, subjects should be made aware that participation is voluntary, that refusal to participate will involve no penalty or loss of benefits, that they may withdraw from the research at any time, and that they may refuse to participate in any part of the research protocol. Subjects may also be told the number of subjects who will be participating in the research and given an opportunity to receive a summary of the results. A copy of a prototype consent form for FBS research is provided in Figure 3.2.

The Special Case of Children's Participation in Research

Children are seen as being particularly vulnerable in the research process and are assumed to be unable to give valid *informed* consent. Thus, special procedures are needed to protect them from potential harm. Involving children directly in research requires the *permission* of their parents and their *assent* (when the child is capable of providing assent) in the place of informed consent.

Permission from parents can be gained by providing them with all the information usually provided to research subjects in informed-consent

(*Figure 3.2 Continued*)

Agreement
  Your signature indicates that, having read the information provided above, you have agreed to participate in the research and that you have received a copy of this form.

_____   _____
Signature   Date

procedures. Based on their understanding of the information, parents are then asked to decide, without coercion, whether or not to allow their child to participate. If permission is granted, an appropriate consent form is completed by the researcher and the parent(s).

Once parental permission is obtained, the proposed research procedures are explained to the children in language that is appropriate to their age, experience, maturity, and condition. This explanation includes a discussion of any discomforts or inconveniences they may experience, and their rights in the research procedure. Their assent is then obtained by having them affirmatively agree to participate in the research; failure to object to participate cannot be construed as assent. (In cases of mature minors, obtaining parental permission is often followed by a full informed-consent procedure with the minor.)

Review boards should ensure that risk to children in research is minimal. In this usage, minimal risk exists when the probability of harm or discomfort anticipated in the proposed research is not greater than that ordinarily encountered in daily life or during the performance of routine physical or psychological examinations or tests. While this is likely to be the case in FBS research, additional protections and precautions must be added when it is not.

If the research involves children who are wards of the state, additional precautions might also be necessary to help to ensure that these children, for whom the state is parent, are not exploited. This is most likely if you are studying children for whom FBS services are aimed at reunification. In these or other circumstances where additional precautions to protect the child might be necessary (e.g., when parents cannot be located, when one is unsure whether permission from both parents is necessary), the agency review board should consult with other similar bodies who have had greater experience in protecting the rights of children in research. Such consultation might be sought from institutional review boards at major universities or child-serving agencies that have had a long history of research or an ongoing research program.

CONCLUSION

The above discussion has highlighted a number of important points. First, despite the importance in FBS of targeting appropriate populations, satisfactory methods of targeting have not yet been established. Until consensus is reached on exclusionary and "imminent risk" criteria, programs and their evaluations will continue to differ substantially from each other, and knowledge about service effectiveness will be compromised.

Second, simple sampling procedures can produce important economies in evaluation. You can generalize to a program's population (but not to other programs) if you use probability techniques. Nonprobability samples are useful and appropriate in the planning stages of an outcome evaluation or when conducting qualitative evaluation.

Third, larger samples have both less error and greater potential for showing program effects. Small programs that serve 100 or fewer people should use their entire population as the sample for the evaluation. Attrition is particularly hazardous for small programs attempting to do rigorous outcome evaluations. As Royse has observed:

> If only one or two caseworkers are employed in a program . . . and if the evaluation period runs for one year, the population of clients served by the program might range from twelve to about fifty.
>
> Even if there were no attrition, twelve cases is too small a sample for a program evaluation, and twenty-four or even thirty-six cases is also pretty darn small. . . . When attrition is a serious problem, it may be difficult to convince others that the program is more successful than less expensive programs. (1992, p. 214)

Finally, subjects must be accorded all available protections. Review of informed consent procedures by an institutional review board or a research committee is a central way to ensure that professional ethics are not compromised in the conduct of evaluations. Only in the context of proper sampling and human subjects' protections can research provide vital knowledge to advance family-based practice.

NOTE

1. Conventional estimates for effect sizes must be viewed with caution as theory and research data previously collected may be used to establish more precisely what is considered to be a "small" versus large effect. I.e., the meaning of the effect size must be viewed within the context of that field of research. (See Cohen, 1988.)

Chapter 4

Assessing Services and Interventions

Identifying and measuring interventions that create change is an enduring challenge in human services. Despite considerable progress since Fischer's (1973) critique of social casework, it is still difficult to isolate the "active ingredient" in interventions with multiple components (Chen, 1990). Nowhere is this problem more pressing than in the field of FBS. Designed to provide comprehensive assistance to troubled families, FBS programs offer a wide variety of services from family therapy to emergency financial aid, and it is seldom clear which, if any, are necessary and sufficient to achieve desired outcomes.

The problem of specifying and measuring interventions is common to all helping professions (Orlinsky & Howard, 1986). In FBS, however, the "therapeutic contract" implied by the structure of the program is particularly important. It determines whether family members are seen together or individually (service unit), how frequently and how long families are seen each week (intensity), what mix of services (concrete and clinical) are provided, and how long services last (duration). One of the features thought to contribute to the success of FBS is that they involve all family members in defining needs and resolving problems (Nelson, Landsman, & Deutelbaum, 1990), a process that is extremely hard to measure. While efforts to describe and measure parental involvement (Sonnichsen, 1994) and empowerment practice (Dunst, Trivette, & Deal, 1988) are under way in several fields, they are not fully developed.

Beyond the aspects of treatment that are defined by the program's structure and policies, specific interventions and therapeutic techniques vary from family to family. Most studies of FBS have measured at least two types of service: clinical and concrete (Fraser, 1990). Using different typologies, several studies have found that counseling was the most frequently provided service. In two studies, less than a quarter of families received concrete services, although these are deemed essential to effective service delivery (Nelson, 1990; Fraser & Haapala, 1988). How-ever, other studies document that a large proportion of families received concrete services, especially transportation, and that in some cases these services were associated with attainment of treatment goals and place-ment prevention (Fraser et al., 1991).

APPROACHES TO STUDYING INTERVENTIONS

Three types of studies that can be used to break down the effects of complex interventions are explored in this chapter: case studies of indi-vidual families, case review studies, and group experimental designs with random assignment to different treatment conditions (Blythe, 1990; Chen, 1990, Ch. 12). Using data from recent studies of FBS programs, this chapter illustrates the strengths and weaknesses of each approach. In addition, since monitoring of services is essential to assure that the program is being faithfully implemented and has not "drifted," different approaches to quality assurance are discussed.

Single-Case Studies

For more than a decade the systematic study of single cases has been promoted as a practical approach to assessing the impact of interven-tions in social work and psychology (Fischer, 1978; Jayaratne & Levy, 1979). As discussed in Chapter 2, these designs involve identifying be-haviors, feelings, or conditions that need to change within a single fami-ly, parent, or child and monitoring them over the course of intervention. In situations where the small number of cases does not allow statistical analysis of grouped data, single-case studies are a practical alternative. They are particularly useful in documenting and assessing the outcomes of highly individualized interventions. Accumulating data from single-subject studies can also assist in monitoring the quality of the program, identifying promising interventions, and contributing information on the effectiveness of the program as a whole (Alter & Evens, 1990; Blythe, 1990; Nuehring & Pascone, 1986).

In single-case studies, you must be able to identify a *specific* interven-tion that you and the family think will help in the situation under study, to identify the point in time when the intervention begins, and to de-scribe it in sufficient detail so that someone else can repeat it. For this reason, generalized interventions such as active listening are not suit-able for this kind of evaluation.

Outcomes can be monitored in a variety of ways including paper and pencil tests (see Chapters 5–7), existing records (e.g., school attendance), and counts of desirable and/or undesirable feelings, events, or behaviors. Counselors using behavioral interventions have devised many ways of counting and recording that can be implemented by the worker, family members, or others in a position to observe the family. For example, Jayaratne & Levy (1979, pp. 76–84) discuss possible observers as well as ways of recording frequency, duration, magnitude, and timing of behaviors in natural and role-play situations.

It is very helpful to begin monitoring the target condition well before the intervention is implemented. However, this may only be feasible if the assessment process in your program typically takes a week or longer. If your program allows for a series of preintervention measurements, or you have access to other data such as school attendance records, you may be able to construct a retrospective baseline or employ a more sophisticated time-series design (Nurius, 1983). In any case, it is very important that you get at least one set of measurements before starting your intervention. For statistical analysis, several preintervention measurements are necessary. However, this is rarely possible if families are at imminent risk of placement.

This approach to evaluation was used in a demonstration project involving intervention with chronically neglecting families known for an extended period of time to the public child welfare agency in a rural county in southern Oregon (Landsman, Nelson, Allen, & Tyler, 1992). Families helped to plan the service program, which centered on weekly parent meetings, concurrent meetings or activities for children, and a meal provided to both project staff and families. According to their individual needs, families also received parent aide services, family therapy, parent education, substance abuse treatment, and other community services. In a successful case in which the family remained intact, a single-subject monitoring design was used to detect possible influences of the intensity and timing of service on family change. The case is described in Figure 4.1.

The success of this family was measured in several ways. There were no additional reports of abuse or neglect, the children in care were returned or relinquished, and no further placements were made. Household management, parental functioning, and child functioning all improved, and the second-oldest son completed his GED. The problems measured by the Family Systems Change Scale (FSCS—see Chapter 5) were rated as not or only slightly problematic by the end of service. The only serious problem noted on the Child Well-Being Scales (CWBS—see Chapter 5) was in supervision of the eleven-year-old girl, with a continuation of moderate behavior problems at termination. These included

> The Thompson family included two married parents, Joanne, 37, and Matt, 34, and her six children ages 1 to 19. The family had been known to the agency for 8 years with a long history of neglect, substance abuse, and a "dysfunctional life-style." The two youngest children had been placed following the arrest of their mother. The oldest child, a boy, was in prison for burglary, the second-oldest son had dropped out of school, and the oldest daughter had been living on the streets of a large city.
>
> Although Matt was employed full time, substance abuse impaired his functioning as a parent and drained family resources. The Thompsons scored in the marginal range on the Childhood Level of Living Scale (Polansky et al., 1983a, 1983b) and at high risk of both neglect and abuse.
>
> At the end of the first quarter of treatment, staff were very satisfied with the family's progress and confident that the two children in foster care would return home. After the 2-year-old was returned, more serious problems were revealed. At 6 months project staff felt the chances of success with this family were poor. During the next 6 months, however, due to their acceptance and ability to provide leadership in the parent group, the parents found the confidence to return to a community college. By the end of the project the family had relinquished the youngest child for adoption, but chances of the remaining children staying in the family were regarded as very good.

Figure 4.1.   Successful intervention with chronic neglect.

incidents of petty shoplifting that did not result in arrests or court involvement.

Graphing the variables for which several measures were available (Figure 4.2) showed a high level of both group and individual family therapy in the first eight months of service. Parent aide activity was maintained at about five hours a month from months four to sixteen. In the last eight months there was very little service to this family.

A second case, described in Figure 4.3, did not have a successful outcome during the project. The graph for this family (Figure 4.4), shows a moderate investment of time by the parent aide in months two to five and by the family therapists and parent aide in months eleven and twelve, after the family had been reported again for neglect, physical abuse, and sexual abuse. Not until month ten did the mother participate in two group meetings and her partner in one, even though they could have joined a group that started in month three.

Since in these cases, as in many others, it was not feasible to delay intervention until an adequate baseline was obtained, monitoring can only show whether the outcome measures changed as interventions were implemented and cannot establish that the intervention was the cause of change. One might deduce from comparing Figures 4.2 and 4.4 that an initial infusion of family therapy and a parenting group, overlapped and

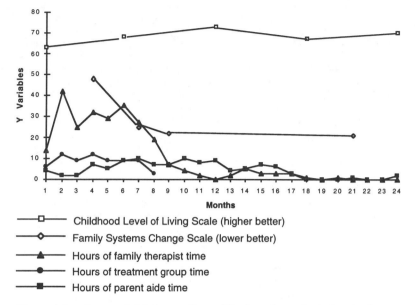

Figure 4.2. Successful intervention with chronic neglect: Service hours and scale scores. [*Source:* M. J. Landsman, K. Nelson, M. Allen, & M. Tyler (1992). *Family-based treatment for chronically neglecting families: The self-sufficiency project.* Iowa City: National Resource Center on Family Based Services.]

followed by six to eight months of parent aide service, is more effective in cases of chronic neglect than parent aide services alone. However, this hypothesis would need to be tested further in single-system studies using more rigorous designs or in group experiments.

Case Reviews

Another approach to studying services uses data from case records and management information systems. Pietrzak, Ramler, Renner, Ford, & Gilbert (1990) describe the process and uses of such case audits. Given reasonably complete case records and/or comparable data in management information systems, agency-based evaluators can describe the services delivered by the program, analyze how services vary according to family characteristics and problems, and investigate the relationship of services to certain outcomes. Suggested in Chapter 2, these types of studies are particularly important in process evaluations to improve service delivery. Although case studies that examine service effectiveness

At the outset of services, Kathy Smith's youngest child Maria, age 2, had been placed due to failure to thrive (persistent weight loss over a 3-month period). The two children in the home, Patricia, 8, and Jason, 7, were having problems with school attendance, and Jason, who was mentally handicapped, was not getting necessary medical treatment. The house was filthy and the living situation unstable as Kathy often moved or other people moved in with the family. At the time, the household included Kathy's boyfriend, Manuel, who was the father of her youngest child. At intake, the family was rated at high risk of neglect and moderate risk of abuse. Both adults had a history of substance abuse and criminal charges. Serious problems were noted on the Child Well-Being Scales (CWBS) (Magura & Moses, 1986), the Childhood Level of Living Scale (CLL) (Polansky et al., 1983a, 1983b), and the Adolescent-Adult Parenting Inventory (Bavolek, 1990d). (See Chapter 7 for further discussion of these scales.)

Although initially agreeing to participate in the project, the parents attended few group sessions and Manuel was not available during home visits. Despite in-home parent training and encouragement from the parent aide, Kathy showed little progress, did not follow through on medical treatment for the children, and often missed scheduled home visits. By the end of treatment, the family's score on CLL had decreased, indicating a worsening and severely neglectful environment for the children, and there had been no change on the Household and Parental Disposition subscales of the CWBS. After abruptly terminating services, Kathy moved her family to New England to attempt a reconciliation with her former husband.

Figure 4.3.   Unsuccessful intervention with chronic neglect.

only after cases are closed are unable to provide definitive answers regarding change and the causes of change, they are frequently used when more complex designs are not practical. However, in assessing the effectiveness of FBS they are vulnerable to many alternative explanations.

Agency-based evaluators who adopt a case review method need a detailed coding scheme to gather the relevant information from case records (or records built into an automated system). If, instead of studying all cases over a certain period of time you are planning to study a sample of cases, you will also need to know something about probability sampling procedures (see Chapter 3) and inferential statistics (see Chapter 12). The following example, although from a large federally funded study, illustrates the kind of case record review that could be implemented by an agency-based evaluator.

In a large descriptive study of eleven FBS programs in six states, trained social work students coded 534 randomly selected case records using a seventeen-page case review instrument (available in Nelson, Emlen, Landsman, & Hutchinson, 1988). In the data analysis, services

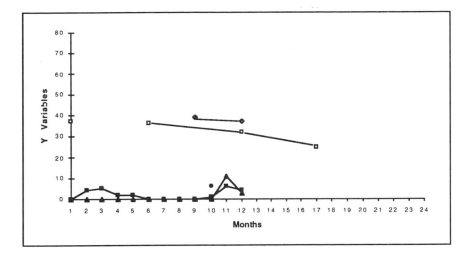

────□──── Childhood Level of Living Scale (higher better)

────◇──── Family Systems Change Scale (lower better)

────▲──── Hours of family therapist time

────●──── Hours of treatment group time

────■──── Hours of parent aide time

Figure 4.4. Unsuccessful intervention with chronic neglect: Service hours and scale scores. [*Source:* M. J. Landsman, K. Nelson, M. Allen, & M. Tyler (1992). *Family-based treatment for chronically neglecting families: The self-sufficiency project.* Iowa City: National Resource Center on Family Based Services.]

were found to vary across sites and according to the reason the case was referred for FBS (Nelson & Landsman, 1992). (This is another example of how site and worker variation are often present and may pose difficulties in an evaluation of FBS. See Chapter 1 for further discussion.) When neglect cases were compared to cases referred for physical or sexual abuse, for example, several differences were found in the type of services provided. Although the average duration of service was similar (Table 4.1), neglect cases more often received concrete and supportive services such as Aid to Families with Dependent Children (AFDC), paraprofessional services, help with money management, and transportation. Neglecting families received concurrent child protective services more often, as well as parent education and skill building services. Altogether, neglecting families received significantly more different kinds of

Table 4.1. A Comparison of FBS Services Provided to Neglect, Physical Abuse, and Sexual Abuse Cases[a]

| | Percentage of cases receiving a service[b] | | | |
Services	Neglect (n = 67)	Physical abuse (n = 101)	Sexual abuse (n = −52)	Total[c] (n = 219)
Family counseling	83.7	89.7	96.7	89.5
Individual counseling	73.4	68.7	55.9	67.1
Information/referral	69.6	52.5	50.0	57.1
Protective services	71.7	54.0	43.2	56.8**
AFDC	72.0	37.9	39.1	48.6***
Parent education	54.1	35.3	25.7	38.8**
Marital counseling	16.8	39.6	40.1	32.8**
Role modeling	42.3	27.7	19.6	30.2*
Accompanied to appointment	38.1	18.9	36.5	28.9**
Paraprofessional services	44.7	22.6	13.5	27.1***
Mental health services	32.0	21.1	29.1	26.3
Self-help/volunteer services	20.0	21.0	41.1	25.5*
Transportation	37.9	21.8	14.9	25.1**
Money management	40.1	15.3	4.8	20.4***

*p < .05.   **p < .01.   ***p < .001.
[a] *Source:* Adapted from K. E. Nelson (1994). Family-based services for families and children at risk of out-of-home placement. In *Child Welfare Research Review,* Volume 1, edited by R. Barth, J. Duerr-Berrick, & N. Gilbert. New York: Columbia University Press, p. 94.
[b] Differences were tested using the χ^2 statistic.
[c] Total N will vary due to weighting of cases.

services and more in-home services than cases involving other types of maltreatment (Nelson, 1994).

While this type of study describes the services provided to different kinds of families and helps to identify services that may be particularly appropriate for certain types of families, it is also important to know which services contribute to desired case outcomes. Because many different services are provided to each family, it is often difficult to assess whether family characteristics, a particular service, or a combination of services have led to a positive outcome. To address this issue, more adventurous evaluators may want to use multivariate statistical methods that control for important family (e.g., education and income) or service (e.g., length and intensity) characteristics to identify combinations of services that contribute to successful case outcomes.

In the study described above, the primary outcome measure available in the case records was whether placement was deemed necessary or had occurred by the end of the service period. Placement included moving in with relatives or neighbors, as well as formal agency placements in family foster care, group homes, or institutions, as long as the placement was in response to the problems that brought the family into service. Controlling for the number of problems, the number of children in the family, placement history, and continuity in caregiving at the start of services, statistical analysis showed that the frequency of the primary caregiver's participation in services and paraprofessional services (such as help in developing housekeeping, budgeting, and/or parenting skills), contributed to placement prevention (Nelson & Landsman, 1992).

This type of study is primarily useful in identifying the types of service provided and suggesting what might work best with different kinds of families. Unless the number of hours each service is provided is available through the agency's service monitoring system, it is seldom possible in a case record review to gauge the intensity and timing of services in order to determine when and in what "dosage" they might be most effective. The ease, however, of gathering data on a relatively large number of cases and of performing simple statistical analyses makes this a cost-effective alternative to more complex research designs.

Experimental Designs

Although random assignment studies using no-treatment control groups may be difficult to implement, random assignment to alternative and equally valued treatments can often be used to test the relative effectiveness of different interventions and service delivery mechanisms (Chapter 2). In the third study reported in this chapter, families in intensive family services (IFS) programs in Oregon and Maryland were randomly assigned to three- or six-month service contracts. (In one site, a treatment group with no formal time limit was also established.) Since the usual time limit for services was three to four months, and many of the workers thought at least some of the families would benefit from longer services, they were willing to participate in a random assignment study (Nelson, Landsman, Tyler, & Richardson, 1995).

The populations in the three study sites differed considerably, as did the structure and staffing of the programs. In Baltimore, a mix of concrete and counseling services was delivered by professional/paraprofessional teams to inner-city families referred for abuse and neglect. According to several measures, families that remained intact improved significantly and achieved higher levels of functioning by the end of services, and no significant differences were found in cost-effectiveness between three-month (**n**=94) and six-month (**n**=98) service contract groups (Nelson et al., 1995).

Two IFS programs were studied in Oregon. In both, the public agency contracted for services with local providers. One program was in an urban area while the other was located in a rural community; both served families with older children. In the rural site, in-office services were provided by private family therapists under contract with the state. No differences were found between the two treatment groups of 39 and 40 families. In the urban site, however, the 55 families who received up to six months of service had significantly fewer and less costly placements at the 12-month follow-up than the 60 families who were under three-month contracts. Although families who remained intact improved significantly in self-reported family functioning and worker-rated parental functioning, the increased effectiveness seen in the six-month group may have been attributable to increases in community and informal support for the families during the second three months of service. Unfortunately, these findings are limited by the loss from the study of a large percentage of families in the urban IFS program who either refused services (40.4%) or declined to participate in the study (21.7%) (Nelson et al., 1995).

This example illustrates a relatively simple factorial methodology for testing the effectiveness of different treatment patterns. Similar procedures can be used to test the effects of caseload size, teaming of workers, and the use of flexible funds or volunteers on case outcomes. While simple experimental designs do not control for worker enthusiasm (or lack of cooperation), tracking measures commonly available in the agency as well as testing interventions about which the workers have a genuine curiosity, can help to uncover or reduce bias.

Useful Research Instruments

Research instruments useful for monitoring program information include service checklists, service inventories, and time logs completed by workers at monthly intervals or when services are terminated. For the experimental study of length of services just described, workers completed an Interventions Checklist covering twenty-one therapeutic, eleven educational, and eight casework interventions. Including interventions common to both family systems and HOMEBUILDERS™-type programs, the two-page instrument, completed monthly, also notes the primary target of the intervention (see Figure 4.5).

A more extensive Clinical Services Checklist was developed for the Family-Based Intensive Treatment (FIT) Project, which studied the

Figure 4.5. Interventions checklist. [*Source:* The National Resource Center of Family Based Services, The University of Iowa School of Social Work, Iowa City. Reprinted with permission.]

Instructions: Indicate the major interventions you used with the family during this month, checking the appropriate column(s) to show which family members were involved. Please check only primary interventions, (e.g., those which were planned in advance or that had a major impact on the family). Do not include incidental interventions with minor impact on the family.

Therapeutic interventions	Primary caretaker	Other adult	Child(ren) at-risk	Other child(ren)
1. Drawing ecomaps/ assessing social support				
2. Confrontation				
3. Behavior rehearsal/role play (practice for future use)				
4. Circular questioning				
5. Structured family inter- view				
6. Identifying behavioral se- quences				
7. Speaking in metaphor				
8. Reframing (relabeling, positive connotation)				
9. Prescribing the symptom				
10. Predicting a relapse				
11. Drawing genograms (mul- tigenerational history)				
12. Encouraging clients to get the family facts				
13. Positive/negative rein- forcement				
14. Tracking or charting be- haviors				
15. Multiple impact therapy				

(*continued*)

Figure 4.5. (Continued)

Therapeutic interventions	Primary caretaker	Other adult	Child(ren) at-risk	Other child(ren)
16. Hypothesizing the function of the symptom (i.e., purpose, effect, or gain)				
17. Coaching verbal or non-verbal expression (e.g., "I" statements, direct requests)				
18. Blocking (e.g., refusing eye contact, moving seats, interrupting)				
19. Unbalancing (allying with subsystem, e.g., telling parents they managed a difficult situation well)				
20. Restraining change (e.g., suggesting clients go slow, speculating on the consequences of change)				
21. Developing a time line (chronology of problems, important events, developmental issues)				
Educational Interventions E.g., the teaching of skills and behaviors so that they become part of the family member(s) repertoire. Do not include interventions carried out by the therapist, but not taught to the family. Can include direct/didactic instruction, role modeling, coaching, cueing, role play, behavioral rehearsal, structured exercises, and homework.				
22. Child behavior management skills (consequences, behavior charts, token economies, PET, STEP)				
23. Other parenting skills (e.g., age-appropriate care and expectations, nurturance, child development)				

(*continued*)

Figure 4.5. (Continued)

Educational interventions	Primary caretaker	Other adult	Child(ren) at-risk	Other child(ren)
24. Communication skills (e.g., "I" messages, active listening, feedback, negotiation)				
25. Cognitive interventions/ self-management skills (self-monitoring, changing "self-talk," values clarification)				
26. Assertiveness/self-advocacy skills (e.g., levels of irritation, assertive responses, accepting "no" from others)				
27. Anger/conflict management skills (e.g., identification of emotions/areas of conflict, fair fighting)				
28. Problem-solving skills (e.g., prioritizing problems, no-lose problem solving, problem ownership)				
29. Home/financial management skills (e.g., cleaning, shopping, cooking, budgeting, daily routine)				
30. Leisure time activities (e.g., teaching how to develop or use)				
31. Sex education (e.g., birth control, avoiding victimization, dealing with sexual training)				
32. Negotiating local service systems (what services are available, how to access)				

(*continued*)

Figure 4.5. (Continued)

Case Management Interventions	Primary caretaker	Other adult	Child(ren) at-risk	Other child(ren)
33. Coordinating services				
34. Accompanying family/ member to appointment				
35. Advocating for the family				
36. Building informal support networks				
37. Developing community resources				
38. Testifying/attending court hearings				
39. Providing or arranging for concrete services				
40. Information and referral (not arranging for ser- vices)				

HOMEBUILDERS™ program in Washington and a similar program in Utah. It includes seventy-four clinical techniques or services such as anger management, reinforcement in parenting, crisis cards, and reframing, derived from the family preservation and HOMEBUILDERS™ literature. Throughout the service period, the workers identified the major services used as well as other services that were used incrementally (Fraser et al., 1991). In addition, a list of twenty-five concrete services including transportation, household goods, and financial assistance was used in the FIT project to record the number of hours spent providing these services (Figure 4.6).

Another use for service checklists is to assess services received by a family before coming to the current program or between termination and follow-up, although the family, not the worker, must provide the information for these time periods. In general little is known about the effect of prior services, except that families with extensive service histories, especially prior placement, usually do less well in FBS (Fraser et al., 1991; Nelson & Landsman, 1992; Yuan & Struckman-Johnson, 1991).

In most studies it has not been possible to track the services received by families after termination from FBS, although it is known that many,

Figure 4.6. Concrete services rating sheet. [*Source:* M. W. Fraser, P. J. Pecora, & D. A. Haapala (1991). *Families in crisis: The impact of intensive family preservation services.* Hawthorne, NY: Aldine de Gruyter.]

Social Research Institute   Behavioral Sciences Institute
Graduate School of Social Work   Federal Way, Washington
University of Utah

_____
                Family

_____
                Worker

_____
        Site   Date

Instructions:

1. Please estimate the number of hours you spent providing concrete services (if any) for this family while the case was open. If you did not spend any time on a service, please leave it blank.

2. The sheet does not include items related to advocacy, relationship building or client reinforcement. Please do *not* use lines 26–28 ("other") to add in services such as: taking a client out for a soda, giving stickers (client reinforcement or relationship building) or referring a client to other services, consulting with other service providers, or attending court (advocacy).

Service Category	Number of Hours
1. Provide transportation (e.g., you drove client to Job Service)	_____
2. Help client get transportation	_____
3. Provide food	_____
4. Help client get food	_____
5. Give financial assistance to client	_____
6. Help client obtain financial assistance (e.g., AFDC, SSI)	_____
7. Provide childcare/babysitting	_____
8. Help client obtain childcare/babysitting	_____
9. Provide clothing	_____
10. Help client obtain clothing	_____
11. Help client obtain legal aid	_____
12. Move client to a new dwelling	_____
13. Help client obtain housing	_____
14. Help client obtain utility benefits or services	_____
15. Do housework/cleaning with client	_____

(*continued*)

Figure 4.6. (Continued)

Service Category	Number of Hours
16. Help arrange homemaker cleaning services	_____
17. Help client obtain medical or dental services (e.g., visiting nurses)	_____
18. Provide a job	_____
19. Help client find a job	_____
20. Provide furniture or other household goods	_____
21. Help client obtain furniture or other household goods	_____
22. Provide toys or recreational equipment	_____
23. Provide recreational activities	_____
24. Arrange for recreational activities (e.g., YMCA, Boy/Girl Scouts)	_____
25. Arrange for lifeskill classes (e.g., driver education classes, other educational programs)	_____
26. Other: _____	_____
27. Other: _____	_____
28. Other: _____	_____

if not most, families do continue with some kind of social service (Nelson & Landsman, 1992). This seriously compromises the ability to attribute longer-term success or failure in a case exclusively to the FBS intervention (Nelson, 1990). A service checklist, developed for an interview study of child neglect, includes 28 services ranging from family counseling to transportation and the family's level of satisfaction with the services they received (see Figure 4.7).

Although lengthy coding schedules are often used in externally funded studies, most agency-based evaluators can gather data on a more concise set of services to answer specific research questions. Often agencies have already developed checklists or time-recording systems that can be used or adapted for this purpose. If you wish to study two or more agencies with different coding systems, common elements can usually be identified and coded in the same way for each agency. If you are starting a new program or revising an existing information-gathering system, instruments such as the ones described in this chapter or available in other published research (e.g., AuClaire & Schwartz, 1986; Littell, Howard, Rzepnicki, Budde, & Pellowe, 1992) can be used to provide a basis for comparing services in your program to those in other programs.

QUALITY ASSURANCE AND QUALITY IMPROVEMENT

Quality assurance, while not a substitute for controlled studies of services and outcomes, can provide ongoing feedback to support and improve services. Currently under development in community mental health, medical social work, and intensive family preservation programs, quality assurance focuses on the structure, processes, and outcomes of services to clients (Coulton, 1991) with the aim of assessing the quality of all components of service delivery in order to identify and correct deficiencies. Quality assurance procedures can include case reviews, peer reviews, supervision, outside consultation, training, continuing education, and conference attendance as well as analysis of quantitative data on client demographics, service utilization, and case disposition (Curtis, 1991). Increasingly, quality assurance is required by both accrediting bodies and funders.

Many of the same issues arise in quality assurance as in more rigorous evaluations of FBS: defining services, assessing the effect of the program's context, determining sufficient versus optimal levels of service, developing appropriate measures, adjusting for type and severity of cases, and coping with inadequate or incomplete information. In assessing the quality of programs, it is important to recognize the interdependence of structure, process, and outcome. Outcomes that cannot be related to the intervention process provide little guidance for practitioners or future programs (Donabedian, 1987).

Much effort has been devoted to developing indicators that can be routinely monitored to assess the quality of service delivery. Vourlekis (1990) and her colleagues have developed a set of indicators to assess quality of care in medical social work across a variety of health care settings. Six indicators were endorsed by more than two-thirds of the practitioners who reviewed them: case finding and access, discharge delays, patient and family involvement in planning, timeliness, readmissions, and teamwork. While the definitions and information to assess these indicators are specific to medical settings, they can easily be translated into terms measurable in FBS.

For example, the HOMEBUILDERS™ program in Washington State is developing similar indicators for a quality assurance program to maintain standards of service in the rapidly expanding area of intensive family preservation services. The Quality Enhancement Systems and Training program (QUEST) includes standards for programs, therapists, intake workers, supervisors, and administrators. Indicators similar to those developed in health care settings include a client population at imminent risk of placement, 24-hour-per-day availability, brevity, unified program philosophy, same-day intake, team backup, and preventing

After checking all of the services received, say, "Now I'd like to ask you how satisfied you were with each service you received in the past year. After I read the service, please tell me if you were 'very satisfied', 'satisfied', 'somewhat dissatisfied,' 'very dissatisfied,' or you had 'no particular feelings one way or the other.'" Now read the services the client reported using in the past year, marking the satisfaction rating with a '1' in the appropriate column.

Services	Ever received as a parent	Received in last year	Very satisfied	Satisfied	Somewhat dissatisfied	Very dissatisfied	No feelings
Family counseling							
Group counseling							
Individual counseling for you							
Individual counseling for one of your children							
Crisis center or "hot line"							
Day treatment							
Alcohol counseling							
Drug abuse counseling							
Psychiatric hospitalization							
School/social work counseling							
Homemaker service							
Youth club							
Big Brothers/Big Sisters							
Parent education class							

Support group, like AA				
Visiting nurse, public health nurse				
Free breakfast - lunch program at school				
Assistance in finding housing				
Emergency housing				
Job training				
Job finding though employ-ment office				
Day care				
Health care at hospital or clinic				
Planned Parenthood/family planning				
Legal aid				
Food pantry / food giveaway				
Battered women's shelter				
Transportation				

Figure 4.7. Family service history and satisfaction survey. [*Source:* K. Nelson, E. Saunders, and M. J. Landsman (1990). *Chronic neglect in perspective: A study of chronically neglecting families in a large metropolitan county.* Iowa City: National Resource Center on Family Based Services.

unnecessary placement. Other standards cover intensity of service, caseloads, flexibility, training, and supervision (Johnston & Marckworth, 1992). The Child Welfare League of America has also published standards of service for FBS and intensive family preservation programs (Child Welfare League of America, 1989).

Extending the concept of quality of service beyond minimum standards and correction of deficiencies, quality improvement (QI) and total quality management strategies help child welfare agencies strive for excellence. Nowhere is the goal of "doing the right thing right the first time, all the time" more important than in child welfare services (Walton, 1986). Consistent with the principles of FBS, QI defines services in terms of consumer needs rather than agency preferences. With an emphasis on supportive, empowering management, QI continuously monitors and tracks services (Joint Commission on Accreditation of Healthcare Organizations, 1991).

Some of the more important areas to monitor in QI include adherence to central organizational philosophy and values, involvement of consumers and all levels of staff in the QI effort, faithful implementation of QI methods, and balance between process and outcomes and between agency and consumer needs. The QI process, however, should not be allowed to overwhelm or divert attention from the agency's central mission or create burdensome committees or paperwork (Seelig & Pecora, under review). QI efforts should establish or reinforce a relationship between compensation and quality, promote high standards and innovative services, and encourage role flexibility across departmental and disciplinary lines. If successful, QI can increase consumer satisfaction, better service outcomes, and improve working relationships with other agencies. Continuous monitoring and documentation of these changes provide positive feedback to staff and validation of program quality to funders.

ASSESSING WORKER PERFORMANCE

Beyond the routine collection of data to monitor and improve program quality, evaluation of the impact of worker values, attitudes, knowledge, skills, and performance may be desirable. Most practitioners believe that the quality of the relationship developed between the family and the worker is an essential determinant of subsequent change. Truax and Carkhuff's (1967) ground-breaking work identified warmth, genuineness, and empathy as common characteristics of successful counselors, regardless of theoretical approach. Their work has been replicated and expanded by Ivey, Ivey, and Simek-Downing (1987). In the field of psychotherapy, a series of recent studies suggests that the "therapeutic alliance" between clients and therapists "not only reflects positive change but may produce it as well" (Lambert & Bergin, 1994, p. 166).

Although detailed qualitative and observational studies using video- or audiotapes of counseling sessions are needed to increase our understanding of successful counseling techniques, two research instruments may be useful in assessing worker orientation and performance in FBS. The first was developed by Pecora, Delewski, Booth, Haapala, & Kinney (1985) to assess the effectiveness of HOMEBUILDERS™ training in changing workers' values and attitudes toward families (see Figure 4.8). Detecting important shifts in attitudes, the instrument has been used in three studies to measure the orientation of FBS workers in different types of programs (AuClaire & Schwartz, 1986; Fraser et al., 1991; Nelson et al., 1988). A comparison of these three studies found that workers agreed on the importance of children remaining in their own homes and of family participation in setting case goals; they concurred less often on the importance of structural features such as 24-hour access, convenient appointments, in-home services, and limiting services to 90 days (Nelson, Landsman, & Deutelbaum, 1990).

A second instrument that assesses family therapy skills may be useful in programs using this type of intervention. The Family Therapist Rating Scale covers five categories of therapist behavior: Structuring, Relationship, Family History, Structural/Process, and Experiential, and is appropriate for use with diverse theoretical orientations. An observer rates the therapist on each of the fifty items on a seven-point scale from "not present" to "maximally effective." The scale has been tested on doctoral students and experienced therapists and was able to differentiate between these two groups in relation to the five categories of behavior, with the experienced therapists scored as more effective (Fredman & Sherman, 1987).

CONCLUSION

While advances have been made in specifying and assessing FBS interventions, a number of problems remain. Perhaps the most serious is access to information. Case records are often incomplete, workers are often reluctant to fill out extra forms, and families are often difficult to locate. Various sources of information (children, workers, families, court, teachers, etc.) are important to tap for these data and multiple sources are essential for providing a fuller picture of service delivery (Personal communication, Marianne Berry, June 14, 1994).

Figure 4.8. Family-based services attitude scale. [*Source:* P. J. Pecora, C. H. Delewski, C. Booth, D. A. Haapala, and J. Kinney (1985). Home-based family-centered services: The impact of training on worker attitudes. *Child Welfare 64*(5), 529–40.

Instructions: Please rate the extent to which you agree with the following items in terms of how family-based services should be provided.

Items	Disagree Strongly 1	2	3	Rating Scale Neutral 4	5	6	Agree Strongly 7
1. Usually disregard previous diagnoses.	1	2	3	4	5	6	7
2. Spend little time focusing on understanding the past.	1	2	3	4	5	6	7
3. Provide "hard services," including moving, cleaning, and grocery shopping with clients.	1	2	3	4	5	6	7
4. Ask clients to set and prioritize their own goals.	1	2	3	4	5	6	7
5. Never insist that all family members participate.	1	2	3	4	5	6	7
6. Focus on dynamics or personalities rather than teach skills.*	1	2	3	4	5	6	7
7. Actively pursue reluctant clients through repeated calls, letters and visits.	1	2	3	4	5	6	7

	1	2	3	4	5	6	7
8. Rarely "confront" clients.	1	2	3	4	5	6	7
9. Never give out home phone number.*	1	2	3	4	5	6	7
10. Rotate to be on call and to be available for emergency visits to clients 24 hours a day, including holidays.	1	2	3	4	5	6	7
11. Routinely work nights and weekends.							
12. Deliver most services in the home environment.	1	2	3	4	5	6	7
13. Schedule appointments at the convenience and preference of clients, not workers.	1	2	3	4	5	6	7
14. Ask clients to evaluate workers.	1	2	3	4	5	6	7
15. See clients within 24 hours.	1	2	3	4	5	6	7
16. Limit in-home services to a 4–6 week period.	1	2	3	4	5	6	7
17. Therapists can do as much harm as they can do good.	1	2	3	4	5	6	7
18. Labeling is productive in working with families.*	1	2	3	4	5	6	7

(continued)

Figure 4.8. (*Continued*)

	Rating Scale						
Items	Disagree Strongly 1	2	3	Neutral 4	5	6	Agree Strongly 7
19. It's our job to motivate clients.	1	2	3	4	5	6	7
20. There are more similarities than differences between clients.	1	2	3	4	5	6	7
21. People are doing the best they can.	1	2	3	4	5	6	7
22. The term "family therapy" has very little meaning when used in a case plan.	1	2	3	4	5	6	7
23. Most kids are better off in their own homes.	1	2	3	4	5	6	7
24. It is important to minimize barriers to clients receiving services.	1	2	3	4	5	6	7
25. Clients have better information about their situation than professionals do.	1	2	3	4	5	6	7
26. If a worker never consults with other staff, something is wrong.	1	2	3	4	5	6	7
27. There are few "right" answers in our casework with individuals and families, only options, with pros and cons.	1	2	3	4	5	6	7

* Items that are reverse-scored.

Even with considerable resources for data collection, evaluators must cope with missing data, and try to assess the characteristics and significance of nonresponses. There is a limit, as well, to an agency-based evaluator's ability to collect detailed information on therapist behavior, time spent on different types of interventions, and services delivered by other providers. Thus it is difficult to study timing, "dosage," and interactions between services. Individual case studies or large externally funded outcome studies are two feasible, if divergent options to obtaining more detailed information.

In addition, the lack of standardization among services and the various ways of recording services makes it difficult to compare the results of different studies. To date, each agency and each study has developed its own service checklists suited to its own purposes. Until there is more agreement on which services are necessary and how to measure them, evaluators should include in their reports detailed descriptions of the most important services and interventions so that others can assess the applicability of the findings to their own programs or service models.

While all of the approaches to gaining a better understanding of services discussed in this chapter have weaknesses as well as strengths, if employed appropriately they can help "unpack," disaggregate, or dismantle the effects of complex interventions. Single-case studies, case record reviews, alternative-treatment experiments, quality assurance, and evaluation of therapeutic techniques can all add to our knowledge of what kinds of interventions work well with different kinds of families. These studies are necessary in agency environments that demand evidence of effectiveness for continued funding. But beyond this, studies of this kind are necessary to develop more effective and efficient services and to fine-tune existing program strategies.

Chapter 5

Assessing Family Functioning

What outcomes for families and children can and should be expected from FBS? Can even the best and most intensive short-term services be expected to solve major family problems? Or do they help willing families make modest behavioral and attitudinal changes that may have long-term impacts? How do poverty, violence, and long-term disadvantage affect a family's ability to respond to FBS? Should we be targeting families with certain characteristics? These are some of the questions facing the field as FBS becomes an established part of the continuum of services for families and children.

Most of the early research on service outcomes focused on placement prevention, both because it seemed to be a clear and quantifiable indicator of program success and because it had readily understandable policy and cost implications. While results of the early studies without control groups were promising, the next generation of experimental studies left doubts as to the efficacy of FBS in preventing child placements (Chapter 1; Rossi, 1992a). Rather than concluding that a programmatic thrust that "feels right" to both families and professionals is ineffective, however, we believe that the field should turn its attention to investigating the impact of FBS on family, child, and parent functioning and the relationship between improvements in functioning and service utilization (including but not limited to placement).

We can take heart from the experiences of the child development field, where early evaluations in the 1960s showed that differences in IQ scores between Head Start children and others were not sustained for more than a few years. Rather than giving up on the program, advocates recognized that IQ scores were not the most appropriate outcome measure for early childhood programs. In concert with advocates and professionals, child development researchers have explored many different outcome measures and methods, and demonstrated the long-term impact of high-quality child care on educational achievement and life success (Belsky, 1990; Haskins, 1989; Berreuta-Clement, Schweinhart, Barnett, Epstein, & Weikart, 1984). As suggested in Chapter 2, bodies of knowledge are built from many different studies over the long term (almost thirty years in the child development field), including false starts and red herrings as well as heralded breakthroughs.

FBS is an equally complex field, defined at this point more by programmatic experimentation and demonstration than by widespread institutionalization. Building evaluation and outcome measurement into large and small-scale demonstrations is clearly crucial not only to justify funding for individual programs, but to build a collective knowledge base. Every program that collects outcome data regularly not only answers its own programmatic questions, but adds incrementally to the field's collective knowledge about the effectiveness and efficiency of FBS.

The next three chapters explore different approaches to assessing and measuring the functioning of families, children, and parents. Such assessment is essential for a full understanding of the impact of FBS programs. Each chapter presents conceptual information, domains of measurement, description of assessment methods, and examples of instruments that may be useful in evaluating FBS programs. [For additional summaries of assessment measures, some of which may be applicable to FBS, see Corcoran (1994), Daro, Abrahams, and Casey (1990), and Pfeiffer, Soldivera, and Norton (1992).]

OUTCOME MEASUREMENT

In simple terms, an outcome is a natural result or consequence of activity. Programmatic outcomes, which may be measured at the individual, family, community, or service system levels, are the results of targeted program interventions. Each FBS program defines its own overall goals, which are translated into specific program outcomes for evaluation purposes. Together, families and workers also develop individualized goals within the parameters of established program goals. The purpose of outcome measurement is to record changes in individual families brought about by program activities or interventions, and to aggregate these changes to determine how successfully a program meets its overall goals. This is different from data collection for descriptive or accountability purposes—to describe clients or services provided or to justify program funding—because it requires measurement of the same attributes at several points in time (see Chapter 2).

As might be expected, measurement of change is more complicated than simple affirmation or denial of an attribute before and after intervention. According to Jones (1991), there are six dimensions of change that may be measured: occurrence, direction, magnitude, rate, duration, and sequence [see Jones (1991) for an excellent discussion of this and other aspects of outcome measurement in FBS].

Another complication is that standardized instruments designed to be sensitive to variability among individuals may not be sensitive to variability within individuals over time or vice versa (Collins & Horn, 1991). Standardized instruments are used because of their demonstrated psychometric properties (the validity and reliability of the instruments), but the very instrument development techniques used to ensure these properties (such as strong test-retest reliability) may decrease sensitivity to change. Therefore, many instruments are designed to find a valid and reliable "true" score rather than to measure variation over time.

Traditionally, however, social programs have aimed at increasing knowledge, changing attitudes, or improving the behavior of individuals. And program goals have been defined in terms of the changes expected in individual children or adults. Although these changes are sometimes difficult to define and measure, this is by and large familiar territory and there are a number of widely used instruments that measure different aspects of individual child and adult functioning (see Chapters 5 and 6 for further discussion of child and parent measures).

Some programs also aim to develop or improve community resources, or to improve service systems (for example, by assuring access or increasing participation). These kinds of systemic goals often prove more difficult to measure, and programs generally rely on simple available indicators such as participation rates or on client report of change in system functioning. (See Appendix A of Chapter 1 for a systems-level example of this approach.)

FBS programs have the additional challenge of measuring change in the *families* who receive services, focusing not just on the individuals involved but on the interactions between individuals, on multigenerational patterns of change, and on the interactions of the family with its environment. The definition of a family may vary among programs, with some focusing on subsystems or dyads rather than the whole family, but every FBS program has some expectations about improving the functioning of family units, beyond the changes expected in individuals. The challenge to the evaluator is to define those changes in terms of expected outcomes and to develop measurement strategies for capturing them.

Measuring changes in families is not only a challenge for established programs with externally funded evaluations. Every FBS program that aims to improve family functioning needs to assess families and collect data on whether and how they change as a result of service intervention.

As discussed earlier in this book, rigorous evaluation often requires comparison of the changes experienced by families served with families unserved or differently served. However, before a program can institute a rigorous evaluation of changes in family functioning, it must be able to define family functioning, specify the changes expected based on its theoretical or conceptual model, design a measurement package that has the potential to capture these changes, assure that the instruments used are sensitive to change over a relatively short time period, and persuade workers to use them consistently. A very tall order!

Every program can and should implement regular data collection processes as soon as possible after start-up and identify instruments that collect meaningful data on program operations and outcomes. However, the complexity of outcome measurement is one of the reasons why we suggest that programs do not begin with rigorous outcome evaluation. Agencies must take the time to become research ready, to investigate instruments, and to plan an evaluation strategy that fits its needs and the needs of the staff and the families it serves. The other reason, of course, is that the program should be ready for evaluation, with most of the service delivery kinks and wrinkles ironed out, before time and money are invested in rigorous outcome research. Implementation (i.e., process or "formative") research is also important. With formative research, the evaluation begins with the program and evolves with the program, testing both its own methods and the program's. This way the evaluation accounts for and documents program implementation and evaluability, and can define a beginning set of outcomes or impacts. This strategy allows the evaluation to inform implementation and thus helps to facilitate maximum effectiveness (Ray Kirk, personal communication, June 17, 1994).

BUILDING FAMILY ASSESSMENTS TO MEET BOTH CLINICAL AND EVALUATION PURPOSES

Because thorough assessment of individual and family functioning is essential for sound service planning and clinical practice, your program should have a family assessment protocol or a set of assessment forms and instruments. Assessment of family functioning for case planning purposes clearly goes well beyond assessment of risks to the safety and well-being of the child(ren) and includes assessment of the family's environment, relationships, resources, and interactions. However, your current clinical assessment tools can provide a starting point for thinking about measuring family functioning for evaluation purposes.

If your program currently uses the same instruments at case opening and at case closing (and, possibly, at some follow-up period), then you already collect data that can be used to evaluate the impact of services on family or individual functioning. If you do not currently collect the same data at several points in time, you can begin your discussions about evaluation by exploring whether it would be useful to repeat some or all of your current clinical family assessment methods at later points in time.

Of course, assessment practices vary enormously across and even within programs, ranging from open-ended to structured, and many programs would need a more standardized format to collect data that would be useful for both clinical and evaluation purposes. Some programs can improve their assessment processes and collect richer evaluation data by adding some standardized instruments to a qualitative psychosocial assessment process, while others might decide to add new topics to their assessment protocols based on specific evaluation questions. Family assessments designed to collect both quantitative and qualitative data are especially rich sources for evaluation purposes because they can balance statistical overviews with explanatory information on the interactions of program processes and client outcomes (Weiss & Halpern, 1990).

Program staff should be involved from the beginning in these discussions, since they not only have the best sense of the information they really need and use but because they also have the most experience with family responses to assessment questions. Engaging staff in collecting and recording data will also be much easier if they understand and agree with both the purposes of data collection and the instruments being used (McCroskey & Nelson, 1989). By the same measure, involving selected client (or former client) families in discussion of data collection and evaluation can help you learn how to collect practical and meaningful assessment data without overwhelming families.

There is no one correct FBS assessment package. The specific family attributes assessed or family variables measured should vary depending on the program's theoretical orientation and desired goals, as well as on the specific needs, desires, cultures, and values of the families served. While assessment of family functioning should be standardized to some extent to allow for analysis across the entire group of families served, it must also be individualized enough to incorporate the family's own goals and cultural values. Practitioners can be very helpful in sensitizing evaluators to the cultural values and expectations of clients served by the program. In this way, assessment protocols are less likely to be unintentionally biased toward white, middle-class values, and miss the strengths of other kinds of families.

Although there are many commonalties among FBS programs, there are also a number of salient differences. For example, a program designed to improve child nurturance will assess families and individuals quite differently than one designed to improve family communication. Some programs collect a good deal of demographic data on families for descriptive purposes or to satisfy funding requirements. Others focus on psychosocial assessment for individual counseling and do not aggregate their data across cases. Some are looking for indications of problem severity, using scales with clinical cutting points to diagnose or guide treatment. Still others focus on concrete service needs so that they can develop appropriate service plans and client contracts.

Regardless of the focus of current family assessment procedures, if your program does not already have one, consider the possibility of building an assessment protocol that combines demographic and clinical data with measurement of family and individual functioning.

ASSESSMENT FOR EVALUATION PURPOSES

While social services often take a shotgun approach to outcome and hope that well-meaning people in well-run programs will do many good things for families, the fact is that we do not have a very convincing track record in documenting our good works. The way to build a more convincing knowledge base is to focus on the specific needs of the families served, to define measurable goals that address those needs, and to use measurement methods that document change in the goal areas targeted by the program.

This is much easier said than done, but it is the inescapable challenge facing FBS over at least the next decade. We must document the effectiveness of services designed to meet specific family needs by measuring change in those areas most critical to a family's functioning and that assure the safety and enhance the well-being of its children.

Many of the basic evaluation issues discussed elsewhere in this book are also important to consider when selecting family functioning measures. You want measures that are valid and reliable, culturally sensitive, and strengths oriented, while avoiding negative labeling. Since there are few, if any, instruments that are equally strong in all respects, we suggest that programs select a set of instruments that can provide a balanced view of family functioning.

It is also crucial to consider multiple perspectives, including the views of professionals (including the FBS worker, the referring worker, teachers, and others) as well as those of various family members, bearing in mind that their different perspectives and roles will lead to differences in their evaluation of family functioning (Kolevzon, Green, Fortune, & Vosler, 1988). Evaluation studies in the child welfare field have not routinely incorporated multiple perspectives, generally relying primarily on worker or caregiver reports. This certainly simplifies data collection, but it tends to underestimate the extent to which family functioning is socially defined and differs according to one's perspective.

In their Los Angeles study, Meezan and McCroskey (1993) explored congruence between reports of family members, FBS workers, elementary school teachers, and trained research interviewers. When looking at so many different views it became clear that role, experience, and perspective shape the lenses through which people view their worlds. Divergence in views is not necessarily an indication that one is right while the other is wrong. Rather, it confirms the fact that family functioning is a complex phenomenon that can and should be viewed from many different angles.

Time frames for measurement are also important. While measurement should be done on at least two different occasions for tracking change, and three points are needed for establishing trends, the specific time frame will vary based on program expectations. Measurement at program entry provides baseline data on family functioning before service. Depending on the length of service, some aspects of functioning may need to be measured during the service delivery period, well before case closure. If achievement of longer-term (or distal) goals is dependent on achievement of shorter-term (or proximal) goals, it will be important to be sure that the family is on track.

For example, if appropriate use of discipline is thought to depend on knowledge of child development, you may need to measure child development knowledge as well as measuring child disciplining. A young mother who has unrealistic expectations of her two-year-old's ability to "behave himself" may continue to react with anger at what she sees as his willful misbehavior until she understands that he is not capable of restraining himself. Of course, she may still be angry even when she understands, but the practice task of helping her deal with her own anger is quite different from that of helping her understand her child's capacities. Measurement of child development knowledge can not only document an achievement, but can help the practitioner plan more effective services for the family.

Follow-up at intervals after case closure will also help programs determine whether family changes are maintained over the longer-term. Unfortunately, since few programs have had the resources for long-term follow-up, we know very little about how changes in family functioning are maintained, lost, or enhanced beyond the service period. Much more research is needed before the field can make any claims at all about the long-term impacts of FBS. For this reason, we urge programs to collect follow-up data whenever possible to determine whether changes made in family functioning during the service period are maintained over time.

DOMAINS OF FAMILY FUNCTIONING

Increasing the ability of the family to meet the needs of its members in different areas of life is an important goal of FBS that needs to be specified and measured. Family functioning can be conceptualized in numerous ways. A sociologist might focus on income, education, family roles, and the socialization of children. A psychologist might be more likely to emphasize family relationships and emotional well-being. Social workers tend to focus on people in their environments, stressing child safety, adequacy of parenting, and the quality of the home environment. While individual characteristics affect the functioning of the family, we focus here on the assessment of functioning of the family group as a whole.

As a group, the family shares a history, a living situation, and characteristic ways of relating to each other that may constitute strengths or create the problems. While it is important through the use of timelines, genograms, and other assessment tools to understand the family's history, intervention programs do not change history. Similarly, risk assessment tools may be helpful in identifying families at risk of future child abuse or neglect, but not every area identified will be the focus of intervention.

In program evaluation, it is more useful to focus on domains of family functioning that are most subject to change: the family's immediate environment including household, neighborhood, and community assets and problems; the resources the family has to draw on in terms of income, employment, social support, and services; the skills necessary to access these resources; and the internal relationships and coping mechanisms the family has developed.

While it is characteristic that FBS programs provide comprehensive services that address all domains of family functioning, it is also true that only a small percentage of families served by a particular program will need assistance in all areas. For example, some families served will have adequate housing, medical care, or parenting skills, while others will need help in these areas. It could also be true that individual family members (i.e., parents) might bear primary responsibility for developing certain skills and accessing specific resources. Therefore, change in these domains would usually be measured at the level of the individual parent or caregiver rather than for the whole family. In contrast, all families develop characteristic patterns of family relationships that pertain to the family as a whole and are subject to intervention. It is, indeed, these patterns of family relationships that many FBS programs seek to change.

Measurement of family functioning is a technology very much under development (see, for example, McCubbin & McCubbin, 1992). There are a number of instruments which address some aspects of functioning, but none are (or perhaps could be) comprehensive. The next section describes and critically analyzes some of the primary instruments currently in use in FBS.

SELECTED INSTRUMENTS

The following section describes nine widely used measures of family functioning. As has been noted, it is important to select measures that are congruent with the treatment philosophy, theory base, and primary goals of your program. In addition, some instruments have been more extensively tested on the kinds of families seen in FBS programs and seem better able to detect change between intake and termination or follow-up and/or differences between treatment and control groups. This section will describe and evaluate some of the instruments most widely used to measure family functioning in treatment programs. The theory base, format, and uses in measuring family functioning will be considered for each.

The Family Adaptability and Cohesion Evaluation Scales (FACES)

The Family Adaptability and Cohesion Evaluation Scales (Olson, Russell, & Sprenkle, 1983) were developed from theory and research and posit two basic dimensions of family functioning: cohesion and adaptability. Adaptability includes leadership, discipline, child control, roles, and rules. Cohesion measures bonding, support, boundaries, and sharing. Both are hypothesized to be curvilinear; optimal functioning is conceptualized as a balance between the extremes of disengagement

> *Theoretical Orientation:* Family systems theory.
> *Populations Tested:* Clinical and nonclinical families; single-parent, step-parent, adoptive, and lesbian families; Latino and African-American families; families with seriously ill, physically handicapped, mentally retarded, substance abusing, and sexually abused members; and juvenile and adult offenders.
> *Format:* Family members self-report: 30 items, 2 subscales (Cohesion and Adaptability/Change).
> *Source:* Dr. David H. Olson, Family Social Science, University of Minnesota, 290 McNeal Hall, 1985 Buford Avenue, St. Paul, MN 55108.

Figure 5.1.   Family Adaptability and Cohesion Evaluation Scales (FACES II).

and enmeshment (Minuchin, 1974) on the Cohesion subscale and between rigidity and chaos on the Adaptability subscale. This circumplex model locates optimal functioning in the center of a circle, with progressively more dysfunction as families move away from balanced to midrange and extreme scores. Sixteen family types, to be used in assessing family functioning, are identified by the model. (See Figure 5.1.)

Research using the FACES scales has been mixed, with FACES I and II markedly better at differentiating functional and dysfunctional families than FACES III. Olson and his colleagues are now developing FACES IV, which will be rated using bipolar scales to better reflect the circumplex model on which the scales are based (Olson, 1991). Until FACES IV is refined, various authors suggest either using only the sum of the items in the FACES III Cohesion subscale (Green, 1989) or trying linear and nonlinear scoring of both subscales to see which works best for your sample (Henggeler, Burr-Harris, Borduin, & McCallum, 1991).

While most of the applications of FACES have been to test the theory behind the scale, to compare it to other measures of family functioning, or to test its ability to differentiate dysfunctional families from normative families, several studies have used FACES to measure change in families after intervention or to compare them to control families. Often used with families of adolescents, FACES II measured significant changes in 200 families with chronic juvenile offenders receiving multisystemic treatment (MST) in Missouri. The treatment included family therapy, school intervention (e.g., facilitating parent-teacher communication and assisting in behavior management), peer intervention (e.g., coaching, integration into prosocial peer groups), individual behavioral therapy, and marital therapy (Henggeler & Borduin, 1990, pp. 229–231). Compared to a randomly assigned control group who received individual counseling, the multisystemic group showed significant reductions in behavior problems and gains in family cohesion and adaptability at termination. Four years after treatment the recidivism rate for the MST youth was 22 percent compared to 72 percent for those who received individual counseling and 87 percent for study dropouts (Borduin et al., 1993).

In another setting, a large private mental health center in California used FACES III to assess the effectiveness of a 90-day Adolescent In-Home Treatment Program to prevent hospitalization of violent/ aggressive or suicidal/depressed adolescents. A clinical team using multiple impact, structural, strategic, and crisis intervention techniques treated 51 families in the first two years of the program. While 79 percent of the families rated themselves in the extreme range of functioning at admission, by termination 50 percent rated themselves in the balanced or midrange and 86 percent had avoided hospitalization (Seelig, Goldman-Hall, & Jerrell, 1992).

However, a study of 453 families receiving Intensive Family Preservation Services in Washington and Utah found that while most of the families scored in the dysfunctional range descriptively, there were no significant differences between family scores at intake and termination (Fraser et al., 1991). The families included about equal numbers of child maltreatment and juvenile justice cases and received very brief (30–45 days) but intensive service based on a cognitive behavioral model. It is not clear whether the FACES III was not appropriate for this model of treatment, whether the service itself was not effective, or if something else might account for this finding.

The Self-Report Family Inventory (SFI)

The Beavers Family Systems Model of Family Functioning (Beavers & Hampson, 1990) is predicated on family systems theory and is based primarily on practice experience with families. Initially, clinician/researchers developed an observational scale to code videotapes of families. Later, they constructed the Self-Report Family Inventory, which can be completed by family members age 12 and over. Using the observational or self-report scales, families can be charted according to health/competence and style. The health/competence dimension differentiates five levels of functioning ranging from optimal to severely dysfunctional. The style dimension identifies three styles of family interaction (centrifugal, mixed, and centripetal) that relate to the tendencies to function as a tightly knit group or a fragmenting set of individuals. Used together these two dimensions identify six configurations of family dysfunction that correspond to standard diagnostic categories, for example, behavior disorder, borderline personality disorder, and schizophrenia (Hampson, Beavers, & Hulgas, 1988). (See Figure 5.2.)

The Beavers scales have been extensively tested and compare favora-

Theoretical Orientation: Family systems theory.
Populations Tested: Clinical and nonclinical families; families with adolescents, seriously ill, mentally ill, or mentally retarded members; African-American and Latino families; foster families.
Format: Family members self-report: 36 items, 6 subscales (Health/Competence, Conflict, Communication, Cohesion, Directive Leadership, Expressiveness).
Source: W. Robert Beavers and Robert B. Hampson (1990). *Successful families: Assessment and intervention.* New York: Norton.

Figure 5.2. Self-Report Family Inventory.

bly to other family rating scales. Green (1989) recommends using either the full scale or the Health/Competence and/or Conflict subscales for clinical research. In addition the SFI appears sensitive to change within individual families and between treatment and control groups. In a study of Oregon's Intensive Family Services, a FBS program based on family systems theory, three quarters of the families scored in the dysfunctional range. The SFI scales showed statistically significant change in family functioning at termination and at a twelve-month follow-up (Nelson, Landsman, Tyler, & Richardson, 1995).

Family Environment Scale (FES)

Another instrument that has been used successfully to measure family change in a variety of settings is the Family Environment Scale (Moos & Moos, 1986). It is part of a set of "social climate" scales that measure the social and environmental characteristics of various settings including work and family. Social climate is defined as "the way an institution maintains or changes itself and provides opportunities for relationships and personal development" (Fredman & Sherman, 1987, p. 82). In this respect, the FES covers a wider range of domains of functioning than FACES or the SFI.

The 90 items include ten subscales grouped into three dimensions: relationships, personal growth, and system maintenance. The relationship dimension includes Cohesion, Expressiveness, and Conflict subscales, which are similar in concept to those in FACES and the SFI. The personal growth dimension measures Independence, Achievement, Intellectual Orientation, Active-Recreational Orientation, and Moral-Religious emphasis. The system maintenance dimension covers Organization and Control in the family. The subscale structure of this scale has not yet been confirmed.

The true/false format used in this scale enables family members to complete the scale in 15 to 20 minutes. However, a shorter form (27 items)

Theoretical Orientation: Family systems, ecological.

Populations Tested: Clinical and nonclinical families; families with seriously ill, mentally ill, and alcoholic members and adolescents; African-American and Latino families, single-parent families.

Format: Family members self-report: 90 items, 10 subscales (Cohesion, Expressiveness, Conflict, Independence, Achievement, Intellectual Orientation, Active/Recreational Orientation, Moral/Religious Orientation, Organization, Control). A 27-item short form including the Cohesion, Expressiveness, and Conflict subscales is also available.

Source: Consulting Psychologists Press, 3803 East Bayshore Road, Palo Alto, CA 94303

Figure 5.3. Family Environment Scale.

that addresses only the relationship dimension may be easier to use in practice. Real, ideal, expected, and children's formats are also available, and the scales have been translated into numerous languages including Spanish, Chinese, and Korean. In English, a sixth-grade reading level is required. (See Figure 5.3.)

The extensive testing of this instrument on differing populations and its apparent sensitivity to differences between groups and over time make it useful for comparing families in FBS programs with other populations. In addition, it has been used successfully with both family systems and behavioral interventions, making it one of the few scales validated in programs with diverse theoretical orientations.

In a study comparing one-person and conjoint family therapy with 37 Cuban-American families of drug-using adolescents, Szapocznik and his colleagues (1983) found significant improvement in both groups in the adolescents' Expressiveness, Achievement Orientation, and Moral-Religious subscale scores and in the families' average scores on Cohesion, Expressiveness, and Conflict. Similarly, Friedman, Tomko, and Utada (1991) found that more positive FES scores predicted better outcomes for 85 Caucasian families with drug-abusing adolescents who received functional family therapy. The FES did not, however, detect change in another study of 33 families who received multisystemic therapy or parent training for physical abuse and neglect, although measures of problems, behavior, and stress did show improvement (Brunk, Henggeler, & Whelan, 1987).

The FES was used in a study of intensive family preservation services in New Jersey (Feldman, 1991b). The services were brief (30 to 45 days) and intensive. Most of the families had adolescent children at risk of placement. With a total sample of 96 families, the family preservation group improved significantly on seven of the ten subscales, with the most change in the Cohesion and Independence subscales. Four of the scales changed from levels typical of distressed families to normative levels. These changes were significantly larger than those in a randomly assigned control group that received standard agency services.

McMaster Family Assessment Device (FAD)

A fourth scale that clinicians have used to evaluate change in family functioning is the McMaster Family Assessment Device. It is based on the McMaster Model of Family Functioning, which includes concepts from systems, communication, and learning theory. Developed through clinical observation and studies, the model covers six dimensions of family functioning: the ability to solve family problems, exchange information, assign and complete tasks, experience appropriate emotions, value each family member's concerns, and maintain behavior standards. In addition to these six dimensions, the 60-item scale has a General Functioning subscale measuring overall family health.

The scales may be completed by adults and teenage family members and take about 20 minutes to complete. As with the FES, the 12-item General Functioning Scale may be used to expedite data collection in clinical settings. Family members rate each item on a strongly agree to strongly disagree continuum; scoring sheets and keys are available (Corcoran & Fischer, 1987; Fredman & Sherman, 1987). The authors have also developed clinical cutting points to identify families in need of treatment. (See Figure 5.4.)

Although the subscale structure has not been confirmed by factor analysis and may not measure independent dimensions of family functioning, the FAD has been used to measure treatment effectiveness in several studies. In a study of twenty-one families receiving family therapy using the Milan systemic model, change in the General Functioning scores of the identified "problem" children were significantly related to achievement of treatment goals (Fleuridas, Rosenthal, Leigh, & Leigh,

---

Theoretical Orientation: Systems, communication, and learning theory.
Populations Tested: Clinical and nonclinical families; families with physically and mentally ill members; elderly couples.
Format: Family members self-report: 60 items, 7 subscales (Problem Solving, Communication, Roles, Affective Responsiveness, Affective Involvement, Behavior Control, General Functioning).
Source: Family Research Program, Butler Hospital, 345 Blackstone Boulevard, Providence, RI 92906.

Figure 5.4.   Family Assessment Device.

1990). Small changes between admission and discharge were also found by Wells and Whittington (1993).

In addition, the FAD was used by Dore (1991b) in her evaluation of 27 family-based children's mental health programs in Pennsylvania. All the children had DSM-IIIR diagnoses—primarily adjustment, attention deficit, conduct, and oppositional defiant disorders. The programs were designed to prevent both crisis placement and long-term residential care. Services lasted an average of 5.8 months. Evaluation of the first 602 families found significant improvements on all FAD subscales (Dore, 1991b). At a 12-month follow-up, 71.4 percent of the families had experienced no posttreatment psychiatric hospitalization. The mother's posttreatment scores on the Behavior Control and General Functioning subscales were highly predictive of child hospitalization.

Comparison of the SFI, FACES-II, FES and FAD Scales

Although each of these four scales measures similar aspects of family functioning and has been used in a variety of treatment settings, they differ in theory base, content, and stability. Even though several of the subscales purport to measure the same concepts, when they are compared to each other it is evident that they do not. Beavers and Hampson (1990) compared the SFI to each of the other scales with mixed results. Table 5.1 shows the subscales that are most highly related to SFI subscales. The scales have high concordance on cohesion, with the Cohesion dimensions of both FACES II and FES significantly correlated to the SFI Cohesion subscale. There is also convergence between the Conflict subscales of the SFI and the FES, but considerably less agreement between

Table 5.1. Interrelationships between the Subscales of Four Measures of Family Functioning[a]

SFI	FACES II[b] (n = 279)	FES (n = 71)	FAD (n = 71)
Health	−.93**	−.73**[b]	.77**[e]
Cohesion	−.81**	−.65**[b]	.61**[e,f]
Expressiveness	−.58**	−.71**[b]	.69**[f]
Conflict	−.69**	.68**[c]	.53**[e,g]
Leadership/Control	−.62**	−.38**[d]	.36**[h]

[a] Correlations based on a normal college sample. Adapted from Beavers and Hampson (1990:207–9).
[b] Cohesion Subscale. [c] Conflict Subscale. [d] Control Subscale.
[e] General Functioning. [f] Affective Responsiveness Subscale.
[g] Affective Involvement Subscale. [h] Behavior Control Subscale

the Leadership/Control subscales of the SFI, FES, and FAD. Dickerson and Coyne (1987) and Schmid, Rosenthal, & Brown (1988) make similar comparisons and find family self-report of cohesion consistent across scales, but low agreement on the control subscales.

Index of Family Relations (IFR)

Although the Index of Family Relations (Hudson, 1982; Hudson, Acklin, & Bartosh, 1980) has not been widely used in studies of FBS, it should be considered for use as a brief, well-documented clinical rating scale. The IFR is part of a multiple-scale Clinical Measurement Package designed to be used in treatment settings.[1] Each scale consists of 25 items that are scored on a continuum from "rarely or none of the time" to "most or all of the time" and each has a cutting point of 30, above which problems are considered to be clinically significant. The scales and their cutting points have been validated on a variety of clinical populations. (See Figure 5.5.)

The IFR was designed to measure the severity or magnitude of family problems; it makes no assumptions about their origins or treatment. Thus, it measures the existence of problems rather than the level of family functioning. If one of the goals of your program is to reduce problems in family functioning, the IFR may be useful in measuring this area, regardless of the program's theoretical orientation.

Child Well-Being Scales (CWBS)

Another instrument that has been used in FBS research is the Child Well-Being Scales (Magura & Moses, 1986). These scales were developed to describe and measure outcomes in child welfare services. Although they were originally conceptualized as a measure of "child well-being," Seaberg (1988) has argued that, since there is a ceiling of "no problem" for

---

Theoretical Orientation: Empirically derived.
Populations Tested: Clinical and nonclinical; single and married.
Format: Family members (12 and over) self-report: 25 items.
Sources: P. S. Nurius and W. W. Hudson (1993). *Human services practice, evaluation, and computers.* Pacific Grove, CA: Brooks/Cole; W. W. Hudson (1982). *The clinical measurement package: A field manual.* Homewood, IL: Dorsey.

Figure 5.5.   Index of Family Relations.

each scale, optimal conditions for child development or well-being are not measured. Therefore, like the IFR, they are best used as a measure of family problems, rather than of family functioning.

The CWBS consists of 43 scales descriptive of the type of problems seen in child welfare agencies. Each subscale has four to five behaviorally specific response categories. Rating most scales requires more knowledge of the family than a research interviewer has, so they must be completed by a worker or supervisor familiar with the case or case record. Not all scales need be used: a subset may be selected to fit the population, service under study, or available data. Seriousness weights have been developed for each category of each scale and scales may be averaged to obtain a score ranging from 1 to 100, which represents the overall severity of the problems facing the family. Thus the scales can be compared across a variety of families with a wide range of problems. (See Figures 5.6 and 5.7.)

Three subscales of the CWBS have been identified through factor analysis. The Household Adequacy subscale (ten items) assesses the adequacy of food, shelter, clothing, cleanliness, and money management in the family. It correlates highly with the Childhood Level of Living Scale developed by Polansky to measure child neglect (see Chapter 7) and is the only scale that relates to the entire family (Landsman et al., 1992; Polansky, Chalmers, Buttenwieser & Williams, 1978). The Parental Disposition subscale (ten items) measures the caregiver's parenting skills, disabilities, recognition of problems, and motivation to solve them, as well as the relationships between children and adults in the family, and is considered in the chapter on parenting. Finally, the Child Performance Subscale reflects the children's average scores for school status/performance and delinquent behavior. Its low reliability may be a result of combining younger and older children, since it better reflects the problems of adolescents.

Although not widely used in child welfare practice due to their length and lack of clinical cutting points, the Child Well-Being Scales and a close

---

Theoretical Orientation: Empirically based.
Populations Tested: Child protective services (neglect, physical and sexual abuse) and juvenile justice.
Format: Worker or case reader scored: 43 items, 3 subscales (Household Adequacy, Parental Disposition, Child Performance).
Source: S. Magura and B. S. Moses (1986). *Outcome measures for child welfare services*. Washington, DC: The Child Welfare League of America.

Figure 5.6. Child Well-Being Scales.

1. Physical Health Care
2. Nutrition/Diet
3. Clothing
4. Personal Hygiene
5. Household Furnishings
6. Overcrowding
7. Household Sanitation
8. Security of Residence
9. Availability of Utilities
10. Physical Safety in Home
11. Mental Health Care
12. Supervision of Younger Children (Under Age 13)
13. Supervision of Teenage Children
14. Arrangements for Substitute Child Care
15. Money Management
16. Parental Capacity for Child Care
17. Parental Relations
18. Continuity of Parenting
19. Parental Recognition of Problems
20. Parental Motivation to Solve Problems
21. Parental Cooperation with Case Planning/Services
22. Support for Principal Caretaker
23. Availability/Accessibility of Services
24. Parental Acceptance of/Affection for Children
25. Parental Approval of Children
26. Parental Expectations of Children
27. Parental Consistency of Discipline
28. Parental Teaching/Stimulating of Children
29. Abusive Physical Discipline
30. Deliberate Deprivation of Food/Water
31. Physical Confinement or Restriction
32. Deliberate "Locking-Out'
33. Sexual Abuse—Parent or Guardian
                 —Other Adult
34. Threat of Abuse
35. Economic Exploitation
36. Protection from Abuse—Intake
                        —Follow-up
37. Adequacy of Education
38. Academic Performance
39. School Attendance
40. Children's Family Relations
41. Children's Misconduct
42. Coping Behavior of Children
43. Children's Disabling Conditions—Degree of Impairment

Figure 5.7. The Child Well-Being Scales.

relative, the Family Risk Scales (Magura, Moses, & Jones, 1987), have been employed in several research projects on family-based child welfare services. Feldman (1991b) used the CWBS and found significant differences before and after services on all subscales except Household Adequacy.

A study of intensive family service programs in Oregon and Maryland that used the Parental Disposition and Household Adequacy scales also found significant changes from pre- to posttest, although these differed by site (Nelson et al., 1995). In this study, for example, the Household Adequacy scale reflected significant changes between intake and termination in the young, primarily African-American families with problems of child abuse and neglect served in the Baltimore program. In addition, both Fraser et al. (1991) and Yuan and Struckman-Johnson (1991) found significant changes on Family Risk Scale items from intake to case termination in families served by intensive family preservation services. Neither of these studies aggregated the items on the Family Risk scales into total family scores.

The CWBS and Family Risk Scales, unlike most of the family functioning scales discussed previously, have the added advantage of being related to placement. All of the studies using the CWLA scales have found the total scores, subscales, or individual scales to be correlated to placement, although the relationships differed according to the populations served (Feldman, 1991; Fraser et al., 1991; Nelson & Landsman, 1992; Theiman, Fuqua, & Linnan, 1990; Yuan & Struckman-Johnson, 1991). In testing the factor-based subscales of the Family Risk Scales, however, Theiman and Dall (1992a) did not find them to be related to risk status or to placement.

Family Systems Change Scale (FSCS)

Another scale administered by workers to assess change during FBS is the Family Systems Change Scale developed by the National Resource Center on Family Based Services. A 12-item scale that can be used to monitor progress monthly or at the end of service, each item on the FSCS is rated as to whether the family stayed the same, got worse, or got better during the service period. The FSCS covers individual behavioral change, systemic change in the family, and change in family-community relations, so it is applicable to a broad range of interventions. In two studies of FBS programs, family scores on the FSCS were significantly related to placement (Nelson & Landsman, 1992; Nelson et al., 1995). While promising, this scale has not been extensively validated with respect to internal consistency and validity.[2]

Goal Attainment Scaling (G.A.S.)

In addition to using a standardized instrument for all families in the program, workers can measure change related to individualized family treatment goals through Goal Attainment Scaling. Used since 1986 to assess treatment effectiveness in mental health settings, G.A.S. lends itself to measuring the achievement of treatment goals at the individual, dyadic, family, or family-environment levels and thus is well-suited to comprehensive FBS programs. It also involves family members in goal-setting and assessing change, a process that is central to many FBS programs. The process of developing goals, weighting them, and assessing change is described in widely available textbooks (e.g., Alter & Evens, 1990; Pietrzak et al., 1990).

Two studies illustrate the use of G.A.S. with family interventions. G.A.S was used in 16 family-focused, home-based intervention programs designed to prevent or remediate developmental disabilities in infants (Simeonsson, Bailey, Huntington, & Brandon, 1991). In addition to assisting in assessment and treatment planning, G.A.S. scores indicated that two-thirds of the treatment goals were attained at or above the expected level. Goal attainment was also significantly related to a decrease in family needs and an increase in positive family functioning.

A modified form of G.A.S was used to assess change in a family treatment program based on the Milan model of systemic family therapy (Fleuridas et al., 1990). G.A.S. scores were significantly correlated with change in other standardized measures of marital and family functioning. The same article gives a detailed example of the use of G.A.S. with an individual family who brought their ten-year-old son for treatment of behavior problems. By the end of treatment, about two-thirds of the parental and child subsystem goals were achieved, but there was no progress in achieving family goals. While relatively easy to use on a case level, aggregating G.A.S. scores across cases presents a number of challenges because of the lack of consistency in goals for various clients.

Family Assessment Form (FAF)

The Family Assessment Form (FAF) was developed at the Children's Bureau of Southern California as a practice-based instrument to assess family functioning, guide development of an appropriate service plan, and reassess functioning at case closing to measure family progress (McCroskey & Nelson, 1989; McCroskey, Nishimoto, & Subramanian, 1991). FBS workers collaborated in instrument development and developed a key that defines the behaviors and family dynamics that anchor each rating.

Theoretical Orientation: Ecological, family systems, practice-based.
Populations Tested: Child protective services.
Format: Worker scored: 104 items; also research interview version available in Spanish and English.
Source: Children's Bureau of Southern California, 3910 Oakwood Avenue, Los Angeles, CA 90004.

Figure 5.8.   Family Assessment Form.

The FAF includes over 100 items, which measure aspects of the family's physical, social, and financial environment; caregiver history and personal characteristics; caregiver's child rearing skills; and interactions between family members. Each item is rated on a nine-point scale ranging from above average (1) to serious risk for child abuse (9). The FAF was not designed as a questionnaire, but as a guide to help workers structure their data collection; it does not presuppose the order of observations or direct the worker's approach to interviewing a family. It does provide a structure for collecting information on psychosocial assessment, history, and current problems (see Figure 5.8).

It was assumed that assessment data would be collected over approximately three in-home visits and that ratings would be made again at termination during an in-home visit. Practitioners report that the FAF is very helpful in recording and structuring numerous observations, helping them to sort through information to develop a focused plan for treatment. It is useful, as well, in training new workers and supervising ongoing cases.

Meezan and McCroskey (1993) have translated the FAF into a research instrument for use in their Los Angeles study of FBS. Based on that study, they have identified six major factors that, taken together, define family functioning:

1. *Interactions between parents and children* is made up of twelve items including consistent and appropriate discipline, bonding and communication with children, and parent taking appropriate authority role.

2. *Living conditions of the family* is made up of four items: safety inside and immediately outside the family's home, cleanliness of the home, and cleanliness of the surrounding area (see Figure 5.9).

3. *Interactions between caregivers* is made up of six items including communication between caregivers, conjoint problem solving, conflict and power.

4. *Supports available to parents* is made up of five items including maintenance of adult relationships, available child care, and medical care.

Figure 5.9. An example of the Family Assessment Form. [*Source:* Children's Bureau of Southern California, 3910 Oakwood Avenue, Los Angeles, CA 90004. Reprinted with permission.]

I. **ENVIRONMENT**

A. **Physical Environment**

1. **CLEANLINESS/ ORDERLINESS—OUTSIDE HOME**

   Refers to litter, garbage, feces, vermin, clutter and odors around exterior of home. Assesses health hazards, physical neglect issues, and impact of physical environment.
   1. above average; feels like a place you want to visit
   2. adequate; clean; orderly; no health hazards; feels comfortable
   3. borderline; mild odors; lots of litter; lots of clutter around yard and house; looks junky; feels like you want to pick up and organize
   4. always smelly; wet and dry litter and garbage; potential health hazards; feels quite uncomfortable
   5. intolerable odors; overflowing trash bins/barrels; rotting food; attracting flies; definite health hazards; not a place you want to visit or be

2. **CLEANLINESS/ ORDERLINESS—INSIDE HOME**

   Refers to litter, garbage, cleanliness, feces, vermin, clutter and odors in home. Does not refer to cleanliness of people in home. Assesses health hazards, physical neglect issues, and impact of physical environment.
   1. above average; very clean; inviting; pleasant place to be
   2. adequate; clean and basically neat

3. borderline; lots of clutter, trash, full garbages; noticeable but tolerable odor; disorderly; generally not clean; could be improved with a couple hours of work; occasional roach problem
4. food particles on floors, tables, chairs; dirty diapers laying around; consistent odors; stained furniture, grease and grime on walls; cobwebs; potential health hazard; roaches; feels very uncomfortable
5. feces (animal or human) on floor; rotting wood; overflowing garbage; intolerable odors; causing difficult breathing; filthy in all areas; multiple vermin; urine-soaked furniture; sticky floors; hesitance about entering or sitting down

3. **SAFETY—OUTSIDE HOME**

   Refers to condition of building's exterior in terms of danger, thoughtfulness as regards to safety precautions and organization. Assesses environmental stressors.
   1. above average; extra safety precaution provided
   2. adequate; some basic safety precautions taken; no problem
   3. generally disorganized exterior; cracks in walls; cracked windows; trash bins, old freezers, etc. carelessly placed
   4. many broken windows in child's reach; rotting floors and walls
   5. extremely dangerous; holes

(*continued*)

Figure 5.9.   *(Continued)*

through walls; missing steps; broken glass in hallways and play areas; many windows broken; dangerous junk all around; i.e., rusting metal, sharp tools, matches	3 one broken window out of child's reach; mold or wet spots on walls; poisons and medications out of sight but within reach of child(ren); overloaded outlets; plumbing problems; few precautions taken
4. SAFETY—INSIDE HOME Refers to condition of building's interior in terms of danger, functioning and safety of plumbing, electricity and gas; thoughtfulness as regards to safety precautions and household organization. Assesses environmental stressors.	4 many broken windows in child's reach; rotting floors or walls; poisons and medications visible and accessible; broken glass on floor; no hot water; wires frayed; no screens on 2nd floor windows for toddlers; generally not safe
1 above average safety precautions taken; poisons and medications locked; outlets plugged; plans for emergency situations	5 extremely dangerous; holes in walls; no or nonfunctioning plumbing; no electricity; many hazards within reach; guns; hunting knives; street drugs; open medication bottles
2 no danger to child(ren); minor cracks in floors, walls, windows; poisons and medications out of reach but not locked; most precautions taken	

5. *Financial conditions of the family* is made up of five items including stress due to the welfare system, financial management, and financial stress.

6. *Developmental stimulation for the children* is made up of four items: toys, learning experiences, sibling interactions, and parents making time for play with their children.

Although the FAF has not been used as widely as some of the instruments mentioned previously, it is promising both as a practice and as a research instrument for FBS programs. Interrater reliability and construct and factor validity have been assessed in the Los Angeles study and the instrument appears to be psychometrically sound, as well as useful for practitioners.[3]

CONCLUSION

Family functioning measures provide both descriptive data on families receiving services and analytic data on the impact of services. This knowledge is essential for policy development, for program design and implementation, and for clinical practice with families.

One idea under discussion in both program and evaluation circles is development of a multipurpose modular assessment instrument, a common intake and assessment form that could be used by many different kinds of programs. This would include a set of key questions in each area of family services (including mental health, health, child care, education, housing, and income). Responses indicating trouble in any service area would trigger a more detailed set of assessment questions in that area. Such a two-phase approach has been tried in some fields of service (e.g., adolescent parenting) but has not been applied broadly to families referred to FBS programs. Such an approach is consistent with the move toward services integration in many communities; it would allow early identification of a broad range of service needs, and provision of a single point of entry for families needing multiple services. However, this kind of broad-based assessment of family functioning and family service needs is still in the planning stages. In the meantime, further experience with promising measures will provide valuable data on family change and direction in the selection of measurement devices for future use.

Although uniformity in instruments for measuring family functioning across programs would make evaluation and cross-program comparisons easier, the field has not yet reached the point where it is possible to recommend that all FBS programs use the same instruments. There is too much uncertainty about the definition of family functioning and too much variation among programs to suggest limiting options. Each program should select and adapt available measures, perhaps supplemented by some of its own making, to match its program theory and goals, population, and desired outcomes.

NOTES

1. The Hudson scales have been compiled for dissemination with other related scales and include the following scales:

- Index of Self-Esteem
- Child's Attitude Toward Father
- Child's Attitude Toward Mother
- Generalized Contentment Scale
- Index of Clinical Stress
- Clinical Anxiety Scale
- Index of Alcohol Involvement
- Index of Peer Relations

- Index of Marital Satisfaction
- Index of Sexual Satisfaction
- Partner Abuse Scale: Non-Physical
- Partner Abuse Scale: Physical
- Index of Family Relations
- Index of Parental Attitudes
- Index of Brother Relations
- Sexual Attitude Scale
- Index of Homophobia
- Children's Behavior Rating Scale
- Global Screening Inventory

For more information, contact Human Services Assessment Consultants (HSAC), P.O. Box 24779, Tempe, AZ 85285–4779.

2.   In its original application, positive scores on the FSCS were found to have an internal reliability of .94 (Cronbach's alpha) and an interrater reliability of .78 (Pearson's *r*).

3.   Researchers at the School of Social Work, University of North Carolina at Chapel Hill have developed a family assessment scale (NCFAS: North Carolina Family Assessment Scale) that is based on some of the features of the Family Assessment Form, Child Well-Being Scales and other measures. While full psychometric testing has yet to be conducted, the scale is being used statewide after extensive development work with FBS practitioners (Ray Kirk and Kellie Reed, personal communication, December 7, 1994).

Chapter 6

Assessing Child Functioning

Improvement of child functioning is an implicit goal of FBS programs. However, programs vary greatly in the amount of attention given to the functioning of individual children. Programs that focus primarily on the family as a unit may assume that improvement in family functioning or in parenting will naturally lead to improvements for children. Another issue is whether programs focus on only one child in the family—the child most "at risk" or known to the referral agency—or on all children in the family. In addition, they assume that more income, upgraded housing, access to health care, and better child care will probably have positive effects on children. These kinds of improvements are more readily observable and may not require sophisticated assessment techniques or measurement instruments. Yet an increasing number of FBS programs are working with youth involved in the mental health and juvenile justice systems, and the desired outcomes for these youth may be more complex.

To add to this complexity, many FBS programs do not evaluate the impact of services on individual children. As a relatively new field, we have focused first on evaluating policy-related goals, making the case that FBS programs can be both good for families (improvements in family functioning) and good for the public purse (reductions in placement). As the field develops, more complete program evaluations should also take on the challenges of fitting assessment measures to program purposes, and teasing out the relationships between actual program procedures and the resulting changes in individual and family functioning. In other words, we need to be able to link what we do with the results— good or bad—shown by children and parents (Dean Fixen, personal communication, June 20, 1994).

One of the primary challenges for clinicians in FBS programs is understanding how to target services to unique family systems, and to intervene in the complex transactions between parents and their children.

117

The research challenge is equally daunting: How does a program document changes in parent-child interactions for individual families and then aggregate results across families? Putting practice and research perspectives together to design service programs and measure their impacts can seem an overwhelming task, and is certainly one that requires patience, trust, and flexibility (Galinsky, Turnbull, Meglin, & Wilner, 1993).

The practice research challenge becomes even more complex when considering the broader ecological contexts of extended families, neighborhoods, service systems, and communities. For example, how does improved parenting affect outcomes for children when families are traumatized by personal life events or live in communities with very few resources? How do the characteristics of the individual child, and the transactions between parent, child, and extended family, influence parenting and child behavior? How do prior experiences with services affect the ability of parents to trust or effectively use services to change their family's circumstances?

Much of the current research on child development is based on a transactional model that "explains behavioral outcomes as the mutual effects of context on child and child on context" (Sameroff & Fiese, 1990, p. 119). As defined by Sameroff and Chandler (1975), the transactional model posits that developmental outcomes are not linear. Rather, they are transactional in nature, the result of dynamic and continuing interactions and processes. Transactional theory requires more complex child assessment strategies to mirror the complexities of child functioning; standardized normative tests or traditional psychometric assessments "lack the theoretical power and empirical specificity necessary to devise a successful intervention program" (Cicchetti & Wagner, 1990, p. 246).

While there are many available instruments designed to measure aspects of child development and functioning, most do not capture the transactional nature of child development. Moreover, they are often long and impractical (Edleson, 1985). Standardized tests are generally used to support a diagnosis, condition, or trait rather than to devise an effective service plan. Thus, many standardized child assessment instruments fail to capture the changes sought by FBS programs. However, they can be used to support both practice and research as part of a multidimensional plan. For example, there has been a great deal of work on the measurement of intelligence, but IQ is more often used as a label than as a key to working with the child or family. Some studies, however, have used standardized tests such as IQ scores to anchor exploration of the long-term impact of familial and environmental factors on children (Sameroff, Seifer, Baldwin, & Baldwin, 1993). And IQ tests can be used to help detect wide disparities in subscales that may indicate organicity, learning or emotional disability, attention deficit disorder, perceptual/motor interference, etc., which *could* lead to more child-centered treatment planning.

FBS programs face many of the same kinds of measurement challenges as early childhood intervention and family support programs: how to build sensitive and comprehensive assessments without being unduly intrusive or overwhelming to families; how to make realistic and practical assessments without falling back on a deficit-oriented diagnosis; how to measure the variables that fit the program's theory and goals rather than those for which standardized instruments are available; and how to link family or child outcomes to particular service strategies. Even with its challenges, however, assessment of child development and functioning is essential for FBS programs that target interventions to individual children, providing essential baseline data for service planning and measuring improvement.

Child assessment may be part of an overall family assessment or it may be aimed at targeted children. Regardless of how it is structured, there are several key issues that should inform development of the assessment approach and the selection of specific assessment protocols:

1. assessment for service planning,
2. evaluation of service outcomes,
3. application of an ecological perspective to child assessment,
4. application of a developmental perspective,
5. increasing knowledge about resilience and vulnerability,
6. the importance of cultural competence, and
7. the relative viewpoints of multiple reporters.

This chapter covers each of these areas and concludes with an outline of the multiple domains of child functioning that may be especially relevant to FBS programs, along with some recommendations and cautions about measurement strategies.

ASSESSMENT FOR SERVICE PLANNING AND EVALUATION

As noted in Chapter 5, assessment serves both clinical and evaluative purposes. First and foremost, a full assessment of the child is needed in order to plan appropriate services. Understanding the child's functioning in multiple domains—including physical, intellectual, emotional, social, and educational functioning—enables FBS programs to address problems in any of these domains. Narrow-range measures, addressing discrete areas such as stress, social competence, or adaptive behavior, may also be useful if there appears to be a particular problem in one area of functioning or if the program focuses on one or more specific areas. If the assessment is repeated at the end of service (or at multiple points during service), it also produces data that can be used to evaluate the results of service. As Cicchetti and Wagner note:

> There are two major reasons to do assessment: prediction and anchoring. Any assessment is implicitly a prediction based on the principles of continuity and representativeness. If a child's relative position on an instrument is not maintained over time, then it is because some other force has acted upon the child. If no change occurs, then we assume that there was no force and the null hypothesis is maintained.
>
> Anchoring refers to the establishment of a base from which one can monitor change. An assessment is done to establish the position of an individual, then an intervention occurs, followed by a subsequent assessment. In this way, the effect of the intervention can be determined experimentally. The purpose of the intervention is, in some sense, to "invalidate" the principle of continuity. (1990, p. 249)

Assessment, as workers know, can also serve therapeutic purposes by increasing the parents' knowledge of the child, calling attention to her/his abilities and strengths, empowering parents to support their child's unique development, and providing models for parent-child interaction in daily situations. A broad-based, multifactor assessment gives the worker the opportunity to include parents and other reporters, and to model interactions with children in many different domains of functioning. For example, asking parents to help you look for developmental indicators gives them important background knowledge about child development as well as purposive activities that they can arrange for their children. Asking them to report on their child's progress at school highlights the importance of home support for school activities. Simply by asking questions or recording information about an area of functioning, the worker underlines the importance of that area for the parent. Workers who recognize the salience of such activities as part of the intervention will want to be actively involved in instrument selection and/or development.

Assessment for Services Versus Assessment of Risk

Assessment for service planning is obviously quite different than risk assessment or assessment for screening purposes. Risk assessment or screening approaches assume that conditions (e.g., a positive toxicity screen at birth), experiences (e.g., previous neglect), or limited competencies (e.g., failure on a screening test) set some children apart from others as being "at risk." Such approaches are based on "population variables" and are generally used to determine program eligibility. They are not comprehensive enough to predict and anchor or to guide service planning that is based on unique "individual variables." Meisels warns against a narrow risk-focused perspective for assessing young children because (1) biological risk is "not a unitary construct" and can be mitigated by other factors, (2) risk alone is not sufficient to cause childhood problems, and (3) single sources of data are "extremely inferential." He recommends a multifactorial approach to assessment, stressing that "the more sources of data that are tapped, the more adequate and useful will be the conclusions drawn from the assessment" (1992, p. 4).

Multifactorial assessments linked to service plans produce richer evaluative data. No time-limited service will be able to address all of the concerns about child functioning that might arise from a full assessment. Depending on the goals of the program and the child's assessed needs, some areas will be targeted for focused intervention, and it is these priority areas where change might be expected. Just as each family is unique, every child in the family will have her/his own constellation of resources and needs. In-depth assessment makes it possible to collect both qualitative and quantitative data for case and program evaluation.

Population Served

Another important consideration is the program's assumptions about the nature of the child population served. According to Hauser-Cram and Shonkoff, there are at least two distinct populations served by family-oriented programs: "children for whom normative development is an achievable goal" and "children for whom atypical development is inevitable" (1988, p. 80). For the first group, children who face risks but who do not have inherent physical or mental limitations, the goal is to prevent problems and maintain developmental progress. For the second group, children with specific disabilities, the goal is to facilitate development and adaptation within limits.

Use of narrow-range assessment instruments, especially those standardized with a normal population, may be appropriate to track development for the first group but will underestimate progress for the second. In fact, "the exclusive use of normative instruments for such youngsters condemns them to automatic failure" (Hauser-Cram & Shonkoff, 1988, p. 80). FBS programs should take this warning to heart when they select measurement instruments; given the wide variety of children served, there may be no single instrument that can capture useful data for all children seen by the program.

The best approach to child assessment will depend on the theory and goals of the FBS program, the population served by the program, the range of services offered, the abilities of the clinical staff, and the evaluation aims of the program. A multifactorial assessment will require interdisciplinary staff training to assure that staff have the skills and knowledge to administer and interpret results. While it would be simpler to administer and evaluate results from a single-factor assessment, we recommend that FBS programs adopt broader-based child assessment strategies. Both service planning and evaluation will benefit in the long run from a comprehensive approach.

While this chapter focuses primarily on use of standardized instruments for assessment, one should not underestimate the utility of *direct observation methods* for measuring change in child or family functioning. (For example, see any issue of the *Journal of Applied Behavior Analysis*.)

Ecological Perspective

The ecological perspective, which has been so influential in the development of early childhood, family support, and FBS programs, also influences evaluation strategies in a number of ways. The first is that it is not possible to predict outcomes without understanding how development and context interact. This means that a program cannot assume that X intervention applied to Y level of functioning will always equal Z result for an individual child, or that average scores will adequately represent the group of children treated. This will be perfectly clear to any experienced worker, but is often overlooked when designing program evaluation strategies. Assessment strategies need to allow for wide variation in outcomes, as unobserved variables and environmental influences can produce unexpected results.

The second implication of the ecological perspective is that we are not *just* measuring single systems (child in family), but nested systems (child in family in program in neighborhood with social support and social services). The nested-systems model

> places the microsystems of immediate experience within a mesosystem of two or more microsystems, [and] is in turn embedded in the exosystem of non-immediate social contact; each of these system levels is, in turn, nested within a macrosystem of socio-cultural mores, values and laws. (Pence, 1988, p. xxiii)

Although no study to date has been designed to examine all of the systems that affect child functioning simultaneously, recognition of their mutual influence can place any one study's or program's contribution in perspective. Clearly, the FBS program is not the only influence on child development and it can only claim to be effective within certain limited boundaries. Broad range assessments allow more complete understanding of context for individual children and families. Yet contextual analysis at the program level remains a significant challenge: one that must be addressed if we are to fully understand how services work for different kinds of children in different kinds of families in different communities.

Many of the families seen by FBS programs have received or are simultaneously receiving services from other providers; information on these collateral services will also enhance child and family assessment. For example, in their study of the relationships between the microsystems of home and day care and their impact on children's language development, Pence and Goelman (as reported by Goelman, 1988) found that a main effect (or linear) explanation of language development did not accurately reflect the important interactions between these two systems. "More troubling, however, was the finding that disproportionate numbers of children from low-resource families were also entering low-resource day care environments. These day care settings, the other major microsystem within which the children participated, also appear to contribute differentially to the child's performance on standardized measures of child development" (p. 28). Simply put, given resources, better educated mothers tended to select better day care settings that encouraged more language usage, and children performed better on tests. If unmeasured, such factors may give an ineffective program the appearance of effectiveness, and vice versa (as discussed in Chapter 2).

Since we know that systems are interactive, it may also be the case that children and families have as much impact on the program as the program has on them. "Thus the program becomes, in the researcher's perceptions—and, thereby, in reality—a social organism that, over time, exhibits greater differentiation as it actively, and sometimes painfully, accommodates to the evolving initiatives, responses, and life circumstances of the families it serves" (Bronfenbrenner, 1988, p. xiii). This kind of dynamism is more likely to be true of active, engaged, and flexible programs—in other words, the best programs are those that continuously adapt to changing needs.

Ironically, evaluating program effectiveness is made more difficult by some of the very factors that enhance program effectiveness. Carefully tracking these programmatic and process variables is essential if we are to understand and evaluate differential developmental outcomes for children and to use this knowledge to improve program design and functioning.

Another implication of the ecological perspective for FBS evaluation is the need to design studies sensitive to the context of the particular program and to select measures that complement each other, without overwhelming service providers, families, or children. Each program must strike its own balance between focus on process and outcome, between measures of familial, parental, and child outcomes, and between qualitative and quantitative measurement techniques.

Developmental Perspective

Implicit in the ecological perspective is the belief that the ongoing development of individual children can be enhanced or blocked by transactions with their environment. Children who have physical or emotional problems, whose caregivers mistreat or neglect them, or who live in very impoverished environments may call on different strengths in order to progress successfully through major developmental stages. Since FBS programs often focus on families whose children have disabling or high-risk conditions, traditional assessment techniques will only tell part of the story. Assessment strategies must not only classify children in terms of age group norms, but must also take into account the unique strengths and challenges of individual children who face very difficult life events.

FBS programs will need to develop different protocols for different age groups, since the appropriate developmental milestones, methods of measurement, and key indicators vary across the life course. Assessment of infants relies almost exclusively on observation and parent report of behavior; assessment of preschool children may include the reports of child care teachers on both behavior and performance; assessment of school-age children should include teachers' reports of school performance, parents' reports of motivation, and self-reports on attitudes; and assessment of adolescents should highlight self-reports of attitudes and behaviors along with adult reports of performance. For all age groups, multiple points of view—both from those with different relationships with the child and those from multiple disciplines—will enrich the FBS worker's judgments about the child.

Assessment approaches appropriate to children at different developmental stages are widely available in the child development literature. For example, Weaver proposes a simple mnemonic where "each initial signifies an area of functioning: P=Physical, I=Intellectual, E=Emotional, E=Educational, and S=Social" (1984, p. 1). He further suggests:

> One practical way of attacking the problem involves taking a sheet of note paper and writing the initials P-I-E-E-S widely spaced down the left margin. Then while perusing the material, one can list possibly significant information under the appropriate initial as one comes across it. The re-

sulting summary list should help the psychologist in several ways during the various stages of assessment. First, the process itself helps fix in one's mind the important dimensions and developmental progressions of the case. Second, marked improvement, deterioration, or failure to develop in any category should be easier to discover. Third, deviance in any one of the major categories automatically raises a major diagnostic question that one must take into account in the overall evaluation. (pp. 3–4)

Other examples of such approaches include interdisciplinary models of infant assessment using an instrument such as the Bayley Scales of Infant Development (McCune, Kalmanson, Fleck, Glazewski, & Sillari, 1990); screening and assessment for disabled and developmentally vulnerable young children (Meisels & Provence, 1989; Poisson et al., 1991); construction of a developmental profile (Zill & Coiro, 1992); assessment of the school-age child (Lucco, 1991); and assessment of adolescent parents and their infants (Moroz & Allen-Meares, 1991).

Resilience and Vulnerability

One of the underlying tenets of FBS programs is that services are more effective when they build on family strengths and resources. A focus on the positive empowers families, while focusing only on problems disempowers and discourages them. Taking this seriously requires a rigorous mental adjustment for many workers (and researchers) who were trained to assess and treat problems, not to identify resources and strengths. It is especially difficult to focus on the positive when assessing children who have been abused or neglected, who are in trouble with the law, or who show emotional or behavioral problems—in other words, the primary child consumers of FBS programs. The combination of troubled histories and current environmental risk can make it seem as though these children don't have a chance, and it is tempting to summarize the case with a list of seemingly insurmountable problems. However, every worker also knows children who have managed to flourish in spite of difficult circumstances.

There is now a considerable body of research on childhood resilience and protective factors that seem to offset risks, as well as on childhood vulnerability. (For a summary of research on protective factors, see Werner, 1990). This research supports a transactional model of child development, which suggests that children can overcome even the most difficult circumstances given their internal strengths and a supportive environment. It also supports the idea that children can use help at any age; there is no single critical stage that determines developmental outcomes.

Werner and Smith found that children in a longitudinal study had individual developmental patterns that changed at different points in their life cycles:

> Some children drew consistently on constitutional resources that allowed them to overcome adverse experiences relatively unscathed. Others went through a period of reorganization after a troubled adolescence which changed their place on the continuum from vulnerability to resiliency. Some individuals who grew up in relatively affluent and supportive home environments in childhood and adolescence became more vulnerable when faced with an accumulation of stressful life events in adulthood. The transactions across time between constitutional characteristics of the individual and aspects of the caregiving environment that were supportive or successful determined the quality of adult adaptation in different domains—at work, in interpersonal relationships, and in the person's overall satisfaction with life. (1992, p. 203)

One of the challenges of child assessment for FBS programs is to find or develop assessment techniques to identify protective factors, both personal and environmental, that enable children to succeed in spite of their problems. Hodges (1993) has developed one such list of the individual, familial, and community factors that can protect children from risk based on the literature in (Table 6.1). A variety of perspectives is emerging in this area as researchers in the juvenile justice field have argued that risk and protective factors are largely the same variables but represent different ends of various continua such as social support and peer relationships (Stouthamer-Loeber et al., 1993).

Culturally Competent Assessment

Another standard of effective assessment is that both the assessor and the assessment instruments must not only be sensitive to the differences between individual children and families, but also to the differences between their own values and those of client families. The need for culturally sensitive practice is clear, underscored dramatically by the skew in the racial makeup of the child welfare and juvenile justice populations. When the culture of the practitioner is different from that of the family served, her/his assumptions and values about how families should work, how parents should behave, and how children should act may be at odds with those of family members. This is a formula for miscommunication, weak worker-client bonds, and poor treatment outcomes.

Although it is clear that evaluation and assessment should be equally

Table 6.1. Protective Factors[a]

Individual Characteristics
Birth order—first born
Health status—healthy during infancy and childhood
Activity level—multiple interests and hobbies, participation and competence
Disposition—good-natured, precocious, mature, inquisitive, willing to take risks, optimistic, hopeful, altruistic, personable, independent
Self-concept—high self-esteem, internal locus of control, ability to give and receive love and affection
Perceptive—quickly assesses dangerous situations and avoids harm
Interpersonal skills—able to create, develop, nurture, and maintain supportive relationships with others, assertive, good social skills, ability to relate to both children and adults, articulate
Cognitive skills—able to focus on positive attributes and ignore negative
Intellectual abilities—high academic achievement

Family Characteristics
Structure—rules and responsibilities for all members
Family relational factors—coherence and attachment, open exchange and expression of feelings and emotions
Parental factors—supervision and monitoring of children, a strong bond to at least one parent figure, a warm and supportive relationship, abundant attention during the first year of life, parental agreement on family values and morals
Family size—four or fewer children spaced at least two years apart
Socioeconomic status—middle to upper SES
Extended family—nurturing relationships with substitute caregivers such as aunts, uncles, and grandparents

Community Characteristics
Positive peer relationships
Extended family in close proximity
Schools—academic and extracurricular participation and achievement, close relationship with a teacher(s)
Reliance on informal network of family, friends, and community leaders for advice

[a] *Source:* V. Hodges (1993). Assessing for strengths and protective factors in child abuse and neglect: Risk assessment with families of color. In *Multicultural guidelines for assessing family strengths and risk factors in child protective services*, edited by P. Pecora and D. English. Seattle: Washington Risk Assessment Project. Washington Department of Health and Social Services, Division of Child and Family Services, and University of Washington School of Social Work.

sensitive to cultural assumptions and values, it is not clear how best to operationalize that sensitivity within a research paradigm. A recent guidebook on cultural competence for evaluators of community-based alcohol and drug prevention programs outlines the multiple possibilities for communication breakdown between evaluators operating from a rigorous "scientific" perspective and practitioners from communities of color operating from a relativist practical perspective (Orlandi, 1992). Possible areas of difficulty range from assumptions about the role of community input in formulating the evaluation agenda (whose questions are most important?), process versus outcome variables (which is most appropriate?), and emphasis on a research versus a service delivery perspective (what is the highest priority?), to inclusion of voices representing special interests in evaluation decision making (who has the say so?). As Orlandi notes:

> When traditionally trained evaluators are presented with a program evaluation challenge, they typically begin by translating it into a series of what, where and when questions. These questions, which deal with the workings of the program under review, are analyzed along dimensions that are infused into those evaluators during their training. These dimensions, which may be thought of as analytic perspectives for establishing an evaluation protocol, are often thought of by the evaluators as being grounded in scientific rigor and, therefore, objective. It is this impression that is often at the heart of the communication breakdown we are describing. Although based substantially on scientific and methodologically rigorous principles, the decisions that are made in establishing an evaluation protocol are far from unbiased and are necessarily subjective in several important respects. (1992, pp. 12–13)

When the basic assumptions do not match, open discussion to clarify differences and reach agreement is very difficult. The best solution is to have people of color, from the community under study, on the evaluation team preferably as leaders, but certainly as team members. When this is not possible, the next best solution is to involve evaluators who are culturally competent. According to Orlandi, cultural competence is "a set of academic and interpersonal skills that allow individuals to increase their understanding and appreciation of cultural differences and similarities within, among, and between groups. This requires a willingness and ability to draw on community-based values, traditions, and customs and to work with knowledgeable persons of and from the community in developing focused interventions, communications and other supports" (Orlandi, 1992, p. vi). And, we would add, in developing evaluation and assessment strategies.

Using Different Points of View

After several decades of research, evidence about the effects of programs that provide therapeutic intervention remains inconclusive at best. While evaluations of some social programs show behavior changes (e.g., job placement for employment training programs, economic self-sufficiency for welfare reform programs), evaluators of counseling, psychotherapy, or parent education programs searching for internal changes in attitudes, values, or states of mind find proof very elusive. As one frustrated evaluator of parent education programs says in explaining his decision to move from traditional designs to more collaborative methods of ecological research: "the parent education 'mouse' was too big for the traditional research 'mousetraps'" (Anglin, 1988, p. 37). (See also Chapter 10.)

Evaluations of therapeutic programs often rely on worker ratings that measure improvement between pre- and posttests or achievement of an acceptable rating at outcome. To overworked program administrators and workers, such tests seem to be simple to administer and tabulate, requiring little training or monitoring of raters. However, they have the obvious limitation of relying on only one point of view, that of the person responsible for providing services, who not only has a vested interest in the outcome but who sees the world through a particular professional and personal lens.

Another difficulty with such instruments is that, without very specific rating anchors or criteria, it is often unclear exactly what standards are to be used in rating, and raters may choose to focus on different aspects of the process (receptiveness to treatment, motivation, amount of effort expended) or its outcome (relative improvement, achievement of an acceptable level). Even though the FBS in-home worker has access to a broader range of information than does a worker who only sees families at office visits, she/he is still limited by the relationship of helper and by the purpose of the visit; she/he does not see the child or family as they appear to themselves or to their friends (Batson, O'Quinn, & Pych, 1982).

One way to develop more compelling proof of changes is to document convergence among reports from multiple reporters. However, if their roles vary, multiple reporters may not see the same things; in fact, it appears that the reporter's point of view is derived from both her/his observations and her/his interpretation of what is seen. In his classic article on disagreement among different kinds of reporters, "A Source of Data Is Not a Measuring Instrument," Fiske explains:

> It seems obvious that very high agreement, close to true consensus, will not be obtained among sources who are using different material for their judgments: a therapist, a spouse, and a co-worker will see the person in different environments. It also seems obvious that the relationships of these individuals to the object-person will inevitably affect their judgment

on all but minor matters. We can obtain agreement among such sources only by asking for perceptions of behaviors (or aspects of behaviors) common to their several experiences with that person: "Does he limp?" "Does he have a deep voice?" (Fiske, 1975, p. 22)

Achenbach, McConaughty, and Howell have concluded, based on a meta-analysis of 269 samples in 119 studies reporting on emotional/behavioral assessments of children, that "no one type of informant typically provides the same data as any other type of informant" (1987, p. 227). There is, however, "strong evidence for considerably higher consistency between pairs of informants who play similar roles with respect to children than between informants who play different roles" (p. 223). McCroskey and Meezan (in press) have found confirmation of this in their Los Angeles study of FBS: at the beginning of service, teachers and in-home workers were more likely to rate children as having serious problems than were parents, and parents, on the average, rated themselves as virtually problem-free while their in-home workers rated them as having problems in multiple areas of functioning. However, a year after the service ended, parents rated themselves as having improved significantly in several areas of functioning as a result of service. Clearly, these groups of raters had their own perspectives and standards of comparison leading them to judgments about family functioning and adequacy.

We therefore strongly recommend that FBS programs include multiple points of view in both their child assessment protocols and in their overall evaluation designs. Reporters should include FBS workers, professionals from other involved agencies (including teachers of school-age children), along with parents, children, and youth themselves. Programs should not expect reports from parents, teachers, children, and others to coincide, but should recognize that each perspective is uniquely valuable in understanding the complex dynamics of child and family change.

DOMAINS OF CHILD ASSESSMENT

There are too many possible child assessment instruments to list in this book; such lists are available, however, in reference books (Pfeiffer & Soldivera, 1992; Weaver, 1984; Corcoran, 1994; Corcoran & Fischer, 1987; Miller, 1991). Instead, we sort the primary indicators of child functioning into five major domains of child functioning that might be of concern to FBS programs. Table 6.2 lists these domains and gives

Table 6.2. Domains of Child Assessment and Selected Instruments[a]

Domain: Physical Health

Bayley Scales of Infant Development

Areas measured	Age range	Format
Mental, motor, infant behavior	1–42 months	Multiple-item, paper-pencil observation inventory

Reference: Bayley (1993)
Source: The Psychological Corporation, Order Service Center, P.O. Box 839954, San Antonio, TX 78283-3954

Denver Developmental Screening Test

Areas measured	Age range	Format
Personal, social, motor, language, adaptive abilities	Birth–6 years	105-item "pick and choose" test

Reference: Frankenburg & Dodds (1967)
Source: Ladoca Publishing Foundation, Laradon Hall Training & Residential Center, East 51st Avenue and Lincoln Street, Denver, CO 80216

Domain: Cognition and Achievement

Bzoch-League Receptive-Expressive Emergent Language Scale

Areas measured	Age range	Format
Expressive and receptive language	Birth–36 months	132-item pencil-paper inventory observed by parent or other adult

Reference: Bzoch & League (1971)
Source: University Park Press, Inc., 300 North Charles Street, Baltimore, MD 21201

Peabody Picture Vocabulary Test-Revised

Areas measured	Age range	Format
Verbal ability, scholastic, aptitude	2.5 years up	175-item "point to" test

Reference: Dunn & Dunn (1959)
Source: American Guidance Service, Publisher's Building, Circle Pines, MN 55014

Standard Progressive Matrices

Areas measured	Age range	Format
Mental ability, nonverbal abstract reasoning	8–65 years	60-item paper-pencil test

Reference: Raven, Court, & Raven (1977)
Source: The Psychological Corporation, Order Service Center, P.O. Box 839954, San Antonio, TX 78283-3954

Table 6.2. *(cont.)*

System of Multicultural Pluralistic Assessment

Areas measured	Age range	Format

Areas measured	Age range	Format
Cognition, sensory-motor, adaptive behavior for children from diverse backgrounds	5–11 years	Parent interview and student assessment materials

Source: The Psychological Corporation, Order Service Center, P.O. Box 839954, San Antonio, TX 78283-3954

Domain: Behavior and Social Well-Being

Adaptive Behavior Social Inventory

Areas measured	Age range	Format

Areas measured	Age range	Format
Adaptive prosocial behaviors, three scales: Express, Comply, Disrupt	Preschool	Interview with primary caretaker of child, using 83 items

Note: This inventory was extensively tested with mothers of different educational levels

Reference: Hogan, Scott & Baver (1992)

Source: Anne E. Hogan 2325 Gulf of Mexico Drive, Longboat Key, FL 34228

Child Behavior Checklist and Youth Self Report

Areas measured	Age range	Format

Areas measured	Age range	Format
Behavioral problems and competencies	4–18 years	1. CBCL—behavior from parent's point of view 2. Teacher Report Form—child's classroom behavior 3. Direct Observation Form—observer form 4. Youth Self Report Form— for 11–18-year-olds

Reference: Achenbach & Edelbrock (1983), Achenbach (1991a, 1991b, 1991c)

Source: University of Vermont, College of Medicine, Department of Psychiatry, Section of Child, Adolescent and Family Psychiatry, 1 South Prospect Street, Burlington, VT 05401 [For an example of application to FBS, see St. Lawrence Youth Association (1994), Wells & Whittington (1993)]

(continued)

Table 6.2. (cont.)

Conflict Behavior Questionnaire (CBQ) or now known as the Interaction Behavior Questionnaire (IBQ)

Areas measured	Age range	Format
Perceived communication conflict between parents and adolescents	Adolescence	1. Parent (75 items) 2. Adolescent (73 items) Two short forms are available using either 20 or 44 items

Reference: Foster et al. (1983)
Source: A. L. Robin & S. L. Foster (1989). Negotiating parent-adolescent conflict: A behavioral-family systems approach. New York: Guilford

Connors Parent Symptom Questionnaire and Teachers Rating Scales

Areas measured	Age range	Format
Behavior problems and classroom behavior	3–17 years	1. Parent—48-item paper-pencil observation inventory 2. Teacher—28-item paper-pencil observation inventory

Reference: Goyette, Conners & Ulrich (1978)
Source: Barkley, R. G. (1981). Hyperactive children: A handbook for diagnosis and treatment. New York: Guilford

Family Relations Test

Areas measured	Age range	Format
Memories and subjective perceptions of interpersonal relationships in family	3–15 years–adult	1. Children's Version—examiner uses figures and cards (20–25 minutes) 2. Adult Version—examiner uses figures and cards (20–25 minutes)

Source: NFER–Nelson Publishing Company, Darville House, 2 Oxford Road East, Windsor, Berkshire SL4IDF, UK

Health Resources Inventory

Areas measured	Age range	Format
Adherence to rules, good student behavior gutsy, peer sociability, frustration tolerance	4–12 years old	A 44-item written instrument with a 5-point scale. Note: most items and the scale are phrased in a positive manner

Reference: Keogh, Juvonen, & Bernheimer (1989)
Source: Barbara Keogh, Graduate School of Education, University of California, Los Angeles

(continued)

Table 6.2.   (*cont.*)

Vineland Adaptive Behavior Scales		
Areas measured	*Age range*	*Format*
Personal and social sufficiency	Birth–adult	1. Interview Edition Survey Form—297 items 2. Classroom Edition—244 items 3. Interview Edition—577 items

Reference: Sparrow, Balla, & Cicchetti (1984)
Source: American Guidance Service, Publisher's Building, Circle Pines, MN 55014

Domain: Psychological and Emotional Well-being

Children's Depression Inventory		
Areas measured	*Age range*	*Format*
Depression	8–13 years	27-item paper-pencil inventory

Reference: Reynolds & Richmond (1985)
Source: Maria Kovacs, Western Psychiatric Institute and Clinic, 3811 O'Hara Street, Pittsburgh, PA 15261

Coopersmith Self-Esteem Inventories		
Areas measured	*Age range*	*Format*
Social self-peers, home-parents, school-academic, general-self	8 years–adult	1. School Form—58-item (8–15 years) 2. School Short Form—25 items 3. Adult Form—25 items (15–adult)

Source: Consulting Psychologists Press, Inc., 577 College Avenue, P.O. Box 60070, Palo Alto, CA 94306

Personality Inventory for Children		
Areas measured	*Age range*	*Format*
Adjustment, development, family relations, anxiety, social skills, achievement, somatic concerns, delinquency, psychosis, intellectual, depression, withdrawal, hyperactivity	3–16 years	600-item paper-pencil inventory completed by parents; 16 primary scales and 17 experimental scales also available

Reference: Wirt et al. (1984)
Source: Western Psychological Services, A Division of Manson Western Corporation, 12031 Wilshire Blvd., Los Angeles, CA 90025

(*continued*)

Table 6.2. *(cont.)*

Home Observation for Measurement of the Environment		
Areas measured	*Age range*	*Format*
Quality of home environment, stimulation available to child	Infant–6 years	1. Infant and Toddler—45 items completed by observer 2. Preschool—55 items completed by observer

Reference: Caldwell and Bradley (1984)
Source: Center for Child Development and Education, College of Education, University of Arkansas at Little Rock, 33rd and University, Little Rock, AK 72204

State-Trait Anxiety Inventory for Children		
Areas measured	*Age range*	*Format*
Anxiety	4–8 years	Two 20-item scales for state and trait anxiety (10–20 minutes)

Source: Consulting Psychologists Press, Inc. 577 College Avenue, P.O. Box 60070, Palo Alto, CA 94306

Domain: Environmental Adequacy

Urban Childhood Level of Living Scale		
Areas measured	*Age range*	*Format*
Quality of care in home, neglect, need for parent education	4–7 years	99-item true-false checklist: Part A—47 items physical care; Part B—52 items on emotional/cognitive care

Reference: Polansky, Chalmers, Buttonwieser and Williams (1978)
Source: Norman Polansky, School of Social Work, University of Georgia, Athens, GA 30601

[a] For further information, see S. J. Weaver (ed.) (1984). *Testing children, a reference guide for effective clinical and psychoeducational assessments.* Kansas City: Test Corporation of America.

examples of the kinds of instruments that might be helpful in measuring aspects of each domain.

Physical Health. Indicators of physical health might include prenatal and perinatal conditions affecting the child's physical and developmental potential, childhood health and illness, nutrition, developmental achievements and delays, and neurological development.

Cognition and Achievement. Indicators of cognition and achievement might include the child's intelligence level, language capacities of the child, and indicators of school performance.

Behavior and Social Well-Being. Indicators of behavior and social well-being might include relationship with caregivers, temperament, adaptive behavior, self-regulatory behavior, peer relations, affective expression, social competence, moral values, oppositional behavior, motivation, and curiosity. Specific adolescent behaviors would include substance use/abuse, employment, teen pregnancy and parenting, school attendance, educational expectations, delinquent peers, delinquency, high school graduation, and postgraduation plans.

Psychological and Emotional Well-Being. Indicators of psychological and emotional well-being might include secure attachment to caregivers, development of an autonomous self, stress levels, self esteem, self-other differentiation, and a wide variety of psychological symptoms.

Environmental Adequacy. Indicators of environmental adequacy might include safety of the child's environment (inside and outside the home), home stimulation available to infants and preschoolers, and parental substance use/abuse.

CONCLUSION

Many FBS programs focus evaluation efforts on documenting outcomes for families, collecting relatively little data on outcomes for individual children (other than placement). However, staff regularly assess children as part of service planning. This chapter has suggested that such clinical assessments, completed at more than one point in time, can be a useful addition to overall program evaluation. It recommends a set of principles that should inform child assessment for both clinical and evaluation purposes. These principles include framing child assessment in an ecological perspective of family and environment, building an understanding of how continuing dynamic transactions influence child development, increasing knowledge about resilience and protective factors, increasing the cultural competence of assessors and using measures that are culturally relevant, and recognizing the unique contributions of multiple reporters.

In FBS programs across the country, more comprehensive assessment of the individual, family, school, peer, and neighborhood factors that affect children and their families is needed. Some programs may be ready and able to develop comprehensive child assessment protocols. Others may be more interested in observing the connections between changes in children, parents, and families. Still others may begin with more limited steps, piloting available child assessment instruments for subgroups of children to test their practicality and utility. Wherever you begin, we suggest a few cautions as you address this complex and challenging task:

1.   Useful child assessment requires a multifaceted approach including multiple domains of child functioning, multiple measures, and multiple sources of information. Given the complexity of the task, the phasing-in of measures, with careful planning, training, and monitoring at each step of the way, will be helpful.

2.   Since programs are limited in the time and attention they can devote to child assessment, they cannot pay equal attention to all domains of child functioning. Select domains that match program theory and goals, and client populations needs for in-depth attention while maintaining a broad-brush approach in other areas. Selection of areas for in-depth attention should follow discussion about what is most important to the program and to the families served.

3.   There should not be so many measures that staff, families, or children are overwhelmed, nor so few that essential information is missed. The theory base of the program should help to determine the important domains of information. Study results that are tied to a theory base can give direction to program improvements, while results that are atheoretical will be of little help in improving clinical services, program design, or policies (Aber, Allen, Carlson, & Cicchetti, 1989).

Development of fine-grained child assessment strategies can improve clinical services as well as provide outcome data to support program development. Data from multidimensional assessment of children can also deepen our understanding of how and for whom FBS programs work.

Chapter 7

Assessing Parent Functioning and Social Support

One of the primary aims of most FBS programs is to improve parenting skills and behaviors. Intimately linked to the ability of parents to provide adequate care for their children is the level of support they receive in their parenting role. Intervention and evaluation in both of these areas are particularly important in cases involving child neglect. Of the hundreds of parenting measures that have been developed since the 1930s, however, only a few have been used for assessing changes in parenting as a result of intervention (Holden & Edwards, 1989). This chapter, therefore, will focus on measures of parenting and social support that have been used in studies with the kinds of issues presented by the families seen in FBS.

Conceptual Background

Belsky (1984a, 1984b) has proposed an ecological model of parenting that includes the multiple interactions of parent, child, and contextual factors. Belsky and Vondra (1989) argue that the personal characteristics of some parents create a predisposition to child maltreatment that is either triggered or buffered by contextual stressors and resources. These, in turn, are partially determined by the characteristics and abilities of the parent and by the attributes of the child (see Figure 7.1).

Although an ecological model of parenting is highly compatible with the philosophy and approach of many FBS programs, most parenting measures have been based on other conceptual frameworks, including psychoanalytic and social learning theory. Indeed, the initial research on parenting behavior was stimulated in the 1930s by Freud's emphasis on the importance of early childhood experiences in personality development (Holden, 1990; Miller & Hauser, 1989).

Patterson and his colleagues, on the other hand, have developed inter-

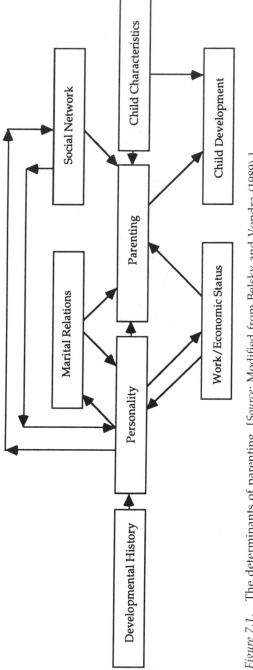

Figure 7.1. The determinants of parenting. [*Source:* Modified from Belsky and Vondra (1989).]

ventions and measures of change in parenting and child behavior based on social learning theory. These focus on the antecedents and consequences of behaviors and on reshaping both parenting and child behavior through reinforcement and contingency management. This work has proven useful in both understanding and intervening in the behavior problems of school-aged children (Goldstein & Keller, 1987; Patterson, Reid, Jones, & Gonger, 1975). In addition, Hansen and MacMillan (1990) have recently developed behavioral measures for the assessment of parental skill deficits that may be useful in evaluating FBS.

As in other areas of assessment, when selecting one or more approaches to measure parental functioning, it is important to be aware of the theoretical framework that guides your conceptualization of a particular aspect of parenting. For example, interventions may focus on "parental locus of control," which reflects parents' beliefs about their ability to control their child's behavior and the "causes" of that behavior. Underpinning this concept are a number of theories including social learning-reinforcement theory, attribution theory, and self-efficacy theory (Koeske & Koeske, 1992). It is important to determine if the theories that guided the development of an instrument are compatible with the practice model of the FBS program being evaluated. If the theory base of the instrument is at variance with that of the practice model, it may not adequately capture changes in parenting that result from your interventions.

Domains of Measurement

Parenting is a complex phenomenon affected by several domains of functioning, all of which may be the subject of intervention, and therefore of evaluation. These domains include knowledge, capacity, acceptance of the parental role, and role performance. Each domain is influenced by the characteristics of the child and by relationships and interactions with others, which determine, among other things, the degree of support the parent receives.

Many instruments have been developed to study parenting knowledge and beliefs, including age-appropriate expectations, knowledge of child development, and beliefs about appropriate discipline. The Adult/Adolescent Parenting Inventory (Bavolek, 1989), discussed later in this chapter, is one example. Others include the Parent Opinion Questionnaire, which has been used in several studies to distinguish abusive from nonabusive parents, and the Family Beliefs Inventory, which measures unreasonable beliefs involved in parent-adolescent conflict (both cited in Hansen & MacMillan, 1990). Choosing an instrument to assess gains in parenting knowledge may be important in your evaluation, since parenting education is widely used in FBS.

Assessment of parenting must also include information about the parent's capacity to provide adequate care. Depression, ill-health, developmental disabilities, low self-esteem, and a sense of lack of control or competence all affect parenting and have been the subject of assessment and intervention. The measurement of these and other areas of individual functioning is highly complex and is itself the subject of innumerable volumes. [See Corcoran (1994), Grotevant & Carlson (1989), Touliatos, Perlmutter, & Strauss (1990) for recent compilations of instruments particularly appropriate for use in evaluating social work practice.]

In addition to knowledge and capacity, parenting requires an acceptance of the parental role. Ambivalence, role-reversal, and rejection of parenting responsibilities have a great deal of influence on the outcome of child welfare services, especially with regard to placement and reunification (Hess & Folaron, 1991). Attachment theory has been especially influential in building support for FBS services to preserve and reunite families, as well as in prevention efforts in child abuse and neglect. A crucial part of family cohesion is the parents' acceptance of and affection for their children. This provides the emotional glue that holds families together through the various developmental stages of childhood (see Chapter 6). Therefore, the assessment of parental warmth and empathy, or coldness and rejection, may be important in planning and evaluating interventions in FBS.

Child protective services and many FBS programs, however, focus primarily on parental role performance. This may be assessed in terms of the physical care of the child and home, appropriate supervision, child protection and safety, or provision of necessary resources such as medical or mental health care. In addition, especially in programs aimed at families with young children, assessing and enhancing intellectual stimulation and cognitive development may be important. Instruments such as the Childhood Level of Living Scale (Polansky et al., 1978; discussed later in this chapter), the Home Observation for Measurement of the Environment (HOME; Caldwell & Bradley, 1984; discussed in Chapter 6), and the Home Accident Prevention Inventory (HAPI; Tertinger, Greene, & Lutzker, 1984) focus primarily on these aspects of parenting.

Reflecting the breadth of concerns in child welfare research, several instruments, most notably the Child Well-Being Scales (Magura & Moses, 1986) and Family Risk Scales (Magura et al., 1987), include items that cover many domains of parental functioning, as well as measures of social support and child functioning. Whether you should use a broad or more narrowly focused instrument in your evaluation will depend on the range of issues presented by the families served by your program and on the specificity of the interventions being evaluated. Table 7.1 provides an overview of the domains of parenting covered by the instruments reviewed in this chapter.

Description of Assessment Methods

Measuring change in parenting presents considerable challenges. A majority of the parenting instruments currently in use measure cognition and behavior, although some investigate parent-child relationships, the home environment, and parental self-perceptions. Most rely on information collected from mothers or children via questionnaires. Only in the mid-1960s did measures to assess the quality of fathers' relationships with their children begin to appear (Holden, 1990).

Holden and Edwards (1989) have questioned the ability of many of the existing instruments to measure change in parenting behavior and attitudes. They found, for example, that 45 mothers gave different responses to an average of four out of ten items on one "exemplary" questionnaire only 15 minutes after its initial administration. The mothers attributed the differences in their responses to vague questions, lack of relevance to the developmental level or temperament of their child, and differences among their children. To improve measurement in this area, the authors recommend using instruments with clear questions embedded in specific contexts and phrased in the first person (i.e., "I" statements).

Although less than 10% of the parenting instruments reviewed by Holden (1990) were designed for direct observation, Wolfe (1988) recommends using observation of structured tasks that may be videotaped and later coded or viewed by the parent for feedback to assess parenting. Due to their ease in administration and applicability in practice situations, only self-report and worker-rated questionnaires are considered in this chapter. However, you may wish to consider observational measures if time and other resources permit [see Wolfe (1988, p. 659) for a discussion of several observational coding systems that can be used to assess (1) verbal and physical behavior, (2) criticism and commands, (3) affect, and (4) quality of interactions].

Issues of Gender, Ethnicity, and Class

As has been discussed in earlier chapters, the effect of gender, ethnicity, and class on measurement has not been thoroughly explored in the evaluation field. Despite the work of Achenbach (1991a, 1991b) and others to norm child assessment measures by gender, it is rare, for

Table 7.1. Domains of Parenting Measured by Selected Instruments

Instruments	Domains					
	Knowledge	Capacity	Acceptance	Performance	Child characteristics	Support
Adult-Adolescent Parenting Inventory (32 items) (Bavolek 1990d)	X		X			
Child Abuse Potential Inventory (160 items) (Milner 1989)		X	X		X	X
Child Well-Being Scales (43 items) (Magura & Moses 1986)		X	X	X	X	
Family Risk Scales (26 items) (Magura, Moses, & Jones 1987)	X	X	X	X	X	X
Childhood Level of Living Scales (99 items) (Polansky, Ammons, & Weathersby 1983)			X	X		
Parenting Stress Index (101 items) (Abidin 1983)		X	X			
Parental Locus of Control Scale (47 items) (Holden 1990)		X	X	X	X	
Parental Acceptance-Rejection Questionnaire (60 items) (Holden & Edwards 1989)			X			

example, to find an instrument that has been normed on a variety of ethnic groups, or on parents with different levels of education and income, in spite of the fact that parenting is influenced by both class (Kohn, 1973) and culture (Korbin, 1981; Scheper-Hughes, 1987). Although the perceptions of mothers and fathers may vary widely (Dore, 1991a), gender differences in measurement have also been largely ignored, and mothers remain the most accessible and frequently used respondents.

Everett, Chipungu, and Leashore (1991) describe the values and worldviews of African-Americans with regard to children and families and advocate an Afrocentric perspective in working with these families. The importance and role of the extended family, orientation to community self-help, strong religious and spiritual beliefs, and emphasis in child rearing on group over individual welfare are factors that affect parenting practices and beliefs in African-American families. Similarly, Mannes (1990) outlines aspects of Native American culture and Fong (1994) discusses Asian family values that profoundly affect parenting and must be taken into account in developing FBS. The same cultural sensitivity required in the delivery of FBS (Hodges, 1991) must be shown in evaluating FBS.

Evaluators, therefore, must scrutinize instrument items for their suitability for certain parents. Are there beliefs, for example, in a parenting scale being considered for use in your study that are not held by the Native American parents you are serving? Will using this scale distort the concept of "effective parenting" for this population? Does the scale require a reading level beyond that of your respondents or assume adherence to middle-class ideas about parenting? Including parents in planning your evaluation and selecting instruments is an excellent way of detecting underlying assumptions in the instruments that may be inappropriate for your population. Reviews of instruments, including those in this chapter, often indicate whether the instrument has been used with differing study populations, whether normative data are available for subgroups, the instruments' required reading level, and whether translations into other languages are available. The next section reviews a number of possible measures that might be used to evaluate FBS programs.

PARENTING INSTRUMENTS

Adult-Adolescent Parenting Inventory (AAPI)

Stephen Bavolek developed the AAPI to measure parenting attitudes and beliefs associated with child abuse and neglect. A review of the literature identified four constructs, confirmed by subsequent factor analysis, that form the basis of the 32-item questionnaire: inappropriate parental expectations of the child, lack of empathy toward children's needs, belief in the value of physical punishment, and parent-child role reversal (Bavolek, 1990d). The AAPI takes about 20 minutes to complete and requires a fifth-grade reading level. It may also be read to respondents with poor reading skills (Bavolek, 1990c). The scale is available in two formats for pre- and posttesting over a short period of time. Norms have been established for males, females, African-Americans, whites, abusive and nonabusive, abused and nonabused respondents, and respondents of different ages (Bavolek, 1989). The AAPI is significantly correlated with the Minnesota Multiphasic Personality Inventory subscale that measures risk of potential child abuse, and it differentiates known populations of abusers from nonabusers, and adults and adolescents who have been abused from those who have not been abused (Bavolek, 1989).[1]

The most extensive testing of the AAPI as a measure of change after intervention has been in Bavolek's own family-based parent "Nurturing Programs" (Bavolek, 1989, 1990e). Both the scale and the program are based on the theory that abusive behavior is learned by observing and experiencing abuse in childhood (Bavolek, 1990d). The programs range from home-based parent education for individual families to groups that include parents and children in social and educational activities (Bavolek, 1990e).

Four evaluations of the Nurturing Programs are especially relevant to FBS. In the first, a group of 171 adults from Head Start programs in seven counties in Wisconsin completed home and group-based nurturing programs, which improved their parenting scores on all four of the AAPI subscales (Bavolek & Dellinger-Bavolek, 1990). In a second study of families referred for abuse from social service departments and Parents Anonymous programs in six sites in the midwest, the 101 parents who completed the 15-week program (83% of those who started it) improved their AAPI scores significantly on all four subscales and also showed significant increases in family cohesion, expressiveness, and independence and a decrease in family conflict on the Family Environment Scale (FES). (See Chapter 5.) The 118 children, ages 6 to 12, who participated in the study showed significant improvement on the FES and several other instruments. At a one-year follow-up, 58% of the families who were active with social services had their cases closed, and only 7% of the total sample had been re-referred for abuse (Bavolek, 1990a, 1990e).

The Nurturing Programs have also been adapted for more specialized populations including families with adolescents and chronically neglecting families. In a third study, of families referred for adolescent abuse/neglect or delinquency, or self-referred for parent-child conflict, the 156 parents who completed the program significantly improved their scores on all four subscales of the AAPI and on the family cohesion, autonomy, communication, family conflict, and anxiety subscales of the FES. The 155 teenagers showed similar changes on the AAPI and on the family conflict and intellectual/cultural subscales of the FES (Bavolek, 1990a, 1990b). Finally, a group of 125 adults in the Salt Lake City area, identified as chronically neglecting by the Utah Division of Family Services, committed to complete the 15-week Nurturing Program. The 82% who with their children completed fifteen weekly group sessions experienced significant increases on all four AAPI subscales (Bavolek, Henderson, & Schultz, 1990).

While the AAPI detected positive outcomes in the Nurturing Programs, it has not yet been used in evaluations of other FBS programs. Caution is warranted since AAPI scores have been found to correlate with amount of formal education (Figoten & Tanner, 1990) and to be unable to distinguish neglecting Native American families from a comparison group of nonneglecting families (Nelson, Landsman, Cross, & Tyler, 1994). Thus, the AAPI may be inappropriate for use with some populations.

Child Abuse Potential Inventory (CAP)

The Child Abuse Potential Inventory was designed to measure both personal and interactional dimensions of parenting in order to assess the risk of physical child abuse. The 160 items (each scored agree or disagree) make up seven factors grouped as personal (Distress, Rigidity, Unhappiness, Loneliness) and interpersonal (Child with Problems, Negative Concept of Child and Self, Problems with Family and Others) (Wolfe, 1988). It also includes three validity scales: faking good, faking bad, and random response. The CAP Inventory requires a third-grade reading level, takes about 20 minutes to administer, and has been translated into Spanish (DePaul, Arruabarrena, & Milner, 1991; Mollerstrom, Patchner, & Milner, 1992).[2]

The CAP Inventory is a general instrument and cannot differentiate between types of abuse and neglect (Milner, 1989). It is reported to accurately classify abusing parents in 80 to 90% of referred cases. CAP Inventory scores have also been found to correlate with future abuse and neglect reports, but not with failure to thrive (Milner, Gold, Ayoub, & Jacewitz, 1984). Extensive testing has shown scores to be related to childhood history of abuse; life stress; and psychological problems such as external locus of control, low self-esteem, high reactivity, ineffective coping, depression, and the five subscales of the Mental Health Index (Milner, Charlesworth, Gold, Gold, & Friesen, 1988). CAP Inventory scores have also been found to be related to family functioning, specifically to the conflict, cohesion, and expressiveness subscales of the FES (Mollerstrom, Patchner, & Milner, 1992). Norms for general and abusive populations are available.

In clinical studies, significant changes in CAP Inventory scores have been found posttreatment and at follow-up. The CAP Inventory was used in an evaluation of a 16-session family life education program serving 79 rural families at high risk of child abuse. The small- and large-group meetings included education, communications skills training, child care, and ancillary income support. Significant decreases in CAP Inventory scores were found at termination and maintained at a seven-week follow-up (Thomasson et al., 1981).

In a study of 76 pregnant adolescents who, in alternating home and clinic visits, received information on prenatal care and parenting skills, medical and social services, and support for four to six months, significant improvements were seen in CAP Inventory scores. In a ten-month follow-up, none of the adolescents were found to have been reported for child abuse or neglect (Fulton, Murphy, & Anderson, 1991).

Wolfe, Edwards, Manion, and Koverloa (1988) used the CAP Inventory to assess changes in attitudes, beliefs, and feelings about parenting in 30 young, single mothers who were receiving child protective services. In accordance with the wishes of the sixteen mothers in the experimental group, training focused on child management skills and included videotaping and desensitization training. Fourteen control mothers received the standard weekly service of two 2-hour information and support groups, which was also provided to the experimental group. At follow-up, experimental group mothers reported fewer problems and CAP scores were reduced to within normal ranges.

Despite these encouraging results, the CAP Inventory has not been used in FBS. It may need to be used in conjunction with other parent-completed instruments such as the AAPI, Parenting Stress Index, or the FES, or with worker/researcher completed measures such as the Child Well-Being Scales, Family Assessment Form, Family Risk Scales, or the Childhood Level of Living Scales (See Chapter 5).

The Parental Disposition Subscale of the Child
Well-Being Scales

As discussed in Chapter 5, the Child Well-Being and related Family Risk Scales[3] have been most frequently used in evaluations of FBS. Since the Parental Disposition Subscale, one of the three subscales of the Child Well-Being Scales (Magura & Moses, 1986), primarily measures parenting, it is discussed at greater length here.

Fourteen questions, grouped by factor analysis into the Parental Disposition Subscale, cover critical areas of parenting such as caretaker capacity to parent; acceptance, approval, and expectations of children; recognition of problems, motivation, and cooperation; discipline and abuse; teaching and stimulation; protection and mental health care. The subscale also includes an item on the children's family relations. The Parental Disposition Subscale was normed on 240 families accepted for child welfare services and has good interitem, interrater, and test-retest reliability (Magura & Moses, 1986, p. 187).

The Parental Disposition Subscale has been most successful in detecting change and predicting placement in studies of FBS programs. In Feldman's (1991b) study of families with adolescents receiving IFPS, the Parental Disposition Subscale showed significantly more posttreatment change in the experimental than the control group. It also showed significant change within the family preservation group. Similar levels of change were observed in a study of a systemically based Intensive Family Service program in Baltimore, which served families with younger children and problems of abuse and neglect (Nelson et al., 1995). Significant changes in Parental Disposition Subscale scores were noted in families who successfully avoided placement at termination and at the twelve month follow-up. In an earlier study of FBS case records, caregivers' initial scores on the Parental Disposition Subscale were found to be related to placement in cases referred for neglect, physical abuse, sexual abuse, status offenses, and delinquency (Nelson & Landsman, 1992).

If programs use the entire Parental Disposition Subscale in their evaluations, results may be compared with other FBS studies. However, subsets of scales may be constructed for specific purposes. Gaudin, Polansky, and Kilpatrick (1992) used 17 CWB scales, 12 representing physical care and five measuring psychological care of children, to discriminate neglecting from nonneglecting families. Nelson et al. (1995) also aggregated 14 scales into a measure of child neglect that showed significant posttreatment change in families receiving FBS in Baltimore.

Childhood Level of Living Scale (CLL)

The Childhood Level of Living Scale was developed to measure positive and negative influences in the home environment of 4- to 7-year-olds, particularly with regard to issues related to child neglect (Wolfe,

1988). The 99-item scale is rated by a social worker familiar with the home environment and includes nine subscales in two general areas: Physical Care (General Positive Care, State of Repair of House, Negligence, Quality of Household Maintenance, and Quality of Health Care and Grooming) and Emotional/Cognitive Care (Encouraging Competency, Inconsistency of Discipline and Coldness, Encouraging Superego Development, and Material Giving). Similarity in ratings have been found in urban and rural areas and among black and white respondents (Polansky, Ammons, & Weathersby, 1983). Normative data and cutoff scores are also available (Polansky et al., 1978; Polansky, Ammons, & Weathersby, 1983; Polansky, Cabral, Magura, & Phillips, 1983).[4]

Several clinical studies have found the CLL sensitive to change in families receiving treatment. In a study of 92 homeless, multiproblem families in New York City who received temporary housing and social services, a significant increase in the number of families providing good or acceptable care was found. Almost all the improvement was in the area of emotional/cognitive care. Most of the young mothers were African-American or Latina with large numbers of children. In Detroit, a similar group of 90 low-income African-American female-headed families who received in-home FBS to prevent out-of-home placement also improved significantly in the emotional/cognitive care that they provided for their children. In both New York and Detroit, considerable stability was observed in the scores of the families rated as severely neglectful (Polansky, Cabral, Magura, & Phillips, 1983). However, probably due to their small numbers and ethnic diversity, 23 families in New Jersey who received intensive services to prevent out-of-home placement failed to show significant improvement on either subscale (Feldman, 1991b).

More recently, the CLL was used to assess family change in six FBS programs treating chronically neglectful families. Nearly three-quarters of the families showed positive change during an average of 18 months of intervention that included parent education, support, and/or family therapy depending on the program. The most change was observed in the first six months of service. Two other sites had similar correlations, but small sample sizes reduced the statistical significance of the findings (DiLeonardi & Johnson, nd). In one of the projects, CLL scores were significantly correlated with CWBS scores and the total scores on both scales were significantly correlated with subsequent reports of neglect (Landsman et al., 1992). Although similar ratings have been found in rural and urban areas and among African-American and white respondents, some researchers and workers have reacted negatively to items in the CLL that reflect middle-class values or require resources beyond the reach of many FBS families.

The Parenting Stress Index (PSI)

Abidin (1983) developed the Parenting Stress Index to assess sources and levels of stress in parents of infants to three-year-olds, although the scale may be used for families with children up to the age of 10. The 101 questions, derived from attachment, temperament, and stress theories, are scored on a 5-point scale by parents. The PSI includes both parent and child factors as well as stressful life events, measured in a separate 19-item scale. It takes about 20–25 minutes to complete using a self-scoring answer sheet (Touliatos et al., 1990, p. 540) and requires a fifth-grade reading level (Wolfe, 1988).[5]

Factor analysis has confirmed six subscales in the child domain (Adaptability, Acceptability, Demandingness, Mood, Distractibility/Hyperactivity, and Reinforces Parent) and seven subscales in the parent domain (Depression, Attachment, Restrictions of Role, Sense of Competence, Social Isolation, Relationship with Spouse, and Parent Health). Reliability ranges from .55 to .80 for the subscales and from .89 to .93 for the total scales. They have also demonstrated test-retest reliability (Loyd & Abidin, 1985). Norms are based on 534 families from small-group pediatric clinics serving both normal and problem children (Miller & Hauser, 1989) and clinical cutoff scores are available (Abidin, 1983). The PSI has been translated into Spanish (Solis & Abidin, 1991).

Although found to discriminate between normal and clinical populations and widely used in assessment, the PSI has not been used to date in studies of FBS. Two studies of parent training, however, indicate that it may be useful in assessing the effectiveness of interventions directed at improving parenting skills. Both studies focused on the parents of 3- to 8-year-olds with behavior problems. In the first, videotaped role modeling was presented to groups of 10 to 15 parents with and without therapist-led group discussion. This intervention was compared to group discussion alone. All treatment conditions were found to reduce parental stress as measured by the PSI and to reduce child behavior problems. Changes were maintained over a one-year follow-up for two-thirds of the parents (Webster-Stratton, Hollinsworth, & Kolpacoff, 1989).

The second study included a comparison of didactic parent education with therapist modeling and role playing. The sample included both low- and middle-income mothers of children with behavior problems. The mothers received eight weeks of training in groups of 6 to 9 in different locations according to their income group. Although child behavior improved in both low- and middle-income families, PSI child domain scores improved only for the middle-income group, even though there was no initial difference between the two groups (Knapp & Deluty,

1989). The PSI may be useful for assessing and measuring change in various areas for parents of preschool children, but care should be taken in using it with low-income groups until additional confirmatory studies have been conducted.

Other Parenting Measures

Although not developed specifically for use in practice, two other scales may be useful to assess change in parenting. The Parental Locus of Control Scale was developed from existing locus of control scales applied specifically to parent-child relationships. The 47 items form five factor-based subscales: Parental Efficacy, Parental Responsibility, Child Control of Parents' Life, Parental Belief in Fate/Chance, and Parental Control of Child's Behavior (Holden, 1990). Although limited data are available, the total scale has good interitem reliability and correlates with other personality measures (Campis, Lyman, & Prentice-Dunn, 1986).

The Parental Acceptance-Rejection Questionnaire (Rohner, Saavedra, & Granum, 1978) measures the concepts of overprotection and rejection of children and is based on psychoanalytic theory (Holden & Edwards, 1989). The 60-item scale is available in child (age 9 to 11), mother, and adult perception forms and is one of the few scales that has been used in cross-cultural research (Miller & Hauser, 1989). Available in Spanish, Czechoslovakian, Hindi, Korean, Swedish, and several African languages, the reliability and validity of the scales have been demonstrated in a number of studies (Rohner, 1986).

PARENT SOCIAL SUPPORT

Relationship of Social Support to Parenting

In the past 15 years, the findings from numerous animal studies, analog experiments, and prospective surveys have suggested that social support is causally related to health maintenance, psychological well-being, and treatment prognosis (for reviews, see Cohen & Wills, 1985; Tracy & Whittaker, 1987; Whittaker & Garbarino, 1983).[6] In particular, Wahler and his colleagues have found that failures in parent training are correlated with "parental insularity," or a lack of social support (Wahler, 1980; Wahler, Leske, & Rogers, 1979). Socioeconomic disadvantage and maternal insularity (an index of daily social contacts weighted by the relative helpfulness of each contact) accounted for 49% of the variance between successful and unsuccessful parenting training outcomes one year following treatment (Dumas & Wahler, 1983).

Furthermore, social support networks that place heavy demands upon families or are the source of criticism have been linked to higher family stress and difficulty in becoming self-sufficient (e.g., Stack, 1974; Tracy & Whittaker, 1990). Recently, Dumas, Wahler, and colleagues have reported that socially isolated parents are doubly at risk of treatment failure—they are isolated and embedded in coercive interactions with bill collectors, landlords, protective services caseworkers, food stamp clerks, counselors, police, and other social-control agents (Dumas, 1984; Dumas & Albin, 1986; Dumas & Wahler, 1983; Wahler & Dumas, 1989). Lack of social support is thought to affect both the psychological and material resources that isolated families may bring to bear in solving financial, housing, health, child care, and other problems. Thus insular families are hypothesized to be more likely to fail to respond to treatment.

Measures of social support are included here because a growing body of literature suggests that parenting behavior is affected strongly by social and environmental conditions (Cochran & Brassard, 1979; Whittaker & Garbarino, 1983). Epidemiological research has shown that noncompliant and delinquent children often come from homes characterized by poverty, family violence, crowding, other aspects of aversive social networks, and poor education (e.g., Bernard, 1990; Loeber & Stouthamer-Loeber, 1986; Patterson, 1985; Wilson, 1987). Research indicates that such families are more likely to fail in treatment or to drop out. Four months after the conclusion of parenting training, Wahler and Afton (1980) found that low-income isolated mothers—women who had few primary social contacts and whose contacts were largely aversive in nature—were less successful in implementing child management strategies than middle-class mothers, who on average reported fewer coercive relationships and more supportive social ties.

Such findings appear to indicate that socially and economically disadvantaged families that lack positive, supportive social networks, particularly those who are trapped in aversive relationships with CPS, other social agencies, the police, neighbors, or relatives, are less likely to respond successfully to parenting training. Yet, these are precisely the kinds of families that FBS are intended to serve.

In a recent report, Wahler and Dumas concluded, "[The] evidence suggests clearly that a mother's ability to fulfill her caretaking responsibilities and, if necessary, to benefit from standardized treatment procedures is related to her level of social support and socioeconomic background" (1989, p. 118). This argues for the inclusion of social support as a focus of service, and, therefore, of evaluation effort.

As a result of the growing recognition of the importance of social support, a number of FBS agencies have included assessment and intervention with social support networks in their array of services. Some programs are expanding their attention to extended families and to helping parents and children through support groups and "family unity" meetings. These meetings assemble extended kin, community helpers, and professionals to encourage family and community members to take responsibility for helping the family at risk (Maxwell & Morris, 1995).

There are a number of challenges to measuring social support because it has many dimensions and levels. For example, a person may receive different types of support from immediate family members, relatives, friends and neighbors, and community groups. According to Barrera (1986), three different forms of social support have been the focus of research:

1. *Social embeddedness:* connections people have with significant others in their immediate environment. These linkages have the potential to serve a social support function in times of crisis. Social embeddedness is believed to be associated with one's sense of belonging to the community, and implies a lack of alienation and social isolation (Gottlieb, 1983; Sarason, 1974).

2. *Perceived social support:* individual perceptions of how much support they are receiving. Measures of perceived social support focus on the individual's cognitive appraisal of his or her social environment. It encompasses the level of confidence he or she has that when support is needed it will be available, offered in a way that is perceived as beneficial, and sufficiently present to meet his or her needs (Tracy, 1990).

3. *Enacted social support:* the actual support provided to a person via certain behaviors or concrete actions. Supportive behaviors can include such activities as listening, expressing concern, lending money, helping with a task, offering suggestions, giving advice, and showing affection. Most measures of enacted support are self-report measures that depend on the recall of past experiences rather than on actual observations of supportive behaviors. Several studies of enacted support have assessed the responsiveness to requests for assistance including the behavioral response that a request receives (Carveth & Gottlieb, 1979; Lefcourt, Martin, & Saleh, 1984; Sandler & Barrera, 1984). (For more information see Streeter & Franklin, 1992.)

Determining which aspects of social support to assess depends on the focus of the FBS interventions in your program. These may include:

1. *Material aid:* providing tangible materials in the form of money and other physical objects;

2. *Behavioral assistance:* sharing of tasks through physical labor;
3. *Intimate interaction:* traditional nondirective counseling behaviors such as listening, caring, expressing esteem and understanding;
4. *Guidance:* offering advice, information, or instruction;
5. *Feedback:* providing individuals with feedback about their behaviors, thoughts, or feelings;
6. *Positive social interaction:* engaging in social interactions for fun and relaxation. (Barrera & Ainlay, 1983, pp. 135–136)

While most of these forms emphasize positive social support, negative social support should also be a major assessment and practice concern, especially since some networks promote and provide opportunities for substance abuse and criminal behavior.

When considering what aspects of social support to examine and what measure to use, a number of dimensions must be considered. These include your conceptualization of support (e.g., social embeddedness, perceived or enacted forms of social supports); the actual types of support provided (e.g., material aid or emotional support); who is providing the social support (e.g., informal versus formal sources); the psychometric qualities of the instrument (validity, test-retest reliability, clinical sensitivity, etc.); and the "clinical utility" of the instrument (e.g., ease of administration and scoring) (Streeter & Franklin, 1992). A practical framework for examining different measures of social support is presented in Table 7.2.

Depending upon the focus of the FBS program with respect to the above areas, the evaluation may or may not include assessment of changes in social support. The parent functioning research reviewed earlier and recent projects (e.g., Tracy, Whittaker, Pugh, Kapp, & Overstreet, in press; Whittaker, Tracy, Overstreet, Mooradian, & Kapp, 1994) suggest that this is an important measurement area.

SELECTED MEASURES OF SOCIAL SUPPORT

Family Relationship Index (FRI)

This social support scale, which is part of the larger Family Environment Scale (FES) discussed in Chapter 5, uses three FES subscales to assess *perceived social support* among family members: cohesion, expressiveness, and conflict (e.g., Holahan & Moos, 1986; Moos, 1986). As such, the FRI differs from more traditional approaches to measuring social support in that it assesses "the degree of closeness, open communication, and conflict that exist among family members" (Streeter & Franklin, 1992, p. 90).[7]

Table 7.2.   A Framework for Assessing Measures of Social Support[a]

Conceptualization of support	Social embeddedness	Social network, social support resources
	Perceived social support	Cognitive appraisal of support
	Enacted social support	Assessment of supportive behaviors
Types of social support	Instrumental	Material aid, financial assistance
	Affective	Emotional support, advice, and guidance
Sources of social support	Informal	Family, friends, peers, colleagues
	Formal	Professional helpers
Psychometric properties	Reliability	Internal consistency
		Test-retest
		Parallel forms
	Validity	Face validity
		Content validity
		Criterion validity
		Construct validity
		Standardized administration protocol
	Standardization and norms	Established norms
Clinical utility	Practical advantage	Time for administration
		Difficulty
		Scoring and interpretation

[a] *Source:*   C. L. Streeter and C. Franklin (1992). Defining and measuring social support: Guidelines for social work practitioners. *Research on Social Work Practice* 2(1), 87. Reprinted with permission.

One advantage of the FRI is that it is combined with other important family functioning information in the FES (Grotevant & Carlson, 1989). This self-report instrument can be completed usually in less than 20 minutes, and scoring is relatively simple, using either a stencil or computer-assisted methods. The FRI has been praised by Streeter and Franklin and others for its ability to assess the perceived quality of social support among family members and for its content, concurrent, predictive, and construct validity:

> The FRI has primarily been used in research studies on the role of family supports in resistance to stress. However, it appears to be useful for clinical assessments with families. It is sensitive to clinical change and provides a good assessment of client progress in treatment. . . . The FRI has been standardized, and a large normative base exists for the measure. (1992, p. 90)

Social Network Map (SNM)

The SNM was developed recently to help FBS therapists and high-risk families assess current levels of social support and family support resources (Tracy, 1990; Tracy & Whittaker, 1990; Whittaker, Tracy, & Marckworth, 1989). The SNM is an example of an instrument that can be used to measure changes in *social embeddedness*—the direct and indirect linkages between family members and others that can be used as resources (Streeter & Franklin, 1992).

More specifically, the SNM is a paper-and-pencil measure that collects information about the size and composition of the network, the extent to which network members provide various types of social support, and the nature of relationships within the network as perceived by the person completing the map (Tracy, 1990, p. 253). Three techniques are used to gather the information: (1) a circular "map" that is filled in with network members in various categories (e.g., neighbors, friends, other family, formal services); (2) cards and slips of paper with network member names prerecorded on them that are sorted by the family; and (3) a social network grid that is used to help interview the person about aspects of the support that they received from each member of her or his network. (See Figures 7.2 and 7.3.) This approach is somewhat like a game, making the process more informal and friendly (Whittaker et al., 1989).[8]

Time of administration varies between 15 minutes and one hour, with an average of 20 minutes. Interrater reliability, measured in terms of overall agreement between sets of therapists administering the instruments with the same respondent, is high (kappa = .81). Rater agreement for some of the more specific variables does vary somewhat (Tracy, Catalano, Whittaker, & Fine, 1990).

The clinical utility of this measure for assessing social embeddedness is promising. FBS staff members have reported that the SNM is easy to administer and that it helped build rapport between them and family members. Additional studies, however, are needed to determine its construct validity and whether it is sensitive to changes in social support over time, particularly those that might occur as a result of FBS.

Recent research using the SNM has indicated that information about the structured aspects of social support (e.g., social network size) "provides little indication of the quality, amount, or experience of social support. . . . Because social support seems to be a perceived event, it is important that social network assessment tools include questions about the experience of social support" (Tracy & Abell, 1994, p. 59). Thus, it is important to include questions about frequency of use, reciprocity between the person and various network members, and satisfaction with support when using this instrument.

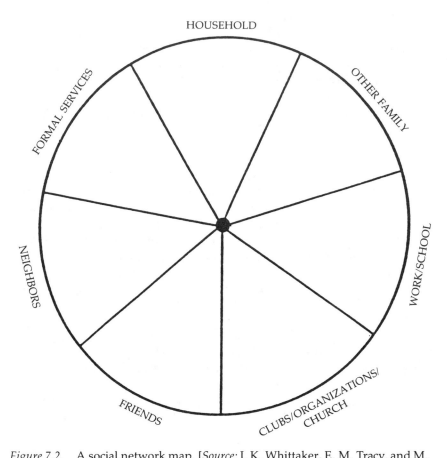

Figure 7.2.   A social network map. [*Source:* J. K. Whittaker, E. M. Tracy, and M. Marckworth (1989). *Family support project.* Seattle and Tacoma, WA: University of Washington, School of Social Work, and Behavioral Sciences Institute. Reprinted with permission.]

Milardo Social Support Inventory (SSI)

The Milardo Social Support Inventory (SSI) primarily measures *enacted social support*, the concrete manifestations of both instrumental and affective support. It was derived from an earlier Inventory of Socially Supportive Behaviors (ISSB) (Barrera, Sandler, & Ramsay, 1981; Tardy, 1985).

In 1983, Milardo revised the ISSB for use with distressed families and added items to measure aversive social interactions. The scale was reduced to 25 items, each with a seven-point response scale: (1) once a day or more, (2) about every other day, (3) about twice a week, (4) about once

ID 999 RESPONDENT Mother NAME	#	Area of Life 1. Household 2. Other family 3. Work/school 4. Organizations 5. Other friends 6. Neighbors 7. Professionals 8 Other	Concrete Support 1. Hardly ever 2. Sometimes 3. Almost always	Emotional Support 1. Hardly ever 2. Sometimes 3. Almost always	Information/ Advice 1. Hardly ever 2. Sometimes 3. Almost always	Critical 1. Hardly ever 2. Sometimes 3. Almost always	Direction of Help 1. Goes both ways 2. You to them 3. Them to you	Closeness 1. Not very close 2. Sort of close 3. Very close	How often seen 0. Does not see 1. Few times yr 2. Monthly 3. Weekly 4. Daily	How Long Known 1. Less than 1 yr 2. From 1-5 yrs 3. More than 5 yrs
Frank	01	1	2	2	2	3	2	3	4	3
Julie	02	1	1	2	1	2	2	2	4	3
Bill	03	1	1	1	1	3	2	1	4	3
Pastor	04	4	2	3	3	1	3	2	3	1
Pastor's wife	05	4	2	2	2	1	1	2	3	1
	06									
	07									
	08									
	09									
	10									
	11									
	12									
	13									
	14									
	15									
	1-6	7	8	9	10	11	12	13	14	15

Figure 7.3. A social network grid with sample data. [*Source:* E. M. Tracy, and J. K. Whittaker (1990). The social network map: 0Assessing social support in clinical practice. *Families in Society* 71(8), 461–70. Reprinted with permission.

a week, (5) about once every two weeks, (6) about once a month, and (7) about once every two months (Milardo, 1983).[9]

The SSI was used in one study of intensive FBS in two states (Fraser et al., 1991). Information about two types of social support was gathered from primary and secondary caregivers. At intake and termination, caregivers filled out one SSI for spousal (or cohabitant) support and one for extended family/non-kin support (including help provided by neighbors, friends, and acquaintances through organizations). On the extended family instrument, respondents were asked to exclude activities that occurred with spouses, live-in companions, children, or professional agency personnel such as mental health therapists, social service workers, or homemakers.

Factor analysis was used to extract three common factors that describe the underlying dimensions of social support among IFPS clients. Intake and exit reports from both primary and secondary caregivers produced remarkably similar structures (see Fraser et al., 1991). The factor scales were comparable to those developed by Barrera and Ainlay (1983) and Milardo (1983).

The first factor was labeled *empathetic friendship* and incorporated elements of nondirective social support and positive social interaction. It contains expressions of intimacy, unconditional acceptance, respect, and trust, and appears to describe the central elements of a confidant relationship—physical affection, listening, and comforting. The second factor was defined by *aversive relationships;* coercion and intrusion characterize this dimension of social relations. Parents who score in the high range on this factor are likely to be embedded in stressful relationships where they are frequently criticized and blamed. The third factor is equivalent to the factor that Barrera called "directive guidance." It was labeled *coaching* and was defined by items that describe helpful guidance and feedback activities such as giving information, teaching, and directive advising.

Changes in social support between treatment intake and exit indicate that IFPS reduced aversive social interactions between spouses (including cohabitants). Also, it appears to have increased empathic friendships with extended kin and network members. Both findings may be due to the attention paid to informal support systems by the IFPS therapist during the intervention period (Spaid, Fraser, & Lewis, 1991, p. 142).

Other Social Support Scales

The National Committee for Preventing Child Abuse has had some success with the Maternal Social Support Index developed by John Pascoe of the Department of Pediatrics, Clinical Science Center, in Madison, Wisconsin (Daro et al., 1990). This 21-item scale has high utility for clinical practice.[10]

Dunst, Jenkins, and Trivette (1984) have developed three additional social support scales that are short and practical. The Family Support Scale measures helpfulness of various sources of support to families rearing a young child, such as parents, spouse, friends, and co-workers. The Inventory of Social Support is used to identify the types of help that are provided to a respondent by the various individuals, groups, and agencies that make up their personal social network. The scale consists of two parts, a frequency of contact section and a matrix indicating both the type and source of assistance (Dunst et al., 1988, pp. 159–163).

The third scale, the Personal Network Matrix, has three parts to assess social needs, resources, and support. Part I asks the person to indicate how often "he or she has contact—face to face, in a group, or by telephone—with different people, groups, and agencies" (Dunst et al., 1988, p. 165). Part II requests the person to list up to ten needs, projects, or aspirations that are considered important enough to devote energy to, and to indicate which people in his or her network provide or have offered help for each of the ten needs, projects, or aspirations. Part III asks the respondent to rate the degree to which they can depend upon different network members for advice, assistance, or any other type of help (see Dunst et al., 1988, p. 165).

In addition, there are two different versions of the scale. One version is "preloaded" with a group of people who are thought to be part of personal networks. The other version asks the respondent to "list the specific persons, groups, and agencies that he or she (a) currently receives help from, and (b) might consider as a possible source of aid and assistance" (Dunst et al., 1988, p. 165).

While none of these three scales have clinical cutoff scores or other types of normative data, they have been used in studies of family support projects, and can provide immediately helpful clinical assessment information for practitioners.[11] (For additional measures and information see Dunst et al., 1988; Miller & Whittaker, 1988; Tracy & Whittaker, 1987. For a children's social support scale see Dubow & Ullman, 1989.)

CONCLUSION

This chapter has presented some approaches to assessing parenting attitudes and skills that are central to the mission of most FBS programs. Much work is still needed to determine which instruments can measure changes in parent functioning resulting from FBS interventions. While it is important to measure social support as part of an evaluation effort, if the agency has few resources for the study this may be secondary to assessing other aspects of parent or family functioning. However, since social support is critical to the effective functioning of most families, it should not be ignored in assessment or intervention. While studies of social support need to be replicated with different client populations and FBS program models, the association between family social supports and healthy functioning is strong enough to merit its inclusion in evaluation studies.

NOTES

1. The *Adult-Adolescent Parenting Inventory* (AAPI) is available from Family Development Resources, Inc. 767 Second Avenue, Eau Claire, WI 54703.
2. The *Child Abuse Potential Inventory* (CAP Inventory) is available from PSYTEC Inc. P.O. Box 564, DeKalb, IL 60115.
3. The *Child Well-Being Scales* (CWB) and Family Risk Scales are available from the Child Welfare League of America c/o CSSC 300 Raritan Center Parkway, Edison, NJ 08818.
4. The *Childhood Level of Living Scale* (CLL) is available from Professor Norman Polansky, School of Social Work, University of Georgia, Athens, GA 30602.
5. The Abidin *Parenting Stress Inventory* (PSI) is available from Pediatric Psychology Press, 320 Terell Road West, Charlottesville, VA 22901.
6. This section is adapted from Fraser et al. (1991), p. 74.
7. The *Family Relationship Index* (FRI) is available from Consulting Psychologists Press, 3803 Bay Shore Road, P.O. Box 10096, Palo Alto, CA 94303.
8. The *Social Network Map* (SNM) is reprinted in Tracy & Whittaker (1990) and is also available from Elizabeth Tracy at the Mandel School of Applied Social Sciences, Case Western Reserve University, 11235 Bellflower Road Cleveland, OH 44106–7164.
9. The Milardo *Social Support Inventory* (SSI) is available from Professor Robert Milardo, Merrill Hall, School of Human Development, University of Maine at Orono, Orono, ME 04469.
10. For a copy of the *Maternal Social Support Index*, write Dr. John Pascoe, at the Department of Pediatrics, Clinical Science Center, 600 Highland Avenue, Madison, WI 53792, or Dr. Deborah Daro at the National Center on the Prevention of Child Abuse, in Chicago.
11. The *Family Support Scale, Inventory of Social Support*, and the *Personal Network Matrix* are presented ready for use, along with limited scoring information, in Dunst et al. (1988), available from Brookline Books, P.O. Box 1046, Cambridge, MA 02238–1046.

Chapter 8

Placement Prevention

Previous chapters have presented a range of outcomes and evaluation measures applicable to FBS, including those relevant to assessing family functioning, household conditions, parenting behaviors, social support, and various aspects of child functioning. However, because of the emphasis that has been placed upon placement prevention in the past by child welfare advocates and more recently by legislative personnel, placement prevention has been the focus of much of the research on FBS; other aspects of program effectiveness have received less attention. Although placement prevention has been widely used as an outcome criterion, it is far from satisfactory as the primary outcome measure for FBS evaluations. In this chapter, a variety of placement-related measures, as well as guidelines for their use, will be presented.

ISSUES IN USING CHILD OR FAMILY PLACEMENT RATES[1]

In and of itself, prevention of child placement is an appealing outcome variable. Child placement has excellent "reliability" because it is basically nonambiguous and is easily verifiable. Reductions in child placement are thought to be associated with dramatic cost savings, and society values family preservation and children's ties to birth family members. And while rates of maltreatment of children in foster family and group care are always a concern, they remain low.

The body of research regarding the benefits of placement versus birth-family care remains contradictory. Further complicating the issue, previous researchers have identified a number of problems associated with using placement prevention rates as a primary measure of success (see for example, Fraser et al., 1991; Jones et al., 1976; Rzepnicki, Schuerman, & Littell, 1991). A few of these are listed below:

- A variety of reasons may account for placement decisions apart from child or family functioning.
- Some placements may be in the best interest of the child and family, while others are not. Distinguishing between the two situations is methodologically difficult.
- Because of the limitations of current risk assessment methods and difficulties in eliciting and screening case referrals, study populations have generally been at low risk of placement, making it very difficult to show prevention effects (see Feldman 1991b; Rzepnicki et al., 1991; Tracy, 1991; Yuan et al., 1990).
- Placement definitions, ways of identifying placements, and follow-up periods differ across studies, making comparisons difficult. It is unclear how long preventive effects should be expected, especially if needed follow-up services are lacking.

Literature reviews and reports indicate that there are mixed findings with respect to placement prevention rates for FBS and IFPS, with differences in placement rates between treatment and comparison groups ranging from 0 to 40% (Feldman, 1991a; Pecora, 1991a; Stein, 1985; Wells & Biegel, 1991). (See Chapter 1.) The summary statistics often cited, however, should be viewed with caution as they provide only a fraction of the research data generated by these major studies. The full reports must be read to understand the particular objectives, findings, limitations, and context of each study including critical factors such as intake criteria, client screening methods, treatment models, program stability, and client characteristics.

While subgroup analyses by child age, type of case, or other variables might reveal significant differences between the treatment and comparison groups in some studies, one might also argue that the field needs other measures of placement-related outcomes that are more sensitive to variations in service. A number of the complexities associated with using placement as an outcome variable will be discussed in the following sections, along with some proposed solutions. These complexities include differing definitions of placement, defining placement as "service failure," organizational and environmental influences on placement rates, problems with current approaches to case screening and decision-making, and the limitations of placement as a measure of success.

Competing Definitions of Placement

Placement must be assessed in the context of competing views about which out-of-home situations represent negative outcomes. In most studies, placement in a foster family, group home, or institutional care is considered a negative outcome. Additionally, a number of other events have been defined as placements or "service failures." These include runaway episodes or placement (1) with relatives, (2) with friends and neighbors, (3) in shelter care, receiving homes, or crisis residential centers, (4) in in-patient psychiatric facilities, (5) in state hospitals, and (6) in other institutions (secure correctional facilities, boarding schools, etc.).

Because most studies have not interviewed families as part of a service follow-up, few studies have been able to accurately report the placement of children with relatives, neighbors, and friends. So the question remains as to how such placements should be viewed and evaluated. Who most controls the decision—parents or the state? Which placements are viewed as negative or positive for children and their parents?

In one sense, these "informal" placements mean that a child's birth family may not remain the central socializing unit in her/his life. Yet in a different sense, the use of a family's social network may prevent placement at public expense and have significant benefits. Children are often able to remain in contact with their birth parents (Duerr-Berrick & Barth, 1994; Le Prohn & Pecora, 1994). They may continue to live in the same neighborhood and to attend the same school. Compared to family foster care, this kind of placement may be less disruptive and may not strain important attachments to peers and adults who act as role models (Lewis & Fraser, 1987). Relative placements may be less costly to the child welfare system and produce many benefits for children (Child Welfare League of America, 1994).

However, recent studies have indicated children in relative care remain longer in placement than children in nonrelative care (Wulczyn & Goerge, 1992) but appear to do at least as well as other children in the foster care system (Wedeven et al., 1994). These findings raise the question as to whether relative placements are positive outcomes if vigorous efforts are not made to reunify children with their birth parents. While placement with relatives has not been counted as a successful outcome in some FBS studies (cf. Fraser et al., 1991), informal placements with neighbors and friends, and runaways are almost always defined as negative.

These criteria for placement are debatable. Some might say that they are too inclusive; others might say they are too exclusive. The decision to use inclusive criteria may be made because researchers want to maximize the number of placements for examination; exclusive criteria may be used to maximize the rate of placement prevention.

Thus, given the current lack of uniform definitions, placement rates are complex and potentially misleading. And as different units of analysis (e.g., children vs. family) are being used across the field, it is important to note that, although counting individual children may provide a more accurate measure of placement avoidance, the removal of even one child from a family constitutes a major disruption and could be viewed from a family perspective as "treatment failure."

Defining Placement as "Service Failure" or as Success

Out-of-home child placement is a complex event. It involves the transfer of certain parental rights to the state, the removal of a child or children from the home, and a disposition decision about type of placement (e.g., foster family care, group home, psychiatric facility, cor rectional center). If a placement occurs, it is usually the culminating event in a series of unsuccessful (or only partially successful) efforts to strengthen the home and protect the child(ren). In this sense, it can be used to denote the failure of FBS efforts. However, the criteria used to define service failure are indeed relative, if not controversial.

Part of the issue relates to who makes the decision about whether and where to place a child. To what degree do the parents and the child lead or participate in that decision-making process? "Once the state takes control, I believe a whole host of things change that, *in themselves*, have detrimental effects on children and families (no matter how good the interventions are and no matter how good a program is)" (Dean Fixen, personal communication, June 20, 1994).

In defining service failure, we must include the location, appropriateness, and desirability of a specific placement. The social desirability of placement has been examined in only a few studies (see for example, Nelson et al., 1988). In some cases, placement may be a desirable alternative for a child and her/his family. However, the appropriateness of various placement options varies in relation to the family's circumstances, the child's situation, community norms, and agency resources (such as whether there is a suitable foster home available). At times, it may be difficult to reach a general consensus as to what constitutes an appropriate and socially desirable placement for a particular child. Other than Wells and Whittington (1993) few studies have interviewed children about their perceptions of FBS. Judging the appropriateness of placement represents a challenge to the field and a major problem to evaluators who elect to use placement as an outcome measure.

But achieving the least restrictive living environment that is possible for a child remains a central objective for many FBS programs. Reducing restrictiveness of placement is therefore an important but complex outcome measure that has not been rigorously employed in many studies, yet it remains one of the more important outcomes to examine both from the perspective of placement appropriateness and cost.

Unfortunately, only a few studies have formally looked at outcomes such as the proportion of shelter care days used compared to other forms of placement (e.g., Yuan et al., 1990), or the use of less restrictive placement options overall (e.g., Kinney & Haapala, 1984; Willems & DeRubeis, 1981). And there are critical methodological challenges that remain to be overcome, such as developing a credible means of determining that a youth should be (or would have been) placed in a particular setting, so that placement diversion can be validly assessed.

Yet this is an important outcome for a small but costly group of highly disturbed youth. The growing literature on "wraparound services" is beginning to describe some of the benefits when children are cared for by relatives or in special nonrelated foster homes (e.g., Burchard & Clarke, 1990; Vandenberg, 1993). The cost differences can be dramatic. For example, even treatment (or therapeutic) foster care rates are much lower than the $40,000–80,000 annual costs of residential treatment. So an FBS program may be very beneficial if it can safely divert youth from psychiatric hospitals, high-security corrections facilities, or intensive residential treatment to relative, foster family, or group home care. In fact, one such home-based program, sponsored by the St. Charles Residential Treatment Center in Milwaukee, has been providing this type of a service for over five years. Clearly, the optimal outcome is some form of permanent care—ideally, return home or adoption. But in certain cases, diversion from residential treatment to family foster care can be cost-effective and the best alternative for that child.[2]

Organizational and Environmental Influences on Placement Rates

Placement is subject to many influences, with a range of factors affecting rates of child placement such as placement availability, worker training, media attention, juvenile court attitudes, and the risk assessment approach used by the child welfare agency (see Figure 8.1).

Variation in placement rates across states (or counties in some states) may represent differences in state policies and resources as much as differences in the effectiveness of placement prevention services. It is one thing to reduce placements in a system where placement rates are declining overall; it is quite another thing to reduce placements in systems where placement rates are stable or increasing. The organizational and environmental context of FBS programs must be assessed, and placement rates should be viewed within the social ecology of changing public policies and practices (Feldman, 1990a; Pecora, 1991c; Tracy, 1990).

Placement incidence statistics for a particular community can be very

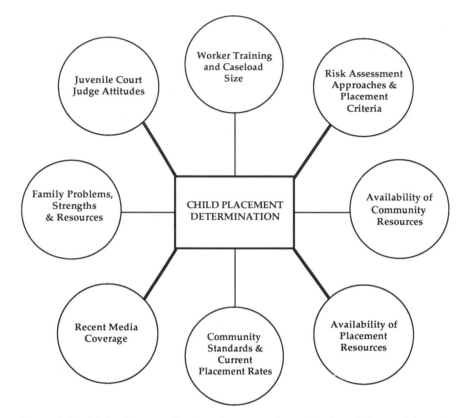

Figure 8.1. Major factors affecting placement determination. [*Source:* Adapted from P. J. Pecora (1991). Using risk assessment technology and other screening methods for determining the need for child placement in family-based services. In *Empowering families: Papers from the fourth annual conference on family-based services*, edited by V. Pina, D. Haapala, & C. Sudia. Riverdale, IL: National Association for Family Based Services, p. 121.]

revealing, as they provide a more accurate picture of the extent to which child placement is used as a service option. For example, at the start of one IFPS research project, foster family care incidence rates did vary by state: placement rates in Washington were five times higher than those in Utah during 1985 (Maximus, 1985). On the basis of these data, it may have been more difficult for children to be placed in foster care in Utah than in Washington. This could have affected the outcome of this evaluation (Fraser et al., 1991).

In addition, public policies clearly affect placement criteria and rates.

Consider the example of two different states that were compared in this same study:

Utah. The child welfare system in Utah adopted a permanency planning approach in the mid-1970s. In each CPS district office, one or more workers were assigned permanency planning functions and received special training and consultation. While the child population rose substantially between 1970 and 1990 in Utah, foster care placement rates did not increase proportionally and instead decreased steadily until 1989, when rates began to increase slowly. This overall decrease was due largely to the emphasis upon preserving families through restricting certain types of placements, and expanding protective supervision and placement prevention services.

In addition, between 1978 and 1982, Utah embarked on a systematic attempt to deinstitutionalize its youth correctional services. The state training school for juvenile offenders was closed and the state's capacity to hold youths in secure confinement was reduced from approximately 500 to 70 beds. Furthermore, beginning in 1983, greater emphasis was placed on licensing relatives or family friends for the placement of especially difficult youth. The number of these "specific" foster home place ments grew disproportionately to other types of placements, and probably accounts for the slight increase in the use of substitute care between 1982 and 1983.

Washington. The State of Washington also adopted permanency planning in the 1970s, but compared to Utah, it was implemented with less intensive training and supervision of its child welfare staff. To further reform child welfare practice, the Family Reconciliation Services program was organized in 1977 to provide community-based services to families as an alternative to foster care placement. However, despite these service initiatives, the number of children in out-of-home care, although declining slightly between 1981 and 1982, rose slowly between 1979 and 1987, at a rate congruent with the increasing child population. With the possible exception of the years 1982–1984 and 1986–1987, the increases in child placement appear to be proportional to population growth.

There was a dramatic increase, however, in the number of placements in 1986–1987. Many experts attribute the increase to tragic case situations such as the death in 1986 of a child who was under state supervision, high child protective service (CPS) caseloads, and a lack of preventive services in many regions of the state. CPS became the focus of much public criticism during this period. Thus, the service program being evaluated was providing services to prevent foster care placement at a time when state CPS workers were very concerned about child injuries, and sensitive to the criticism being directed at the Department of Health and Human Services by citizen groups and the media.

Comparing environmental influences in Utah and Washington. Placement rates in the two states should be assessed in the context of these different public policy environments. In Utah, there was a concerted attempt to provide services to families so that children and youth might be maintained in their own homes. In Washington, while the child welfare system had implemented a range of preventive services, for at least part of the study period, CPS workers were especially concerned about child safety and the public social service system was under intense public scrutiny. In addition, there was decided skepticism in the juvenile justice system about the capacity of service providers to help delinquent youth and their families; juvenile justice legislation focused on public protection and established judicial sentencing guidelines for youth. (For more information about Washington's juvenile justice system, see Schram, McKelvy, Schneider, & Griswold, 1981.)

Overall, it appears that environmental influences operated to reduce placements more in Utah than in Washington. From one perspective, this means that it should have been easier to prevent child placement in Washington because so many more children were being placed. But, maintaining placement prevention efforts in this environment might be more difficult. Given these differences and the influence that other environmental factors may exert, comparisons of placement prevention rates between states (or counties in county-administered programs) should be viewed with caution unless the contexts are fully described and their impact is known.

Screening Cases for Family-Based Services

Another major limitation to using placement prevention as an outcome variable was discussed in Chapter 3, but bears repeating. A growing number of FBS programs state that they will serve only families where the children or adolescents are in danger of being placed at some point in the future (e.g., immediately, within one week, within one year). The validity and reliability of the processes that workers in child welfare use to make decisions about the need for placement are not very high (Stein & Rzepnicki, 1984), and a number of problems regarding adherence to FBS intake criteria have been noted (Feldman, 1990a; Jones, 1985; Tracy, 1991).

Determining what criteria and screening process to use is a complex decision. For many cases, the process might involve assessing the risk of future child maltreatment. For other cases, it may be determining how much risk this child poses to herself or others through substance abuse, delinquency or other behaviors. In addition, families might be identified as appropriate for service only when a referring worker, with approval pending from a judge, plans to place a child outside the home in non-shelter care within five days. Developing decision-making protocols has been hampered by the lack of valid conceptual frameworks for decision-making and of reliable and valid assessment instruments (English & Pecora, 1994; Stein & Rzepnicki, 1983; Wald & Woolverton, 1990), although a number of groups have been developing resources in this area (e.g., Haapala, Kinney & McDade, 1988; Holder & Corey, 1986).

As mentioned in Chapter 3, to use "risk of imminent placement" as a valid intake criterion, agencies need to develop explicit decision-making rules and possibly interdepartmental screening committees who work closely with the court so that the consistency and validity of these decisions can be more easily examined and refined. Program administrators and staff members will need to move practice technology beyond an "art form" to a more precise approach that can be documented. Unfortunately, the complexity of family problems, cultural issues, interactive factors, explosive combinations of risk elements, the need to analyze family strengths, and other issues will make this a difficult task.

Placement Prevention Is a Restrictive Measure of Treatment Success

The primary outcome measure in many early FBS studies was child placement. Placement avoidance was often declared only when a family remained intact or utilized a relative to help care for a child. Conversely, failure was declared when a family experienced a nonrelative placement. This measure of success may have elevated "failure" or "placement rates" in these studies by the inclusion of children who ran away from home or who went to live with neighbors or friends. In addition, although multiple outcome measures were used to assess the effects of the FBS program, the stability of the child's living situation was not determined. Both the *quality* and *stability* of placements are important outcome variables (see, for example, Fanshel et al., 1989, 1990). Without such considerations being taken into account, placement remains a crude outcome measure, and placement rates in different studies of FBS programs cannot be compared.

Further, in one study, placements of two weeks' duration or more involving any form of substitute care (including shelter care, inpatient psychiatric treatment, and juvenile corrections-related dispositions) were all counted as service failures (Fraser et al., 1991). Some of the children in the study returned to their families three to six weeks after removal. Thus, the placement outcomes reported in that study do not differentiate between short- versus long-term placements, and the failure rate may be increased by including shorter term placements. And the social desirability of those placements was not assessed. Furthermore, other than querying parents and IFPS staff members, it was not possible to distinguish between placements that should have been prevented and those which were in the best interest of the child and his/her family.

Thus, dichotomous measures such as placed/not placed are limited in important ways. First, they are fairly crude—families who drop out of treatment or experience placement within two to three weeks of intake are classified in the same way as families who experience placement many months after successfully completing treatment. Consider the case of the child who is placed in foster care 11 months after participating with her/his family in a FBS program. Relatively speaking, such families might be considered successful for ten months (assuming a four-week FBS program), but because a child is placed in the eleventh month after FBS intake, the family's treatment is declared a failure when a dichotomous measure is used. By aggregating families who fail early in the treatment evaluation period with those who stay together for extended periods but eventually experience a placement, important information is lost.

Second, most definitions of placement do not take into account the type of placement used. In 1979, the HOMEBUILDERS™ program began a project to work with families containing children who were severely emotionally disturbed. These children were about to be placed in a psychiatric inpatient facility. Using a dichotomous outcome measure, 6 of the 25 children were placed or classified as "failures." However, 3 of the 6 children were placed in group homes, and 1 of these 3 children quickly returned home (Kinney & Haapala, 1984). From the perspective of the restrictiveness of placement, these three cases might be viewed as partial successes, for IFPS resulted in the use of a nonpsychiatric, less restrictive, and less expensive placement resource. Outcome studies that focus solely on the proportion of children placed cannot analyze the relative merits and desirability of different placement outcomes.

We may need to look beyond the children at risk of imminent placement for additional indicators of service impact. For example, some practitioners report that while it was not possible to prevent placement of an older child, placement of younger siblings is frequently not required as they grow older because parents are able to use some of the skills learned from FBS staff members *before* things become too bad with younger children (Bonita Lantz, personal communication, October 18,

1993). Treatment effect might therefore be delayed. Tracking outcomes such as these requires longitudinal studies that go beyond the typical one-year follow-up of recent FBS studies.

Finally an alternative approach to the measurement of failure and success in FBS involves measurement strategies that permit the specification of success in varying degrees. Two such measures are the number of days in placement and time-to-placement or the "hazard rate" for placement.

Days in Placement

The FBS field needs measures of placement-related outcomes that are more sensitive to variations in service. Days in placement, therefore, remains an important supplementary outcome criterion. A number of studies have found that children in FBS treatment groups spent significantly fewer days in placement than comparison group children (e.g., AuClaire & Schwartz, 1986, pp. 39–40; Nelson, 1984; Yuan et al., 1990). This outcome measure has also been used in FBS studies of family reunification (Walton et al., 1993).

This approach involves tracking the number of days that a child spends out of home during both the FBS treatment and the designated "official" follow-up period(s). Differences in placement rate utilization, *by day*, are then compared. It is hypothesized that as a result of the service, the FBS-treated children will spend more days living safely with their families compared to control group children, as assessed by days in the home without self-reported or agency-reported child maltreatment.

Time-to-Placement and "Hazard Rates" for Treatment Failure

Treatment success may be represented as the amount of time that has elapsed between intake and placement or, in the event that no placement has occurred, between intake and the end of a follow-up period. The use of such a measure permits the calculation of a "hazard rate" as an outcome measure.

The hazard rate is the probability that a child will be placed at time t given that the child was at risk at time t. At any point during a follow-up period, the risk of placement for each child may be expressed as the odds of service failure. For example, if out of a sample of 200 children, 20 are placed in the first week of treatment, the odds of treatment failure are 20/200 or 1/10. In the second week, if 18 children are placed, then the odds of failure are 18/180, or still 1/10, because the sample at risk was reduced by 20, the number of children who experienced a placement in the first week.[3]

Hazard rates may change as a function of time. One might posit, for example, that the risk of placement would be higher just after intake and treatment termination compared to during the course of treatment and during the months following treatment. The former are points in time when families are making major changes.

The hazard rate might also differ for families with different social or demographic characteristics. For example, the hazard rate may be higher for families with children who have had prior placements, as opposed to families whose children have never been placed out of the home. Thus, the hazard rate may change as a function of time and explanatory variables. (For a discussion of issues related to hazard rates, see Allison, 1984; Fraser et al., 1994; Fraser, Pecora, Popuang, & Haapala, 1992.)

WAYS OF USING PLACEMENT RATES

Fundamental Principles

Child placement rates can be more validly used as one of a study's outcome measures if the following conditions are met. First, if cases are randomly assigned to the treatment and control groups, so that each child has a roughly equal chance of placement (see Chapters 1 and 2). In addition, if placement is supposed to be "imminent" then the intake criteria should be defined clearly and applied as objectively as possible so that the children in both groups have a high likelihood of being placed without FBS intervention (see Chapter 3).

As mentioned previously, the use of interagency placement screening committees or only accepting cases in which a judge has already determined that the child should be placed would in part clarify and bring greater rigor to case screening (cf. Feldman, 1991b; Pecora, 1991c; Tracy, 1991). These strategies alone, however, may not be sufficient, as a number of studies have reported substantial problems with referral rates, types of cases referred, and worker compliance with screening guidelines.

Second, it is essential to clearly define the unit of analysis (i.e., focus or measuring unit) as a child or a family. Focusing on individual children at risk is generally the most valid and sensitive unit of analysis because, for example, only one of the family's three children who are at risk may be placed—a partial success. However, using data for more than one child in a family is problematic in some analyses as there is interdependence among certain measures. Nonetheless, tracking the outcomes of all children in a family—even those not thought to be at risk of imminent placement—may be wise, albeit difficult.

Third, some distinction should be drawn between placements that were truly necessary during or after FBS versus those that were due to the failure of the FBS program. This is difficult, as the views of children, parents, therapists, supervisors, allied professionals, and/or "FBS experts" may differ. But better discrimination of the "true successes" from the "true failures" is necessary. Case review methods such as the "Professional Review Action Group" (PRAG), where a diverse group of agency staff members systematically analyzes services and outcomes from a set of cases have proven effective for evaluating decision-making and analyzing service failures in foster care (Hess & Folaron, 1993).

Fourth, it is important to track the number and timing of true service failures. When did the greatest number of placements occur? These important data may indicate the need for improving client engagement, for referral to other services immediately after the termination of FBS, or for more long-term or different follow-up services (see Figure 8.2).

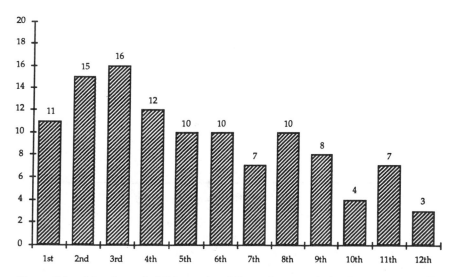

Figure 8.2. Number of child service failures by month in the aggregate 12-month follow-up sample (*n*=342). [*Source:* P. J. Pecora, M. W. Fraser, R. B. Bennett, and D. A. Haapala (1991). Placement rates of children and families served by the Intensive Family Preservation Services programs. In *Families in crisis: The impact of intensive family preservation services,* edited by M. W. Fraser, P. J. Pecora, & D. A. Haapala. Hawthorne, NY: Aldine de Gruyter, p. 165. Reprinted with permission.]

The type and restrictiveness of the placement location should also be tracked (see Figure 8.3). How many youth were placed in family foster care versus group care? Where did the children end up at service termination? After 12 months? Ideally, as discussed earlier, a comparison should be made between the projected placement type and the actual placement location. For example, children who were projected to need residential treatment may have ended up remaining with their families or being placed in treatment foster care instead. These placement diver-

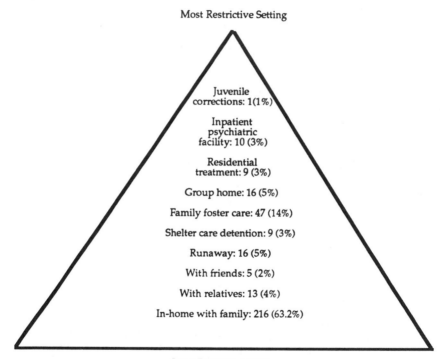

Most Restrictive Setting

Juvenile corrections: 1(1%)

Inpatient psychiatric facility: 10 (3%)

Residential treatment: 9 (3%)

Group home: 16 (5%)

Family foster care: 47 (14%)

Shelter care detention: 9 (3%)

Runaway: 16 (5%)

With friends: 5 (2%)

With relatives: 13 (4%)

In-home with family: 216 (63.2%)

Least Restrictive Setting

Figure 8.3. Placement outcomes for children included in the 12-month follow-up sample for Utah and Washington (*n*=342). [Data based upon the three oldest children living at home identified as being at risk of placement, which constitutes 95.5% of children at risk of removal in the study. The most restrictive placement location for each child was recorded. [*Source:* Adapted from P. J. Pecora, M. W. Fraser, R. B. Bennett, and D. A. Haapala (1991). Placement rates of children and families served by the Intensive Family Preservation Services programs. In *Families in crisis: The impact of intensive family preservation services,* edited by M. W. Fraser, P. J. Pecora, & D. A. Haapala. Hawthorne, NY: Aldine de Gruyter, p. 165. Reprinted with permission.]

sions from more restrictive settings can be counted as program successes. While validly projecting placement location is complex, it allows for a broader range of success criteria to be used.

Finally, it is critical that placement data be examined in relation to various demographic and other variables, such as child age, gender, ethnicity, use of controlled substances, and type of maltreatment. It is almost certain that FBS programs will vary in terms of effectiveness depending upon these variables. Using both bivariate *and* multivariate approaches and randomly selecting one child per family as the unit of analysis will allow you to begin to determine what service works best in specific conditions.

CONCLUSION

Various types of placement-related outcome criteria need to be considered by FBS program evaluators, even if placement prevention is not the major focus of the program. Clearly, placement prevention should be viewed cautiously as it is a simplistically seductive outcome measure. In the absence of a complete understanding of the context in which the measure is used, it can be misleading and therefore dangerous. For example, placement prevention can become an agency-centered measure rather than a child- or family-centered measure, which can adversely influence practice (Ray Kirk, personal communication, June 18, 1994). However, while the complexities and challenges of this outcome measure are great, they must be met in order to address the concerns of policymakers.

NOTES

1. Portions of this section are adapted from Pecora, Fraser, Bennett, & Haapala (1991, pp. 149–152).
2. Other positive outcomes may be adoption or the successful efforts of many long-term family foster care programs to maintain youth in foster families rather than in institutional settings (see, for example, Fanshel et al., 1990).
3. A hazard rate may be computed by plotting the log-odds of placement for each child for every day of risk.

Chapter 9

Measuring Program Efficiency

Cost-effectiveness and benefit-cost analyses are means of assessing a program's efficiency. *Benefit-cost analysis* is an important evaluative approach because of the interest in funding social programs with the largest net benefits (benefits minus costs) (Plotnick, 1994). Policymakers want to support the programs in which they receive good value in relation to the dollars being invested. In contrast, if the evaluation objective is to determine what type of program can most efficiently achieve a certain service objective or produce a benefit that is not easily quantified, then *cost-effectiveness analysis* is often used.

Efficiency assessments provide a frame of reference for relating costs to program results. In benefit-cost analyses, both program inputs and outcomes are measured in monetary terms; in cost-effectiveness analyses, inputs are estimated in monetary terms and outcomes in terms of actual impact (for example, number of days in care or improvements in reading scores). Benefit-cost and cost-effectiveness analyses provide information for making decisions on the allocation of resources; in addition, they are often useful in gaining the support of planning groups and political constituencies who determine the fate of social intervention efforts (Rossi & Freeman, 1993).

These types of efficiency analyses require technical expertise and preplanning in selecting methods for tracking costs, establishing time horizons, and estimating benefits in terms of "shadow prices" (See Table 9.1 for definitions of key terms). Yet, it is critical that the purpose for conducting such an analysis be thought through carefully, as various program alternatives must be possible for the comparisons to be useful for decision-making (Levin, 1983).[1]

Table 9.1. Key Concepts for Measuring Efficiency[a]

Accounting perspectives	Perspectives underlying decisions on which categories of goods and services to include as costs or benefits in an analysis.
Benefits	Net project outcomes, usually translated into monetary terms. Benefits may include both direct and indirect effects.
Benefits-to-costs ratio	The total discounted benefits divided by the total discounted costs.
Cost-benefit analysis	Analytical procedure for determining the economic efficiency of a program, expressed as the relationship between costs and outcomes, usually measured in monetary terms.
Cost-effectiveness	The efficacy of a program in achieving given intervention outcomes in relation to the program costs.
Costs	Inputs, both direct and indirect, required to produce an intervention.
Discounting	The treatment of time in valuing costs and benefits, that is, the adjustment of costs and benefits to their present values, requiring a choice of discount rate and time frame.
Distributional effects	Effects of programs that result in a redistribution of resources in the general population.
Ex ante efficiency analysis	An efficiency analysis undertaken prior to program implementation, usually as part of program planning, to estimate net outcome in relation to costs.
Ex post efficiency analysis	An efficiency analysis undertaken subsequent to knowing a program's net outcome effects.
Externalities	Effects of a program that impose costs on persons or groups who are not targets.
Internal rate of return	The calculated value for the discount rate necessary for total discounted program benefits to equal total discounted program costs.
Net benefits	The total discounted benefits minus the total discounted costs (also called *net rate of return*).
Opportunity costs	The value of opportunities forgone because of an intervention project.
Shadow prices	Imputed or estimated costs of goods and services not valued accurately in the marketplace. Shadow prices are also used when market prices exist but are inappropriate due to regulation or externalities.

[a] *Source:* P. H. Rossi and H. E. Freeman (1993). *Evaluation: A systematic approach*, 5th ed. Newbury Park, CA: Sage, p. 362. Reprinted with permission.

180

COST-EFFECTIVENESS MEASUREMENT

With cost-effectiveness, two or more programs with similar goals are compared. Only programs with identical goals can be compared, and a common measure of effectiveness must be used (Levin, 1983, p. 18). Thus cost-effectiveness is generally limited to comparing programs in relationship to a single outcome, such as child maltreatment or placement.

Cost-effectiveness analysis can help policymakers decide which service approach may be most efficient by comparing the unit cost of service per family of various programs (e.g., number of placements prevented or families reunified per dollar of cost). For example, the X program has a cost of $5,000 per family served, while the Y program has a cost of $7,000 per family served. If the intake criteria, type of families served, consumer satisfaction ratings, overall program quality, service outcome, and other important characteristics of the two programs were similar, a legislature might be persuaded to fund the X program instead of the Y program because of its *cost-effectiveness*.

One requisite of a valid cost-effectiveness analysis (and benefit-cost analysis for that matter) is the ability of the evaluator to estimate (or in the case of post hoc analyses to actually measure) the impact(s) of the program. If the program has had no significant effects, it is senseless to conduct any type of efficiency analysis (Rossi & Freeman, 1993). Because of its emphasis upon what it costs for various programs to achieve a single common service objective, cost-effectiveness analysis produces a focused comparison. Thus, when programs have multiple objectives (and therefore benefits), this approach is not as effective as benefit-cost analysis (Plotnick, 1994).

BENEFIT-COST ANALYSIS

Overview

The basic objective of benefit-cost analysis is to assess how much in the way of immediate and longer-range benefits is achieved by investing in a particular service approach. To accomplish this requires quantifying various benefits of the service, and the full costs of providing the service. Child placement is an expensive service that may be reduced or prevented if an FBS program is able to target high-risk children and effectively serve them.

Complexities of Benefit-Cost Analysis

Designing and conducting a benefit-cost analysis as part of an evaluation of FBS requires special technical expertise. One of the significant challenges involves handling "costs" or benefits that cannot be quantified in monetary terms (e.g., increases in self-esteem or social skills). For example, an FBS placement prevention program might save government funds in the long run if a significant proportion of children in foster care (say 10%) were found to eventually become homeless adults without employment skills or the emotional stability to work productively. Thus, certain persons or some aspects of society may gain more from the service than others. Handling these differences is complex (Plotnick, 1994).

The monetary benefits of the service may be calculated in a variety of ways, but the value of the benefits will likely need to be "discounted" if they are received later, because benefits received in the future will be worth less than if those dollars were invested today. For example, if a community receives $5,000 in benefits two years from now, that sum of money is not as valuable as receiving $5,000 today because the community does not have the ability to use or invest those funds. Thus, part of conducting a benefit-cost analysis involves specifying what benefits will be accrued when, and how far into the future they will be accrued.

When benefits would start and the length of time that they would be received is often referred to as determining a "time horizon." Benefits are generally judged to be worth less in the future because of the effects of inflation on their value and because of the increased costs of the goods or services that they will be used to purchase.

While some benefit and cost projections are relatively straightforward, there are "uncertainties" and "risks" that must be considered as part of estimating or projecting the benefits and costs. In addition, the components are "valued" differently depending upon the nature of the program, the orientation of the person doing the valuing, and other conditions. (For a more technical discussion, see Zerbe & Dively, 1994.) The basic steps in benefit-cost analysis are displayed in Table 9.2.

Identify Benefits That Can Be Attributed to the Program

A program creates benefits when it produces results with a positive value to society. For example, an independent living program that raises the earnings of participants produces a benefit: the increase in earnings measures the value of the extra production in the economy. Benefits also accrue when a program prevents or reduces harm that otherwise would

Table 9.2. Basic Steps in Benefit-Cost Analysis

1. Identify benefits that can be attributed to the program.
2. Determine how long each benefit will last.
3. Choose and apply a discount rate.
4. Look for secondary effects.
5. Incorporate distributional effects into the analysis.
6. Compare the benefits and costs for the treatment and control groups.
7. Calculate the benefit-cost rate for the treatment and control groups.

have occurred. FBS programs (and many other social services) are likely to create benefits in this fashion.

One of the first steps in this process involves identifying broadly who benefits from the program, even if those persons are not directly served by the program. What positive results can occur and who receives those benefits? What harm is prevented? What skills are learned and why are they valuable? You need to estimate such things as the benefits of increased school attendance, better academic performance, and less conflict in the community. How does society as a whole benefit? Are local, state, or federal funds saved for other purposes?

Thinking broadly and creatively in this area is important, as discussed by Plotnick:

> At the early stages of designing a program evaluation, developing a comprehensive list of possible benefits can be of value because it may suggest a promising avenue of research and data collection that might otherwise have been overlooked. It would indicate which other social outcomes besides the direct program goals should be measured and examined to see if the intervention affects them. As a pragmatic matter, limits on time and resources will prevent evaluators from investigating the existence and size of all possible benefits. Findings from earlier studies and theoretical considerations will be needed to decide which types of benefit warrant primary attention. (1994, pp. 343–344)

The easiest approach is to estimate the "willingness of someone to pay" for an outcome or action (Plotnick, 1994). This can be directly or indirectly quantified. An example of a directly quantifiable benefit is when the recipient of the service directly gains in income from decreased absenteeism from her job due to a child's misbehavior. Other benefits are usually achieved as well, such as the funds saved in preventing a child from being placed. One can also estimate the value of a benefit in "market terms" (i.e., the current going rate). Using econometric estimation procedures, estimating monetary benefits by asking potential consumers, and analyzing political choices are other methods that can be used (see Rossi & Freeman, 1993; Thompson, 1980).

Some benefits can be quantified but are not directly measured in monetary terms. In these cases, either the current market value does not reflect the true cost of purchasing that benefit or there is no actual market price. Consequently, a monetary value may be derived by multiplying the change in outcome by a "shadow price" (Levin, 1983, pp. 63–64). If an FBS program works with families to prevent further physical abuse, the average cost of medical care associated with subsequent incidents of abuse can be used to estimate the value of the program's ability to reduce future abuse. Similarly, funds might be saved in diverting a child from a special alternative education setting when her behavior has improved sufficiently to stay within a traditional school setting.

Other benefits cannot be so easily converted into monetary figures. For example, what is the monetary value of a child's ability to sleep securely at night because of the prevention of placement trauma? Does it involve a savings of some of the costs of treating enuresis or encopresis, therapy for lowering anxiety, or counseling to alleviate grief for the loss of family member companionship? These benefits need to be identified and summarized (see Weisbrod, 1981). Thus a comprehensive benefit-cost analysis includes a complete listing of benefits that can be quantified and some estimate of the size of those that cannot be converted to monetary terms.[2] This is important to assess early in the study:

> In some cases measured monetary benefits will exceed costs. Evidence that nonmonetary benefits exist would strengthen the argument in favor of funding the intervention, but such evidence probably would not be crucial to the decision. Ahead of time, however, there is a pragmatic as well as intellectual reason to seriously consider nonmonetary benefits along with the monetary ones. If the analysis finds that measured monetary benefits are *less* than monetary costs, demonstrating that there are other quantified, but nonmonetary benefits may tip judgments in favor of the program. For example, suppose on a per client basis a drug use prevention program's monetary benefits are $50 less than its monetary costs. The program also reduces stress and domestic violence, and raises commitment to pro-social values. The $50 shortfall implicitly asks a decision maker: is it worth $50 per case to obtain these gains? Are we willing to pay $50 to obtain these real, but nonfinancial, benefits of the program? A policymaker might well answer "yes." On the other hand, if the financial shortfall were $400, the policymaker might decide those benefits are not worth $400, given other uses of the funds, or might investigate finding ways to reduce costs while still obtaining similar benefits. The benefit-cost analysis has presented much of the relevant information for informed decision making. (Plotnick, 1994, pp. 345–346)

Determine How Long Each Benefit Will Last

If successful, an FBS intervention may generate favorable benefits that will persist for some period of time. How long is each benefit expected to last? Do the benefits increase or decrease over time? If they decrease what is their rate of "decay" compared to that of persons not treated by FBS? For example, to estimate how long each benefit is expected to last, an evaluation team might examine differences in key outcomes between treatment and control groups over the study period. To project beyond the study period, we would consider the trend during the observation period. If the difference narrows, we can derive a "decay" rate and project the difference to narrow steadily until it reaches zero at some year in the future. If the difference remained roughly constant, we would project a constant difference. Similarly, a widening difference could be projected to grow at the rate observed during the posttreatment period. To establish trend lines, we would compare outcomes of treatment and control groups over the study period and also review trend data reported in previous research on related interventions. Because making these extrapolations is complex and subject to uncertainty, a research team would need to project future benefits using different trend lines. In other words, you would assess the sensitivity of the benefit estimates to assumptions about different trends (Plotnick, 1994).

Choose and Apply a "Discount" Rate

Evaluators cannot simply sum each year's benefits to derive total program benefits for all years. A dollar received now can be invested and will be worth more than a dollar received at any time in the future. Thus, a dollar of benefit received in the first year of the intervention is more valuable than a dollar of benefit received in the future. You need to apply a "discount rate" (an interest rate) to convert the benefits in each time period into their "present value." Summing the present values for all periods will yield the total monetary benefits of the intervention.

For example, if the average length of foster care placement in a state is 24 months for certain types of youth, and your program prevents a child from being placed, you cannot just add up the monthly costs of placement for 24 months. You would have to convert the placement cost saving (a benefit) into its *present value* by applying a discount rate (an interest rate) in order to adjust this amount to its *present value* (see Plotnick, 1994; Gramlich, 1990).

The formula for estimating the present value of a future cost outlay (which is how we estimate the "benefits" gained in the future in this situation) is $PV=C/(1+r)^{t-1}$. In this formula, PV stands for present value; C denotes the cost (of the foster care being prevented); r denotes the discount rate, which is the rate of interest used to reduce the present value of a deferred cost; and t is the year in which the cost outlay will be made, where it is equal to 1 for this year, 2 for the next year, 3 for the following year, etc. (Levin, 1983, p.97). For example, family stipend costs for a foster care placement that would be prevented by an FBS program intervention are $5,000 in year 2. If a common discount rate of 10% is used, the present value formula is $PV=\$5,000/(1+0.10)^1=\$5,000/1.10=\$4,545$. So the present value of a service cost of $5,000 that would be expended in year 2 is $4,545. This would be one of the cost savings or benefits of the FBS intervention.

Recent reviews of the empirical and theoretical discount rate literature (Zerbe, 1992; Zerbe & Dively, 1994) can be used to select a rate for various types of situations. Zerbe (1992) also suggests procedures for conducting a sensitivity analysis, as well as the appropriate range of rates. Because you may have to choose among different rates, as with the trend line analysis for projecting future benefits, you may need to calculate the present value of benefits using a range of discount rates.

Estimating Program Costs

What is the full set of costs involved in providing a particular FBS intervention? Evaluators include not only the direct costs of the intervention, but also the supervision, administrative overhead, community services, family, and other resources expended or invested during the intervention.

> Economic reasoning asserts that a program creates costs when it uses any kind of real resource that could have been used for some other worthwhile purpose. That is, the resources had "opportunity costs" that were foregone [sic] by choosing to use them in the program. Parallel to the treatment of benefits, one counts costs independently of which persons bear them. (Plotnick, 1994, p. 349)

At times, the evaluator needs to include a cost based on the actual market value of the goods or services included in program costs. These costs are referred to as "shadow prices" or "accounting prices" (Rossi & Freeman, 1993). For example, what would be the true cost of replacing a highly skilled but underpaid staff development coordinator for an FBS program who currently is paid $25,000 per year? The current cost is $25,000, yet it may require a salary of $35,000 to replace the coordinator with someone as well qualified. Estimated depreciation of assets, such as office buildings or equipment, is another cost that should be accounted for, along with the time spent by volunteers.

Generally, the costs of a program are easier to measure than the benefits of the program, but some costs may not be easily quantified, such as the loss of staff weekend leisure time if many FBS therapists work weekends. Estimating costs also includes assessing the *negative side effects* of the program. For example, one might need to estimate the costs of alleviating the damage to a few children because of maltreatment that occurs during the course of an ultimately but not initially successful FBS intervention with physically abusive or neglectful parents. Finally, if cost estimates for one or more components differ, you may need to assess how differences in these estimates will affect the benefit-cost ratios. This is known as "sensitivity analysis" and various techniques exist for this procedure (see Levin, 1983).

Look for Secondary Effects

The program being evaluated may have secondary effects that produce extra benefits *or* costs. These effects are also known as "externalities." Does the FBS program cause a better public image for a public agency as a supporter of families? Does a series of controversial cases increase service delivery costs because FBS staff members are reluctant to close cases? Does it change state-wide placement patterns? These are just three examples of secondary effects that should be considered when calculating benefits (see Appendix in Chapter 1, Rossi & Freeman, 1993).

Incorporate Distributional Effects into the Analysis

Until this point, our discussion has ignored the reality that the benefits and costs of any social service program, including FBS, will not be distributed evenly to all members of society: they will likely create gains for some and losses for others. It is especially important to consider the difference between benefits and costs from three perspectives: that of the participants (in this case, the children and their families), that of nonparticipants (who would pay for most of the program's expenses, if it were to be widely adopted and publicly funded), and that of society as a whole.

The social perspective accounts for gains and losses to all members of society. Clearly, we want benefits to exceed costs from this perspective, or else the resources devoted to the FBS program would be better used to provide other services. For political, administrative, and ethical reasons, it is important to determine whether the program also passes a

benefit-cost test from the perspectives of both participants and nonparticipants. Nonparticipants (the taxpayers in general) are more likely to
support a program if it makes them better off, so one should investigate
whether a publicly funded FBS program would save taxpayers money
over the long run. Potential participants will only want to enroll in a
program if it is likely to make them better off, as well. Thus, we should
also investigate whether the children and their families gain net benefits
from the FBS. While we might hypothesize that certain FBS programs
will pass a benefit-cost test from all three perspectives, this must be
empirically determined.

The public child welfare agency has a somewhat different perspective
than the nonparticipant (taxpayer). From the agency perspective a program impact that leads to less use of services from a different agency
(such as special education services) is neither a benefit nor a cost. Yet it
clearly is an overall benefit. Knowing benefits and costs from the agency's point of view has important bureaucratic and political uses and is
worth estimating, but it must be recognized that this does not yield a
complete picture of benefits and costs sufficient for deciding whether
the project is an improvement over another service approach.

*Compare the Benefits and Costs for the Treatment
and Control Groups*

Once all cost and benefits estimates are completed, the difference in
costs between two approaches is compared to the difference in benefits
to determine if the FBS intervention improves on the alternative service
approach. As indicated above, one can conduct the comparison from
several perspectives. If, for example, it is found that the FBS intervention costs $3,000 more per child, but yields $5,000 more in benefits than
an alternative approach, then based on benefit-cost criteria the FBS approach is better.

For example, a program that requires a huge amount of volunteer time
from the community may "cost" the community more than the benefits
it receives. A more controversial approach to estimating costs involves
weighting gains and losses more heavily for some groups and less heavily for others. Most often, both benefits and costs are weighted more
heavily for low-income persons. There are a variety of complexities associated with these weighting approaches that are beyond the scope of this
chapter, but weighting should be used with caution since it may be
difficult for the reader to see the effects of alternative weights unless
they are fully described (see Plotnick, 1994).

A more straightforward approach displays the relative benefits and

Table 9.3. A Sampling of Benefits and Costs of an FBS Placement Prevention Program from Three Perspectives[a]

Benefits and Costs	Participants	Nonparticipants/ program sponsor	Society
Benefits			
Increase in earnings[b]	$ 1,500[c]	$ 2,000[d]	
Taxes collected		200	
Savings in foster care placement payments[e]		8,100	8,100
Lower administrative costs for foster care program		800	800
(Subtotal)	($1,500)	($9,100)	($10,900)
Costs			
FBS program operating costs per family served		4,000	4,000
Taxes paid	500		
Loss of income support payments	700		
(Subtotal)	($1,200)	($4,000)	($4,000)
Benefit/cost ratio	1,500/1,200 = 1.25	9,100/4,000 = 2.27	10,900/4,000 = 2.72
Net benefit	$ 300	$ 5,100	$ 6,900

[a] Adapted from Plotnick (1994), and Rossi and Freeman (1993:384). Note that this example is simplified in that benefits and costs are not placed within a specific time frame and discount rates have not been applied.
[b] Increase in parent earnings is based on a decrease in the number of days late to work or absent because of child crises at home.
[c] Net earnings.
[d] Gross earnings.
[e] Placements last on average about 18 months (18 × $450 per month=$8,100).

losses for each group side by side, so that the reader can view and weigh the balance between them. In Table 9.3, note that nonparticipants have a net gain of $5,100, based on this simplified example. Society gains $6,900 worth of benefits. While not true in this example, this type of presentation may show that some groups will gain and others will lose. Thus, the various perspectives of different groups must be analyzed and displayed appropriately.

Calculate the Benefit-Cost Ratios for the Treatment and Control Groups

If the evaluation study uses both treatment and control groups, "the *difference* in costs between the two treatments must be compared to the *difference* in benefits to determine if the new intervention improves on the conventional one" (Plotnick, 1994 p. 21). In a hypothetical comparison of short- and long-term programs, a three-month family reunification program for kinship care providers utilizing an intensive set of services may cost $8,000. Since children are more quickly reunified, however, the program produces an estimated benefit of $24,000. (The benefit-cost ratio is 3/1 or 3.) In contrast, a 12-month, less intensive intervention costing 25% more ($12,000) may result in children being reunified later and in slightly fewer numbers. Benefits in this second case might be estimated at $16,000 for a benefit-cost ratio of 4/3 (or 1.33). Comparing the difference in costs (the long-term program is $4,000 higher) to the difference in benefits ($8,000 fewer dollars saved) produces a benefit-cost ratio of 2/1 (or 2) in favor of the shorter, more intensive program.

CONCLUSION

The basic steps in benefit-cost analysis are relatively straightforward, but a number of complexities (e.g., time horizons, present-value calculations), together with the political nature of decision making regarding program funding, render this type of evaluation difficult to conduct. Nevertheless, measuring program efficiency in this way is extremely important for many evaluation studies. Unfortunately, virtually no rigorous cost-effectiveness or benefit-cost analyses have been conducted for FBS programs to date. Thus, information for establishing the relative efficiency of these programs has not been available. Since these types of analyses require considerable specialized expertise, outside consultation is strongly recommended if you are contemplating an efficiency analysis.

NOTES

1.   For certain types of situations where benefits cannot be expressed in pecuniary terms, cost-utility analyses are used, where relative values are placed on certain outcomes after the probability of their occurrence is calculated. See Levin (1983, pp. 26–30).

2.   For more information, see Levin (1983), Rossi and Freeman (1993), Zerbe and Dively (1994).

Chapter 10

Constructivist Research: A Qualitative Approach

MARY K. RODWELL

Earlier chapters have outlined some of the key issues in evaluating FBS programs. They have noted that clarity about program elements and procedures is central to evaluating programs and that the stage of program development helps to determine not only whether a program can be evaluated, but the type of evaluation that should be undertaken. This chapter will present yet another consideration in designing FBS evaluation studies: the use of alternative or emerging evaluation approaches that involve qualitative methods.

Why Do Qualitative Research?

Patton (1987) suggests that qualitative data puts "flesh on the bones" of quantitative results. Over the last several years there has been a growing realization that qualitative methods can add depth, detail, and meaning to quantitative studies in social services (LaRossa, 1988; Austin, 1991; Whittaker, 1991; Fraser & Haapala, 1988; Gilgun, Handel, & Daly, 1993). Qualitative data can flesh out the meaning of statistical relationships (Glaser & Strauss, 1967; Glisson, 1990). Interviews with a subsample of respondents can provide additional detail in the interpretation of evaluation results. However, qualitative methods in FBS evaluation can be more than an addendum to traditional program evaluation designs and methods—they can be an entire methodological approach unto themselves.

While there have been few qualitative studies of FBS published to date (for exceptions see Haapala, 1983; Fraser & Haapala, 1988), qualitative methodologies may allow us to move beyond the cost-effectiveness and cost-benefit conundrums present in quantitative research. They allow us to look at intangible issues of importance to practitioners, including the "meaning" of service; how families experience FBS; and whether families feel empowered by them. Qualitative methods can be used to uncover and understand why some families flourish in FBS while others founder. With qualitative methods of evaluation, we may be able to begin to understand important FBS phenomena such as the nature of the helping process as experienced from a multiplicity of perspectives (see Wells & Freer, 1994).

Qualitative methods may be more congruent with clinical ways of knowing and evaluating other peoples' experiences. What did the process feel like? What had meaning for whom? They may also provide a fresh perspective on things about which quite a bit is already known. But probably the most important advantage of qualitative methods is that the interpretive results are less reductionistic than those found with more traditional quantitative methods; the consumer of the evaluation can expect to have a more intricate, complex, or "thick" description of the evaluation issues under investigation (Geertz, 1973; Guba & Lincoln, 1981; Zeller, 1987).

Qualitative methods are congruent with FBS principles. As outlined in the Introduction and Chapter 1, these principles include an investment in a child's family with services that are complete, comprehensive, and intensive; delivered in the home; directed at any problem identified by the family who remains in charge at all times; and utilize family strengths and resources. Evaluation undertaken from the qualitative perspective discussed in this chapter produces a comprehensive view of what is important from the perspectives of the major participants in the helping process. Maximum power remains with the participants, who shape not only the appropriate evaluation questions, but the evaluation results. The participants, particularly the families, remain in charge of the evaluation process.

Underlying Assumptions

The assumptions of qualitative evaluation strategies contrast markedly with the traditional postpositivist paradigm of conventional inquiry. The assumptions upon which the approach is built are:

1. *The nature of reality.* There are multiple "constructed" realities that can be understood only with full details of the family and service context.
2. *The relationship of knower to known.* The inquirer and the "object of inquiry" interact and influence one another. There can be no objective distance between knower and known.

3. *Limited generalization.* The aim of research is to develop a charac-teristic body of knowledge in the form of tentative suppositions that describe the individual case. Broad generalizations to other groups or situations are generally not possible.

4. *The impossibility of causal linkages.* All entities (e.g., families) are in a state of mutual influence and shaping so that it is impossible to distinguish causes from effects.

5. *Inquiry is value-bound.* The inquirer's values are expressed in the choice of a problem to study and in the framing, bounding, and focusing of research questions. Values influence the choice of the paradigm that guides the definition of the problem, the theory utilized in collecting and analyzing data, and the interpretation of findings.

Qualitative methodology focuses on multiple constructed realities, rath-er than a single reality. Based on this, it is sometimes called "constructi-vist" inquiry (Guba, 1985; Guba & Lincoln 1989; Rodwell, 1990). Realities are studied holistically to gain understanding—control and prediction are not the aims of this methodology. And understanding is idiographic, based on the case being studied.

Because of these assumptions, proponents of constructivism have a very different view of the evaluation process and product (Guba & Lin-coln 1989). They argue that "truth" is a matter of consensus among informed and sophisticated participants, not of correspondence with an objective reality. They further argue that "facts" have no meaning except within a value framework; hence, there cannot be an "objective" assess-ment of any proposition. In this paradigm "causes" and "effects" do not exist except by imputation.

Constructivists also believe that interventions are not stable; when they are introduced into a particular context they will be at least as much affected (changed) by that context as they are likely to affect the context. Therefore, it is their position that change cannot be engineered; it is a nonlinear process that involves the introduction of new informa-tion, and increasing sophistication in the use of this information until the people involved create constructions of reality, which continually change. Accountability, therefore, is a relative matter and impacts all interacting parties equally. Since phenomena can be understood only within the context in which they are studied, findings from one context cannot be generalized to another.

Thus, from the constructivist perspective, evaluation produces data in which facts and values are inextricably linked. Valuing is an essential part of the evaluation process and provides the basis for an attributed meaning about that which is under investigation. Accountability for program effectiveness or failure is shared by a conglomerate of mutual and simultaneous shapers; no single factor or group of factors can be uniquely singled out for praise or blame. Consequently, evaluators are subjective partners with stakeholders in the literal creation of data. Evaluators are orchestrators of a negotiation process that aims to culminate in consensus on better informed and more sophisticated constructions about the meanings of situations and the outcomes of services. Finally, evaluation data derived from constructivist inquiry have neither special status nor legitimation; they represent simply another "construction" to be taken into account in the move toward consensus.

Research Questions Appropriate for Constructivist Evaluation

The individual and subjective focus of constructivist evaluation, which is in the frame of reference of the participants, makes it uniquely suited for evaluation questions that are principally subjective and focused on the full understanding of multiple perspectives. Also appropriate for constructivist approaches are attempts to understand the subjective meaning that lies behind a social action—why certain behaviors are preferred or rejected.

The following research objectives are congruent with the constructivist paradigm and methodology:

1.   *When the goal is to understand the internal dynamics of program operations (process evaluation).*   This includes questions such as, What factors are important in making this FBS what it is? What are the strengths and weaknesses of the program? How do families come to the program and how do they move through the services? What do staff do with families when they are in the families' homes?

2.   *When the goal is to understand how the program is perceived by important groups.*   This includes how the expectations of funders compare to those of referral agencies. Are the expectations of the referring agencies the same as those of the courts? The families? What is the meaning of the different perceptions that may emerge?

3.   *When there is a sense that emergent or unmet needs are affecting the quality of the service process and outcomes.*   These questions might relate to the meaning of unmet needs from a variety of perspectives. Does the lack of community-based drug treatment make home-based services more difficult to deliver? Are interventions other than what we are currently providing necessary to keep families together?

4.   *When there is a sense that something is happening, missing, or needed, but the shape of the question is unknown.*   Questions may include: What

does the program or worker need to know, do, or understand in order to be helpful with a subgroup of families or an individual family? What does the referral source think about the service? What do the neighbors, the school, the minister think about the family's progress?

5. *When the goal is to understand or document individual client outcomes (case studies).* Discussed earlier, case studies can serve to aid in understanding the "typical," the "unusual," the "difficult," the "politically hot" case. Questions about the match between individualized needs and program services might also be appropriate.

Is This Program Evaluable by Constructivist Means?

To determine evaluability, Guba and Lincoln (1989) have provided some guidelines. At a minimum, all parties must agree to work from a position of integrity. No deliberate attempts to lie, mislead, or otherwise misconstruct are appropriate. In addition, all parties should have at least a basic level of communication skills and a willingness to share power. The commitment in terms of time must be present, and participants must be willing to change and to reconsider value positions if results warrant it. Those who believe in FBS no matter what the cost, research result, or consequence will not be able to carry out the meaningful negotiations that are expected during the inquiry process.

Organizations that are not collegial will not support the collaborative, teaching/learning nature of the constructivist process. These programs probably cannot withstand the consequences of the shared responsibility and empowerment that a constructivist evaluation can engender. In addition, programs that are uncomfortable with continual evolution will not benefit initially from an evaluation process that is continuous, ambiguous, divergent, and essentially unending (unending because the results of the educational process continue to reverberate over time). The program that benefits most from a constructivist evaluation is one that can allow and support mutual respect among all stakeholding groups and can take the actions that this type of evaluation will inspire.

EXPECTATIONS FOR THE CONSTRUCTIVIST INQUIRY PROCESS

When we speak of qualitative evaluation, we mean the type of research that, for the most part, produces nonquantitative findings. While some numbers may be reported, nonmathematical means and analytic procedures are preferred to produce findings that are expressed in words. Narrative, not numbers, is the essence of qualitative evaluation. In addition, based on the underlying assumptions of constructivism, there are specific expectations related to the evaluation process, the rigor involved, and the means of reporting results. The methodological consequences of the constructivist perspective are outlined in Table 10.1.

The mutual interaction of the inquirer and the respondent, as well as the value basis of the inquiry, influence the research process in a variety of ways. First, constructivistic inquirers tend to employ a particular research design. It is emergent and evolves as the problem is formulated by the researcher and the primary stakeholders, whose identities also emerge as sampling evolves purposefully. The researcher, in collaboration with the research participants (all of whom are stakeholders; Gold, 1983), determine what the primary question is and the perspectives to be tapped in order to reconstruct a full, rich description of the phenomenon under investigation.

Second, constructivists use a particular set of methodological strategies for data collection, analysis, and reporting of results. These strategies, identified by Lincoln (1985), involve data collection in a natural setting with the evaluator as the primary research instrument. Qualita-

Table 10.1. Consequences of the Constructivist Assumptions for the Research Process

For the research design	Emergent design[a]
	Problem-determined boundaries
	Purposive sampling
For data collection	Qualitative methods
	Human instrument
	Tacit knowledge[b]
For data analysis	Grounded theory[c]
	Inductive data analysis
For reporting results	Case study reporting mode
	Idiographic interpretation[d]
	Tentative application
For research rigor	Trustworthiness
	Negotiated outcomes
	Authenticity

[a] An emergent design is characterized by the lack of a predetermined fixed format for the research. Instead, the design develops as participants and data are identified.
[b] Tacit knowledge is intuitive knowledge that has not been given propositional or word form.
[c] Grounded theory is developed through data analysis. Theory grows from the data.
[d] Idiographic interpretation is an interpretation that is derived from the perspective of a person in the situation (e.g., a child in the family being studied).

tive methods, particularly interviewing and participant-observation, are preferred. They allow for probing the tacit, or intuitive, knowledge of the respondents. In keeping with the emergent nature of the process, data are analyzed inductively throughout the research process in order to produce grounded theory, theory that grows from the data and is tested in the research process (Glaser & Strauss, 1967). Results are reported in a case study format to provide a rich description of the phenomenon under study.

Lastly, Lincoln and Guba (1985; Guba, 1981) have suggested that conventional methods for establishing rigor and control in research cannot be applied to constructivist inquiry because of the relativistic assumptions upon which it is based. They offer four aspects of "trustworthiness" that should be used to judge the success of constructivist research: credibility, dependability, confirmability, and transferability. Efforts to establish trustworthiness are intended to establish the truth value, applicability, consistency, and neutrality of the results (Lincoln & Guba, 1985; Lincoln & Guba, 1986; Schwandt & Halpern, 1988). The four aspects of trustworthiness, and the techniques used to increase the probability that these criteria can be met, are explored below.

Credibility

Credibility is achieved through prolonged engagement, persistent observation, triangulation, peer debriefing, and member checks. Prolonged engagement with and persistent observation of the stakeholders (in the context of the phenomenon under investigation) leads to credibility in understanding the depth and scope of the issues involved. Information gathered from noting, watching, and taking into account the physical and psychosocial dynamics present in the environment, plus any other data collected, is validated through triangulation. Triangulation is accomplished through the use of multiple sources, methods, investigators, and/or theories to test for the existence of consistent, distortion free information (Denzin, 1978). For example, information from a parent interview about the reason for a family's referral to FBS could be compared to the information in files or with the perspective of the FBS worker to test for consistency. Different perspectives, however, might be expected.

Peer debriefing is also advised for credibility (Lincoln & Guba, 1985). The FBS evaluator might choose another person familiar with qualitative evaluation and knowledgeable about FBS to act as a peer reviewer. The purposes of debriefing are multiple:

> to ask the difficult questions which the inquirer might otherwise avoid ("to keep the inquirer honest"), to explore methodological next steps with

someone who has no ax to grind, and to provide a sympathetic listening
point for personal catharsis. (Lincoln & Guba, 1985, p. 283)

Both the evaluator and the peer reviewer keep journals to record the
content and process of each session to document how the evaluator's
thinking about decisions and inquiry activities were clarified.

Member checking is the ongoing formal and informal testing of the
accuracy and meaning of the data collected. This is done with the participants from whom the data were obtained (Lincoln & Guba, 1985). This
allows participants to correct data, challenge interpretations, provide
new data, assess overall adequacy, and confirm the evaluator's initial
constructions and reconstructions. The FBS evaluator might check the
accuracy of his or her understanding of the worker's behavior in the
home with the family involved or with another family, worker, or
administrator.

The final member check has the same general function as the ongoing
check, but specifically targets the final case report. Participants are invited to assess the overall adequacy of the portrayals. It is not necessary
to include all participants in this final process; criteria for selection
emerge from the process itself. Willingness to participate, the ability to
judge the interpretations, and the capacity to articulate support or objec-
tions to the portrayals may be appropriate criteria for member selection.

Dependability

Assessing dependability involves looking for instability and design-
induced changes in the research process. It helps to demonstrate the
appropriateness of the data collection decisions that were made and
the methodological shifts that occurred during an emergent process.
The evaluator documents all methodological decisions in a methodological log (including those involving data analysis) so that they can be
submitted to a dependability audit of the inquiry process completed by
an outside auditor (discussed below).

Confirmability

Confirmability demonstrates that the results are linked to the data. It
is established through an audit trail, which traces findings from raw
data, documentary evidence, interview summaries, data analysis, methodological and reflexive journals, plus any other evidence used in a
study (Schwandt & Halpern, 1988). The outside auditor will use an audit

trail to undertake a systematic review of the procedures used and the decisions and interpretations made in order to attest to the quality of the inquiry process and product.

Transferability

Finally, transferability allows for the tentative application of findings to other contexts (i.e., a limited form of generalization). It measures how well the working hypotheses of one inquiry hold in other environments. To be transferable, the case study must contain sufficient description to allow a reader to determine if transfer of the findings to another known context is possible. For example, a thorough, rich description of the setting, the clients, and the workers would be necessary for informed readers to decide if the FBS program being evaluated was sufficiently similar to their own for the findings to be of use.

Authenticity

In addition to trustworthiness, authenticity is a more recently developed criterion for rigor implied by constructivist assumptions. Authenticity (Guba & Lincoln, 1989; Lincoln & Guba, 1986) differs markedly from trustworthiness. It focuses on the integrity and quality of the interactive process of the constructivist evaluation itself rather than on its product and includes assessment of the following:

- *Fairness:* Evenhanded representation of all viewpoints. To establish fairness the case study must reflect a balanced view that presents all constructions and the values that undergird them.
- *Ontological authenticity:* Increased awareness of the complexity of the program's social environment (i.e., consciousness raising). The evaluation process should increase participant appreciation of the complexities of the phenomenon under study.
- *Educative authenticity:* Increased understanding of and respect for the value systems of others and their impact on other stakeholder's viewpoints. Understanding and respect result when participants gain an appreciation for the constructions created by others and how these constructions are rooted in their different value systems and points of view.
- *Catalytic authenticity:* Change (reshaping) of the program. Change can be seen in the degree to which the inquiry process facilitates and stimulates action.

Tactical authenticity: Empowerment or redistribution of power among stakeholders which is achieved through stimulation to effective action.

PRINCIPLES OF CONSTRUCTIVIST EVALUATION

Although qualitative research rests on equal involvement and value of all participants, the evaluator should be responsible for the following aspects of constructivist inquiry (Guba & Lincoln, 1989; Chambers, Wedel, & Rodwell, 1992):

Identifying the full array of potential participants who might have a stake in the projected evaluation. At a minimum this should include referral sources, funders, administrators, staff (including support staff), and the adults and children who are service recipients. The design should always be open to including new stakeholders whenever they come to the evaluator's attention. The goal is maximum variation in the information sources (Patton, 1980). For this type of evaluation, it is assumed that no useful understanding can be derived by an evaluator who does not thoroughly experience the contexts, offices, homes, communities, and views of all of the stakeholders.

Eliciting from each stakeholder group their constructions about the FBS program and the range of claims, concerns, and issues they wish to raise in relation to it. Through this process it is believed that an insider's view of what is important and what should be pursued in the evaluation will emerge. Framing and bounding the research in this way prevent the evaluator or the evaluation contractor from being the only one shaping the focus of the evaluation.

Providing a context and methodology through which different perspectives, claims, concerns, and issues can be understood, critiqued, and taken into account. The context of the evaluation must always include the participant in his or her own environment—the home, the office, the community in which FBS is delivered. Various qualitative methods of data collection and data analysis allow for the various voices to be heard.

Generating consensus with respect to as many constructions (and their related claims, concerns, and issues) as possible. This forms the major content of the final report. Note that generalizability of findings is not a matter of fundamental concern. Instead, negotiation between the stakeholders determines the conclusions of the FBS evaluation.

Creating a forum for negotiation on items about which there is no, or incomplete, consensus and mediating a process to attend to unresolved differences. The researcher's goal is to reduce differences. Those themes or interpretations where consensus exists become a part of the final report. Those remaining unresolved may serve to set the stage for another round of evaluative negotiation or become a part of a minority report.

Developing a report that communicates to all stakeholders the consensus on constructions. This report is intended to convey the reality in a "factual" sense, but it should also clarify the meaning and interpretations of those facts. It should not simply be about the FBS program, but how the various groups make sense of it and why. The case report is an ideal format for this purpose (Zeller, 1987).

Recycling the evaluation to revisit the unresolved constructions and questions that were raised as the result of the evaluative process. Returning to a prior question with new information or greater sophistication because of the research process should not just be a possibility but an expectation. According to Guba and Lincoln (1989), constructivist evaluations never stop; they merely pause.

WHEN AND WHERE TO UNDERTAKE ALTERNATIVE FORMS OF EVALUATION

Constructivist evaluation is an intensely personal, introspective experience that provides a fit between the science and the art of inquiry, while allowing for divergent values and personal styles. According to Barreth (1986), constructivism is a process of convergence, punctuated by periods of divergence within which there is a constant loss of focus. With this come feelings of uncertainty and loss of an internal standard by which to judge the work. Because the process is ever emerging, there is a consistent lack of clarity, so the evaluator may be overwhelmed and frustrated by the wealth of information. Constructivist evaluation is not for the fainthearted. We would not want you to underestimate the tasks involved in constructivist FBS evaluation.

On the other hand, while it may not be for every evaluator nor for every program, when it is successful it can be as powerful as an intervention. It is powerful because the findings have real contextual meaning and therefore real political consequences. The methodology produces changes of various kinds (Skrtic, 1985; Chambers, Wedel, & Rodwell, 1992). The questions that surface as a result of the emergent process cause all stakeholders to reconsider the issues from new points of view. Many participants will say, "I have never thought about this before" or "I can now understand why someone might feel that way." It is developmental and educational for all involved.

OVERVIEW OF PHASES OF AN EMERGENT
EVALUATION METHOD

A constructivist evaluation by its nature is emergent. That is, aside from some prior working hypotheses of the evaluator about the phenomenon to be studied, the precise evaluation questions and processes *emerge* during the inquiry. According to Guba and Lincoln, "when one does not know in advance what information is to be collected, it is literally impossible to design an inquiry that will provide it" (1989, p. 55). However, utilizing stakeholder inputs (claims, concerns, and issues) to organize the evaluation typically involves three phases.

Phase 1. The first phase, *orientation and overview,* is necessary even if the evaluator is extremely familiar with the FBS program and its principal stakeholding groups. The evaluator should enter the process without an a priori theory or question—potential participants should tell the evaluator what he or she ought to know. Thus the objective of this phase is to obtain enough information from the stakeholding perspectives to identify what is important to follow up on in detail in the next phase. Using prior ethnography (Spradley, 1979) the researcher "hangs out" in the evaluation environment, noting, watching, and taking into account the physical and psychosocial dynamics of the environment.

In addition, through somewhat directed interviewing of those who appear during the ethnographic process, the FBS evaluator focuses on discovering details about the agency, the community, and the larger environmental contexts that affect the FBS program. The evaluator identifies the important stakeholding groups other than the FBS workers (parents, educators, mental health professionals, and law enforcement personnel) who could be tapped in later phases of the inquiry. Initial questions should identify differing ideas about what the evaluator should know about FBS including, for example, concerns about the intensity and intrusiveness of in-home services or skepticism about its real usefulness in preventing out-of-home care.

Phase 2. *Focused exploration* moves from general discovery to more targeted probing. Analysis of data from the first phase allows general themes to emerge that require further investigation. In FBS "eligibility for service," "treatment success," "establishing trust," "increased communication and parenting skills," "placement decisions," and "maintaining and strengthening family bonds" are examples of themes that may require follow-up. More structured interviewing and observation of participants who have been selected through purposive methods, with a view toward maximum variation in the participant viewpoints, concerns, and issues, provide in-depth information about the elements that appeared to be salient during the first phase of the study.

Phase 3 and beyond. The last phase, *comprehensive member check,* occurs after analysis of data from the second phase and the writing of a preliminary case study. This provisional report is shared with the participants to "obtain confirmation that the report has captured the data as constructed by the informants, or to correct, amend, or extend it, that is, to establish the credibility of the case" (Lincoln & Guba, 1985, p. 236). Consensus about what is contained in the document, though desirable, is not necessary. What is necessary is sufficient negotiation between the evaluator and the stakeholders so that the areas of disagreement are clear and become a part of the final document. The equal partners in the evaluation should be comfortable that perspectives have been accurately captured before the outside audit.

After the audit, the final case study is written, thus closing the third phase of the process. But closure of Phase III is not really the end of an evaluation. The teaching/learning process that occurs during evaluation should continue with continued organizational learning and program refinement (Chambers, Wedel, & Rodwell, 1992).

RESEARCHER AS INSTRUMENT

Constructivist evaluation requires not only a knowledge of research methods, but humor, flexibility, and creativity. The evaluator should be capable of combining personal past history, knowledge gained through experience and education, and the experiences of the stakeholders to create a tacit understanding of the verbal and nonverbal data uncovered during the evaluation. It is the evaluator's task to move this to propositional or word form in order to ascribe meaning to the data.

Interpretation results from the insight and understanding the evaluator gains from feelings, behaviors, thoughts, actions (witnessed or felt), records, and documents (seen, heard, read, tasted, smelled, sensed, experienced, and discovered; Cook & Reichardt, 1979; Guba & Lincoln, 1984; Kirk & Miller, 1986; Leininger, 1985; Reinharz, 1979). An evaluation

of family-based services that involves direct evaluator/participant interaction requires prior knowledge, skills, attitudes, and experience in FBS,
the systems involved in service delivery (including the policy at various
levels that encourages or discourages this type of service), and constructivist evaluation methodology (Lincoln & Guba, 1985). At a minimum,
the evaluator should be capable of developing trust, establishing honest
communication, questioning appropriately, taking notes, and transcrib-
ing into a journal (Agar, 1986; Douglas, 1985; Fielding & Fielding, 1986;
Lincoln & Guba, 1985).[1]

DATA COLLECTION TECHNIQUES

In FBS constructivist evaluation, the three important techniques of
data collection are interviews (including triangulation), participant-
observation, and observation.[2]

The Interview

The interview is a conversation with a purpose. It is used to obtain
here-and-now constructions of persons, events, activities, organizations, feelings, motivations, claims, concerns, or past reconstructions
and projections as they are expected to be experienced in the future
(Lincoln & Guba, 1985, p. 268). Further, interviews can verify, revise,
and extend information obtained from other sources, human and non-
human, through triangulation. Interviews also allow for the verification
and amplification of the constructions developed by the evaluator. (For
more information, see Chambers, Wedel & Rodwell, 1992.) While the
interview may be structured so the problem is defined by the evaluator,
it may (and most probably will) be unstructured, with a nonstandar-
dized format and nonnormative responses. In the FBS evaluation the
interviewee's definition, structure, and account of what is relevant
are stressed because the interviewer is concerned with the unique, the
idiosyncratic, and the wholly individual viewpoint (Guba & Lincoln,
1981).

Participant-Observation

Participant-observation occurs when the evaluator enters the scene
and participates in what is being observed, analyzed, and reported on.
In the case of FBS constructivist evaluation, the evaluator is an actor,

audience, player, and spectator—shaping and being shaped by the evaluation process. By participating in the work and practice environments, by visiting homes and watching/participating in sessions, the FBS evaluator becomes a part of the social worlds that will be described in the final report. The evaluator not only observes events but also experiences firsthand the emotions and concerns of the people and the program that he or she is trying to understand.

For constructivist evaluation to be successful, it is imperative that the participants be aware of the evaluator's role and allow the evaluator to acquire data. At times, it may be difficult for the evaluator to balance the requirements of being both a participant and an observer, but the intimacy that this allows far outshadows the potential loss of perspective. Validating information against at least one other source (for example another interview) and/or method (for example, an observation in addition to an interview) should guard against serious distortions that might arise as a result of dual roles.

Observation

Another data collection mechanism is pure observation (sometimes called persistent observation; Skrtic, 1985). Here the evaluator notes, watches, and takes into account the physical and psychosocial dynamics at the time and place of observation. The evaluator watches a session in the home to learn about the style and skills of the therapist and to learn from the family in their home environment. These observations should be overt, planned, and scheduled, requiring the same informed consent and practices as interviews and participant-observations.

DATA MANAGEMENT

Data collected from these processes should be recorded in two field journals (condensed and expanded). According to Lofland (1971) the accounts of the interviews and observations should include a concrete description of what occurred, without interpretation or inference. Spradley (1980) suggests a condensed journal during the actual interview or observation recording direct quotes, specific behaviors, specific words, and key phrases. These are then transferred to the expanded version (much like a social work process recording with dialogue, nonverbal behaviors, and evaluator reactions) within 24 hours of the experience to assure recall and accuracy.

Inexperienced evaluators may doubt their capacity to reproduce data accurately and may prefer the fidelity provided by video or audio recording to assure that important information is not lost. However, data overload, or the inability to distinguish important from irrelevant data, may result unless the researcher has screened data, a process that occurs naturally when field notes are collected.

Constructivist evaluators should maintain a separate personal log (sometimes called a reflexive journal; Lincoln & Guba, 1985), to record their impressions of participants, analytic ideas, thoughts, personal reactions, and notes regarding further needed information. This is a record of the evaluator's feelings and reactions to the participants and the social context. It serves to track evaluator emotions and interpretation, and provides evidence about the role of the evaluator in the final construction of the report and audit. It is primarily in the reflexive journal that the evaluator begins to see tacit knowledge taking propositional form in the shape of tentative insights and next-step ideas. All records of data collected and data sources are systematically maintained to aid in data analysis and the audit.

Data Analysis

Data collection and data analysis interact in constructivist evaluation (Lincoln & Guba, 1985). Data analysis begins with the first data collected and facilitates the development of the emerging design. Data from the first phase of an FBS evaluation provide the evaluator with ideas about who should be contacted (sampling) and how data would be best collected (through interviews, participant-observation, observation, or other qualitative means). Working hypotheses (Cronbach, 1975; Lincoln & Guba, 1985) or tentative "hunches" about the uniqueness of the situation emerge from the initial data and serve to ground the theory about the phenomenon under study as it evolves. Early data analysis also gives direction to the more structured data collection of the second phase of the inquiry process.

From this description it should be clear that inductive data analysis, from the specific to the general, is preferred to deductive data analysis, at least in the early stages of the FBS constructivist evaluation. Later, as the evaluation reveals patterns and major dimensions of interest, the evaluator focuses on verifying what appears to have emerged (a more deductive approach). The evaluator must consciously work back and forth between parts and wholes in a "sorting" and "putting-back-together" process (Patton, 1980).

Data are analyzed from the specific raw units of information to subsuming categories. The constant comparative method, developed by Glaser and Strauss (1967) and later modified by Lincoln and Guba (1985), whereby every datum is compared with every other datum, is used. Information that is relevant and applicable to the FBS evaluation is identified in the accumulated data.

From that information, units are created that represent the smallest piece of information that can be understood by someone with minimal knowledge or experience in family-based services. The unit can be as short as a word or as long as several paragraphs, but it must stand alone without requiring further explanation.

A partial text of an interview with a parent participating in an FBS evaluation, displayed in Figure 10.1, will serve as an example of how units can be derived: The seven units found in Figure 10.1 should be handled separately and coded in such a way as to allow tracking to the original data source. The coding should also capture important characteristics of stakeholders that could be useful in later analysis (e.g., what female parents say as compared to male parents). A typical coding system for data units is displayed in Figure 10.2.

Through constant comparison, relevant themes (categories) emerge by comparing each data unit with all other data units (sorting), and bringing together into provisional categories those units that relate to the same content (lumping). Decision rules or definitions of the categories are developed to justify the inclusion of each data unit in the particular category. Categories and their decision rules should be nonredun-

---

Instead of pulling the kid, teach the parent. Maybe the system will have to pull the kid but they need to see what parents can do. If parents don't have common sense enough to make it using what's available they should be taught. Even if it takes digging in the trash to get what's needed. They need to be able to turn their situation to their advantage. The program should educate the parents for survival. What the program offers now is wrong. They need to provide commonsense survival stuff.

[Instead of pulling the kid, teach the parent.]
[Maybe the system will have to pull the kid but they need to see what parents can do.]
[If parents don't have common sense enough to make it using what's available they should be taught.]
[Even if it takes digging in the trash to get what's needed.]
[They need to be able to turn their situation to their advantage.]
[The program should educate the parents for survival.]
[What the program offers now is wrong.]
[They need to provide common sense survival stuff.]

Figure 10.1. Text of a parent interview.

> (site).(respondent type).(interview # with respondent).(interview # out of total at site).(verbal)(data unit #)
> **Example:**   1.FP.1.6.V51
> **Interpretation:**   Site #1, female parent, first interview with respondent, sixth interview total at site, verbal data, fifty-first data unit.

Figure 10.2.   Example of a coding system for data units.

dant and exclusive; however, data units may be included in more than one category. Decision rules should be used not only to justify inclusion of data units in one category instead of another, but to render the category set internally consistent (Bulmer, 1979). They can be the basis for later tests of replicability and logic during the auditing review process and serve as an organizing structure to guide the development of the final case report.

Examples of categories, decision rules, and data units created from the earlier statement by the parent participating in an FBS evaluation are displayed in Figure 10.3. With the inclusion of more data as the process unfolds the preliminary categories may be restructured to make better sense of the data. Subcategories will naturally evolve as the information becomes more complex. Thus, changes in categories and decision rules should be recorded in the methodological journal for the dependability audit.[3]

> *Parental responsibility* (category):   Include all delimiters for holding parents accountable (decision rule).
> [Even if it takes digging in the trash to get what's needed. They (the parents) need to be able to turn their situation to their advantage.](data unit)
>
> *Program standards*:   Include all aspects for expectations for program service delivery.
> [Instead of pulling the kid, teach the parent.]
> [Maybe the system will have to pull the kid but they need to see what parents can do.]
> [If parents don't have commonsense enough to make it using what's available they should be taught.]
> [The program should educate the parents for survival.]
> [They (the program) need to provide commonsense survival stuff.]
>
> *Program evaluation*:   Include overall descriptive evaluations of the program.
> [What the program offers now is wrong.]

Figure 10.3.   Examples of data categories, decision rules, and data units.

Computer-Assisted Data Analysis Technologies

The traditional method of analysis of word data, no matter which perspective guides the data collection or analysis, has been a transfer of field notes to index cards. The cards are then sorted in whatever way the evaluator wishes to pursue the analysis. This aspect alone may scare away potential qualitative analysts because any evaluation of reasonable size will produce 3,000 to 6,000 data cards.

Clearly, this up-close-and-personal management allows the evaluator to become very familiar with the data, but loss of cards, disorganization, and general confusion can also result. The data coding and analysis process is laborious, but informative. Students, with close supervision, can often be of tremendous help in completing this research task. In addition, several computer-based programs have been developed to lessen these problems.[4]

Reporting Findings

The final stage of data analysis is the development of the case study (Lincoln & Guba, 1985). The categories developed and an index of documents serve as the source for a provisional, overall outline of the study. The case report should, at a minimum, consist of three parts: (a) general program/context description, (b) problems/issues, and, (c) lessons to be learned. Support material, such as data units, records, and documents, should be cross referenced to this outline and the subsequent final report. For peer review, a preliminary draft should be developed and evaluated for adequacy of the representation of the program; the existence of errors of fact or interpretations; omissions; the clarity of the writer's interpretations as distinct from the respondents'; confidentiality and protection of anonymity; and elimination of irrelevant or particularly controversial issues. Charts, diagrams, tables, or photographs can be used to condense and enhance the presentation of the data (Wolcott, 1990), but should not be seen as a substitute for the thick rich description (Geertz, 1973) that the case study should provide.

Respondents to the evaluation should be invited to assess the accuracy of the report as well as to participate in ongoing member checks that correct the data, challenge interpretations, provide new data, and confirm the evaluator's reconstruction of their constructions. For example, throughout the process the FBS evaluator might have tested the information gained from one worker about agency expectations with another worker or a family member to allow for clarity.

The final member check of the case report has basically the same purpose. All participants (or some subsample of respondents if total participation is not feasible) should be invited to assess the overall adequacy of the portrayals. The assessment may be done formally or informally, individually or in groups. The goal is to facilitate accurate assessment of the preliminary case study from the participant perspective. Negotiated results of this member check provide the basis for the final case study report.

Prior to final publication and dissemination of the report, an outside independent audit of the process and the resultant product is suggested (Lincoln & Guba, 1985). The audit involves a formal examination and checking of the records of data collected, data analyzed, decision rules, analytic categories, interpretation, and conclusions (Lincoln & Guba, 1985; Skrtic, 1985; Halpern, 1983; Schwandt & Halpern, 1988). The intent is to verify the consistency, appropriateness, and accuracy of the content and the procedures for analysis through a dependability and confirmability audit.

Based on the review of the evidence, the auditor comments on the degree to which the procedures used fall into generally accepted constructivist practice (dependability). An examination of the data and the evaluator's reconstruction of it results in confirmability of the case report. This process serves to attest to the degree of rigor, technical accuracy, and trustworthiness of the evaluation process.

The final product must reflect multiple perspectives and the interactive nature of the process itself. It should allow the reader to become an interactive partner in understanding the issues and drawing implications. The reader should be able to become involved, not just remain an at-a-distance observer. Finally, the study should empower, activate, and stimulate the reader to responsiveness or action, especially when the case report may have applicability in his or her own context. At the least, it should stimulate readers to reexamine their positions.[5]

Though constructivist evaluation attends little to generalizability, findings from one FBS program may have meaning in another. The degree to which working hypotheses hold outside the time and contexts within which they were found depends upon the degree of similarity between the *sending* (the FBS evaluation in question) and *receiving* (a reader of the case report) contexts (Lincoln & Guba, 1985, p. 316; Skrtic, 1985, p. 200). To some extent then, a grounded theory (Strauss & Corbin, 1990), one that is inductively derived from the study, may emerge. If the FBS evaluation accurately captures the multiple realities of the program and its context, then the lessons learned might aid in understanding FBS in another environment. If the descriptions of the multiple constructions of the FBS program provide sufficient information about its context, then the informed reader who knows his or her own context should be able to reach a conclusion about whether transfer into another context is possible.

SPECIAL CHALLENGES OF QUALITATIVE AND CONSTRUCTIVIST RESEARCH

Qualitative evaluation tends to attract the same criticisms as quantitative evaluation, including lack of rigor and inability to generalize. On the other hand, the auditing process may be criticized for misplaced rigor, with the suggestion that it is not necessary or relevant because qualitative methods, by their very nature, are not rigorous.

A special challenge unique to constructivist research is the redistribution of power that naturally results from the process. The evaluator of an FBS program will only be in charge at the beginning of the first interview. Empowerment will result not only from the collaboration and mutual education that the process produces, but also from the changes

Table 10.2. Contract for Constructivist Evaluation

1. Identify the sponsor of the evaluation, who is the a priori power in the evaluative process, to all stakeholders.
2. Identify, in writing and from the perspective of the sponsor, the program to be evaluated with clear understanding that the sponsor's construction of the program may not match that of other stakeholders and will certainly change in the emergent process.
3. State the purpose of the evaluation. Is it process (formative) or outcome (summative) oriented?
4. Document the agreement of the sponsor to adhere to the conditions necessary for constructivist evaluation: working from positions of integrity; willingness to share power; willingness to change given persuasive information; willingness to reconsider value positions as appropriate; and willingness to make the time and energy commitment required.
5. State the intent of the evaluator to seek out and involve all relevant stakeholders who will also be asked to comply with item 4.
6. Describe briefly the methodology to be used, including its emergent nature.
7. Guarantee access to records and documents. This should specify how they will be accessed, what use can be made of them, and procedure if access is blocked.
8. State the evaluator's intent to protect confidentiality and anonymity of information sources insofar as possible given the nature of a negotiated process.
9. Describe the reporting mode to be utilized. Preference is given to the case report with its capacity for thick description, but other types of reports may be necessary for different stakeholding groups and should be specified as much as possible before the process begins.
10. Develop a listing of other specifications that might include a budget, the evaluators, and a tentative schedule.

that should result. The status quo will not be maintained in a constructivist evaluation. Evaluators and sponsors should be aware of this prior to undertaking this type of evaluation.

It is recommended that a specific contract for constructivist evaluation be drawn up to protect all parties from misunderstanding or erroneous expectations. Guba and Lincoln (1989) provide clear instructions in this respect (see Table 10.2).

Table 10.3.   Additional Qualitative Techniques

Case Studies

These serve a specific purpose such as understanding dropouts, successes, or failures. A case study can be of a person, an event, a program, a time period, a critical incident, or a community. Regardless of the unit of analysis, the goal is in-depth description with great detail and context.

Patton (1987) suggests, depending on the evaluation purpose, the following selection criteria: extreme or deviant cases, maximum variation, homogeneity, typical cases, and critical cases. Critical cases may be particularly important for FBS (especially in programs with limited resources) in that the goal is to understand what happened in a specific positive or negative situation. Data gathering is then limited to understanding only that case.

Case analysis includes all data (interview data, observational data, records, impressions, statements of others). The case data are pulled together, organized, and condensed into a case record, which is then used to construct the case study, which should be descriptive, analytic, interpretive, and evaluative. The goal is a holistic portrayal of the unit of study.

Focus Groups

These groups generally involve eight to twelve individuals who discuss a particular topic under the direction of a moderator. The moderator's role is to assure appropriate participation and to limit the discussion to a small number of issues. The moderator must be well trained in group dynamics and interview skills. Typically lasting from one to three hours, focus groups can be conducted in a variety of settings from homes to offices, including conference telephone calls. The focus group can contain a transcriber, but more often the sessions are taped for later analysis. Data are elicited through more or less directive probes by the moderator. The degree of direction is dependent upon the questions of interest, focused exploration, or confirmation. The more sharply focused the evaluation the more direct the questions.

Record Review

This represents a rich and often neglected data source in evaluation (Lincoln & Guba, 1985). Evaluations based on record review could include content analysis of case records or in-depth analysis of data available in the agency's management information system.

Existing records are available to the evaluator at relatively low cost. They are nonreactive and can be stable sources of information; but they can vary in quality. Because they were not prepared for the evaluation, they may contain insufficient or biased information. There is also the problem of selective survival of information. Evaluation using only what remains in records may present an incomplete account of events or behaviors.

Additional Resources for the Qualitative Researcher

Many programs may not have the opportunity or the desire to enter into a fully developed constructivist research experience, but may wish to take advantage of other qualitative methods to enhance traditional FBS evaluation efforts.[6] Table 10.3 provides brief descriptions of the more appropriate strategies for FBS program evaluation.

CONCLUSION

What has been discussed in this chapter is based on different meta-theoretical assumptions regarding the nature of science and society. Because of this, the constructivist evaluation report is not expected to contain a rational explanation of social affairs (the traditional scientific perspective), but an understanding of the nature of the social world at the level of intersubjectively shared meaning of experience. Quantitative methods aimed at prediction and control fit more comfortably with the belief system of traditional science. Even qualitative methods, which by nature are subjective, will consistently fall shy of expected standards of rigor in traditional science. The evaluator choosing to mix qualitative and quantitative methods must be aware of the challenges this will create if the qualitative product is measured against traditional evaluation standards.

NOTES

1. For more details about the *interpersonal skills* in data collection techniques, the reader may wish to refer to Corimer and Corimer (1979), Dexter (1970), Egan (1982), Knapp (1972), Spradley (1979).
2. For those readers requiring more details about *word data collection* such as persistent observation, document and record review, and historical research, refer to Bogdon and Taylor (1975), Silverman (1985), Strauss and Corbin (1990), Van Maanen, Dabbs, and Faulkner (1982), Whyte (1984).
3. Detailed information about *qualitative data analysis* can be found in Bulmer (1979), Holsti (1969), Miles and Hubberman (1994), Rosengren (1981), Strauss and Corbin (1990).
4. Some spreadsheet programs, like *Excel*, allow sorting of words if the sorting is not very complex. There are also a series of programs designed for use with an IBM-compatible computer. Perhaps the most "user friendly" is *Ethnograph* with clear instructions and means to move from raw data to categories with little difficulty. It is the only program that does not require the establish-

ment of analysis parameters prior to data entry and analysis. *Lotus Agenda* provides a type of automated day timer/scheduler. The subprograms TACT or OCP will produce concordances, indexes, and frequency counts of words in machine-readable text. It will also allow the creation of categories, but because the text must be marked, the analysis is rather cumbersome. *Chat* allows various ways of manipulation, organizing, coding, and counting of language units. Because of its level of technicality it is recommended that *Chat* users attend a *Chat* seminar prior to launching a qualitative analysis. Finally, those evaluators with access to a MacIntosh computer may use *HyperQual*. It has the same general capacity in manipulating word data as programs designed for an IBM environment.

5.   More discussion of *data display and reporting methods* can be found in Chilcott (1987), Miles and Hubberman (1994), Smith (1987), Van Maanen (1988).

6.   For more details on other qualitative methods, the following guides are provided. For more on *focus groups* see Stewart and Shamdasani, (1990), Krueger (1988), VanGundy (1988), Greenbaum (1988). For *case record analysis* see Bailey (1978), Carmines and Zeller (1979), Cochran (1978), Rosenthal and Glass (1984).

Chapter 11

The Management and Impact of Family-Based Services Evaluations: Doing Research in the Real World

Previous chapters in this book have discussed the basics of planning an FBS evaluation. Now, all that is needed is to implement the decisions that have been made. It sounds easy! But, in reality, evaluating "action programs" (Weiss, 1972a, 1972b)—with real program environments, real programs, real workers, real evaluators, real clients, and real research protocols—is significantly more difficult than it first appears. Real-world settings have three characteristics that often lead to implementation problems in conducting research: (1) there are usually multiple and con-flicting interests around the evaluation, (2) many people have a stake in the design, execution, and results of the evaluation, and (3) evaluation is not only a research process, but a political process (Rossi & Freeman, 1993).

As a general rule those preparing for an evaluation should anticipate that "what *can* go wrong *will* go wrong," and must be prepared to deal with problems as they arise. Unless this is done, the evaluation will not be completed successfully, and the energy, time, and money spent in its planning will have been wasted. Further, the evaluation questions will remain unanswered or may be answered incorrectly.

This chapter describes some of the implementation problems faced by evaluators in this field. We recognize that not all of these problems will be encountered, and that some evaluations will face implementation issues that are not described. Our aim is to sensitize the reader's "re-search antennae" so that problems can be anticipated or resolved when they first arise, and an evaluation "meltdown" can be avoided.

All of the authors of this book have taught evaluation research meth-odology and each of us has discussed the pitfalls present in implement-ing research plans. Yet we know that discussing these issues didactically often does not convey to our students the reality that "these things really happen." In order to convey this to our readers, we have chosen to use an actual case example to illustrate the points we will make. Thus, the chapter begins by calling your attention to the Appendix at the end of this chapter, which is a shortened, revised version of a research proposal for a project conducted by two of the authors. Each major area of this proposal will be discussed in terms of the implementation issues that arose and how obstacles were or were not overcome.

In the service model of the programs evaluated, families were seen by trained professional and paraprofessional staff over a three-month period. Frequency of contact with the families ranged from one to seven hours per week, depending on the family's need and the intervention phase (Kubosa-Munro & Sladen, 1987). Thus, these programs fit into the category of family-centered services rather than intensive family-centered services (see Chapter 1; Child Welfare League of America, 1989).

IMPLEMENTATION ISSUES

On the surface, the proposal in the Appendix to this chapter articulates a research plan that meets most of the criteria for conducting good FBS evaluations. According to Rossi (1992a), evaluations should use randomized experimental designs, adopt behavioral criteria for program success, avoid "risk of imminent placement" as the sampling criterion, have a sample containing variety in age of children and types of problems, include programs across a number of sites, exclude a minimum of families from the program and research, and be able to specify the services received by the control group. But, designing an "ideal" study is one thing; carrying it out is quite another.

Agreement on Goals and Objectives

In beginning an outcome evaluation, you need to specify the goals and objectives of the program and reach consensus between the various stakeholders about them. Unless this is done, the evaluation is likely to fail at one or more levels: policymakers, including those at the local level, may see the research as meaningless and therefore disregard the findings; program funders may come to believe that their support was used for inappropriate purposes; program administrators may conclude that the findings from the evaluation cannot inform their operational decisions; and staff may find that participating in the evaluation had little payoff for them in terms of practice. While in some evaluations outcomes are specified by funders or policymakers, the programs under study were unusual in that the agencies were free, within the limits imposed by the various stakeholders, to define and operationalize their goals.

Change in family functioning was designated as the paramount goal. The agencies were most concerned about the effects of their programs on the families and children they served, and wanted to know whether specific domains of family functioning were affected by their services. Outcomes regarding placement prevention, re-reports of child abuse/ neglect, and length of involvement with the public child welfare system, while seen as proxy measures for family functioning, were less important for a number of reasons.

First, leading professionals had expressed concern that the welfare of children not be narrowly equated with placement avoidance (McGowan, 1990; Wald, 1988; Frankel, 1988). In-home family services, it was believed, should be seen as part of a continuum of services to enhance the welfare of children (Brown, Finch, Northern, Taylor, & Weil, 1982; Brown & Weil, 1992; McGowan & Meezan, 1983). Second, it was recognized that the use of placement resources was, in part, influenced by factors other than the condition of the family (e.g., the availability of placement resources, the intensity of family supervision). Third, placement was not considered negative under all circumstances: some families might need and benefit from the placement of their children. Finally, placement was seen as a "program accountability," rather than as a "service improvement" outcome (Jones, 1991, p. 181), and these agencies were most interested in answering the question, How can we improve the services we provide?

Yet program accountability measures could not be ignored given the policy arena in which this research was being conducted. The Department of Children's Service (DCS, the public child welfare agency) needed to have program accountability questions answered. And placement had been the primary outcome measure used in this field up until this time. Measures of placement thus took on importance beyond the service agencies' concern and were incorporated into the research design.

Because service improvement outcomes were of most concern to the agencies, it is not surprising that factors associated with positive outcome were also important. The identification of such factors could provide important information about which families should be targeted for services in an environment of scarce resources.

Although questions regarding improvement in functioning and behavior of children in school were not originally a concern of either the agencies or the researchers, this arena was a priority of the funding agency. The Stuart Foundations have a long history of concern about school performance, and they urged that this goal be incorporated into the research.

The fifth research question was of concern primarily to the researchers. The Family Assessment Form (FAF) is a practice-based instrument developed in collaboration between workers and one of the researchers (McCroskey & Nelson, 1989; McCroskey et al., 1991). If this instrument could be converted to research use, and its psychometric properties found acceptable, then the field would have another instrument at its disposal in evaluating FBS programs. (See Chapter 5 for more information on the FAF.)

Finally, the effectiveness of earlier intervention was of concern to both the agencies and policymakers. If the results of this evaluation supported earlier intervention, then resources might be better allocated to preventive services for troubled but not yet abusing/neglecting families.

Reaching consensus on goals and objectives was not an easy task. It involved a number of steps jointly taken by stakeholders. First, overarching program goals were enumerated. Second, from among these goals, those of greater import to the various stakeholders were specified. Third, these specific goals were narrowed and operationalized so that measures could be chosen. Finally, the goals were revisited in order to ensure that they were reasonable for the program.

This process was successfully accomplished only with the *full* and sustained involvement of all of the stakeholders in the program and its evaluation. Numerous meetings of the stakeholders were held, with participation by line staff, agency supervisors and administrators, DCS administrative personnel, the researchers, and representatives of the foundation. While these deliberations were lengthy, time-consuming, and at times uncomfortable, they resulted in the investment of all the parties in the processes and outcomes of the study.

Clearly, in determining goals and objectives, compromises were necessary and occurred. An example will give the reader a sense of the process that allowed this critical task to be successfully accomplished.

While the agencies' staffs and administrators rejected many of the program accountability goals that were being used in the field, they recognized that in order for the program and its evaluation to be credible, they had to be addressed since these were among the most important questions that DCS wanted answered. The compromise reached involved expending fewer resources in this area by using data collected from the DCS management information system. This strategy accommodated both the FBS agencies' commitment to change in family functioning as the primary outcome and DCS's desire for program accountability measures. However, it also resulted in limited placement data, since the information system did not record the full array of possible placements (e.g., runaway behavior, private psychiatric placements, unpaid placement with relatives).

It should be clear from the above discussion that setting goals and objectives for a program evaluation is not easy: agreeing on what is to be evaluated, narrowing and operationalizing broad goals, and accommodating all the parties in the choice of goals and objectives are necessary if all stakeholders in an evaluation are to invest their talents and resources in a project. This can only be accomplished through open and frank discussions with the major stakeholders, where respect is granted to all. In this process, a team committed to the evaluation emerges and the successful execution of the project becomes possible. Without team building, you can anticipate serious problems at every stage of the evaluation.

Choice of Measures

As noted in the proposal, a significant amount of data was collected through the FAF in research interviews and on worker-completed forms. Some might question the use of this instrument since it had not been "standardized," its psychometric properties at the time of the project's initiation were unknown, it had not been normed on a known population, it covered some of the same domains as better established measures [e.g., the Child Well Being Scales (Magura & Moses, 1986) and the Family Risk Scales (Magura et al., 1987)], and it had not been disseminated widely.

Yet the use of this instrument to measure family functioning was almost a forgone conclusion. The instrument had been developed at one of the service agencies and was in use there as a practice tool (McCroskey & Nelson, 1989). For researchers to ignore the investment the agency had in this instrument would have negated three years of agency work. This might well have reduced investment in the evaluation, undermined data collection, and led to dismissal of the study's findings as irrelevant to agency practice. It would also have created a situation where workers were "double recording"—once for their practice and a second time for the evaluation. This undoubtedly would have engendered resentment on the part of workers, with all of the attendant consequences including inaccurate reporting of data or outright refusal to cooperate.

Since the FAF was normally completed by the worker, it was necessary to transform it into a research instrument that could be administered by an outside interviewer. This would not only help to ensure the "objectivity" of the data, but would further the development of the FAF as a research tool. As Rossi (1992a) has argued, there is a preference for data to be collected by research workers who do not bear responsibility for service delivery.

However, since the FAF was still in development, it was agreed that other well-established, standardized instruments would be used to collect all additional information regarding the family's environment, child and adult functioning, and service satisfaction. On balance, this compromise probably enhanced the credibility of the evaluation.

Choice of Design

The research design called for the use of random assignment to a service group and a control group that would receive "normal" agency services. It also included a follow-up with families 12 months after the close of service. The choice of a 12-month follow-up was based on the resources available to the project, the need to complete the project in a timely manner, and similarity to follow-up periods in other controlled studies of FBS (Feldman, 1990a; Fraser et al., 1991; McDonald & Associates, 1990), not on how long treatment effects were expected to persist.

While experimental design is "the preferred strategy for the assessment of the impact of social programs" (Rossi, 1992b, p. 78), there are many barriers to successful implementation. As Rossi notes:

> [P]erhaps the most difficult obstacles to overcome are political in character: random assignment reduces the discretionary control exercised by program personnel. Placing a family into a control condition often appears to program personnel to involve the withholding of program benefits from needy and deserving clients, a process that borders on the unethical. (1992b, p. 79)

Almost immediately, the evaluation encountered a number of these political problems. Referrals "dried up" upon the implementation of random assignment. This occurred despite strenuous efforts to gain the cooperation of DCS program staff, including numerous presentations to the referring workers, meetings with supervisory personnel, and the full agreement of DCS administrative staff that design rigor should be maintained. The FBS agencies made extraordinary efforts, including individual meetings with workers, recognition of workers who made referrals, and agency receptions for DCS workers. None of these efforts worked.

It appears that several issues were responsible for the initial lack of response by DCS line workers. First, it was discovered that under ordinary circumstances, contrary to agency policy, workers did not obtain a release of information before referrals to voluntary agencies were made. Workers often circumvented this requirement by giving their clients a list of potential service providers and asking them to contact the agency directly. In this way, workers did not reveal the client's name to a service provider.

Second, the project required compliance with informed-consent procedures (see Chapter 3) that proved burdensome to the DCS worker. The extra time involved in explaining the service and the research component, and the additional paperwork required to obtain written consent, deterred workers from cooperating with the referral process. Since project services were in place prior to the initiation of the research component, workers also questioned whether the knowledge gained from the research was worth the additional paperwork burdens placed upon them and their clients.

Finally, once referred for FBS, clients had only a 50% chance of receiving FBS services. This placed workers in the awkward position of referring clients for service only to have them assigned to the control group. In these cases, workers believed they lost personal credibility with their clients. Further, they had to do additional work in order to link control group clients with other services. And some workers felt that "withholding" service in this manner was unethical.

The lack of referrals caused a significant problem (some might say crisis) for the FBS programs and the research. In the end, the problem was resolved through the use of leverage; the foundation, which had committed substantial funds to both the service component and the research, met with top and middle-level administrators of DCS to reiterate the importance of the project and the investment they had made in it, and to discuss ways in which the problem could be overcome. This meeting led to swift intervention by DCS administrators, and referrals to the project began to flow at an appropriate pace.

This experience taught us a valuable but costly lesson about the importance of early participation of administrative and line staff in planning research. In the end, the research component of the project was set back almost a full year by the initial lack of referrals and the amount of time it took to correct the problem. This forced us to decrease sample sizes for the study, and undoubtedly created ill will on the part of some of the stakeholders.

Random assignment to alternative services, as called for in this design, also created data collection problems. In order to be able to check whether workers serving comparison group cases are not overcompensating for their clients (Cook & Campbell, 1979), projects must collect a considerable amount of "process" data—data that describe the characteristics of the clients and the services they receive. Obtaining these data is not as easy as it might sound, particularly for members of the comparison group who in this study received "normal" agency service and were referred to other voluntary agencies. While the records for the FBS group were complete and a summary was kept of the services they received, this was not so for the control group. DCS records contained only an overview of services they provided directly and the service referrals they made to private agencies—they did not contain information about the services actually received. The study was thus limited, like other studies in the field, in assuming that

> the kinds of service and the dosage levels [for the comparison group] were different and inferior at least in quantity. . . . [W]e cannot tell whether the experimental treatment was sufficiently different from the control condition. (Rossi, 1992b, pp. 94–95)

Had it been logistically and fiscally possible, services to comparison cases would have been tracked through a case reading in the provider agencies to assess the full range and extent of services received by this group. Unfortunately, this was beyond both the scope and resources of the project.

Sampling Criteria

Recall that the project was designed to serve the full range of DCS cases. Families were eliminated from consideration only if there was not at least one child present in the home, if they refused service when offered by the DCS worker, or if they were incapable of understanding and/or participating in case planning. The decision to include the full range of cases in the sample ran counter to the wisdom in the field at the time—programs providing intensive family-based services, and studies looking at their effectiveness, had attempted to confine their samples to families in which there was "risk of imminent placement."

The concept of "risk of imminent placement" was rejected as a criterion for sample selection only after careful consideration. It was believed that this criterion would be difficult to operationalize and even more difficult to implement (Feldman, 1990b; Fraser et al., 1991; Rossi, 1992a, 1992b; Schuerman, Rzepnicki, Littell & Budde, 1992a; Tracy, 1991).

Further, services were initially conceptualized as a way to improve family functioning, not primarily as a way to prevent placement: we were interested in discovering the factors associated with improved family functioning in order to refine their service and define an appropriate target population. Limiting cases to those at risk of imminent placement would have narrowed the range of cases available for study, and thus would have decreased the possibility of discovering which families were most likely to benefit as a result of service.

The decision to include a wide range of cases had the full backing of the agencies and the funding source, who also wanted to know how to target services. After discussion and negotiation regarding accountability and reporting procedures, DCS endorsed these criteria. While DCS had initially objected to referring their "most difficult" cases, they came to see FBS as a significant enhancement of their service network.

The decision to eliminate risk of imminent placement and to minimize other exclusionary criteria had consequences for the FBS programs and the research. There was no way of knowing what criteria various DCS workers used in referring families. Some might have referred only their most difficult cases, others might have referred a full range of cases, and still others only their "easier" cases. Thus, in the end, the target population of these services was the cases actually referred, and this sample heterogeneity made the analysis of these data quite complicated. It took a great deal of time and effort to discern the effects of the program on various sub-populations within the sample, and these analyses were limited by the reduced sample size.

Sample Attrition

The original proposal called for a total of 180 families to be referred to *each* of the FBS agencies. It was anticipated that, over the course of the project, about one-third of these families would be lost to the study, leaving a final sample size of 240 on whom complete data would be available. This final sample size (according to the power analysis performed) would have allowed statistical tests to detect small to moderate differences between the service and comparison groups, and moderate differences in most of the subgroup analyses that were planned.

In fact, sample loss between time 1 and time 2 was about 20%; between time 2 and time 3 this rate of loss continued, for a total attrition (time 1 to time 3) during the course of the study of about 35%.

However, for totally unexpected reasons, overall sample attrition between referral for service and the end of the follow-up period was much higher than expected (58%, 152 of 360 families remained at time 3). While approximately 360 families were referred to the agencies and were randomly assigned to either the experimental or control group, engaging these families *at time 1, prior to the receipt of any services,* proved to be inordinately difficult. Between referral to FBS and the initial interview,

120 families were lost, producing a 33% attrition rate *before data collection at time 1.*

Two factors associated with this attrition rate were not anticipated. First, many families could not be located after referral. The inability to locate families at the point when mandated services were supposed to begin was extremely troubling, yet few service or research projects report such data. Barth is one of the few to discuss this as an issue; attrition at the beginning of service in his study was only somewhat less than that encountered in this study (Barth, 1989). Others writing about FBS refer to this issue, but often do not cite figures (Feldman, 1990b).

The second major reason for subject loss at time 1 was the unwillingness of families to participate in the research. This occurred despite the fact that families had been told about the research component by both their DCS workers and FBS workers (for service cases) prior to contact with the research interviewer. Approximately 30 families, evenly divided between the service and comparison groups, were lost to the sample through refusal to participate.

The project attempted to minimize sample loss in a number of ways once a family participated at time 1. First, at the point of the first research contact, each family was asked to provide a list of people (and their phone numbers) who were always likely to know their whereabouts. Contacting relatives and friends proved particularly helpful in locating families in the sample. Second, while the case remained open with the public child protective system, DCS could sometimes provide new addresses when a family could not be located. However, once a case was closed, it was no longer tracked. Thus, this procedure was less useful for the follow-up period.

Finally, families were given vouchers for $25 of groceries or clothing to compensate them for the interview time. (Cash payments would have affected families' public assistance payments.) While this compensation recognized the importance of their time and their contribution to the project, and was not meant to be coercive, it clearly had an effect on participation. Families, at times, actually called the project to ask when their interview was due.

Unexpectedly, loss and attrition also affected the teacher sample even though a similar $25 compensation was offered to them. The school systems changes that were going on at the time of the study point to the effects that "historical" events can have on research plans. Collecting data even from "stable" populations such as teachers is affected by program changes that make major demands on their time: a move to a year-round school calendar, seasonal employment, strikes and labor negotiations, turnover, and severe budget cuts that limited the amount of time teachers were willing to spend on activities outside the classroom.

In all, interviews were conducted with less than 50% of the teachers who had children in the study; even fewer children had teacher reports at multiple points in time.

Somewhat surprisingly, sample attrition also occurred during the case reading phase of the study. More than one in five (22%) of the case records of the families in study could not be located by DCS personnel, who in numerous attempts exhausted all potential sources and locations within the department. This problem has been encountered by others doing research in Los Angeles county and jurisdictions across the country (McDonald & Associates, 1990). It is sad commentary on the state of record keeping in many large child welfare systems, and it is a fact of life that affects the accuracy and representativeness of findings in many evaluations.

Sample loss and attrition create challenges in data analysis, and statistical consultation may be necessary to deal with these problems. For example, differential sample loss from the service and comparison groups needs to be checked and compensated for statistically in order to draw accurate conclusions from the evaluation. Also, even if a large number of subjects were initially sampled, attrition may so reduce statistical power that relationships that are, in fact, significant will not be recognized. This is particularly a problem with data from multiple methods and sources—which is preferred in evaluation research. Despite having complete data from one data source, missing data from another source will eliminate that subject from certain analyses, thus reducing statistical power.

Data Collection

The actual process of collecting data for this study presented its own set of challenges, which included training the data collectors, working with the FBS agencies so that the worker-completed FAFs and service data were received in a timely way and contained all of the appropriate information, collaborating with DCS to gain access to family records, and arranging for the transfer of data from the DCS management information system. In addition, interviewers had to be sensitized both to their potential impact on clients and to issues concerning their own safety.

The interviewers were trained in social work, experienced in FBS, and were similar in ethnic background to the families in the study. While this increased personnel costs, we believe it contributed to greater sensitivity, more reliable judgments on the FAF, and increased validity of data collected from families of different ethnic backgrounds.

Training in the use of these specific research instruments was accomplished in a number of ways, including a daylong orientation, two days of in-house role playing, pretesting both the interview and interviewing techniques in the field, supervised field practice (in pretest), and completion of consistency checks. After the initial training, interviewers met periodically to review common problems and concerns with the senior project staff. In addition, each interview was checked for completeness, consistency, and accuracy, and a sample of interview tapes was recoded by a second interviewer. This served as both additional training and as a way of establishing the interrater reliability of the instrument.

Retired DCS personnel were chosen to read cases and trained in a similar way. One DCS staff member with considerable agency experience was assigned to the project on an as-needed basis to gather the case records from various DCS offices and storage facilities so that they could be read in a central place.

In addition, the researchers had to be briefed on the types of information and the specific data elements available through the two management information systems currently in use by the department. Specification of needed data elements and arrangements to transfer the information involved numerous discussions and agreements with DCS personnel in the management information section.

The data collection plan also required the participating agencies to supply the project with the worker-completed FAFs and service information data. Project personnel kept track of which case FAFs and service summaries were received, checked them for completeness, and sought missing information from workers.

All of these processes required the development of an evaluation management structure. We believe that these processes ran smoothly for two reasons. First, we were fortunate to maintain almost our entire staff for the four years of the project. We believe that this was due, in part, to the fact that (1) project personnel were treated as partners in the research process and understood the crucial role they played, (2) project personnel were highly invested in the topic under study, (3) dissertation opportunities were made available to doctoral students, (4) staff replacement was accomplished by promoting from within, (5) frequent staff meetings were held so that problems, concerns, and frustrations could be aired and resolved in a timely manner, and (6) staff were provided with an amount of work consistent with their needs and availability. Second, since the research was conducted as a collaborative effort between the researchers, the service agencies, and DCS, each of these partners was committed to its successful implementation. Thus, each was amenable to responding to the demands of the project and to committing time and personnel to its completion.

Project Management

It should be clear by now that a research study can be a logistical nightmare. The need to maintain relationships with stakeholders, the number of data collection points, the accumulation of a rolling sample, the number of data sources, and the sheer amount of data requires teamwork. Staffing for this project included two senior principal investigators who shared responsibility for the overall direction of the work (equivalent to 25% time each), a project associate who was responsible for the day-to-day operations of the project including assigning and checking interviews and case readings (67% time), a data manager/analyst (50% time), between three and seven interviewers depending on the stage of the project (about seven hours per week each for about three years), four case readers (seven hours per week each for about six months), and access to the support staff of a major university for budget management, equipment purchase, and occasional secretarial support.

Project management was facilitated through regular as well as ad hoc staff meetings. Meetings of senior staff monitored overall progress, discussed obstacles to task completion, identified strategies to overcome them, and set future goals. Regular meetings with interviewers and case readers addressed problems and possible solutions to issues of data collection.

Due to the length of the project, proximate goals and time lines to measure progress toward these goals were needed. While the general sample selection process was out of the control of the investigators, other project goals and time lines for their completion were well articulated through the use of specific timelines. A sample timeline from the third-year proposal for this project is presented in Figure 11.1.

Data Analysis

In order to even begin to answer the major research questions of an evaluation, a number of steps have to be taken prior to the actual analysis of the data. This involves cleaning the data, checking the reliability and validity of the standardized instruments used, establishing interrater reliability, and determining the psychometric properties of newly devised instruments (see Chapter 12). While researchers understand the importance of these steps, agencies, anxious for results and unfamiliar with these necessities, can become frustrated with these preliminary analytic tasks.

It thus becomes the role of the researchers to educate their partners. While this takes time and energy, it is crucial if trust is to be maintained

```
Rolling Data collection on families—Time 1 ......... August, 1991
Rolling Data collection on families—Time 2 ......... Through Dec. 1991
Rolling Data collection on families—Time 3 ......... June 1991—Sept. 1992
Rolling Data collection from teachers—Time 1 ...... Completed Sept. 1991
Rolling Data collection from teachers—Time 3 ...... July 1991—Oct. 1992
Case Record Review ............................. Sept. 1992—Jan. 1993
DCS Information System Run—Time 3 ............. January 1993
Coding and data entry .......................... Through March 1993
Time 1 Analysis ................................ Sept.—Dec. 1991
Time 2 Analysis ................................ Jan.—March 1992
Time 1/Time 2 Change Analysis .................. April—June 1992
Worker/Research FAF comparison ................ Jan.—April 1992
Time 3 analysis ................................ Jan.—March 1993
Time 1/Time 3 Change Analysis .................. March—May 1993
Time 2/Time 3 Change Analysis .................. April—June 1993
Factors Associated with Change Analysis .......... July—Sept. 1993
Additional Analyses as Needed ................... Oct.—Dec. 1993
Final Report Writing ............................ Jan.—April 1994
Final Report Submitted .......................... April 30, 1994
```

Figure 11.1. Project Timeline. [*Source:* Adapted from W. Meezan and J. Mc-
Croskey J. (1991). An evaluation of the home-based services programs of
Children's Bureau of Los Angeles and Hathaway Children's Services: Third
year proposal submitted to the Stuart Foundations, University of Southern
California, School of Social Work, Los Angeles.]

between the parties in the evaluation. If agencies do not understand the
intricacies of these preliminary steps, and the time it takes to complete
them, they may feel "locked out" of the process and disenfranchised by it.

Once these preliminary steps are completed, work on answering the
research questions can begin. Obviously, the order in which data are
available dictate, to some extent, the order of the data analysis. However, when multiple questions can be addressed simultaneously from
the same data set, prioritization becomes important. In any evaluation,
the various stakeholders have varying information needs; some answers
are of higher priority to some stakeholders than to others. Thus, consultation is again needed to set analytic priorities.

It was decided that while the funding source would be kept informed
of the progress made in answering the research questions, the evaluation's two primary stakeholders, the agencies and the researchers,
would negotiate the order of the analytic questions to be answered. The
result was consistent with the discussions that led to the prioritization of
the research questions; it was decided that the service improvement
questions would be the first to be addressed; program accountability
questions would be put off until these were answered.

As the findings emerged, results were reported to the stakeholders as quickly as possible, so that their interpretation could be incorporated into the evaluation report. Further, flexibility was required, as questions that were initially given a lower priority emerged as critical to understanding and interpreting unanticipated findings. For example, it became clear that determining the congruence of information collected by the research interviewer and the data provided by the worker was crucial to understanding the major outcomes of the program. Thus, this question was explored "out of turn."

IMPACT OF RESEARCH

On Families

Our experience indicates that, for the most part, the research interviews had a positive impact on the families and a negligible impact on teachers. The families informally reported to both their workers and the interviewers that the long and complex interview gave them a neutral party to "tell their story to." Some reported that it made them think of things in different ways. Certainly, the $25 compensation helped with financial troubles. Over the course of the study, we wondered whether the interview itself was not an intervention, since many of the families had never before had such an experience.

Some of the service workers reported that the research interview "stirred up" feelings that staff were able to use in the therapeutic process—that it had helped clients to clarify issues that could then be dealt with in the worker-client relationship. This, however, led to concern for the families in the comparison group. What were the effects of the interview be on them? Who did they have to help them with these feelings?

It should be noted, however, that for some of the families, the research interview created confusion about the roles of the three new people in their lives: their DCS worker, the FBS worker, and the research interviewer. Why did they ask some of the same questions, many of which were personal? While all parties attempted to explain their various roles, some families remained confused, and this confusion had to be dealt with.

On Interviewers

The research interviewers, although they were professionals, had to learn the differences between a therapeutic role and a research role.

Many times they felt frustrated because they "wanted to help" although they knew that their primary role was to gather information. They had to adjust to the fact that they had to leave the families basically "as they found them" and to remain nonjudgmental about some of the situations they encountered. This was accomplished through debriefing with senior personnel throughout their experience.

The interviewers had to be further sensitized to safety issues. While many of them were confident about their ability to protect themselves, they were encouraged, when necessary, to reschedule interviews in safer environments if dangerous situations emerged.

On Program and Program Personnel

By definition, an evaluation will have an impact on program staff and service delivery. Perhaps the most frequent effect is staff resistance and anxiety related to being evaluated. Workers are concerned that their practices are being judged and are aware that evaluation results may provide "evidence on which to base decisions about maintaining, institutionalizing, and expanding successful programs and modifying or abandoning unsuccessful ones" (Weiss, 1977b, p. 328).

In this evaluation, staff in the FBS agencies showed little or no resistance to the evaluation process. Groundwork done at both agencies included the importance of the evaluation and its potential to contribute to knowledge and to policy decisions; reassurance that the knowledge gained from the evaluation would be used to improve the program rather than judge staff performance; commitment of the agency executives to the improvement of practice and policy; trust in the research team that was built over a long period of time; confidence that the program was up and running smoothly and was ready for evaluation; and, most importantly, the involvement of workers in every step of planning the evaluation and incorporation of their concerns into our final plans.

Being "research ready," and believing that they were contributing to a meaningful endeavor affected the way some of the workers performed their job tasks. Some reported that knowing that someone from outside the agency was evaluating their program led them to be more conscientious, more timely, and more thoughtful in their case planning and implementation. DCS workers involved with comparison group cases may have attempted to make up for the fact that their clients did not receive "enhanced" services by providing greater attention and more services to these cases. Such "compensatory rivalry" (Cook & Campbell, 1979) is not uncommon in field experiments. While neither of these phenomena is easily measured, anecdotal evidence indicates that both took place.

The evaluation also changed practice, supervision, and support within the FBS agencies in ways that were unanticipated at the time the evaluation was begun. The initial lack of referrals from DCS spurred more personalized and aggressive strategies to obtain cooperation. FBS workers were confronted by their counterparts at DCS with charges that the random assignment was unethical, illegal, and even cruel, feelings shared by some of the FBS workers even though they had a much better understanding of the benefits that could be derived from this procedure. Both groups of workers, however, believed that the services would have greater impact if they were able to use their professional judgment regarding who would be accepted into the program.

After numerous meetings to overcome these feelings, the FBS workers went out of their way to describe the program and its expected benefits in order to increase referrals. While these personal contacts placed significant demands on the FBS workers (with only minor payoffs in terms of actual referrals), they improved communication between workers in the public and voluntary sector about cases of mutual concern. This improved communication and the personal relationships established continue to provide benefits for the agencies.

In addition, because the evaluation required that the FBS agencies serve a greater number of cases referred by DCS than by community services, the types of families served changed. Workers reported that DCS families, at least initially, were generally less motivated, less amenable to the treatment provided, and more defensive and angry than families referred by the other community agencies. This had a demoralizing effect on the workers, as they sometimes experienced less immediate engagement and progress than they were used to.

This change in the mix of cases also heightened awareness of safety. The FBS programs served an increasing number of families who lived in dangerous, violent, drug-involved communities in Los Angeles. While staff safety had always been a concern of the agencies, the pressure to engage and keep the research families in the sample led to a heightened awareness of the potential dangers of doing home-based work. The agencies' responses included informal discussions, supervision, training, more teaming of workers, more attention to the timing of visits, and, when necessary, arranging visits in less dangerous situations. Over the course of the project, workers by and large reported that they developed more confidence and skill in coping with dangerous situations.

The shift in caseload mix also had consequences for the agencies, who became concerned that their responsiveness to community needs may have been diminished by shifting their caseloads toward the public child protective agency. While the agencies made efforts to maintain their relationships with other community agencies, they correctly believed that their reputation for responsiveness to all referral sources would need to be reestablished. After the study concluded this was accomplished, and the agencies again have appropriate, responsive relationships with other community agencies.

But perhaps the most unpredicted and positive impact of the evaluation is the incorporation of evaluation methodology into the culture of both agencies. Administrators, supervisors, and other programs within the agencies (foster care, residential treatment, etc.) were motivated and excited by the benefits of knowing whether their practices are effective, and a healthy spirit of competition to evaluate practice has been engendered. Both agencies now have research committees and evaluation has become part of their culture, a development that can only have a positive impact on services and clients.

CONDITIONS NECESSARY FOR SUCCESSFUL IMPLEMENTATION

From all that has been said in this chapter, a number of principles emerge that enhance the possibility that an evaluation will be successfully implemented. This is not to say that all will go smoothly if they are present. Rather, they may remove some of the most obvious barriers to the successful implementation of an evaluation study.

First, there must be a commitment on the part of all of the stakeholders to *experimentation* in order to improve services and change policy; evaluations are best undertaken when the parties involved have a commitment to policy and program change. Without a commitment to learning about what works and what does not for whom, and changing, modifying, or discontinuing programs based on the results of the evaluation, it is senseless to undertake an evaluation.

Second, evaluations are most successful when they are a part of the agency's normal activities. Ideally, social service programs would be constantly evaluating themselves, so that program and practice modifications based on ongoing data collection and analysis become routine. When incorporated into everyday activities, the collection of evaluation data is perceived as part of good professional practice rather than as threatening or intrusive. And readily and consistently available data become helpful to administrators and program personnel at all levels. In this sense, the research study itself becomes an "intervention" that affects services, and those effects should be recognized.

Third, if evaluation is not part of an agency's normal activities, the agency should be "research ready" before undertaking an evaluation or becoming part of an outside evaluation. This means that (1) the program has agreed-upon goals and measurable objectives that are meaningful to the staff, (2) the program as designed and delivered consistently addresses these objectives, (3) program stability has been achieved, (4) measurements relevant to the program's goals and objectives have been agreed to, (5) the consequences of the research design are understood, and (6) data collection is not intrusive but incorporated into normal recording activities. To establish the partnership necessary for a successful evaluation, full and complete involvement of staff at all levels and at every step of the process is required. A meaningful evaluation can only take place if the agency and its staff are committed to it and believe they will profit from it.

Fourth, programs should not oversell a single goal or cost savings. As Schuerman et al. have noted "a program which is oversold must eventually answer to the evaluation data" (1991, p. 198) and to policymakers. If claims cannot be substantiated, promising service models may lose political support before their full potential has been explored. Therefore, it is important for programs to define their potential impacts broadly but modestly, and for evaluations to use multiple outcome measures to explore all of the potential impacts of a program.

Finally, evaluations cannot be done "on the cheap." It takes resources to spend the time to form partnerships and agree on goals, design, measures, procedures, and protocols; to hire and retain sufficient and adequately prepared staff; to collect and analyze data; to manage project operations; to deal with the unexpected situations that inevitably arise; and to disseminate findings. Too often, evaluations are an afterthought, required of programs by their funding sources ex post facto. If you are planning to carry out an in-house evaluation, your agency must dedicate sufficient resources for hiring staff qualified to plan and carry out such work (responsibility for this task cannot simply be added to an overburdened staff member's role) and for purchasing the supplies and equipment necessary to collect data, track project activities, and analyze results. Agencies new to evaluation should consult with those with more experience in the evaluation process on staff qualifications and equipment needs.

In addition, consultation from experts (faculty and advanced doctoral students at universities, private research concerns, or private individuals) should be available to in-house staff during the planning and execution of the study. There are particular advantages when academic–public service linkages are fostered. The agency benefits from advice on evaluation methodology and implementation; the faculty consultant can bring the vicissitudes of doing practice research in the real world back to the classroom. No matter who is retained, the agency must have confidence in the person's research knowledge, management abilities, and concern for the agency's interests.

In-house agency expertise is needed even if an external evaluation is planned. Often, outside researchers are not well acquainted with the specific agencies or programs they will be evaluating. Agencies must therefore be prepared to help the researchers tailor, shape, and narrow their research strategies to fit the specific program being studied. This requires in-house expertise or consultation from someone who is known and trusted. Evaluations can be meaningless, or worse, detrimental when predetermined goals and research methodologies are overlaid on unique agency programs. But by paying attention to the cautions and principles discussed in this chapter, and other literature, agencies can substantially increase the likelihood of completing a rewarding evaluation study that staff at all levels of the organization will benefit from.

Appendix to Chapter 11

A Sample Research Proposal[1]

This three-year research plan addresses the evaluation of the in-home family support programs at Children's Bureau of Los Angeles and Hathaway Children's Service. It is based on the multifaceted service delivery goals of the two agencies and on a review of the research in this important emerging field of practice. We believe, along with the program staff, that research on the placement outcomes of such programs, while mixed (AuClaire and Schwartz, 1986; Jones, 1985) has demonstrated their potential for the child welfare system and has helped to develop an initial funding base for them.

We believe that the next necessary step is to construct methodologically sound experimental studies that address the *multiple* potential effects of such programs on family and child functioning as well as their potential long-term effects on the family unit. We believe that the concept of family functioning should be broadly based, using an ecological framework, and should include the family's environment, characteristics and behaviors of both parents and children, interactions between family members, and risks of child abuse and neglect.

Research Questions

The proposed research is designed to answer the following questions:

1.   Is there a change in the functioning of abusive/neglectful families over time and can such changes be attributed to the program inputs?

2.   To what extent is participation in the service program associated with decreased need for other child welfare services, including Department of Children's Services (DCS) supervision and out-of-home placement?

3.   What factors are associated with positive outcomes for families participating in the experimental programs of these agencies?

4.   Is there a relationship between improved family functioning and improved school behavior and performance in elementary-school-aged children?

5.   Can an emerging, promising practice instrument be adapted to meet the needs of researchers in the field? Are there differences in the ratings of family functioning when information is collected by practitioners as opposed to research interviewers?

6.   Are there differences between families referred to the programs by DCS and families referred by other sources in terms of family characteristics, problem severity, and outcomes?

Research Methodology

The design for this study is a variation of the classic experimental design (Campbell & Stanley, 1963). Random assignment to experimental and control groups from DCS referrals will be used. However, the design will vary from the classic experimental design in a number of ways.

First, the control group will receive "normal agency services" rather than no treatment (Cook & Campbell, 1979). The use of this procedure allows for the fact that services are mandated for this entire population. It further eliminates any ethical problems that may be present with a "no-service" condition.

Second, both the experimental and control groups will be followed for a period of time beyond the end of the experimental treatment. The follow-up will take place approximately twelve months after the end of treatment (approximately fifteen months after entrance into the service or comparison program). The proposed study therefore adds a longitudinal component and thus allows the researchers to answer questions regarding the longer-term effects of the program and the delayed effects of the program.

Sampling

The desired final sample, after any attrition, is 240 families (120 randomly assigned to each of the experimental and comparison groups) who are referred for service to DCS for child abuse or neglect, where at least one child is present in the home. Since some attrition in the sample is anticipated, due both to the unwillingness of families to participate in the research and the inability to locate families at the one-year follow-up, agencies are being asked to sample a total of 180 families for each group. This allows the desired sample size to be maintained even with an expected attrition rate of about 33%.

Eligibility for random assignment is limited by only three criteria: (1) families must have at least one minor child living at home, (2) families are eliminated from consideration for assignment to either the experimental or control group if they refuse service, or (3) if they are totally incapable of understanding and/or participating in case planning.

Setting the sampling frame in the described way guarantees significant heterogeneity in the sample. This heterogeneity allows important within-group analyses to be conducted and thus allows beginning answers to the class of questions that can be framed as Who improves due to services?

One advantage of setting the sample size in the experimental group at 120 is that it allows comparisons to be made between DCS-and non-DCS-referred children. Each program is expected to serve at least 120 families during the next year of the funding period. If 85 from each agency are DCS referrals and 35 are not, important comparisons can be made between the groups on outcome variables.

Based on a power analysis, a sample size of 120 in each group will not allow "small" effects to be detected (Cohen, 1988). However, it will allow for smaller than moderate effects to be detected in the primary analysis comparing experimental with control groups, at least moderate effects to be detected in analyses involving change in the experimental group, and moderate effects to be detected in comparisons between DCS- and non-DCS-referred service families.

Instrumentation

The following considerations guided selection of instruments: (1) A single assessment of family functioning should not be used; rather measures covering a variety of domains will be employed. (2) Where possible, a variety of informants will be used. (3) Where possible, multiple methods of data collection will be utilized. (4) When necessary and available, measures that are appropriate for use over time will be utilized.

Sources of Data

The Family Interview. This interview schedule, which will be constructed by the researchers and includes some standardized measures, will be based on the Family Assessment Form (FAF), and will occur at all three points in time (t_1, t_2, and t_3). This instrument, normally completed by social workers in the participating agencies as part of their assessment, will be converted so that the information necessary for its completion can be gathered in a research interview. Such a conversion will probably have some effects on the psychometric properties of the FAF, which will require systematic assessment. However, the opportunity for assessing these changes, as well as the interrater reliability between social work staff and researchers, will be readily available.

The two primary characteristics of the instrument that distinguish it from others currently in use in family-based services are its ecological orientation and its practice base. The instrument assesses the family's physical, social, and financial environment; the parent's (or other caregiver's) history, personal characteristics, and child-rearing skills; the child's developmental status and behavior; and the interactions between adults and children in the family.

During the parent interview, mothers whose "study" child is six years old or over will be asked to respond to the Child Behavior Checklist (Achenbach & Edelbrock, 1984). This checklist consists of 118 behavior problems and 20 social competence items. Behavior dimensions that are tapped are somewhat different for boys and girls, but include, for both, depression, social withdrawal, somatic complaints, aggression, hyperactivity, and delinquency.

In homes in which the study child is under the age of six, the HOME Inventory will be administered (Caldwell & Bradley, 1984). This instrument, which involves both direct questioning and observation of parent-child interaction, measures a number of dimensions thought to be important to optimal child development.

At the end of each interview, mothers will also be asked to complete the Brief Symptom Inventory (Derogatis, Lipman, & Covi 1973). This standardized instrument measures the presence of psychiatric symptomatology along a number of dimensions including depression and anxiety.

Included in the family interview at time 2 (termination of service for the service group) with the family will also be information regarding services received and service satisfaction. Satisfaction will be measured through the use of an instrument based on the Client Satisfaction Questionnaire (Larsen, Attkisson, Hargreaves, & Nguyn, 1979).

Worker Assessment. Data from the FAF will be recorded at opening and closing of services by workers for all service cases. Workers will also provide data on services used by families.

Data From Case Records. In addition to family-and agency-provided service information data, the DCS case records will be read at follow-up (t_3) to collect information on all cases regarding a number of areas. Included here will be such information as DCS's initial intake information: the risk assessment completed by DCS worker, the complaint that led to the abuse/neglect report, whether the court was involved with the family, the length of DCS involvement with the family and whether there were subsequent openings, and services received through both DCS and other service-providing agencies.

Data from Information Systems. Data regarding initial or subsequent reports of child abuse, placement histories, etc., will be collected through the DCS management information system at follow-up (t_3). Searches for relevant information will be conducted for both the service and comparison group children, as well as for non-DCS-referred children who are being served by the project agencies.

Teacher Interview. A teacher interview, covering both the academic and behavioral status of the child, will be conducted at the beginning of service and at the one-year follow-up (t_1 and t_3) for both experimental and control group children of *elementary* school age. Academic domains will be covered in the interview. In addition, teachers will be asked to complete the Teacher Report Form, a teacher version of the Child Behavior Checklist described above (Achenbach & Edelbrock, 1986).

NOTE

1. Adapted from Meezan, W. & McCroskey, J. (1989). An evaluation of the home-based services programs of Children's Bureau of Los Angeles and Hathaway Children's Services: A proposal submitted to the Stuart Foundations. Los Angeles: University of Southern California, School of Social Work.

Chapter 12

Analyzing Findings and Writing Reports

The purpose of analysis is to distill simplicities from complexities, and the purpose of a report is to present the analysis in a fluid, clear way. Good reports discuss the findings in a persuasive fashion. Poor ones leave the reader feeling inundated with data. The key to both analysis and report writing is "making sense" of the data and this chapter will describe this process.

Whether qualitative or quantitative data are collected, a plan for data analysis is as necessary as a map in a strange country. Without one, you can make your way, but it will take more time. With one, you can be more efficient. The data analysis should be planned at the same time that the evaluation instruments and design are selected. It is a central part of a research design, because it specifies the means for making sense of raw data.

The precise steps in the plan will vary by the kind of data collected. As discussed earlier, qualitative analysis is characterized by categorizing and cross-classifying. Although there is substantial variation, quantitative data analysis often consists of comparable steps. It is quite common for a quantitative evaluator to construct multivariable indexes and to cross-classify indexes in an attempt to identify patterns in the data. Both qualitative and quantitative researchers look for central themes in the data.

In the next few pages, we will focus on the analysis of quantitative data and the data analysis plan. Qualitative analysis is discussed in Chapter 10. Because much agency-level research is quantitative in nature, the goal of this chapter is to provide readers with a template for conducting small agency-based studies, including writing up the findings to inform stakeholders. We will discuss the components of a data analysis plan, a strategy for statistical analysis, and the central elements of evaluation reports. In short, we will describe the "making-sense" process.

THE DATA ANALYSIS PLAN

The data analysis plan has five steps: (1) specify the measurements, (2) decide on the level of statistical significance and the methods for estimating clinical significance, (3) make a plan for statistical analysis, (4) devise a raw data examination and correction protocol, and, (5) develop a data-coding and entry protocol. The plan should begin when the research design is being formulated. On the basis of prior studies, theory, practice wisdom, and just plain hunches, major variables are specified. Then hypotheses are advanced about the expected relationships among these variables. These hypotheses and the properties of the variables themselves constitute the measurement model for the study. They determine the kind of statistical procedures to be employed. In this chapter, we will not discuss specific statistical procedures. There are many statistics books for that. Rather, we will discuss the intervening and sometimes abstruse steps between the specification of major variables and the presentation of statistical findings in a report.

In the following section, the data analysis plan listed above will be described. There are many alternative approaches to an analysis of data. Our recommendations chart one path through these alternatives. Some evaluators prefer to give their raw data to a professional "data entry" company, which will enter and check the data for accuracy, and then return a "clean" data disk for statistical analysis. The approach that we describe assumes that evaluators will code and enter data themselves. It also assumes that the best way to analyze data is from the univariate to the bivariate to the multivariate. We think that this system leads to greater knowledge about the data and reduces the risk that multivariate procedures will be employed inappropriately. After discussing the data analysis plan, steps in statistical analysis and the process of writing research reports are discussed.

Step 1: Specify the Measures

In Step 1, the evaluator specifies the major variables and how they will be measured. Defining the problem and reviewing the literature lead to central concepts—or a conceptual framework—in a study. Lacking a conceptual framework, the evaluator is functionally blind. He or she selects variables on the basis of intuition and opportunity. With such an approach, the chances are high that a study will provide no strategically useful information for stakeholders.

A conceptual framework defines relationships between major variables. It is from the conceptual framework that the difficult and tedious work of operationalizing measures begins. Each measure in a study must be constructed in advance. Simple measures may consist of a single indicator. For abstract concepts such as family communication, a host of measures may be combined in indexes. Each measure and its defining elements are mapped in Step 1.

Step 2: Define Significance

How do we determine whether a difference is big enough to be significant? Evaluators usually do two things. First, they attempt to determine whether the observed difference could have occurred by chance alone. Once they have determined that a difference is so big that it could not have occurred as a result of mere variation in the data, they then ask: Is the difference big enough to make a clinical or practical difference? After specifying the measures, data analysis plans should articulate strategies for the estimation of both statistical and clinical significance.

Statistical Significance. The purpose of estimating statistical significance is to determine whether a result could have occurred by chance in the population of interest. Because samples from populations can vary, statistical tests are used to infer whether differences in populations (say, for example, the difference in placement outcomes for children of different ethnic backgrounds) are likely to exist. The null hypothesis is always that a difference does not exist. Evaluators try to reduce the chances of making what is called a Type I error, of rejecting the null hypothesis when, in fact, it is true. Most FBS research has used an $\alpha = .05$ criterion, where α is the probability of a Type I mistake. In the social and health sciences, researchers usually call differences at the .05 level "statistically significant." This means that with 5 samples out of 100 one might conclude that a difference exists when it does not. Any probability level less than .05—for example, .045 or .001—also indicates that differences in the population of interest are significant. At the start of all studies, evaluators must decide on the level of statistical significance, and in FBS research $\alpha = .05$ has usually been used.

Clinical Significance. Unfortunately, statistical significance is influenced by more than differences between groups. The amount of variation in the data and the size of the sample can produce statistically significant findings when pragmatic observers might conclude that no meaningful difference exists. A difference may be statistically significant, but as far as families go, it may have no practical value. Statistical significance is often overemphasized, and evaluators often choose alternative criteria by which to assess findings. They may make explicit decisions about clinical significance or present the data clearly enough so others can make those determinations.

244 Analyzing Findings and Writing Reports

A data analysis plan should include the criteria to be used for assessing clinical or practical significance. The criteria may be qualitative or quantitative. Suppose the difference between children whose families participated in an FBS program and those whose families did not was measured by the number of days in the home after some point in time. If 3,000 children were followed, a difference between the FBS and non-FBS groups of, say, seven days in a year might prove to be statistically significant. Is it clinically significant? How might alternative criteria be applied?

First, one might estimate the strength of the relationship between some important element of treatment, for example, parenting skills and days in the home. Because statistical significance does not indicate the strength and form of relationships, the first step in estimating the practical significance of a finding is to compute the correlation between key variables and outcomes. Is the correlation high? Is it in the expected direction? Tests of the strength expected of relationships build the argument that findings have practical significance.

Second, the cost of extra days of foster or group care might be examined. Is the cost difference large in a practical sense? Would a state legislator consider it to be significant? Can the program be considered cost-effective in relation to another "successful" FBS program with different results in terms of placement days?

Third, one might choose some scale of family functioning and measure all families on it. If the FBS and non-FBS families differ statistically significantly, one might further ask: What proportion in each group fall above some arbitrary clinical threshold? Scales such as the Achenbach Child Behavior Checklist have clinical cut points above which children are thought to be functioning poorly. Even with small samples where statistical analysis may be inappropriate, cut points for clinical significance may be identified.

With the increasing complexity of statistical analyses, it is easy to forget the simple questions. Were the differences large enough to be persuasive to stakeholders? Do the differences truly affect children, families, and workers? Good data analysis plans should include estimates of the strength of relationships and should declare alternative criteria to be used in establishing clinical significance.

Step 3: Make a Plan for Statistical Analysis

Once measures and criteria for significance have been identified, the next step in creating a data analysis plan is to specify the kinds of statistical tests to be used. All measures have measurement properties and these properties determine the range of statistical procedures that may be available to the evaluator. Common statistical tests like χ^2 and *t*-tests may or may not be appropriate. Different levels of measurement have been defined by statisticians. These levels of measurement are used to determine the kind of statistical tests to be undertaken after the data have been collected:

- *Nominal* classifies characteristics or persons into categories (e.g., females or males).
- *Ordinal* ranks characteristics or persons along some underlying dimension (e.g., poor, average, superior).
- *Interval* has the same qualities as ordinal level of measurement, and in addition, distances between numbers on a scale are equal (e.g., net worth in dollars).
- *Ratio* has the same qualities as interval level of measurement, and in addition, has a true zero (e.g., age in years).

The data analysis plan should include a table that shows each major hypothesis, the measures used to express each concept, and the statistical tests or procedures to be used to test the hypothesis. Tables such as Table 12.1 are a part of many research proposals, whether the proposal describes an FBS evaluation, a dissertation, or a research grant.

The plan may involve testing hypotheses one by one or all at once. When relationships are examined one by one, the analyses are usually described as bivariate. In an experiment, a comparison of maltreatment outcomes in the treatment and control groups would be considered bivariate because, as indicated in the second hypothesis of Table 12.1, two variables (group and child maltreatment) are examined. When third, fourth, or fifth variables are included, the tests are considered to be multivariate. An evaluator might wish to examine placement outcomes by gender in an experiment. This would involve three variables: group (treatment or control), outcome (e.g., child maltreatment), and gender. This would necessitate the use of a multivariate statistical procedure like multiple regression, analysis of variance, or LISREL.

The choice of a statistical procedure is based on the number of variables to be examined, the number of cases, and the level of measurement of each variable. Such factors as distributional properties of variables may further affect the statistics chosen. As shown in the third hypothesis of Table 12.1, a simple examination of the correlation between placement outcomes and age can involve several different statistical procedures, each with its own distinct advantages and disadvantages. Because the options are many and risks of error high, consultation is indispensable in the selection of statistical procedures. We recommend that FBS eval-

Table 12.1. Plan for Statistical Analysis

Hypotheses	Measures	Level of measurement	Procedure or statistic
Effective parental monitoring will be negatively associated with school antisocial behavior	Parental monitoring: Parent phone interview Interviewer impressions	Interval level index	Pearson *r*
	School antisocial behavior: Negative playground Social skills scale Academic time engaged Attendance Discipline contacts	Interval level index	Pearson *r*
Compared to children who receive routine child welfare services, children whose families receive FPS will be at less risk of child maltreatment	Group: FPS treatment versus routine child welfare services	Nominal	χ^2 test
	Child maltreatment: Official reports of child abuse and neglect	Nominal	χ^2 test
In a sample of children whose families received FPS, age will be significantly correlated with placement outcomes	Age in years	Interval	*t*-test or point biserial correlation
	Placement outcomes: Placement in foster care subsequent to FPS	Nominal (placed or not)	
	Days in foster care placements subsequent to FPS	Interval	Pearson correlation

uators consult with an experienced university- or agency-based program evaluator at the design and analysis phases of a project.

Step 4: Devise a Raw Data Examination and Correction Protocol

Part of the data analysis plan involves devising a protocol for examining and correcting all incoming questionnaires and schedules. No matter how good the interviewers or how conscientious the observers, they make mistakes. It may be helpful to appoint a staff member as the "data manager." It is the data manager's responsibility to examine each returned questionnaire or rating form. When errors are found, he or she should seek out the correct information immediately by contacting interviewers or observers. If information on particular questions or items is consistently incorrect, this suggests that the item is flawed or that the data collectors need additional training.

As discussed in Chapter 11, training of data gatherers can occur formally in structured settings or informally in weekly staff meetings. Both are important. We encourage FBS evaluators to involve data collection staff in regular project meetings. Errors can be reduced by establishing a protocol in which raw data are reviewed by the same person and time is allocated each week to review and discuss data collection problems.

Step 5:   Develop a Data Coding and Entry Protocol

Omissions and errors in raw data are common. Consequently, a data entry protocol must be developed to establish procedures for coding and entering information. Without such a protocol, the data entry person will be forced to make on-the-spot decisions. Over time, these decisions are likely to be inconsistent, and the data will contain errors that may bias the findings.

Data entry has been substantially simplified by the recent development of electronic data entry protocols. With electronic protocols, a template for each variable is established. If an out-of-range value is entered, the computer automatically warns the typist, making possible immediate correction. Electronic protocols can also be used by two or more data entry staff so that comparison of the entries is possible. The protocol will automatically flag entries that do not match. Doubly entered data are likely to contain fewer typographical errors, as it is not likely that different people will make exactly the same typographical errors.

ANALYZING THE DATA

Even with a carefully constructed plan, data analysis is a formidable process, but many evaluators regard this as the most exciting part of a study. It is here that hundreds of hours of work begin to reach fruition. However, it is here also that major mistakes can be made. To reduce the risk of error, a four-step process of examining the data, making transformations, conducting tests, and assessing significance is described below.

Step 1:   Examine the Univariate Data

Even with a scrupulously followed data entry protocol, double entry, and a skillful data manager, errors will creep into the data, and once there, they are hard to detect. The best way to identify errors is to conduct a univariate data analysis. Using a standard computer program it is easy to estimate means, standard deviations, medians, upper and lower limits, and a variety of helpful descriptive statistics. A univariate analysis should expose out-of-range errors, but it will not expose errors that are within the normal range of a variable. These can only be discovered by careful comparison of the original values with those in the data. This is an important limitation of univariate analyses, for a too common explanation of stunningly new and different findings is error. It is advisable, therefore, to compare univariate findings with those in previous studies. Look for obvious differences. When they are found, be a skeptic and check the accuracy of the data entry. Even with careful data entry protocols, errors can produce unusual findings.

Adjusting Missing Data. Missing data are ubiquitous. Of course, the best option is to have no missing data, to track down a respondent and obtain a valid response. In part, this is the data manager's job, but he or she is unlikely to be entirely successful. Critical decisions must be made about missing data. Should cases that have missing values be thrown out? This could reduce the sample size, reducing the power to detect differences. Can cases be thrown out on an analysis-by-analysis basis? This has the limitation of producing different samples for different analyses. If done extensively, differing results can be due to differing sample sizes. Can mean scores be used to replace missing values? This reduces the variation in the data and affects power, the ability to detect a true difference when there is one. Alternatively, can a score for the missing value be estimated on the basis of the characteristics of the respondent? This is be a viable option only if characteristics are highly correlated with the true value of the missing information. Methods of treating missing data should be determined with statistical consultation.

The Problem of Outliers. Most statistics are designed for samples where there is a normal or bell-shaped distribution of scores, and in fact, many variables used by FBS evaluators are normally distributed. But some are not. The most common reason for such "distributional problems" is outliers. Outliers are individual scores that fall three or more standard deviations beyond the mean. When an outlier is observed, an evaluator has only one choice: Investigate! In human services, families are often seen at extreme moments. Outliers can be real in the sense that they are valid indicators of the extraordinary conditions that children and families face. If an outlier validly represents an extreme circumstance, it should be left in the data.

However, outliers can also represent errors. The respondent or interviewer may have misunderstood a question, he or she may have recorded an answer incorrectly, or the data entry staff member may have made a keystroke error. Many times the only way to determine whether an outlier is a valid indicator of an extreme circumstance is to contact respondents, to examine the original instrument, and to cross-check data entry. Because outliers can affect correlations, statistical analyses should not be undertaken until all outliers have been thoroughly studied.

Step 2: Make Transformations and Construct Scales

Outliers are not the only cause of distributional problems. Some variables in FBS research are simply poorly distributed. Delinquency, for example, is rarely normally distributed. Most children commit small antisocial acts as a part of normal development. They are occasionally oppositional in the home and school, cheat on a test, or take something from their parents without permission. Fewer children engage in shoplifting or vandalism. Even fewer children steal cars or break into shops and businesses. And far fewer carry weapons or join gangs. Although delinquency is not normally distributed, it is still an important variable. The evaluator can take several steps to salvage such a variable for analysis.

Making Transformations. When a variable is poorly distributed, it can be reconstructed using arithmetic operations that convert raw scores into new numbers that have better properties for analysis. Delinquency, for example, is often considered to be a "log normal" variable. This means that, when the log of each child's delinquency score is taken, the variable loses some of its problematic characteristics. It becomes more normally distributed. Making log, square root, arcsine, quadratic, and other kinds of transformations can significantly improve statistical analyses, but it complicates interpretation.

Recoding Variables. Another common statistical practice is collapsing a variable into a smaller number of categories. Recoding occurs for a variable such as Religious Affiliation, when Methodists, Lutherans, and Baptists are collapsed into a new category called Protestants. Whenever a variable is recoded, information is lost. Unless there are too few cases for separate analysis (e.g., only five Methodists, three Lutherans, and eight Baptists), recoding should be avoided.

There is an exception to this rule. Sometimes the distribution of a variable will be so poor that a transformation cannot be used. If a variable such as Age were distributed so that 50% of the sample was under the age of 6, 25% was between the ages of 15 and 30, and 25% was over

40, it would be advisable to collapse Age into three categories. Alternatively, one might conduct three separate analyses: one for children under the age of 6; one for young adults aged 15 to 30 years; and one for middle-aged adults over 40 years. Transformations cannot remedy lack of variation, and it is occasionally necessary to recode poorly distributed variables or to conduct analyses for subgroupings of a sample.

Family-Focused Measures.   FBS evaluators often wish to construct a score for an entire family. In family research, it makes sense to measure some things at the family level. Family size and income are common family-level variables. But many family concepts are not so easy to measure. How, for example, does one measure the value that a family places on formal education? One option is to rely on the report of a single family member, say the person who bears the greater responsibility for child care. However, family members—particularly children—see many things differently. Should the views of children be included? In our view, the data analysis plan should be flexible enough to incorporate the views of many family members. In addition to creating a coding scheme for each family member, this requires the construction of indices that combine information from different family members.

Constructing Scales and Indices.   The things that interest stakeholders are often complex. They are expressed as constructs and are measured with a variety of variables. Parent-child attachment, family cohesion, parenting skill, child monitoring, antisocial behavior, and child maltreatment are all constructs that require multiple measures. To measure such constructs, variables and even entire instruments must be collapsed into scales.

While the creation of complex scales is beyond the scope of this book (for information on scale development, see DeVellis, 1991), simple family-based indices may be constructed easily. The simplest involves computing the mean score for a particular variable from the raw scores of each family member. This family "average" is used to represent the family value for a variable of interest.

Other more complex approaches involve computing the discrepancy between various family members' scores and using this discrepancy to represent the family. For example, one might ask family members to rate family communication on a 10-point scale. Once done, the evaluator might then compute a discrepancy score between parent(s) and child(ren) (or any other subgrouping of family members). A small number would suggest agreement within the family, whereas a large number would suggest that there is disagreement between parent(s) and child(ren). A variety of these kinds of measures is being developed. Some are based on weighted averages of other indexes. Others include transforming raw scores using arithmetic operations (like Euclidean distances). Still others are based on random sampling of family members (for more information, see Draper & Marcos, 1990; Grotevant & Carlson, 1989; L'Abate, 1994; L'Abate & Bagarozzi, 1993; Touliatos, Perlmutter, & Straus, 1990).

Step 3: Conduct Statistical Analyses

The purpose of statistical analysis is to distill from the many pieces of information gathered in a study those few pieces that are important. Used correctly, statistics identify central tendencies and patterns within the data. Three sequenced steps usually characterize statistical analyses: (a) description of the sample, (b) bivariate analysis, and (c) multivariate analysis. In the next few paragraphs, each step is described briefly.

Descriptive Analysis. Using univariate statistics, descriptive analysis reports the aggregate characteristics of the sample. Once transformations have been made and scales estimated, descriptive statistics are computed. The mean, median, and mode are used to describe central tendencies. The standard deviation and variance describe the amount of variation in the data. The range and frequencies portray the actual distribution of the findings. A good descriptive analysis reports means and standard deviations for interval and ratio level variables and cell counts and percentages for ordinal and nominal variables. You should select those variables that will interest various stakeholders and those that will be used later in analyses or reports.

Bivariate Analysis. The richness of many data sets is revealed in bivariate analysis. Bivariate analyses not only show differences between groups—as in *t*-tests between experimental and control groups—but correlation between variables. Correlation is the basis for much multivariate analysis. The strength of correlations points to central themes that may have practice or policy implications.

Multivariate Analysis. Multivariate analysis sorts out the relationships between many variables simultaneously. It is almost always the case that several variables will be correlated with an outcome and that these variables will not be independent of one another. This creates a knotty problem. How do we sort out what is important? Because findings are woven tightly together in a complex mass of correlations, bivariate analyses may introduce more confusion than clarity.

Multivariate statistics were designed to identify patterns in correlation matrices. Technically, a wide variety of analytic strategies may be used, but ultimately all multivariate procedures attempt to distill important patterns from the data. Such patterns are often impossible to discern by visual inspection of univariate or bivariate findings.

Different multivariate approaches work with different kinds of data. For example, multiple regression is used with an interval-level outcome measure and explanatory variables. Logit or probit regression is used with a nominal or ordinal outcome measure, and event history analysis with a time-dependent outcome (e.g., length of time to placement). There are dozens of sophisticated multivariate statistical methods (discriminant analysis, factor analysis, cluster analysis, LISREL, and so on), and in choosing them, statistical consultation is indispensable. Selection of the proper statistical technique is critical for the detection of patterns in the data and is often of major importance in producing a report that has meaning for policymakers.

Step 4: Explore the Substantive Significance of Findings

The final step in the data analysis process is the exploration of the substantive or practice value of findings. Statistical analyses are subject to a variety of influences. The order in which variables are entered into equations, the size of standard deviations, the presence of outliers, the lack of linearity, and a host of other factors can lead to elegant findings that are fictional. Statistics are merely one way of making a logical argument that a particular pattern exists. Because of a growing sense that statistical analyses provide only one (albeit important) way to view data, evaluators are turning to two additional ways or corroborating findings. These involve the estimation of effect sizes and clinical significance (Rubin & Babbie, 1989, pp. 457–458).

Effect Sizes. In experiments and, to a lesser degree, other types of studies, it is becoming increasingly important to estimate "effect" sizes. Statistical significance in an experiment is influenced by the mean difference between the experimental and control groups, the standard deviations of both groups, and the comparative sample sizes. Thus, a small difference might prove to be statistically significant because a sample size was large or a standard deviation was small. Effect size (ES) was developed to convert group differences into a common measure for comparison across studies.

As ES for an interval or ratio level outcome measure such as Days in the Home is estimated by:

$$ES = (\mu_t - \mu_c)/s$$

The symbols μ_t and μ_c represent the mean scores for the average Days in the Home of children in the treatment and control populations, and s is the pooled standard deviation of each group.

There are different formulas for different kinds of effect sizes. An arcsine transformation may be used, for example, with proportional outcomes. This would be appropriate for FBS studies that use the proportion of children placed or not placed as an outcome:

$$ESp = f_t - f_c$$

The symbol ES_p represents the estimator for a difference in proportions, and f_t and f_c are the arcsine transformations of the proportions of treatment and control children who experience an outcome event (e.g., placement or abuse) subsequent to receiving services (Lipsey, 1990, p. 87).

Because effect sizes are in a z-score format, it is possible to compare them across studies. Although there are some confounds in making such comparisons, effect sizes that are less than .30 are considered small, while effect sizes larger than .50 or .55 are considered large (Cohen, 1988; Lipsey, 1990, p. 56).

Clinical Significance. In determining clinical significance, an evaluator addresses a basic question: Are the findings significant in some practical way? Statistical significance does not indicate the strength of an association. It merely indicates that an observed difference could not have occurred by chance. Both the strength and the form of relationships should be estimated.

To address the real-world significance of FBS programs, evaluators often establish separate criteria for clinical significance. Value judgments must be made about findings. If a family-based delinquency prevention program produces a 1% reduction in property crimes, it is not likely to be found effective. But if property crimes could be reduced by 1% nationally, legislators might look upon such a program quite favorably. On the other hand, statistically significant differences may be viewed as insignificant from a substantive perspective. If a program reduces the number of property offenses for an average offender from 17.2 in a typical year to 11.5, a policy-maker might conclude that society continues to be at too great a risk with such a program.

Ultimately, the findings must be addressed from a value perspective. You can do this by using established criteria, by exploring the issue of clinical significance in the Discussion Section of the research report, or by just reporting the data and allowing others to draw interpretations. Many scales have "clinical" or "problem" cut points and scores above these established cut points are considered substantively significant. The proportion of families falling above and below these cut points can be used to augment arguments for clinical significance. In addition, the views of family members and other experts in the field can be brought to bear upon the issue of substantive significance. Reports and anecdotes from consumers about the apparent effectiveness of services can be especially persuasive, as can analyses that illuminate the cost of service relative to its outcomes and to the cost of alternative services.

Summary

As discussed earlier, data analysis may be broken down into four steps. By examining the univariate characteristics of variables, an evaluator determines whether the statistics selected in the data analysis plan are appropriate. Assumptions must be met, and when they are not, transformations may be used. At the same time, outliers are investigated and the measurement properties of scales and indexes are tested.

In the four-step model, a bottom-up approach was described. Following univariate analyses and "data manipulation" (making transformations, recoding skewed variables, and constructing scales or indexes), bivariate and multivariate analyses are undertaken according to the data analysis plan. Additional analyses may estimate the substantive impact of services in terms of effect sizes, clinically meaningful cut points, and costs.

All this constitutes the findings that make up the meat of research reports. The final step in making sense of the data involves communicating the findings to stakeholders and others. While the jargon and economy of statistics makes sense to technical experts, the making-sense process is not complete until reports that interpret the findings for others are written.

THE RESEARCH REPORT

Writing is a skill, a craft, and an art. It takes practice. There is a latent structure in much writing. Moreover, in writing research reports, there is both a latent structure and a distinctive style. In this section, we will focus on this structure and style.

The Structure of a Research Report

Good writing comes from good organization and from using a simple structure for research reports. Before beginning to write, many evaluators outline the steps that will take the reader from the beginning of a report to its end. In reporting the results of an evaluation, you may wish to use the time-tested format shown in Figure 12.1. This format provides

---

GUIDELINES FOR AN EVALUATION MANUSCRIPT

  I. Title Page
     A. Title
     B. Author's Name and Affiliation
  II. Executive Summary
 III. Introduction Section
     A. Briefly Describe the Problem. Use Data.
     B. Briefly Discuss the Relevant Literature
     C. State the Purpose of the Report, including Hypotheses (If Any)
  IV. Methods Section
     A. Briefly Describe Subjects or Sample in Terms of:
        1. Sample Size(s)
        2. Sampling Criteria
           a. Inclusionary Criteria
           b. Exclusionary Criteria
        3. Dropouts, Refusals
        4. Demographic Characteristics of Participants
        5. Informed-Consent Procedures
     B. Briefly Describe Research Procedures (As Appropriate)
        1. Design
        2. Program Description
        3. Outcomes Measures
        4. Explanatory or Independent Measures (Other Than FBS Treatment)
  V. Results Section
     A. Describe the Main Findings
     B. Present Data to Support Findings and Conclusions
  VI. Discussion Section
     A. Discuss Support for Hypotheses
     B. Describe Theoretical Implications
     C. Describe Practice or Policy Implications
     D. Acknowledge Limitations of the Design
     E. Suggest Implications for Future Research
 VII. References

Figure 12.1. Components of an evaluation or research report. Adapted from: American Psychological Association (1983). *Publication Manual*, 3rd ed. Washington, DC: Author.

a template for developing reports based on most quantitative research designs. As described in Chapter 10, reports from qualitative studies have more narrative and employ alternative formats.

A research report usually has seven sections. Each section is designed to show the reader the different elements of a study—from purpose, through literature review, to findings and implications. The data and findings should be presented cautiously. This lets readers assess for themselves the importance of the findings. Theoretical, practice, policy, and research implications should take into account the limitations of the design. In the next few paragraphs, we will describe the major sections of a research report.

Title. The title should describe the central purpose of the report. It should be sufficiently explanatory that a person who picks up a report and reads the cover page will know immediately the issues and ideas addressed in the manuscript. Bad titles have too many words and leave the reader uninformed, for example:

A NIMH Study of User Response to CATI

Excess words (like "study"), acronyms (like NIMH and CATI), and abstruse language (like "user response") condemn this paper to a small audience. A better title might read:

Advances in Telephone Survey Methods

To be sure, this is not a topic that generates widespread interest, but this title at least lets readers know the main topic covered by the paper.

Executive Summary. The Executive Summary is the most widely read section of many reports and will determine whether readers approach the report with enthusiasm or passivity (or continue to read it at all). The abstract should be a precise summary of the problem, design, findings, and implications. It should stand alone, avoiding abbreviations, acronyms, and technical language that require definition.

Introduction. Most FBS evaluations are oriented toward social problems, and the particular problem addressed by the report should be identified immediately. Use the problem to engage the reader:

> Failure rates in FBS have been high for drug-involved children and their families. Recent data suggest that as many as three in five families with drug involvement will drop out of FBS. The purpose of this report is to . . .

The introduction should briefly state the purpose of the report and summarize relevant literature. It should make use of both local and national data. In general, the goal of a good introduction is to state the purpose of the study and to show how the study builds logically upon previous studies. If findings from previous studies are equivocal, the writer should acknowledge conflicting reports.

In longer research reports, introductions are followed by detailed literature reviews. They focus on characteristics of the social problem and prior attempts to address it. Often the research methods of major studies are reviewed. In these reports, the literature review includes description of research designs, major measures, sample sizes, and findings. In shorter research reports, the literature review is often a brief summary of central findings.

Methods Section. The Methods Section describes the research design. As shown in Figure 12.1, it has many different subsections. At least five topics should be addressed under Subjects. In addition to giving the sample sizes, sampling criteria should be described. In FBS evaluations, inclusionary and exclusionary criteria are common. It is also appropriate to discuss the characteristics of families that refused to participate in the study or dropped out during data collection. Many evaluators compare such families to those who stayed involved and develop small appendices on "bias due to dropout." Further, procedures to protect family members' informed consent should also be described.

The Methods Section summarizes the conduct of the study. Procedures to ensure that FBS was delivered consistently over time and, if relevant, across sites should be explained. Staff training and characteristics, plus the central elements of the service, should be briefly described. Finally, the selection of measures should be discussed. If instruments were used, their reliability and validity for FBS populations should be reviewed in an Appendix. In short, the Methods Section both describes and defends the decisions that an evaluator made about the research design.

Results or Findings Section. The Results Section summarizes the main findings. Tables and figures should include enough detail so that critics can determine whether methods were used correctly. When statistics are presented, information about the size of the test statistic, the degrees of freedom, the significance level, and, if appropriate, the direction of the relationship should be presented. Findings that relate to hypotheses or main purposes of the research should be presented. It may be better to produce several reports on small topics, than to produce one large report.

Discussion Section. The Discussion Section is where the writer is given comparatively free reign. Here, you may offer interpretations, cast findings in the context of theory, respond to critics, outline limitations, and draw implications. (See Chapter 13 for some cautions regarding drawing conclusions from research.) If your reports began with a discussion of a social problem, you should return to it in the Discussion Section. The writer should indicate how the study contributes to knowledge about the problem. Some readers may disagree with the answer, but writers have license to interpret their findings, make inferences about relationships, and point out directions for future research.

The Style of a Research Report

Styles are changing. In the past, it was viewed as inappropriate to use first and second person in a research report. A research report was supposed to be impersonal in the same way that science was thought to be impersonal and objective. Third-person and passive voice dominated. The problem is that this makes for boring reading.

Our advice is to try to strike a balance in the use of tense and voice. In general, most research reports use past tense, because the data have been collected weeks or months ago. They also tend to be in the third person. However, extensive use of past tense and third person detract from a report. We suggest that you use a bit of present tense, particularly if the time elapsing between data collection and report writing is not more than two years. Variety leads to effective writing.

The goal of research writing is clear communication. Without sacrificing precision, scientific writing can have style. But it should also be unambiguous, concise, and fluid (for more on this topic, see Alley, 1987). Albert Einstein, clearly one of the preeminent scientists of the twentieth century, wrote with descriptive richness that translated difficult concepts into easily understood images. In describing the mechanics of space and time, Einstein wrote:

> I stand at the window of a railway carriage which is traveling uniformly, and I drop a stone on the embankment, without throwing it. Then, disregarding the influence of air resistance, I see the stone descend in a straight line. A pedestrian who observes the misdeed from the footpath notices that the stone falls to earth in a parabolic curve. I now ask: Do the "positions" traversed by the stone lie "in reality" on a straight line or on a parabola? (1961, p. 9)

Although it describes an enormously complex operation, Einstein's paragraph communicates in a clear, fluid fashion. He used an image to engage the reader; used carefully, they can enhance the effectiveness of research writing. To write this way requires hard work, but it makes for an effective manuscript. And the creation of an effective manuscript is the final challenge in making sense of the data.

CONCLUSION

The process of making sense of the data starts at the beginning of the study. As a study is being formulated, a data analysis plan should be devised. While these plans may vary in composition, most plans will include the specification of measurement model, criteria for statistical and clinical significance, statistical procedures being used, and protocols for data entry and coding. By doing this groundwork, small problems can be identified and resolved before they grow into large problems.

Statistical analysis is itself a process of uncovering and distilling simplicities from complexities. It begins with simple univariate analyses to describe the characteristics of the sample. Then it proceeds to bivariate analyses. These may take the form of comparisons across groups of the estimation of correlation between critical variables and constructs. Only when bivariate patterns are fully known should evaluators begin the work of building multivariate models. Finally, statistical analysis is not complete until the substantive significance of the findings is explored. This involves estimating effect sizes and clinical significance.

A well-targeted and clearly written report has the potential to influence public policy. However, this does not always happen. How the data are presented, who is involved in interpreting the research findings, and the context and design of the study itself are important. In the next chapter, guest author Charles Gershenson addresses these issues.

Chapter 13

Social Policy and Evaluation: An Evolving Symbiosis

CHARLES GERSHENSON

Local, state, and federal governments are continually endeavoring to address changing social conditions with social policies that improve the general welfare of families and children. While policymakers work in complex bureaucratic organizations clothed in centuries of history and culture, social scientists engaged in evaluation studies work in less complex organizational structures clothed in the staid traditions of academia and scientific entrepreneurship. Yet, increasingly, policymakers and evaluators are forming a symbiotic relationship. This chapter will describe the nature and pitfalls of this curious relationship. It will provide a cautionary note about the multiple roles of evaluators, and will posit some practical ways of improving the usefulness of evaluation data.

EVALUATION AND POLICY

Conceptual Framework

The task of evaluating FBS and the concepts presented in this book should be viewed within a larger conceptual framework. Evaluation is a scientific process that generates information to address policy, practice, and administrative concerns. These concerns arise continually in a dynamic society, beginning with the identification of a social issue by the mass media, by an advocacy group, or at times from research.

Once the issue is identified, "practice wisdom," research (literature review, examining published data, retrieving data from management

261

information systems, quick surveys, purposive sampling of informed people, etc.), and other analytical tools are used to *define the problem*. This includes specification of the social problem by determining its scope and trend, the consequences for the involved individuals, families, and communities, the present and future costs to society, first approximation to causal factors (hunches), and the status of current efforts to resolve the issue.

After the social problem is defined and considered significant, a policy decision is made to search for alternative solutions. This may entail using an "on-the-shelf" study that has indications of effectiveness. More often, there is no such study and a series of demonstration studies are launched that are targeted to the defined social issue. These studies are truly experimental, and evaluation efforts that focus on program outcomes are critical. Part of this phase may involve social "research and development" (R&D) oriented evaluation efforts to refine an intervention model before it is ready to be proposed to policymakers for implementation on a wider basis (Rothman, 1980).

When there is sufficient evidence that alternative solutions are available, then the task flows back to the policymakers to assess the evaluative evidence, the costs, the organizational requirements, the people and training required, the impact on the existing network of services and policies, *and its priority in relation to other social needs* (the political context).

Legislative action codifies the policy decision in reference to the social issue. With complementary action to provide funds, the implementation of the policy is then assigned to the agency administrator. Process evaluation provides the administrator with the necessary information about whether the implementation is basically in accord with the "proven" demonstrations. Process evaluation is a component of internalized quality assurance procedures, which include detection of "side-effects." These studies involve analyses of program integrity (e.g., validity, stability over time, consistency of services across staff and offices). This implementation may take from three to five years, depending on the complexity of the task, the competence of the leadership and staff, and the resources available.

After program implementation is relatively stable, there is a clear understanding of the interventive process, and the administrator is "proud" of the new program, an impact evaluation is used to measure its effect on the defined social issue. Issues of costs are examined throughout the implementation and operational phases of the program.

This social change paradigm links social issues to policies and program implementation in a reciprocal manner, with circular causality in which different evaluation modalities are used to enhance the information flow necessary for critical decision-making.

What Should We Expect from Program "Evaluation"?

Both the research and policy communities are currently in a state of confusion about what is expected from "evaluation." Greater status is attached to "outcome" and "impact" research, with little understanding of the purpose of different types of research and the need for other forms of evaluation. Process, or formative, evaluation is not taken seriously and is most often superficially implemented. Imagine the consequences to pharmaceutical firms if there were only sporadic efforts at controlling the quality of manufactured drugs. *Because we have confidence in their quality* we can use them in clinical trials to measure effectiveness. This is true for all "hard" services whether they be housing units, food stamps, or AFDC checks.

When services depend on the interaction of provider/consumer, as in social services, mental health, and education, the use of "outcome" measures is meaningless unless there is some awareness of the quality of the interaction. That is the difficult and complex task of process evaluation. The interaction is the "social pill" that is meant to help vulnerable people and families. Typically, at best, all we can do is provide crude counts of intensity—contact hours per defined period of time—and training curricula that are supposed to delimit and define the nature and content of interaction. What is inside these social pills remains a black box. Here is a role for the service-oriented and qualitative research components of evaluation. Here is where the evaluation of FBS is weakest. Here is where greater emphasis should be placed in the next generation of studies. A more definitive set of findings with respect to outcomes will remain elusive until we understand the social pills that are being dispensed.

Thus, as discussed in Chapter 1, it is important to understand the intervention itself before moving to assess other major evaluation domains such as program impact on youth and families, and public policy. The interrelationship of these domains may be addressed by "system" evaluation efforts, which were described in the Appendix to Chapter 1.

Policy Issues

Evaluation is a scientific process for generating specific information to guide policy, administrative, and judicial decisions. Policymakers are usually lawyers or administrators rather than social scientists; evaluators are almost always social scientists. Increasingly, however, lawyers who are involved in class action suits against failing human service systems have taken on evaluative roles or are using evaluation data produced by others. These class action lawsuits have introduced the judiciary as policymakers, thereby involving every branch of government in the utilization of evaluation in the decision-making process. The executive, legislative, and judiciary branches of government rely increasingly upon findings from evaluation studies to articulate social policies, guide legislation, and inform consent decrees.

As late as 1965 the definition of social policy was unclear. Alternative definitions were developed during the 1960s and 1970s. The U.S. Children's Bureau of the Department Health and Human Services initiated a study conducted to define social policy and to develop an analytical framework for policy analysis. After developing a theory of social policy, Gil (1990, pp. 23–24) offered the definition in Table 13.1.

This definition links the objectives of social policies to broad institutional processes and social outcomes. It provides the holistic framework

---

Table 13.1. Definition of Social Policy[a]

Social policies are guiding principles for ways of life, motivated by basic and perceived human needs. They were derived by people from the structures, dynamics, and values of their ways of life, and they serve to maintain or change these ways. Social policies tend to, but need not, be codified in formal legal instruments. All extant social policies of a given society at a given time, constitute an interrelated, yet not necessarily internally consistent system of social policies.

Social policies operate through the following essential institutional processes and their manifold interactions:
    a. development, management, and conservation of natural and human created resources;
    b. organization of work and production of life-sustaining and life-enhancing, concrete and non-concrete, goods and services;
    c. exchange and distribution of life-sustaining and life-enhancing goods and services, and of social, civil, and political rights and responsibilities;
    d. governance and legitimization;
    e. reproduction, socialization, and social control.

Through the operations and interactions of these essential institutional processes, social policies shape the following linked outcome variables of ways of life:
    a. circumstances of living of individuals, groups, and classes;
    b. power of individuals, groups, and classes;
    c. nature and quality of human relations among individuals, groups, and classes;
    d. overall quality of life.

---

[a] *Source:* Gil (1990:23–24).

for any evaluation directed at informing policy formulation. An evaluation informs the policymaker about objectives, service processes, and outcomes as they relate to a specified social issue or problem (see Chapter 2). In practice, evaluation outcomes focus on circumstances of living and quality of life, but rarely include power and quality of human relations.

POLICY PROCESS AND EVALUATION

The National Academy of Sciences published a seminal volume in 1978, *Knowledge and Policy: The Uncertain Connection* (Lynn, 1978). The chapter by Weiss, "Improving the Linkage between Social Research and Public Policy," is an excellent, thoughtful, and comprehensive analysis of the difficulties in linking research to policy development. It points out the different motives of the respective individuals involved: the policymaker seeking ways to make "wiser decisions" and the researcher seeking ways to advance knowledge for policymakers.

Paraphrasing Weiss (1978), the following are "Principles of Policy-Research Connections" (with examples from FBS in brackets):

1. "Social scientists often have grandiose expectations, perhaps tainted with self-interest, of the potential effects of social research on policy" (p. 35). [Evaluators hope to produce the seminal study that conclusively proves the worth of FBS.]

2. When research is used for problem-solving types of evaluation, "It is assumed that both policy makers and researchers tend to agree on what the desired end should be; the contribution of research is to help the identification and selection of the appropriate means to reach that goal" (p. 28). [Yet too often in FBS the most important outcome criteria are not agreed upon, or if shared, the criteria may not fit the program model.]

3. "The less able policy makers are to crystallize their information needs, the less likely they are to use the research effectively" (p. 44). [Federal and state officials posed vague demands of FBS programs in the 1980s.]

4. "Different [institutional] locations create different perceptions of policy issues. Each set of actors in the policy process responds to the incentives and rewards of their own positions" (p. 46). [Witness the policy tug of war between voluntary FBS agencies and legislators in California, Illinois, and other states.]

5. "Researchers often choose and conceptualize problems in terms

of the methodologies in which they are proficient" (p. 44). [There is a dearth of small, controlled clinical trials and rigorous qualitative investigations in FBS.]

6. "Researchers are affected by the state of their science; its maturity in theory, knowledge, and method sets limits on the authoritativeness of their research" (p. 37). [More sophisticated statistical analyses are only recently being applied in FBS.]

7. "The way in which research is funded affects its formulation" (p. 49). [This is one of the reasons why early federal research on FBS did not result in the use of experimental designs.]

8. "[T]he writing of research reports tends to be turgid" (p. 51). [This clearly inhibits FBS practitioners' use of research data.]

9. "Some research findings provide no clear-cut conclusions" (p. 52). [Many of the FBS studies fall into this grouping.]

10. "In moving from analysis of data to recommendations for action, researchers must leave the world of fact and science" (p. 55). [A note of caution that needs to be clearly highlighted in many FBS reports.]

11. "Dissemination tends to be nobody's job" (p. 57). [Witness the many "fugitive" reports of FBS studies.]

12. "Whatever research shows, the political climate places limits on what kinds of changes will be countenanced, how fast, and at what cost" (p. 60). [See, for example, how fast FBS were expanded in Michigan and Iowa.]

13. "If they [researchers] have done a relevant and competent study, if it reaches the people who can use it, and if it is intelligible to them, then they have done their job" (p. 62). [These are some of the lessons from the Oregon Permanency Planning Project and Head Start from which the FBS field can benefit.]

Weiss concentrated on the translation of policy issues into research questions and the retranslation of answers into policy recommendations. The former provides the foundation for the design and conduct of evaluations and the latter derives its authority from the findings. This cryptological task is the most important contribution of evaluation to the policy decision process.

LIMITATIONS IN THE EVALUATION APPROACH FOR POLICY

Social policies in a democratic society are promulgated primarily through a contentious and adversarial process, which includes an examination of alternatives. People disagree on all aspects of social policy:

defining the social issue, specifying objectives and means to achieve them, and implementation. These disagreements are manifested in the various information streams that converge upon the policymaker. Evaluation studies are only one of a number of these streams, which may include anecdotal testimonials, historical material, polling surveys, census data, economic data, social data, mass media stories, petitions, and "wise-person" judgments.

Complexity and the Need for Critical Tests

Evaluation, unlike some of the other information streams, is based on social science research principles to ensure valid findings. It uses a social science research paradigm in which it is assumed that a social problem is addressed by a specified intervention to achieve desired outcomes. Basically, it posits a linear cause-and-effect relationship, sometimes expressed as a regression equation. This "general linear model" is well understood by the evaluator and policymaker. It is deceptively and seductively simple, and it seldom models well the dynamics of human service delivery systems or their clients (Cronbach & Associates, 1980).

For many decades, policymakers, educators, and the public have been concerned about the quality of public education. The use of more resources has been the most common solution, but in 1981 the effectiveness of this approach was challenged in an article by Hanushek (cited in Spencer & Wiley, 1981). He concluded, after reviewing 130 evaluation studies that used the linear regression model that there was no relationship between expenditures and the achievement of students. This was challenged by Spencer and Wiley (1981), who questioned the linear assumptions used in evaluation studies. Anderson puzzled, "Why do we, as a policy analytic community, replicate experiments for 15 years without devising 'critical tests' to help answer the prior methodological question of whether such production models either are able to measure real effects or are just a silly waste of time?" (1983, p. 298). In FBS, the growing use of nonlinear models (see, e.g., Fraser et al., 1991), qualitative methods (Chapter 10), and systems-level analyses (Appendix for Chapter 1) holds much potential for improvement.

Values and Politics as Critical Factors

As described in the previous chapters, the task of designing a study is both complex and difficult. Every stage of the process—from describing the problem, formation of the research design, specifying the measurement procedures, selecting the statistical methods, choosing sampling procedures, dealing with missing data and cases, setting probability levels, defining criteria for practical significance, interpreting the findings, to making recommendations—requires *value* judgments. Evaluation studies, no matter how closely they adhere to scientific principles, are saturated with value judgments, any one of which can be questioned. This questioning of latent decisions, values, and assumptions in studies happens frequently in congressional hearings. For example, in a report for the U.S. House of Representatives, Select Committee on Children, Youth, and Families, the majority (Democrats) projected the 1995 foster population based on an annual increase of 7.2%, using 1985 as the base year. The "Dissenting Views" of the minority (Republican) members stated, "Choosing which year to begin with is significant. By excluding 1980, the majority projects a 7.2% annual increase in foster care children to 1995. But if we included 1980, we would find a 1.5% rate of increase. Obviously, the number of children projected to be in foster care would be much lower." As of 1993, the APWA currently estimates that there were 460,000 children in foster care. The majority estimate was 481,000, the minority estimate was 366,000, and my estimate (never published) was 458,000 using a 6.9% annual increase (U.S. House of Representatives, Select Committee on Children Youth, and Families, 1990).

When dealing with legislative bodies, most of the real work is done by the staff of the various committees that review specific legislative proposals. In many instances, staff are social scientists well versed in social science concepts. Many are graduates of policy schools, Bush Foundation policy centers, and academic departments of economics, sociology, psychology, political science and public administration (with a few from social work). They critically examine evaluation studies, review the literature, and know which foundations or individuals to call upon for a supportive or critical review of evaluation findings.

All Evaluations Are Questioned and Criticized

Those who support the findings of a research effort tend to approve the way in which the study was executed, and those with opposing views have little difficulty in pointing out the study's limitations. While this has a partisan flavor, it does not differ basically from the disagreements within professions where the process for expressing differences of opinion is less confrontational and often reduced to protracted debate in journals. As Lynn wrote, "Policy making that takes place within the framework of an adversary process can hardly be scientific or rational" (1978, p. 16). Despite this contentiousness and the lack of a "definitive" set of findings, Congress continues to provide resources for program evaluation, as there appears to be no better alternative for generating needed information.

ARE EVALUATION FINDINGS MEANINGFUL?

Evaluation is "exoteric research" while social research includes both esoteric and exoteric research. Exoteric research, which is problem-oriented research, is conducted to produce specific information that will inform policy analysis. Research findings are expected to be relevant, usable, and stable over short time periods. Information lacking any of these characteristics has little, if any, utility.

Findings from evaluation research are frequently expressed in probability terms and effect sizes. Yet many policymakers understand only percentages, means, medians, and correlation. Beyond that, when other statistics are used, they are fully dependent upon the evaluator for interpretation. For example, how does one refer to or use data significant at the 10% level, the 5% level, and the .1% (.001) level, all in the same study? And what does it mean that some relationships are "not significant"? Some evaluators confuse policymakers and themselves by using the term "not significant" when they mean "not determinable" due to unacceptably low statistical power.

This statistical babble is further confused by defensive statements: "Findings need to be interpreted with great caution." "The reader is urged to recognize the limitations of the data due to lack of random sampling." "While we have lost 60 percent of our sample due to attrition, our analysis of the remaining 40 percent shows." The policymaker cannot deal with this ambiguity and uncertainty. Fortunately, policymakers rarely see these statements buried in the research report as they concentrate on the findings and recommendations. By the time some investigators draft these sections of reports, cautionary amnesia has set in, and all findings are reported with greater certitude.

A more serious problem for the policymaker is understanding what the researcher means by *significant*. The evaluator's *significant* most often refers to probability levels obtained from using "tests of significance" to generalize findings from the study sample to the larger population. While this significance is necessary for the policymaker, it is not sufficient. Some misinterpret the word *significant*, thinking it means *important*. But as discussed in Chapter 12, the policymaker needs to know the effect size and whether it is large enough to be cost-effective. Practical or program significance cannot be ignored, for this is what the policymaker is seeking.

Most evaluation findings that are statistically significant have effect sizes between 10 and 40%, skewed heavily toward 10%. The policymaker is usually not aware of this and believes that statistical significance implies program significance. Since program significance is a value judgment, this has to be determined by specifying the minimum effect size, in advance, by the policy or program staff members. It should not be left by default to the evaluator.

FRAMING EVALUATION RECOMMENDATIONS

As noted previously, the translation of evaluation findings to policy recommendations requires a shift away from the conservative canons of social science. To what? Advocacy! Whose responsibility is this task? Who has the capacity and competence to translate evaluation findings into recommendations? Should the recommendations for the policymaker be based solely on the findings or should the findings be the core foundation of a larger information base and set in a context of social and economic costs, values, and ethics?

At times during the 1980s, the U.S. Children's Bureau's Request for Proposals (RFP) for evaluation studies would specify that the evaluator *should not include recommendations* in the final report. Too often, it was found that when recommendations were requested the evaluator would prepare a list that contained some relevant suggestions combined with a wish list of non sequiturs. Many recommendations were simplistic, and did not recognize the complexity of service delivery systems and the political climate. There was rarely an admission that the findings are indeterminate, or of little or no value to the policymaker. Nor is the general recommendation to support further research viewed as other than self-serving. When made, such recommendations need to be specific as to the nature of the research, approximate cost, time frame, and usefulness of the expected findings.

The choice the funding agency makes either to select a principal investigator who is excellent in methodology but naive about the subject area or to select someone who is well informed and experienced in the subject area and moderately good in methodology is important. To get excellence in both areas in a single individual is rare. Currently there are more people who are well qualified in methodology and very few who really know child welfare systems.

Recommendations from the naive investigator reflect a narrow perspective that generally lacks an historical base and is informed primarily by the study's findings, with little regard to the social change process and context. In contrast, the knowledgeable investigator has a broader understanding of the findings, but invariably has accumulated biases. There is no simple solution to this dilemma—resorting to a team structure combining methodologists, program experts, and policymakers appears to offer a feasible solution.

Perhaps another solution involves shifting roles somewhat—the evaluator's task should be completed with a well-written and understandable description of the study emphasizing the *findings,* thereby allowing advocates and policymakers to draw their own conclusions. Let the evaluator remain the scientist and let the advocate, having read and understood the scientific findings, make the recommendations. Otherwise, the scientist has become an advocate who truly understands the findings and their limitations. Allowing a "halo effect" to mislead the public and policymaker into believing that the evaluator's recommendations, per se, are necessarily valid, cogent, feasible, or timely is a serious mistake.

Yet, the whole purpose of evaluation is to contribute to knowledge in a way that informs the policy decision process. Recommendations must flow from the study, even in the extreme case of suggesting that the study findings be ignored. What additional information is necessary to assist in the formulation of recommendations? Answers to, or at least an awareness of, the questions of concern to the policy analyst listed in Table 13.2 would assist in the construction of recommendations as well as for testing the appropriateness, feasibility, and validity of the final policy recommendations.

TIME FRAMES AND LAGS

Both the policymaker and the evaluator watch the clock. But the clocks have different dials: the analog clock of the policymaker spans two years while that of the evaluator measures five years. Policymakers need to act quickly (Weiss, 1987), before the next election, the next appointment, the next promotion, and/or the next crisis. Evaluators' clocks require five years, most often reduced to two to three years due to pressures from administrators, politicians, or funders, for the *initial study,* let alone replication. Policy formulation takes a great deal of time in a democratic society, but the policymakers need information as soon as a social issue or problem emerges. Consequently, more frequently than we would like to believe, policy decisions are made on available information, no matter how limited or questionable.

Evaluators, conducting their studies in ecologically valid environ-

Table 13.2. Questions of Concern to Policy Analysts

1. Who are the primary stakeholders affected by the recommendations? Who gains and who loses power, status, resources, or jobs?
2. Is the evidence convincing that there is a sufficient effect size to merit system changes? (The question is posed in this peculiar manner as effect size is determined *after and not before* the service is completed.)
3. Do the findings lead to changes of an existing program, service, or delivery system or lead to a new system?
4. What is the likely decrease in program effectiveness of the "multiplier effect" when shifting from a demonstration at a limited site to broad based implementation?
5. What resources and amount of time will be required to develop the necessary infrastructure to support the proposed changes? Particularly important is a management information system.
6. How receptive is the political and social climate to proposed changes? The social climate includes both those providing services and those expected to utilize them. Of great importance is the impact on the "street-level bureaucrat" who, in the final analysis, implements policy.
7. Who trains the trainers? Is there a developed training curriculum? How many people can be trained within a fixed time limit? Are the required skills and knowledge alien to staff, significantly different from their training and work experience?
8. What is the learning curve for implementing changes and how long will it take for the staff to be "proud" of their program?
9. What are the costs for implementation? Operation? How will it be financed? Using old or new dollars?
10. What are the opportunity costs? What alternatives exist and what are their respective merits and negatives? There is usually at least one alternative: improve the quality of the existing program through improved administration, improved training of staff, improved salaries and working conditions, and a continuous quality improvement (CQI) process.
11. What are the possible negative side-effects and how are they to be minimized? Positive side-effects?
12. What was the role and character of the leadership in the evaluated program? Is it transferable?
13. What is the history of program changes that addressed the issue? Can the system tolerate another change?
14. Are the findings supported by other studies, clinical practice, or simulated modeling?
15. What is the impact of proposed changes on the larger delivery system?

ments (the real world) cannot control the social context in which they generate data. This social context introduces time lags throughout the evaluation process, from the time it takes to approve a contract for an evaluation study, to review and approval of the final report draft and its transmission to the policymakers. More serious are the time lags that occur in implementing a program or service. As discussed in Chapter 11, the initial recruitment and training of staff take more time than anticipated, initial referrals are slow until the project achieves credibility, community agreements take an inordinate amount of time to consummate, and the development of management procedures and information systems is slowed by the burden posed for everyone.

Time itself is an issue—in terms of the amount of time necessary to study programs, to frame critical policy questions, and to evaluate critical outcomes, such as child abuse, arrest, or placement. What is a reasonable amount of time to allow for a relatively rare event to occur? During the service? Immediately after termination of an FBS intervention? One year? Two years? A lifetime? A generation? What time frames are appropriate for FBS studies? Is FBS a psychosocial vaccine or a crisis intervention service—is it expected to "protect" the family for years to come or to help them cope with a current situation?

Previous FBS studies have assessed outcomes over as long as two years. Does the policymaker have a different time frame? Policymakers often expect long-term solutions based on inexpensive, short-term interventions. There are too many problems on their agenda for repeated attention to what they perceive as the same problem. Congress was led to believe, and wanted to believe, that passage of P.L. 96–272, the Adoption Assistance and Child Welfare Act of 1980, would reduce the problem of "drift" for children in foster care and promote the adoption of children with special needs. "Reasonable efforts" to avoid child placement was more a hope than a designated program. Thirteen years later, Congress provided additional funds for "reasonable efforts" by providing funds for family preservation and support services.

These changes in child welfare policy illustrate the disjointed and incremental nature of social change and policy development. An incremental change perspective requires a long time span. Policies that support incremental changes are more likely to be approved than those which seek to completely overhaul existing policies and programs (witness the national health care debate!).

EVALUATION AND CHILD WELFARE LEGISLATION

Policies are formulated and implemented. Legislated policies never reflect a single set of recommendations, no matter how well thought through. The political process requires bargaining, compromises, and concern for constituencies. The resultant policy may be prescriptive or general. The former allows little latitude and the latter great latitude in implementation. The nature of the recommendations has great impact on policymakers' choices.

The Adoption Assistance and Child Welfare Act of 1980 is a good example of what happens in the policy process. There was clear understanding of what was necessary to move children out of foster care into permanent placements based on the Oregon Project (Emlen et al., 1978). Prescriptive foster care protections and monies were legislated to reduce the time children remained in foster care. However, there was little information available on how to prevent placement. This lack of information led to a "reasonable efforts" clause without further specification and without any earmarking of funds for the purpose.

By 1993 there was a great deal more information concerning "reasonable efforts" to avoid placement by strengthening families using family support and family preservation services. This new body of information, the result of many evaluations for more than a decade, contributed significantly to the 1993 legislation, which authorized approximately $1.2 billion in federal and matching state funds for family preservation and family support service through 1998 (Omnibus Budget Reconciliation Act, 1993). Again, because there was useful information, the legislation was framed in a prescriptive mode to make certain that the states and local communities understood the policy decisions Congress had made. Approximately an additional $17 million was earmarked by the administration for evaluation and $10 million for training and technical assistance. The next set of challenges associated with this legislation includes evaluating the implementation and effects of these programs in ways that reflect the community context and the degree of program maturity.

CONCLUSION

Policy formulation and policy changes are increasingly informed by studies and testimonials of exemplary programs, innovative service demonstrations, and occasional large-scale, multisite, natural "experiments." Program administrators and advocates rely on testimonials when information based on the scientific gathering and analysis of data are unavailable. Evaluators rely on the outcomes of their research designs that attempt to adhere to scientific principles in data generation and analysis.

Both approaches have their merits and weaknesses. As the authors of this volume have shown in the previous chapters, the goal is to shift from the testimonial approach toward a fuller and more valid documentation of the service process and results arising from a formal evaluation study. The problems encountered by the evaluator are many, as are the problems faced by the frontline worker who first steps across the threshold of a home to meet a family with ambivalent or hostile feelings. In essence, both practitioners and evaluators must work collaboratively to produce findings that are relevant for policy formulation.

Administrators and clinical practitioners will improve service delivery in their FBS programs through a careful reading of the collective wisdom of the contributing authors while simultaneously achieving greater control and direction of the evaluation process. This will strengthen and enhance the validity of study recommendations because they will be based on findings translated by the very practitioners who know the past practices, experience the current practices, and are responsible for implementing future practices.

Evaluators, particularly those who have had little experience with FBS, will learn the many nuances of this service that have challenged their predecessors. The people who have contributed to this volume have encountered the problems and frustrations usually experienced in complex evaluation studies. Their wisdom enables the next generation of evaluators to advance and improve upon the design, methodology, and interpretation of study findings. This cannot be done in isolation: the evaluator is an important team member and joins the practitioners in understanding what is being done, its consequences, and how to improve FBS

As with the Head Start research, it is important to take a long-term view of evaluation in this program area. Persistent attention to improving program implementation, service consistency, and quality assurance, while refining the research designs and measures, will help produce useful data about the cost-effectiveness of FBS programs.

Afterword

Family-based programs face a number of challenges. On one hand are those challenges posed by skeptics who ask: "Can a single welfare mother who has been beating her children, or failing to feed and bathe them, be turned into a responsible parent as the result of a one- to three-month infusion of counseling, free food, cash, furniture, rent vouchers, and housekeeping services?" (MacDonald, 1994, p. 45). On the other hand are challenges raised by reform-oriented policymakers who envision a revolutionary restructuring of traditional services. They ask: Can the concept of family-centered services be used to change the nature of child welfare, mental health, and juvenile justice practice? As suggested by guest author Charles Gershenson, evaluation studies will occupy a central role in responding to these challenges.

The field is approaching a watershed time. In spite of lingering and important questions regarding the effectiveness of FBS, a new wave of family support and family preservation programs is being developed under the Family Preservation and Support Services Program of the Omnibus Budget Reconciliation Act of 1993. In response to this legislation, a wide array of service reforms has been initiated

At the state level, family-based, integrated service systems are emerging. In Idaho, for example, the values and practices of family preservation have been applied to systemwide reform, which integrates child protective, juvenile justice, child mental health, JOBS, adoption, and substance abuse services in a single family-centered practice model with a common administrative structure. Work units at the Idaho Division of Family and Children's Services now contain staff from all program areas—CPS through substance abuse—and apply a team approach to serving families.[1] In Maryland, the Families Now initiative has defined four levels of family-based child welfare services that correspond to different levels of family need. Level I consists of intensive family services (IFS) provided for up to three months with caseloads of six families; Level II consists of IFS provided up to six months with caseloads of ten families; Level III consists of family-centered protective services provided up to twelve months with caseloads of fifteen families; and Level IV provides an intensive family reunification service for six months with caseloads of five families. Other states such as North Carolina and Ore-

gon are undertaking early intervention experiments with family resource centers and family support programs.

Similar reforms are being implemented by county and city agencies. In
Los Angeles, networks of community-based agencies are being organized
to provide a broad range of family preservation services including child
care, housing, transportation, and substance abuse treatment, as well as
more traditional in-home counseling and training. And even longstand-
ing FBS programs, such as the state of Washington's HOMEBUILDERS™,
are formulating new structures to extend the traditional four- to six-week
service period for certain families in need of longer services. The spirit of
reform is affecting nearly every state and agency. And despite the recent
major legislative shifts, there may be opportunities to strengthen the
income, housing, medical, and other basic supports that FBS program
advocates have said are critical to long-term family functioning.

With this new series of field-initiated reforms and experiments, some
programs are bound to be more successful than others. Because large
studies often are vulnerable to site differences that cannot be controlled,
many small evaluations with rigorous designs will be needed to map the
successes and failures. This new generation of studies must address a
range of questions that extend beyond, Did it work? These questions
include: Was the program successfully implemented? If not, why not? If
it was successfully implemented, was it effective? How much did it cost
relative to other programs? And if it did work, what were the correlates
of success? Who seemed to benefit from service and who did not? Which
elements of service contributed the most to success with specific issues?

In this book, we have tried to lay the groundwork for studies to
answer such questions. To respond to both the visionaries and the skeptics, evaluations that use strong methods must be brought to bear upon
both enduring and emerging questions about family-based services.

Peter J. Pecora
Mark W. Fraser
Kristine E. Nelson
Jacquelyn McCroskey
William Meezan

NOTE

1.   As this book goes to press, some newly appointed government officials in
Idaho are proposing to separate juvenile justice from the larger social services
department, which would reduce the affectiveness of the current organizational
structure which emphasizes coordinated services.

References

Aber, J., Allen, J., Carlson, V., & Cicchetti, D. (1989). The effects of maltreatment on development during early childhood: Recent studies and their theoretical, clinical and policy implications. Pp. 579–619 in *Child maltreatment: Theory and research on the causes and consequences of child abuse and neglect*, edited by D. Cicchetti & V. Carlson. New York: Cambridge University Press.

Abidin, R. R. (1983). *Parenting stress index: Manual*. Charlottesville, VA: Pediatric Psychology Press.

Achenbach, T. M. (1991a). *Manual for the child behavior checklist/4–18 and 1991 profile*. Burlington: University of Vermont Department of Psychiatry.

Achenbach, T. M. (1991b). *Manual for the teacher's report form and 1991 profile*. Burlington: University of Vermont Department of Psychiatry.

Achenbach, T. M. (1991c). *Manual for the youth self-report and 1991 profile*. Burlington: University of Vermont Department of Psychiatry.

Achenbach, T. M., & Edelbrock, C. (1983). *Manual for the child behavior checklist and revised child behavior profile*. Burlington, VT: Thomas A. Achenbach.

Achenbach, T. M., & Edelbrock, C. (1986). *Manual for the teacher's report form and teacher version of the child behavior profile*. Burlington: University of Vermont Department of Psychiatry.

Achenbach, T. M., McConaughty, S., & Howell, C. (1987). Child/adolescent behavioral and emotional problems: Implications of cross-informant correlations for situational specificity. *Psychological Bulletin 101*(2), 213–232.

Adnopoz, J., & Nagler, S. F. (1993) Supporting HIV infected children in their own families through family-centered practice. Pp. 119–128 in *Advancing family preservation practice*, edited by E. S. Morton & R. K. Grigsby. Newbury Park, CA: Sage.

Agar, M. H. (1986). *Speaking of ethnography*. Beverly Hills, CA: Sage.

Alexander, J. F., & Parsons, B. V. (1982). *Functional family therapy*. Monterey, CA: Brooks/Cole.

Alley, M. (1987). *The craft of scientific writing*. Englewood Cliffs, NJ: Prentice-Hall.

Allison, P. D. (1984). *Event history analysis: Regression for longitudinal event data*. Quantitative Applications in the Social Sciences Series Paper #46. Beverly Hills, CA: Sage.

Alter, C., & Evens, W. (1990). *Evaluating your practice: A guide to self-assessment*. New York: Springer.

American Psychological Association. (1982). *Ethical principles in the conduct of research with human participants*. Washington, DC: Author.

American Psychological Association. (1983). *Publication Manual*, 3rd ed. Washington, DC: Author.

Anderson, D. F. (1983). Disentangling statistical artifacts from hard conclusions. *Journal of Policy Analysis and Management* 2(2), 296–302.

Anglin J. (1988). The parent networks project: Toward a collaborative methodology of ecological research. Pp. 35–48 in *Ecological research with families and children: From concepts to methodology,* edited by A. Pence. New York: Teachers College Press.

AuClaire, P., & Schwartz, I. M. (1986). *An evaluation of the effectiveness of intensive home-based services as an alternative to placement for adolescents and their families.* Minneapolis: Hennepin County Community Services Department, and the University of Minnesota, Hubert H. Humphrey Institute of Public Affairs.

AuClaire, P., & Schwartz, I. M. (1987). Are home-based services effective? A public child welfare agency's experiment. *Children Today 5,* 16–21.

Austin, D. (1991). Comments on research development in social work. *Social Work Research and Abstracts* 27(1), 38–41.

Austin, M. J., Cox, G., Gottlieb, N., Hawkins, J. D., Kruzich. J. M., & Rauch, R. (1982). *Evaluating your agency's programs.* Newbury Park, CA: Sage.

Bailey, K. D. (1978). *Methods of social research,* 2nd ed. New York: Free Press.

Baird, C., & Neuenfeldt, D. (1988). Development of risk indices for the Alaska Department of Health and Social Services. In *Validation research in CPS risk assessment: Three recent studies,* edited by T. Tatara (Occasional monograph series of APWA Social R&D Department, No. 2). Washington, DC: American Public Welfare Association.

Barkley, R. G. (1981). *Hyperactive children: A handbook for diagnosis and treatment.* New York: Guilford.

Barrera, M., Jr. (1986). Distinctions between social support concepts, measures and models. *American Journal of Community Psychology 14,* 413–416.

Barrera, M., Jr., & Ainlay, S. L. (1983). The structure of social support: A conceptual and empirical analysis. *Journal of Community Psychology 11,* 133–143.

Barrera, M., Jr., Sandler, I. N., & Ramsay, T. B. (1981). Preliminary development of a scale of social support: Studies on college students. *American Journal of Community Psychology 9,* 435–447.

Barreth, D. G. (1986). *Experiences of naturalistic inquirers during inquiry.* Unpublished doctoral dissertation, Indiana University, Bloomington.

Barth, R. P. (1991). Theories guiding home-based intensive family preservation services. Pp. 89–112 in *Reaching high-risk families: Intensive family preservation in human services,* edited by J. K. Whittaker, J. Kinney, E. M. Tracy, & C. Booth. Hawthorne, NY: Aldine de Gruyter.

Basch, C. E., Sliepcevich, E. M., Gold, R. S., Duncan, D. F., & Kolbe, L. J. (1985). Avoiding Type III errors in health education program evaluations: A case study. *Health Education Quarterly* 12(4), 315–331.

Bath, H. I., & Haapala, D. A. (1994). Family preservation services: What does the outcome research really tell us? *Social Services Review* 68(3), 386–404.

Bath, H. I., Richey, C. A., & Haapala, D. A. (1992). Child age and outcome correlates in intensive family preservation services. *Children and Youth Services Review* 14(5), 389–406.

Batson, C., O'Quin, K., & Pych, V. (1982). An attribution theory analysis of trained helper inferences about clients' needs. Pp. 59–101 in *Basic processes in helping relationships*, edited by T. Wills. New York: Academic Press.

Bavolek, S. J. (1989). Assessing and teaching high-risk parenting attitudes. *Early Child Development and Care 42*, 99–112.

Bavolek, S. J. (1990a). Assessing the impact of the Nurturing Programs in treating abusive parenting practices. Pp. 22–25 in *Research and validation report: Adult-Adolescent Parenting Inventory*, edited by S. J. Bavolek. Park City, UT: Family Development Resources.

Bavolek, S. J. (1990b). Building nurturing interactions in families experiencing parent-adolescent conflict. Pp. 30–36 in *Research and validation report of the Nurturing Programs*, edited by S. J. Bavolek. Park City, UT: Family Development Resources.

Bavolek, S. J. (1990c). Comprehensive research summary of the Adult-Adolescent Parenting Inventory (AAPI). Pp. 1–3 in *Research and validation report: Adult-Adolescent Parenting Inventory*, edited by S. J. Bavolek. Park City, UT: Family Development Resources.

Bavolek, S. J. (1990d). Identification of known abusive parenting and child rearing practices. Pp. 4–8 in *Research and validation report: Adult-Adolescent Parenting Inventory*, edited by S. J. Bavolek. Park City, UT: Family Development Resources.

Bavolek, S. J., ed. (1990e). *Research and validation report of the Nurturing Programs.* Park City, UT: Family Development Resources.

Bavolek, S. J., & Dellinger-Bavolek, J. (1990). Increasing the nurturing parenting skills of families in Head Start. Pp. 22–29 in *Research and validation report of the Nurturing Programs*, edited by S. J. Bavolek. Park City, UT: Family Development Resources.

Bavolek, S. J., Henderson, H. L., & Schultz, B. B. (1990). A training project designed to reduce the incidence of child neglect. Pp. 44–54 in *Research and validation report of the Nurturing Programs*, edited by S. J. Bavolek. Park City, UT: Family Development Resources.

Bayley, N. (1993). *Bayley scales of infant development*, 2nd ed. New York: Psychological Corporation.

Beavers, W. R., & Hampson, R. B (1990). *Successful families: Assessment and intervention.* New York: W. W. Norton.

Belsky, J. (1984a). The determinants of parenting: A process model. *Child Development 55*, 83–96.

Belsky, J. (1984b). Two waves of day care research: Developmental effects and conditions of quality. Pp. 1–34 in *The child and the day care setting*, edited by R. C. Ainslie. New York: Praeger.

Belsky, J. (1990). Parental and nonparental child care and children's socioeconomic development: A decade in review. *Journal of Marriage and the Family 52*(4), 885–903.

Belsky, J., & Vondra, J. (1989). Lessons from child abuse: The determinants of parenting. Pp. 153–202 in *Child maltreatment: Theory and research on the causes and consequences of child abuse and neglect*, edited by D. Cicchetti & V. Carlson. New York: Cambridge University Press.

Bernard, T. J. (1990). Angry aggression among the 'truly disadvantaged.' *Criminology 28*(1), 73–96.

Berreuta-Clement, J. R., Schweinhart, L .S. Barnett, W. S., Epstein, A. S., & Weikart, D. P. (1984). *Changed lives, the effects of the Perry Preschool Program on youths through age 19.* Ypsilanti, MI: High/Scope.

Berry, M. (1994). *Keeping families together.* New York: Garland.

Bickman, L. (1990). Study design. Pp. 132–166 in *Preserving families: Evaluation resources for practitioners and policymakers,* edited by Y. T. Yuan & M. Rivest. Newbury Park, CA: Sage.

Biegel, D. E., Farkas, K. J., Abell, N., Goodin, J., & Friedman, B. (1988). *Social support networks and bibliography 1983–1987.* New York: Greenwood.

Bielawski, B., & Epstein, I. (1984). Assessing program stabilization: An extension of the "differential evaluation" model. *Administration in Social Work 8*(4), 13–23.

Bingham, R. D., & Felbinger, C. L. (1989). *Evaluation in practice—A methodological approach.* White Plains, NY: Longman.

Bloom, M., & Fischer, J. (1982). *Evaluating practice. Guidelines for the accountable professional.* Englewood Cliffs, NJ: Prentice-Hall.

Blythe, B. J. (1990). Applying practice research methods in intensive family preservation services. Pp. 147–164 in *Reaching high-risk families: Intensive family preservation in human services,* edited by J. K. Whittaker, J. Kinney, E. M. Tracy, & C. Booth. Hawthorne, NY: Aldine de Gruyter.

Blythe, B. J., Salley, M. P., & Jayaratne, S. (1994). A review of intensive family preservation services research. *Social Work Research 18*(4), 213–224.

Bogdon, R., & Taylor, S. J. (1975). *Introduction to qualitative research methods: A phenomenological approach to the social sciences.* New York: Wiley.

Borduin, C. M., Mann, B. J., Cone, L., Henggeler, S. W., Fucci, B. R., Blaske, D. M., & Williams, R. A. (1993). Multisystemic treatment of serious juvenile offenders: Longterm prevention of criminality and violent offending. Manuscript submitted for publication.

Breakey, G., & Pratt, B. (1991). Healthy growth for Hawaii's "healthy start": Toward a systematic statewide approach to the prevention of child abuse and neglect. *Zero to Three* (April).

Brieland, D. (1987). History and evolution of social work practice. Pp. 739–754 in *Encyclopedia of Social Work,* 18th ed., Vol. 1. Silver Spring, MD: National Association of Social Workers.

Bronfenbrenner, U. (1979). *The ecology of human development.* Cambridge, MA: Harvard University Press.

Bronfenbrenner, U. (1988). Foreword. Pp. ix–xix in *Ecological research with families and children, From concepts to methodology,* edited by A. Pence. New York: Teachers College Press.

Brown, G., ed. (1968). *The multi-problem dilemma.* Metuchen, NJ: Scarecrow.

Brown, J., Finch, W. A., Northern, H., Taylor, S. H., & Weil, M. (1982). *Child/Family/Neighborhood.* New York: Child Welfare League of America.

Brown, J., & M. Weil, eds. (1992). *Family Practice: A Curriculum Plan for Social Services.* Washington, DC: Child Welfare League of America.

Brunk, M., Henggeler, S. W., & Whelan, J. B. (1987). Comparison of multisystemic therapy and parent training in the brief treatment of child abuse and neglect. *Journal of Consulting and Clinical Psychology 55,* 171–178.

Bryce, M., & Lloyd, J. C., eds. (1981). *Treating families in the home: An alternative to placement.* Springfield, IL: Charles C. Thomas.

Buchard, J. D., & Clarke, R. T. (1990). The role of individualized care in a service delivery system for children and adolescents with severely maladjusted behavior. *Journal of Health Administration 17*(1), 48–60.

Bulmer, H. (1979). Concepts in the analysis of qualitative data. *Sociological Review 27*, 651–677.

Burchard, J. D., & Clarke, R. T. (1990). The role of individualized care in a service delivery system for children and adolescents with severely maladjusted behavior. *Journal of Mental Health Administration 17*, 48–60.

Bzoch, K., & League, R. (1971). *The Bzoch-League receptive-expressive emergent language scale: For the measurement of language skills in infancy.* Baltimore, MD: University Park Press.

Cabral, R. J., & Callard, E. D. (1982). A home-based program to serve high-risk families. *Journal of Home Economics 74*(3), 14–19.

Caldwell, B., & Bradley R. (1984). *The HOME observation for measurement of the environment.* Little Rock: University of Arkansas, School of Education.

Campbell, D. T., & Stanley, J. (1963). *Experimental and quasi-experimental designs for research.* Chicago: Rand McNally.

Campis, L. K., Lyman, R. D., & Prentice-Dunn, S. (1986). The parental locus of control scale: Development and validation. *Journal of Clinical Child Psychology 15*, 260–267.

Carmines, E. G., & Zeller, R. A. (1979). *Reliability and validity assessment.* Beverly Hills: Sage.

Carveth, W. B., & Gottlieb, B. H. (1979). The measurement of social support and its relation to stress. *Canadian Journal of Behavioral Science 11*, 179–187.

Chambers, D. E., Wedel, K. R., & Rodwell, M. K. (1992). *Evaluating social programs.* Needham Heights, MA: Allyn & Bacon.

Chen, H. (1990). *Theory-driven evaluation.* Newbury Park, CA: Sage.

Chilcott, J. H. (1987). Where are you coming from and where are you going? The reporting of ethnographic research. *American Educational Research Journal 24*, 199–218.

Child Welfare League of America. (1989). *Standards for service to strengthen and preserve families with children.* Washington, D.C.: Author.

Child Welfare League of America. (1994). *Kinship care: A natural bridge.* Washington, DC: Author.

Cicchetti, D., & Wagner, S. (1990). Alternative assessment strategies for the evaluation of infants and toddlers: An organizational perspective. Pp. 246–277 in *Handbook of early childhood intervention*, edited by S. Meisels & J. Shonkoff. Cambridge, MA: Cambridge University Press.

Cochran, M., & Brassard, J. (1979). Child development and personal social networks. *Child Development 50*, 601–616.

Cochran, N. (1978). Grandma Moses and the 'corruption' of data. *Evaluation Quarterly 2*(3), 363–373.

Cohen, J. (1988). *Statistical power analysis for the behavioral sciences*, 2nd ed. Hillside, NJ: Lawrence Erlbaum Associates.

Cohen, S., & Wills, T. A. (1985). Stress, social support, and the buffering hypothesis. *Psychological Bulletin 98*, 310–357.

Collins, L. M., & Horn, J. L. (1991). *Best methods for the analysis of change: Recent advances, unanswered questions, future directions.* Washington, DC: American Psychological Association.

Compher, J. V. (1983). Home services to families to prevent child placement. *Social Work 28*(5), 360–364.

Cook, T. D., & Campbell, D. T. (1979). *Quasi-experimentation: Design and analysis issues for field settings.* Chicago: Rand McNally.

Cook, T., & Reichardt, C., eds. (1979). *Qualitative and quantitative methods in evaluation research,* Vol. 1. Beverly Hills, CA: Sage.

Corcoran, K. J. (1993). Practice evaluation: Problems and promises of single-system designs in clinical practice. *Journal of Social Service Research 18*(1/2), 147–159.

Corcoran, K. J. (1994). *Measures for clinical practice: A sourcebook.* Vol.1: *Couples, Families, & Children.* New York: Free Press.

Corcoran, K. J. , & Fischer, J. (1987). *Measures for clinical practice: A sourcebook.* New York: Free Press.

Corimer, W. H., & Corimer, L. S. (1979). *Interviewing strategies for helpers.* Monterey, CA: Brooks/Cole.

Coulton, C. J. (1991). Developing and implementing quality assurance programs. Pp. 251–266 in *Skills for effective human services management,* edited by R. L. Edwards & J. A. Yankey. Silver Spring, MD: NASW Press.

Cronbach, L. J. (1975). Beyond the two disciplines of scientific psychology. *American Psychologist 30,* 116–127.

Cronbach, L. J., & Associates. (1980). *Toward reform of program evaluation.* San Francisco: Jossey-Bass.

Curtis, P. A. (1991). Quality assurance, program evaluation and research in a child welfare agency setting. *Research and Evaluation in Group Care 1*(2), 13–15.

Danish, S. J., D'Angell, A. R., & Hauer, A. L. (1980). *Helping skills,* 2nd ed. New York: Human Sciences Press.

Daro, D., Abrahams, N., & Casey, K. (1990). *Parenting program manual.* Chicago, IL: The National Committee for the Prevention of Child Abuse.

Denzin, N. K. (1978). *Sociological methods.* New York: McGraw-Hill.

Denzin, N. K., & Lincoln, Y. S., eds. (1994). *Handbook of qualitative research.* Thousand Oaks, CA: Sage.

DePaul, J., Arruabarrena, I., & Milner, J. S. (1991). Validacion de una version espanola del Child Abuse Potential Inventory para su uso en Espana. *Child Abuse and Neglect 15,* 495–504.

Derogatis, L. R., Lipman, R. J., & Covi, L. (1973). The SCL-90: An outpatient psychiatric rating scale. *Psychopharmacology Bulletin 9,* 13–28.

DeVellis, R. F. (1991). *Scale development: Theory and applications.* Newbury Park, CA: Sage.

Dexter, L. A (1970). *Elite and specialized interviewing.* Evanston, IL.: Northwestern University Press.

Dickerson, V. C., & Coyne, J. C. (1987). Family cohesion and control: A multitrait-multimethod study. *Journal of Consulting and Clinical Psychology 13,* 275–285.

Di Leonardi, J. W., & Johnson, P. (n.d.). *Evaluation of the chronic neglect consortium: Final report.* Chicago: Children's Home and Aid Society of Illinois.

Dillman, D. A. (1978). *Mail and telephone surveys: The total design method.* New York: Wiley.

Donabedian, A. (1987). Commentary on some studies of the quality of care. *Health Care Financing Review, Annual Supplement*, 75–85.

Dore, M. M. (1991a). Context and structure of practice: Implications for research. Pp. 121–137 in *Family preservation services: Research and evaluation*, edited by K. Wells & D. E. Biegel. Newbury Park, CA: Sage.

Dore, M. M. (1991b). *Family-based mental health services programs and outcomes*. Philadelphia: Philadelphia Child Guidance Clinic.

Doueck, H. J., Bronson, D. E., & Levine, M. (1992). Evaluating risk assessment implementation in child protection: Issues for consideration. *Child Abuse & Neglect 16*, 637–646.

Douglas, J. D. (1985). *Creative interviewing*. Beverly Hills, CA: Sage.

Draper, T. W., & Marcos, A. C., eds. (1990). *Family variables: Conceptualization, measurement, and use*. Newbury Park, CA: Sage.

Dubow, E. F., & Ullman, D. G. (1989). Assessing social support in elementary school children: The survey of children's social support. *Journal of Clinical Child Psychology 18*, 52–64.

Duerr-Berrick, J., & Barth, R. P. (1994). Research on kinship foster care: What do we know? Where do we go from here? *Children and Youth Services Review 16*(1/2), 1–5.

Dumas, J. E. (1984). Interactional correlates of treatment outcome in behavioral parenting training. *Journal of Consulting and Clinical Psychology 52*(6), 946–954.

Dumas, J. E., & Albin, J. B. (1986). Parent training outcome: Does active parental involvement matter? *Behavioral Research and Therapy 24*(2), 227–230.

Dumas, J. E., & Wahler, R. G. (1983). Predictors of treatment outcome in parenting training: Mother insularity and socioeconomic disadvantage. *Behavioral Assessment 5*, 301–313.

Dunn, L., & Dunn, L. (1959). *Peabody picture vocabulary test*. Circle Pines, MN: American Guidance Service.

Dunst, C. J., Jenkins, V., & Trivette, C. M. (1984). Family support scale: Reliability and validity. *Journal of Individual Family, and Community Wellness 1*, 45–52.

Dunst, C. J., Trivette, C. M., & Deal, A. G. (1988). *Enabling and empowering families: Principles and guidelines for practice*. Cambridge, MA: Brookline.

Egan, G. (1982). *The skilled helper*, 2nd ed. Monterey, CA: Brooks/Cole.

Einstein, A. (1961). *Relativity: The special and the general theory, a popular exposition*. New York: Crown.

Emlen, A., Lahti, J., Downs, G., McKay, A., & Downs, S. (1978). *Overcoming barriers to planning for children in foster care*. DHEW Publication No. (OHDS) 78–30138. Washington, DC: U.S. Department of Health and Human Services, U.S. Children's Bureau.

English, D. J., & Pecora, P. J. (1994). Risk assessment as a practice method in child protective services. *Child Welfare 73*(5), 451–473.

Everett, J. E., Chipungu, S. S., & Leashore, B. R. (1991). *Child welfare: An Africentric perspective*. New Brunswick, NJ: Rutgers University Press.

Fanshel, D. (1992). Foster care as a two-tiered system. *Children and Youth Services Review 14*, 49–60.

Fanshel, D., Finch, S. J., & Grundy, J. F. (1989). Modes of exit from foster family care and adjustment of time of departures of children with unstable life histories. *Child Welfare 68*(4), 391–402.

Fanshel, D., Finch, S. J., & Grundy, J. F. (1990). *Foster children in a life course perspective*. New York: Columbia University Press.

Fanshel, D., & Shinn, E. B. (1978). *Children in foster care: A longitudinal investigation*. New York: Columbia University Press.

Farrow, F. (1991). Services to families: The view from the states. *Families in Society: Journal of Contemporary Human Services 72*(5), 268–275.

Fein, E., & Maluccio, A. N. (1992). Permanency planning: Another Remedy in jeopardy? *Social Service Review 66*(3), 335–348,

Feldman, L. H. (1990a). *Evaluating the impact of family preservation services in New Jersey.* Trenton: New Jersey Division of Youth and Family Services, Bureau of Research, Evaluation and Quality Assurance.

Feldman, L. H. (1990b). Target problem definition. Pp. 16–38 in *Preserving families: Evaluation resources for practitioners and policymakers*, edited by Y. T. Yuan & M. Rivest. Newbury Park, CA: Sage.

Feldman, L. H. (1991a). Evaluating the impact of intensive family preservation services in New Jersey. Pp. 47–71 in *Family preservation Services: Research and Evaluation*, edited by K. Wells & D. E. Biegel. Newbury Park, CA: Sage.

Feldman, L. H. (1991b). *Assessing the effectiveness of family preservation services in New Jersey within an ecological context.* Trenton: Bureau of Research, Evaluation and Quality Assurance, New Jersey Division of Youth and Family Services.

Fielding, N. G., & Fielding, J. L. (1986). *Linking data*. Beverly Hills, CA: Sage.

Figoten, S. S., & Tanner, L. T. (1990). Primary prevention of child abuse and neglect: Identification and education of potentially abusive parents (abstract). In *Research and validation report: Adult-Adolescent Parenting Inventory*, (p. 42), edited by S. J. Bavolek. Park City, UT: Family Development Resources.

Fischer, J. (1973). Is social work effective?: A review. *Social Work 18*, 5–20.

Fischer, J. (1978). *Effective casework practice: An eclectic approach*. New York: McGraw-Hill.

Fiske, D. (1975). A source of data is not a measuring instrument, *Journal of Abnormal Psychology 84*(1), 20–23.

Fleuridas, C., Rosenthal, D. M., Leigh, G. K., & Leigh, T. E. (1990). Family goal recording: An adaptation of G. A. S. *Journal of Marital and Family Therapy 16*, 389–406.

Fong, R. (1994). Family preservation: Making it work for Asians. *Child Welfare 73*(4), 331–341.

Forsythe, P. W. (1992). Homebuilders and family preservation. *Children and Youth Services Review 14*, 37–47.

Foster, S. L., Prinz, R. J., & O'Leary, K. D. (1983). Impact of problem-solving communication training and generalization procedures on family conflict. *Child and Family Behavior Therapy 5*, 1–23.

Frankel, H. (1988). Family centered, home-based services in child protection: A review of the research. *Social Service Review 62*(1), 137–157.

Frankenburg W., & Dodds, J. (1967). The Denver developmental screening test. *Journal of Pediatrics 71*, 181–191.

Fraser, M. (1990). Assessing the effectiveness of family preservation programs:

Implications for agency-based research. Paper presented at the Family Preservation Institute for Social Work University Educators, Kansas City, MO, August.

Fraser, M. W., Jenson, J. M., Kiefer, D., & Popuang, P. (1994). Statistical methods for the analysis of critical life events. *Social Work Research 18*(3), 163–177.

Fraser, M. W., & Haapala, D. A. (1988). Home-based family treatment: A quantitative-qualitative assessment. *Journal of Applied Social Sciences 12*(1), 1–23.

Fraser, M. W., Pecora, P. J., & Haapala, D. A. (1991). *Families in crisis: The impact of intensive family preservation services.* Hawthorne, NY: Aldine de Gruyter.

Fraser, M. W., Pecora, P. J., Popuang, C., & Haapala, D. A. (1992). Event history analysis: A proportional hazards perspective on modeling outcomes in intensive family preservation services. *Journal of Social Service Research 16*(1/2), 123–158.

Fraser, M. W., Taylor, M., Jackson, R., & O'Jack, J. (1991). Many ways of knowing? *Social Work Research & Abstract 27*(4), 5–15.

Fredman, N., & Sherman, R. (1987). *Handbook of measurements for marriage and family therapy.* New York: Bruner/Mazel.

Frey, J. H. (1983). *Survey research by telephone.* Beverly Hills, CA: Sage.

Friedman, A. S., Tomko, L. A., & Utada, A. (1991). Client and family characteristics that predict better family outcome for adolescent drug abusers. *Family Dynamics of Addiction Quarterly 1*, 77–93.

Fulton, A. M., Murphy, K. R., & Anderson, S. L. (1991). Increasing adolescent mothers' knowledge of child development: An intervention program. *Adolescence 26*(101), 73–81.

Gabor, P., & Grinnell, R.M. (1993). *Evaluation and quality improvement in the social services.* Needham Heights, MA: Allyn & Bacon.

Galinsky, M., Turnbull, J., Meglin, D., & Wilner, M. (1993). Confronting the reality of collaborative practice research: Issues of practice, design, measurement, and team development, *Social Work 38*(4), 440–449.

Garbarino, J., Schellenbach, C. J., Sebes, J., & Associates (1986). *Troubled youth, troubled families: Understanding families at risk for adolescent maltreatment.* Hawthorne, NY: Aldine de Gruyter.

Gaudin, J. M., Jr., Polansky, N., & Kilpatrick, A. C. (1992). The Child Well-Being Scales: A field trial. *Child Welfare 71*(4), 319–328.

Geertz, C. (1973). Thick description: Toward an interpretive theory of culture. Pp. 3–30 in *The interpretation of cultures*, edited by C. Geertz. New York: Basic Books.

Geismar, L., & Ayers, B. (1958). *Families in trouble.* St. Paul, MN: Family-Centered Project.

Geismar, L., & Krisberg, J. (1966). The family life improvement project: An experiment in preventive intervention. *Social Casework 47*(6), 563–570.

Gershenson, C. P. (1993). The child well-being conundrum. *Readings: A Journal of Reviews and Commentary in Mental Health* (June), 8–11.

Gil, D. G. (1990) *Unravelling social policy.* Rochester, VT: Schenkman Books.

Gilgun, J. F., Handel, G., & Daly, K., eds. (1993). *Qualitative methods in family research.* Newbury Park, CA: Sage.

Glaser, B. G., & Strauss, A. L. (1967). *The discovery of grounded theory: Strategies for qualitative research.* Hawthorne, NY: Aldine de Gruyter.

Glisson, C. (1990). Commentary: Distinguishing and combining qualitative and quantitative methods. Pp. 184–193 in *Advances in clinical social work research,* edited by L. Videka-Sherman & W. J. Reid. Silver Spring, MD: NASW Press.

Goelman, H. (1988). The relationship between structure and process variables in home and day care settings on children's language development. Pp. 9–19 in *Ecological research with families and children, From concepts to methodology,* edited by A. Pence. New York: Teachers College Press.

Gold, N. (1983). Stakeholders and program evaluations: Characterizations and reflections. In *Stakeholder-based evaluation,* edited by A. Bryk. San Francisco: Jossey-Bass.

Goldstein, A. P., & Keller, H. (1987). *Aggressive behavior: Assessment and intervention.* Oxford: Pergamon.

Gomby, D. S., Larson, C. S., Lewit, E. M., & Behrman, R. E. (1993). Home visiting: Analysis and recommendations. *Future of Children–Home Visiting* 3(3, Winter), 6–22.

Gordon, D. A., Arbuthnot, J., Gustofson, K. E., & McGreen, P. (1988). Home-based behavioral-systems family therapy with disadvantaged juvenile delinquents, *American Journal of Family Therapy* 16, 243–255.

Gottlieb, B. (1983). *Social support strategies: Guidelines for mental health practice.* Beverly Hills, CA: Sage.

Gottlieb, B. (1988). *Marshaling social support.* Beverly Hills, CA: Sage.

Goyette, C., Conners, C., & Ulrich, R. (1978). Normative data on revised Conners Parent and Teacher Rating scales, *Journal of Abnormal Child Psychology* 6, 221–236.

Gramlich, E. (1990). *A guide to benefit-cost analysis.* Englewood Cliffs, NJ: Prentice-Hall.

Green, R. G. (1989). Choosing family measurement devices for practice and research. *Social Service Review* 63, 304–320.

Greenbaum, T. L. (1988). *The practical handbook and guide to focus group research.* Lexington, MA: D.C. Heath.

Grinnell, R. M. (1993). *Social work research and evaluation,* 4th ed. Itasca, IL: F.E. Peacock.

Grotevant, H. D., & Carlson, C. I. (1989). *Family assessment: A guide to methods and measures.* New York: Guilford.

Gruber, A. R. (1973). *Foster home care in Massachusetts: A study of children—Their biological and foster parents.* Boston: Governor's Commission on Adoption and Foster Care.

Guba, E. (1981). Criteria for assessing the trustworthiness of naturalistic inquiries. *Educational Communications and Technology Journal* 29, 75–92.

Guba, E. (1985). Perspectives on public policy: What can happen as a result of policy? (mimeograph).

Guba, E. G., & Lincoln, Y. M. (1981). *Effective evaluation.* San Francisco: Jossey-Bass.

Guba, E. G., & Lincoln, Y. M. (1984) Do inquiry paradigms imply inquiry methodologies? Pp. 89–115 in *Ethnography in educational evaluation,* edited by D. L. Fetterman. Beverly Hills, CA: Sage.

Guba, E. G., & Lincoln, Y. M. (1989). *Fourth generation evaluation.* Newbury Park, CA: Sage.

Haapala, D. A. (1983). *Perceived helpfulness, attributed critical incident responsibility, and a discrimination of home-based family therapy treatment outcomes: Homebuilders model.* Report prepared for the Department of Health and Human Services, Administration for Children, Youth and Families (Grant #90-CW-626 OHDS). Federal Way, WA: Behavioral Sciences Institute.

Haapala, D. A., & Kinney, J. M. (1988). Avoiding out-of-home placement of high-risk status offenders through the use of intensive home-based family preservation services. *Criminal Justice and Behavior 15*(3), 334–348.

Haapala, D. A., Kinney, J., & McDade, K. (1988). *Referring families to intensive home-based family reservation services: A guide book* (draft). Federal Way, WA: Behavioral Sciences Institute.

Haapala, D. A., McDade, K., & Johnston, B. (1988). *Preventing the dissolution of special needs adoption families through the use of intensive home-based family preservation services: The Homebuilders Model.* Clinical Services Final Report from the Homebuilders Adoption Services Continuum Project. Federal Way, WA: Behavioral Sciences Institute.

Halper, G., & Jones, M. A. (1981). *Serving families at risk of dissolution: Public preventive services in New York City.* New York: Human Resources Administration.

Halpern, E. S. (1983). *Auditing naturalistic inquiries: The development and application of a model.* Unpublished doctoral dissertation, Indiana University, Bloomington.

Hampson, R. B., Beavers, W. R., & Hulgas, Y. F. (1988). Commentary: Comparing the Beavers and circumplex models of family functioning. *Family Process 27*, 85–92.

Hansen, D. J., & MacMillan, V. M. (1990). Behavioral assessment of child abusive and neglectful families: Recent developments and current issues. *Behavior Modification 14*, 255–278.

Haskins, R. (1989). Beyond metaphor: The efficacy of early childhood education. *American Psychologist 44*(2), 274–282.

Hauser-Cram, P., & Shonkoff, J. (1988). Rethinking the assessment of child-focused outcomes. Pp. 73–94 in *Evaluating family programs*, edited by H. B. Weiss & F. H. Jacobs. Hawthorne, NY: Aldine de Gruyter.

Hayes, J. R., & Joseph, J. A. (1985). *Home-based family centered project evaluation.* Columbus, OH: Metropolitan Human Services Commission.

Henggeler, S. W., & Borduin, C. M. (1990). *Family therapy and beyond: A multisystemic approach to treating the behavior problems of children and adolescents.* Pacific Grove, CA: Brooks/Cole.

Henggeler, S. W., Burr-Harris, A. W., Borduin, C. M., & McCallum, G. (1991). Use of the family adaptability and cohesion evaluation scales in child clinical research. *Journal of Abnormal Child Psychology 19*, 53–63.

Henggeler, S. W., Melton, G. B., & Smith, L. A. (1992). Family preservation using multisystemic therapy: An effective alternative to incarcerating serious juvenile offenders. *Journal of Consulting and Clinical Psychology 60*(6), 953–961.

Henggeler, S. W., Melton, G. B., Smith, L. A., Schoenwald, S. K., & Hanley, J. H. (1993). Family preservation using multisystemic treatment: Long-term follow-up to a clinical trial with serious juvenile offenders. *Journal of Child & Family Studies, 2*, 283–293.

Henggeler, S. W., & Schoenwald, S. K. (1993). Multisystemic therapy with juvenile offenders: An effective family-based treatment. *Family Psychologist 9*, 24–26.

Hennepin County Community Services Department. (1980). *Family study project: Demonstration and research in intensive services to families.* Minneapolis: Author.

Hess, P. M., & Folaron, G. (1991). Ambivalences: A challenge to permanency for children. *Child Welfare 70*, 403–424.

Hess, P. M., & Folaron, G. (1993). *The Professional Review Action Group (PRAG) model: A user's guide.* Washington, DC: Child Welfare League of America.

Heying, K. R. (1985). Family-based, in-home services for the severely emotionally disturbed child. *Child Welfare 64*(5), 519–527.

Hinckley, E. C., & Ellis, W. F. (1985). An effective alternative to residential placement: Home-based services. *Journal of Clinical Child Psychology 14*(3), 209–213.

Hodges, V. G. (1991). Providing culturally sensitive intensive family preservation services to ethnic minority families. Pp. 95–116 in *Intensive family preservation services: An instructional sourcebook*, edited by E. M. Tracy, D. A. Haapala, J. Kinney, & P. J. Pecora. Cleveland, OH: Mandel School of Applied Social Sciences, Case Western Reserve University.

Hodges, V. G. (1993). Assessing for strengths and protective factors in child abuse and neglect: Risk assessment with families of color. Pp. II.1–II.11 in *Multicultural guidelines for assessing family strengths and risk factors in child protective services*, edited by P. Pecora & D. English. Seattle: DCFS Research Office, Washington Risk Assessment Project.

Hodges, V. G., Guterman, N. B., Blythe, B. J., & Bronson, D. E. (1989). Intensive aftercare services for children. *Social Casework 70*(7), 397–404.

Hogan, A. E., Scott, K. G., & Bauer, C. R. (1992). The Adaptive Social Behavior Inventory (ASBI): A new assessment of social competence in high-risk three-year-olds. *Journal of Psychoeducational Assessment 10*, 230–239.

Holahan, C. J., & Moos, R. H. (1986). Personality, coping, and family resources in social resistance: A longitudinal analysis. *Journal of Personality and Social Psychology 51*, 389–395.

Holden, G. W. (1990). Parenthood. Pp. 285–338 in *Handbook of Family Measurement Techniques*, edited by J. Touliatos, B. F. Perlmutter, & M. A. Strauss. Newbury Park, CA: Sage.

Holden, G. W., & Edwards, L. A. (1989). Parental attitudes toward child rearing: Instruments, issues, and implications. *Psychological Bulletin 106*, 29–58.

Holder, W., & Corey, M. (1986). *Child protective services risk management: A decisionmaking handbook.* Charlotte, NC: ACTION for Child Protection.

Holsti, O. R. (1969). *Content analysis for the social sciences and humanities.* Reading, MA: Addison-Wesley.

Hudson, W. H., Acklin, J. D., & Bartosh, J. C. (1980). Assessing discord in family relationships. *Social Work Research and Abstracts 20*, 21–29.

Hudson, W. H. (1982). *The clinical measurement package: A field manual*. Homewood, IL: Dorsey.

Ivey, A. E., Ivey, M. B., & Simek-Downing, L. (1987). *Counseling and psychotherapy: Integrating skills, theory and practice*. Englewood Cliffs, NJ: Prentice-Hall.

Jacobs, F. H. (1988) The five-tiered approach to evaluation: Context and implementation. Pp. 37–68 in *Evaluating family programs*, edited by H. B. Weiss & F. H. Jacobs. Hawthorne, NY: Aldine de Gruyter.

Jayaratne, S., & Levy, R. L. (1979). *Empirical clinical practice*. New York: Columbia University Press.

Jenson, J., & Whittaker, J. K. (1987). Parental involvement in children's residential treatment: From pre-placement to aftercare. *Children and Youth Services Review 9*, 81–100.

Johnston, B., & Marckworth, P. (1992). Quality enhancement: A new approach to family preservation supervisory training and evaluation. Pp. 23–32 in *Empowering families: Papers from the fifth annual conference on family-based services*, edited by J. Zamosky. Riverdale, IA: National Association for Family Based Services.

Joint Commission on Accreditation of Healthcare Organizations. (1991). *An introduction to quality improvement in health care: The transition from QA to CQI*. Oakbrook Terrace, IL: Author.

Jones, M. A. (1985). *A second chance for families five years later: Follow-up of a program to prevent foster care*. New York: Child Welfare League of America.

Jones, M. A. (1991). Measuring outcomes. Pp. 159–186 in *Family preservation services: Research and evaluation*, edited by K. Wells & D. E. Biegel. Newbury Park, CA: Sage.

Jones, M. A., Neuman, R., & Shyne, A. W. (1976). *A second chance for families: Evaluation of a program to reduce foster care*. New York: Child Welfare League of America.

Kagan, J., Powell, D. R., Weissbourd, B., & Zigler, E., eds. (1987). *America's Family Support Programs*. New Haven, CT: Yale University Press.

Kagan, S. L., & Weissbourd, B., eds. (1994). *Putting families first: America's family support movement and the challenge of change*. San Francisco: Jossey-Bass.

Kendall, P. C., & Grove, W. M. (1988). Normative comparisons in therapy outcome. *Behavioral Assessment 10*, 147–158.

Keogh, B. K., Juvonen, J., & Bernheimer, L. (1989). Assessing children's competence: Mothers' and teachers' ratings of competent behavior. *Psychological Assessment 1*(3), 224–229.

Kettner, P. M., Moroney, R. M., & Martin, L. L. (1990). *Designing and managing programs: An effectiveness-based approach*. Newbury Park, CA: Sage.

King, J. A., Morris, L. L., & Fitz-Gibbon, C. T. (1987). *How to assess program implementation*. Newbury Park, CA: Sage.

Kinney, J. M., & Haapala, D. (1984). *First year Homebuilders mental health project report* (mimeograph). Federal Way, WA: Behavioral Sciences Institute.

Kinney, J. M., Haapala, D., & Booth, C. (1991) *Keeping families together: The Homebuilders model*. Hawthorne, NY: Aldine de Gruyter.

Kinney, J. M., Madsen, B., Fleming, T., & Haapala, D. A. (1977). Homebuilders: Keeping families together. *Journal of Consulting and Clinical Psychology 45*(4), 667–673.

Kirk. J., & Miller, M. L. (1986). *Reliability and validity in qualitative research*. Beverly Hills, CA: Sage.

Knapp, M. L. (1972). *Nonverbal communication in human interaction*. New York: Holt, Rinehart, & Winston.

Knapp, P. A., & Deluty, R. H. (1989). Relative effectiveness of two behavioral parent training programs. *Journal of Clinical Child Psychology 18*, 314–322.

Knitzer, J., Allen, M. L., & McGowan, B. (1978). *Children without homes: An examination of public responsibility to children in out-of-home care*. Washington, DC: Children's Defense Fund.

Koeske, G. F., & Koeske, R. D. (1992). Parenting locus of control: Measurement, construct validation, and a proposed conceptual model. *Social Work Research & Abstracts 28*(3), 37–46.

Kohn, M. L. (1973). Social class and parent-child relationships: An interpretation. Pp. 18–30 in *Socialization*, edited by S. Scarr-Salapatek & P. Salapatek,. Columbus, OH: Charles E. Merrill.

Kolevzon, M. S., Green, R. G., Fortune, A. E., & Vosler, N. R. (1988). Evaluating family therapy: Divergent methods, divergent findings. *Journal of Marital and Family Therapy 14*(3), 277–286.

Korbin, J. (1981). *Child abuse and neglect: Cross-cultural perspectives*. Berkeley: University of California Press.

Kraemer, H. C., & Thiemann, S. (1987). *How many subjects?: Statistical power analysis in research*. Newbury Park, CA: Sage.

Krueger, R. A. (1988). *Focus groups: A practical guide for allied research*. Newbury Park, CA: Sage.

Kubosa-Munro, L., & Sladen, A. (1989). Abstract of the Stuart funded in-home family support programs. Mimeograph.

Lahti, J. (1982). A follow-up study of foster children in permanent placements. *Social Service Review 56*, 556–571.

Lambert, M. J., & Bergin, A. E. (1994). The effectiveness of psychotherapy. Pp. 143–189 in *Handbook of Psychotherapy and Behavior Change*, 4th ed., edited by A. E. Bergin & S. L. Garfield. New York: Wiley.

Landsman, M. J., Nelson, K., Allen, M., & Tyler, M. (1992). *Family-based treatment for chronically neglecting families: The self-sufficiency project*. Iowa City, IA: National Resource Center on Family Based Services.

LaRossa, R. (1988). Renewing our faith in qualitative family research. *Journal of Contemporary Ethnography 17*, 243–260.

Larsen, D. L., Attkisson, C. C., Hargreaves, W. A., & Nguyn, T. D. (1979). Assessment of client/patient satisfaction: Development of a general scale. *Evaluation and Program Planning Review 2*, 197–207.

Le Prohn, N. S., & Pecora, P. J. (1994). *The Casey foster parent study: Research summary*. Seattle, WA: The Casey Family Program.

Lefcourt, H. M., Martin, R. A., & Saleh, W. E. (1984). Locus of control and social support: Interactive moderators of stress. *Journal of Personality and Social Psychology 47*, 378–389.

Leininger, M. M. (1985). *Qualitative research methods in nursing*. New York: Grune & Stratton.

Levin, H. M. (1983). *Cost-effectiveness: A primer*. Beverly Hills, CA: Sage.

Levine, C., & Beck, I., eds. (1988). *Programs to strengthen families: A resource guide.* Chicago: Family Resource Coalition.

Levine, R. A. (1964). Treatment in the home. *Social Work 9*(1), 19–28.

Lewis, R. E. (1991). What are the characteristics of intensive family preservation services? Pp. 93–108 in *Families in crisis: The impact of intensive family preservation services*, edited by M. W. Fraser, P. J. Pecora, & D. A. Haapala. Hawthorne, NY: Aldine de Gruyter.

Lewis, R. E., & Fraser, M. (1987). Blending informal and formal helping networks in foster care. *Children and Youth Services Review 9*, 153–169.

Lincoln, Y. S., ed. (1985). *Organizational theory and inquiry: The paradigm revolution.* Beverly Hills, CA: Sage.

Lincoln, Y. S., & Guba, E. G. (1985). *Naturalistic inquiry.* Beverly Hills, CA: Sage.

Lincoln, Y. S., & Guba, E. G. (1986). But is it rigorous?: Trustworthiness and authenticity in naturalistic evaluation. Pp. 73–84 in *Naturalistic evaluation. New Directions for Program Evaluation*, no. 30, edited by D. D. Williams. San Francisco: Jossey-Bass.

Lipsey, M. W. (1990). *Design sensitivity: Statistical power for experimental research.* Newbury Park, CA: Sage.

Littell, J. H., & Fong, E. (1992). Recent findings on selected program outcomes. Pp. 57–75 in *An Interim Report from the Evaluation of the Illinois Family First Placement Prevention Program*, edited by J. R. Schuerman, T. L, Rzepnicki, & J. H. Littell. Chicago: Chapin Hall Center for Children at the University of Chicago.

Littell, J. H., Howard, J., Rzepnicki, T. L., Budde, S., & Pellowe, D., with J. H. Schuerman & P. Johnson. (1992). *Intervention with families in the Illinois family preservation program.* Chicago: Chapin Hall Center for Children.

Littell, J. H., Kim, J. L., Fong, E., & Jones, T. (1992). *Effects of the Illinois Family First Program on selected outcomes for various kinds of cases* (mimeograph). Chicago: The University of Chicago, Chapin Hall Center for Children.

Loeber, R., & Stouthammer-Loeber, M. (1986). Family factors as correlates and predictors of juvenile conduct problems and delinquency. Pp. 29–149 in *Crime and Justice*, Vol. 7, edited by M. Tonry & N. Morris. Chicago: University of Chicago Press.

Lofland, J. (1971). Styles of reporting qualitative field research. *American Sociologist 9*, 101–111.

Loyd, B. H., & Abidin, R. R. (1985). Revision of the Parenting Stress Index. *Journal of Pediatric Psychology 10*, 169–177.

Lucco, A. (1991). Assessment of the school-age child, *Families in Society 72*(7), 394–408.

Lynn, L., Jr., ed. (1978). Pp. 12–22 in *The question of relevance. Knowledge and policy: The uncertain connection.* Washington, DC: National Academy of Sciences.

L'Abate, L. (1994). *Family evaluation: A psychological approach.* Thousand Oaks, CA: Sage.

L'Abate, L., & Bagarozzi, D. A. (1993). *Sourcebook for marriage and family evaluation.* New York: Brunner/Mazel.

Maas, H., & Engler, R. (1959). *Children in need of parents*. New York: Columbia University Press.

Magazino, C. J. (1983). Services to children and families at risk of separation. Pp. 211–254 in *Child welfare: Current dilemmas, future directions*, edited by B. G. McGowan & W. Meezan. Itasca, IL: F. E. Peacock.

Magura, S. (1981). Are services to prevent foster care effective? *Children and Youth Services Review 3*(3), 193–212.

Magura, S., & De Rubeis, R. (1980). *The effectiveness of preventive services for families with abused, neglected and disturbed children: Second year evaluation of Hudson County Project*. Trenton. NJ: Division of Youth and Family Services, Bureau of Research.

Magura, S., & Moses, B. S. (1984). Clients as evaluators in child protective services. *Child Welfare 63*(2), 99–112.

Magura, S., & Moses, B. S. (1986). *Outcome measures for child welfare services: Theory and applications*. Washington, DC: Child Welfare League of America.

Magura, S., Moses, B. S., & Jones, M. A. (1987). *Assessing risk and measuring change in families: The family risk scales*. Washington, DC: Child Welfare League of America.

Maluccio, A. N. (1991). The optimism of policy choices in child welfare. *American Journal of Orthopsychiatry 61*(4), 606–609.

Mannes, M. (1990). Linking family preservation and Indian child welfare: A historical perspective and the contemporary context. In *Family preservation and Indian child welfare*, edited by M. Mannes. Albuquerque, NM: American Indian Law Center.

Maximus, Inc. (1985). *Child welfare statistical fact book. 1985: Substitute care*. Washington, DC: U.S. Department of Health and Human Services, Administration for Children, Youth and Families, Office of Human Development Services.

Maxwell, G. M., & Morris, A. (1985). Deciding about justice for young people in New Zealand: The involvement of families, victims, and culture. In *Child Welfare in Canada: Research and Policy Implications*, edited by J. Hudson & B. Galaway. Toronto: Thompson Educational Publishing.

Maybanks, S., & Bryce, M., eds. (1979). *Home-based services for children and families: Policy, practice, and research*. Springfield, IL: Charles C. Thomas.

McCroskey, J., & Meezan, W. (in press). Family preservation and family functioning. Washington, DC: Child Welfare League of America.

McCroskey, J., & Meezan, W. (1993). Outcomes of home-based services: Effects on family functioning, child behavior and child placement. Paper presented at Empowering Families through Building Our Ecology, Fort Lauderdale, FL.

McCroskey, J., & Nelson, J. (1989). Practice-based research in a family support program: The family connection project example. *Child Welfare 67*, 574–589.

McCroskey, J., Nishimoto, R., & Subramanian, K. (1991) Assessment in family support programs: Initial reliability and validity testing of the family assessment form. *Child Welfare 70*, 19–34.

McCubbin, H. I., & McCubbin, M. A. (1992). Research utilization in social work practice of family treatment. Pp. 149–192 in *Research utilization in the social services: Innovations for practice and administration*, edited by A. J. Grasso and I. Epstein. New York: Haworth Press.

McCune, L., Kalmanson, B., Fleck, M., Glazewski, B., & Sillari, J. (1990). An interdisciplinary model of infant assessment. Pp. 219–245 in *Handbook of early childhood intervention*, edited by S. Meisels & J. Shonkoff. Cambridge, MA: Cambridge University Press.

MacDonald, H. (1994). The ideology of "family preservation." *Public Interest 115*, 45–60.

McDonald & Associates (1990). *Evaluation of AB 1562 In-Home Care Demonstration Project. Volume I: Final Report.* Sacramento, CA: Walter McDonald and Associates.

McGowan, B. G. (1990). Family-based services and public policy: Context and implications. Pp. 65–87 in *Reaching high-risk families: Intensive family preservation in human services*, edited by J. K. Whittaker, J. Kinney, E. M. Tracy, & C. Booth. Hawthorne, NY: Aldine de Gruyter.

McGowan, B. G., & Meezan, W., eds. (1983). *Child welfare: Current dilemmas, future directions.* Itasca Il: F.E. Peacock.

Meezan, W., & McCroskey, J. (1989). An evaluation of the home-based services programs of Children's Bureau of Los Angeles and Hathaway Children's Services: A proposal submitted to the Stuart Foundations, University of Southern California, School of Social Work, Los Angeles.

Meezan, W., & McCroskey, J. (1991). An evaluation of the home-based services programs of Children's Bureau of Los Angeles and Hathaway Children's Services: Third year proposal submitted to the Stuart Foundations, University of Southern California, School of Social Work, Los Angeles.

Meezan, W., & McCroskey, J. (1993). Research on intensive family services. Paper presented to the annual grantees meeting, Children's Bureau, Administration for Children, Youth and Families, Department of Health and Human Services, Washington, D.C.

Meezan, W., & McCroskey, J. (in press). *Family Preservation and Family Functioning.* Washington, DC: Child Welfare League of America.

Meisels A., & Provence, S. (1989). *Screening and assessment: Guidelines for identifying young disabled and developmentally vulnerable children and their families.* Washington, DC: National Center for Clinical Infant Programs.

Meisels, S. (1992). Early intervention: A matter of context. *Zero to Three 12*(3), 1–6.

Milardo, R. M. (1983). Social networks and pair relationships: A review of substantive and measurement issues. *Sociology and Social Research 68*(1), 1–18.

Miles, M. B., & Hubberman, A. M. (1994). *Qualitative data analysis: A sourcebook of new methods.* (2nd ed.). Newbury Park, CA: Sage.

Miller, D. (1991). *Handbook of research design and social measurement*, 5th ed., Part 6. Beverly Hills, CA: Sage.

Miller, J. L., & Whittaker, J. K. (1988). Social services and Social support: Blended programs for families at risk of child maltreatment. *Child Welfare 67*(2), 161–174.

Miller, P. A., & Hauser, R. (1989). Self-report measures of parent-child relationships. Pp. 111–149 in *Family Assessment: A Guide to Methods and Measures*, edited by H. D. Grotevan. New York: Guilford.

Milner, J. S. (1989). Applications of the Child Abuse Potential Inventory. *Journal of Clinical Psychology 45*, 450–454.

Milner, J. S., Charlesworth, J. R., Gold, R. G., Gold, S. R., & Friesen, M. R.

(1988). Convergent validity of the Child Abuse Potential Inventory. *Journal of Clinical Psychology 44*, 281–285.

Milner, J. S., Gold, R. G., Ayoub, C., & Jacewitz, M. M. (1984). Predictive validity of the Child Abuse Potential Inventory. *Journal of Consulting and Clinical Psychology 52*, 879–884.

Minuchin, S. (1974). *Families and family therapy.* Cambridge, MA: Harvard University Press.

Mnookin, R. H. (1973). Foster care: In whose best interest? *Harvard Educational Review 43*(4), 599–638.

Mollerstrom, W. W., Patchner, M. A., & Milner, J. S. (1992). Family functioning and child abuse potential. *Journal of Clinical Psychology 48*, 445–454.

Moos, R. H. (1986). Manual for the Family Environment Scales, 2nd ed. Palo Alto, CA: Consulting Psychologists Press.

Moos, R. H., & Moos, B. S. (1986). *Family environment scale manual*, 2nd ed. Palo Alto, CA: Consulting Psychologists Press.

Moroz, K., & Allen-Meares, P. (1991). Assessing adolescent parents and their infants: Individualized family service planning, *Families in Society 72*(8), 461–468.

Murphy, J. M., Jellinek, M., Quinn, D., Smith, G., Poitrast, F. G., & Goshko, M. (1991). Substance abuse and serious child mistreatment: Prevalence, risk, and outcome in a court sample. *Child Abuse & Neglect 15*(3) 197–211.

Nasuti, J. P., & Pecora, P. J. (1993). Risk assessment scales in child protection: A test of the internal consistency and interrater reliability of one statewide system. *Social Work Research and Abstracts 29*(2), 28–33.

National Alliance for Restructuring Education. (1993). *A framework for improving outcomes for children and families.* Washington, DC: The Harvard Project on Effective Services, The Center for the Study of Social Policy, & The National Center for Education and the Economy.

National Commission on Children. (1991). *Beyond rhetoric: A new American agenda for children and families.* Washington, DC: Author.

Nelson, D. W. (1991). The public policy implications of family preservation. In *Family preservation services research and evaluation* (pp. 207–222), edited by K. Wells and D. E. Piegel. Newbury Park, CA: Sage Publications.

Nelson, J. P. (1984). *An experimental evaluation of a home-based family-centered program model in a public child protection agency.* Unpublished Ph.D. thesis. University of Minnesota, School of Social Work.

Nelson, K. (1990). How do we know that family-based services are effective? *Prevention Report* (Fall), 1–3.

Nelson, K. E. (1994). Family-based services for families and children at risk of out-of-home placement. Pp. 83–108 in *Child Welfare Research Review,* Volume 1, edited by R. Barth, J. Duerr-Berrick, & N. Gilbert. New York: Columbia University Press.

Nelson, K. E., Emlen, A., Landsman, M., & Hutchinson, J. (1988). *Factors contributing to success and failure in family based child welfare services: Final report* (OHDS Grant # 90-CW-0732). Iowa City: National Resource Center on Family Based Services, School of Social Work, University of Iowa.

Nelson, K. E., & Landsman, M. J. (1992). *Alternative models of family preservation: Family-based services in context.* Springfield, IL: Charles C. Thomas.

Nelson, K. E., Landsman, M., Cross, T., & Tyler, M. (1994). *Family functioning of neglectful families: Final report*. Iowa City: National Resource Center on Family Based Services, The University of Iowa.

Nelson, K. E., Landsman, M. J., & Deutelbaum, W. (1990). Three models of family-centered placement prevention services. *Child Welfare 69*(1), 3–21.

Nelson, K. E., Landsman, M., Tyler, M., & Richardson, B. (1995). *Length of services and cost effectiveness of intensive family services: Final report*. Iowa City: University of Iowa, School of Social Work, National Resource Center on Family Based Services.

Nelson, K. E., Saunders, E., & Landsman, M. J. (1990). *Chronic neglect in perspective: A study of chronically neglecting families in a large metropolitan county*. Iowa City: National Resource Center on Family Based Services.

Nuehring, E. M., & Pascone, A. B. (1986). Single subject evaluation: A tool for quality assurance. *Social Work 31*, 359–365.

Nurius, P. S. (1983). Use of time-series analysis in the evaluation of change due to intervention. *Journal of Applied Behavioral Science 19*, 215–228.

Nurius, P. S., & Hudson, W. W. (1993). *Human services practice, evaluation, and computers*. Pacific Grove, CA: Brooks/Cole.

Olds, D. L., Henderson, C. R., Chamberlin, R., & Tatelbaum, R. (1986). Preventing child abuse and neglect: A randomized trial of nurse home visitation. *Pediatrics 78*, 65–78.

Olds, D. L., & Kitzman, H. (1993). Review of research on home visiting for pregnant women and parents of young children. *Future of Children—Home Visiting 3*(3, Winter), 53–92.

Olson, D. H. (1991). Commentary: Three dimensional (3-D) circumplex model and revised scoring of FACES III. *Family Process 30*, 74–79.

Olson, D. H., Russell, C. S., & Sprenkle, D. H. (1983). Circumplex model of marital and family systems: VI. Theoretical update. *Family Process 22*, 69–83.

Omnibus Budget Reconciliation Act (OBRA) (1993). Human Resources and Income Security, Part I of Subchapter C, Sec. 1711. Entitlement Funding for Services Designed to Strengthen and Preserve Families. Washington, DC: U.S. Government Printing Office.

Orlandi M., ed. (1992). *Cultural competence for evaluators*. Rockville, MD: Office for Substance Abuse Prevention.

Orlinsky, D. E., & Howard, K. I. (1986). Process and outcome in psychotherapy. Pp. 311–384 in *Handbook of Psychotherapy and Behavior Change*, 3rd ed., edited by S. L. Garfield & A. E. Bergin. New York: Wiley.

Overton, A. (1953). Serving families who don't want help. *Social Casework 34*, 304–309.

Patterson, G. R. (1985). Beyond technology: The next stage in developing an empirical base for parent training. In *Handbook of Family Psychology and Therapy*, Vol. 2, edited by L. L'Abate. Homewood, IL: Dorsey.

Patterson, G. R., Reid, J. G., Jones, R. R., & Gonger, R. E. (1975). *A social learning approach to family intervention*, Vol 1. Eugene, OR: Castalia.

Patton, M .Q. (1980). *Qualitative evaluation methods*. Beverly Hills, CA: Sage.

Patton, M. Q. (1987). *How to use qualitative methods in evaluation*. Newbury Park, CA: Sage.

Patton, M. Q. (1990). *Qualitative evaluation and research methods*, 2nd ed. Newbury Park, CA: Sage.

Pecora, P. J. (1991a). Family preservation and home-based services: A select literature review. Pp. 23–24 in *Families in crisis: Findings from the family-based intensive treatment project*, edited by M. W. Fraser, P. J. Pecora, & D. A. Haapala. Hawthorne, NY: Aldine de Gruyter.

Pecora, P. J. (1991b). Investigating allegations of child maltreatment: The strengths and limitations of current risk assessment systems. *Child and Youth Services 15*(2), 73–92.

Pecora, P. J. (1991c). Using risk assessment technology and other screening methods for determining the need for child placement in family-based services. Pp. 119–129 in *Empowering families: Papers from the fourth annual conference on family-based services*, edited by V. Pina, D. Haapala, & C. Sudia. Riverdale, IL: National Association for Family Based Services.

Pecora, P. J. (1995). Assessing the impact of family-based services. Pp. 100–112. In *Child Welfare in Canada: Research and Policy Implications*, edited by J. Hudson & B. Galaway. Toronto: Thompson Educational Publishing.

Pecora, P. J., Bartlomé, J. A., Magana, V. L., & Sperry, C. K. (1991a). How consumers view intensive family preservation services. Pp. 225–271 in *Families in crisis: The impact of intensive family preservation services*, edited by M. W. Fraser, P. J. Pecora, & D. A. Haapala. Hawthorne, NY: Aldine de Gruyter.

Pecora, P. J., Delewski, C. H., Booth, C., Haapala, D. A., & Kinney, J. (1985). Home-based family-centered services: The impact of training on worker attitudes. *Child Welfare 64*(5), 529–540.

Pecora, P. J., Fraser, M. W., & Haapala, D. H. (1991b). Intensive, home-based family preservation services: Client outcomes and issues for program design. Pp. 3–32 in *Family preservation services: Research and evaluation*, edited by K. Wells & D. E. Biegel. Newbury Park, CA: Sage.

Pecora, P. J., Fraser, M. W., Bennett, R. B., & Haapala, D. A. (1991). Placement rates of children and families served by the Intensive Family Preservation Services programs. Pp. 149–179 in *Families in crisis: The impact of intensive family preservation services*, edited by M. W. Fraser, P. J. Pecora, & D. A. Haapala. Hawthorne, NY: Aldine de Gruyter.

Pecora, P. J., Haapala, D. A., & Fraser, M. W. (1991c). Comparing intensive family preservation services with other family-based service programs. Pp. 117–142 in *Intensive family preservation services: An instructional sourcebook*, edited by E. M. Tracy, D. A. Haapala, J. Kinney, & P. J. Pecora. Cleveland, OH: Mandel School of Applied Social Sciences, Case Western Reserve University.

Pence, A. (1988). Introduction. Pp. ix–xxix in *Ecological research with families and children, From concepts to methodology*, edited by A. Pence. New York: Teachers College Press.

Pfeiffer, S. I., Soldivera, S., & Norton, J. (1992). *A consumer's guide to mental health outcome measures*. Devon, PA: Devereux Foundation.

Pietrzak, J., Ramler, M., Renner, T., Ford, L., & Gilbert, N. (1990). *Practical program evaluation*. Newbury Park, CA: Sage.

Pine, B. A. (1986). Child welfare reform and the political process. *Social Service Review 60*(3), 339–359.

Plotnick, R. D. (1994) Applying benefit-cost analysis to substance abuse prevention programs. *International Journal of Addictions 29*(3), 339–359.

Poisson, S., DeGangi, G., Nathanson, B., Craft, P., Williams, D., Castellan, J., & West, A. (1991). *Emotional and sensory processing problems: Assessment and treatment approaches for young children and their families.* Rockville, MD: Reginald S. Lourie Center for Infants and Young Children.

Polansky, N. A., Ammons, P. W., & Weathersby, B. L. (1983a). Is there an American standard of child care? *Social Work 28*, 341–346.

Polansky, N., Cabral, R. J., Magura, S., & Phillips, M. H. (1983b). Comparative norms for the Childhood Level of Living Scale. *Journal of Social Service Research 6*(3/4), 45–55.

Polansky, N. A., Chalmers, M. A., Buttenweiser, E., & Williams, D. P. (1978). Assessing adequacy of child caring: An urban scale. *Child Welfare 57*, 439–449.

Polansky, N. A., Chalmers, M. A., Buttenweiser, E., & Williams, D. P. (1982). *Damaged parents: An anatomy of child neglect.* Chicago, IL: University of Chicago Press.

Polansky, N. A., Gaudin, J. M., Jr., & Kilpatrick, A. C. (1992) Family radicals. *Children and Youth Services Review 14*, 19–26

Raven, J., Court, J., & Raven, J. (1977). *Manual for raven's progressive matrices and vocabulary scales.* London: H. K. Lewis.

Reid, W. J. (1993). Fitting the single-system design to family treatment. *Journal of Social Service Research 18*(1/2), 83–99.

Reinharz, S. (1979). *On becoming a social scientist.* San Francisco: Jossey-Bass.

Reynolds, C., & Richmond, B. (1985). *Revised children's manifest anxiety scale manual.* Los Angeles: Western Psychological Services.

Robin, A. L., & Foster, S. L. (1989). *Negotiating parent-adolescent conflict. A behavioral-family systems approach.* New York: Guilford.

Rodwell, M. K. (1990). Person/environment construct: Positivist versus naturalist, dilemma or opportunity for health social work research and practice? *Social Science & Medicine 31*(1), 27–34.

Rohner, R. P. (1986). *The warmth dimension: Foundations of parental acceptance-rejection theory.* Beverly Hills, CA: Sage.

Rohner, R. P., Saavedra, J. M., & Granum, E. O. (1978). Development and validation of the parental acceptance-rejection questionnaire. *JSAS Catalog of Selected Documents in Psychology 8*, 1635.

Rosenberg, S. A., McTate, G. A., & Robinson, C. C. (1982). *Intensive services to families-at-risk project.* Unpublished manuscript, Nebraska Department of Public Welfare, & University of Nebraska Medical Center, Omaha.

Rosengren, K. E., ed. (1981). *Advances in content analysis.* Beverly Hills, CA: Sage.

Rosenthal, J. A., & Glass, G. V. (1984). Comparative impacts of alternatives to adolescent placement. *Journal of Social Science Research 13*, 19–38.

Rossi, P. H. (1992a). Assessing family preservation programs. *Children & Youth Services Review 14*(1/2), 77–97.

Rossi, P. H. (1992b). Some critical comments on current evaluations of programs for the amelioration of persistent poverty. *Focus 14*(1), 22–24. University of Wisconsin–Madison: Institute for Research on Poverty.

Rossi, P. H. (1992c). Strategies for evaluation. *Children and Youth Services Review 14*(1/2), 167–191.

Rossi, P. H., & Freeman, H. E. (1993). *Evaluation: A systematic approach*, 5th ed. Newbury Park, CA: Sage.

Rothman, J. (1980). *Social R & D: Research and development in the human services.* Englewood Cliffs, NJ: Prentice-Hall.

Royse, D. (1992). *Program evaluation: An introduction.* Chicago: Nelson Hall.

Rubin, A., & Babbie, E. (1989). *Research methods for social work.* Belmont, CA: Wadsworth.

Rubin, A., & Babbie, E. (1993). *Research methods for social work,* 2nd ed. Pacific Grove, CA: Brooks/Cole.

Rzepnicki, T. L. (1987). Recidivism of foster children returned to their own homes: A review and new directions for research. *Social Service Review 61*(1), 56–70.

Rzepnicki, T. L., Schuerman, J. R., & Littell, J. (1991). Issues in evaluating intensive family preservation services. Pp. 71–93 in *Intensive family preservation services: An instructional sourcebook,* edited by E. M. Tracy, D. A. Haapala, J. Kinney, & P. J. Pecora. Cleveland, OH: Mandel School of Applied Social Sciences, Case Western Reserve University.

Rzepnicki, T. L., Schuerman, J. R., Littell, J. H., Chak, A., & Lopez, M. (1994). An experimental study of family preservation services: Early findings from a parent study. Pp. 60–82 in *Child Welfare Research Review,* Vol. 1, edited by R. Barth, J. Duerr-Berrick, & N. Gilbert. New York: Columbia University Press.

Saint Lawrence Youth Association (1994). *Community support services—Annual report.* Kingston, Ontario: Author.

Sameroff, A. J., & Chandler, M. (1975). Reproductive risk and the continuum of caretaking casualty. Pp. 187–244 in *Review of child development research,* Vol. 4, edited by F. Horowitz, F. Hetherington, S. Scarr-Salapatek, and G. Siegel. Chicago: University of Chicago Press.

Sameroff, A. J., & Fiese, B. H. (1990). Transactional regulation and early intervention. Pp. 119–149 in *Handbook of early childhood intervention,* edited by S. Meisels & J. Shonkoff. Cambridge, MA: Cambridge University Press.

Sameroff, A., Seifer, R., Baldwin, A., & Baldwin, C. (1993). Stability of intelligence from preschool to adolescence: The influence of social and family risk factors, *Child Development 64,* 80–97.

Sandler, I. N., & Barrera, M., Jr. (1984). Toward a multimethod approach to assessing the effects of social support. *American Journal of Community Psychology 12,* 37–52.

Sarason, S. B (1974). *The psychological sense of community: Prospect for a community psychology.* San Francisco: Jossey-Bass.

Scanlon, J. W., Horst, P., Nay, J. N., Schmidt, R. E., & Waller, J. D. (1977). Evaluability assessment: Avoiding Type III and IV errors. Pp. 264–284 in *Evaluation management: A source book of readings,* edited by G. R. Gilbert & P. J. Conklin. Charlottesville: United States Civil Service Commission.

Scheper-Hughes, N. (1987). The cultural politics of child survival. Pp. 1–29 in *Child survival: Anthropological perspectives on the treatment and maltreatment of children,* edited by N. Scheper-Hughes. Boston: D. Reidel with Kluwer Academic Publishers Group.

Schinke, S. P. (1981). Ethics. Pp. 57–70 in *Social work research and evaluation,* edited by R. M. Grinnell. Itasca, IL: F.E. Peacock.

Schmid, K. D., Rosenthal, S. L., & Brown, E. B. (1988). A comparison of self-report measures of two family dimensions: Control and cohesion. *American Journal of Family Therapy 16*, 73–77.

Schram, D. D., McKelvy, J. G., Schneider, A, L., & Griswold, D. B. (1981). *Preliminary findings: Assessment of the juvenile justice code.* Urban Policy Research and Institute of Policy Analysis (National Institute of Juvenile Justice and Delinquency Prevention, Grant No. 79-JN-AX-0028).

Schuerman, J. R., Mullen, E., Stagner, M., & Johnson, P. (1989). First generation expert systems in social welfare. *Computers in Human Services 4*, 111–122.

Schuerman, J. R., Rzepnicki, T. L., & Littell, J. H. (1991). From Chicago to Little Egypt: Lessons from an evaluation of a family preservation program. Pp. 187–206 in *Family preservation services: Research and evaluation*, edited by K. Wells & D. E. Biegel. Newbury Park, CA: Sage.

Schuerman, J. R., Rzepnicki, T. L., & Littell, J. H. (1994). *Putting families first—An experiment in family preservation.* Hawthorne, NY: Aldine de Gruyter.

Schuerman, J. R., Rzepnicki, T. L., Littell, J. H., & Budde, S. (1992a). Implementation issues. *Children and Youth Services Review 14* (1/2), 193–206.

Schuerman, J. R., Rzepnicki, T. L., Littell, J. H., & Budde, S. (1992b). Preliminary results of the evaluation of the Illinois family first project. Paper Presented at the 6th Annual Empowering Families Conference, National Association of Family-Based Services, Seattle WA.

Schuerman, J. R., Rzepnicki, T. L., Littell, J. H., & Chak, A. (1993). *Evaluation of the Illinois Family First placement prevention program: Final report.* Chicago: Chapin Hall Center for Children, The University of Chicago.

Schwandt, T. S., & Halpern, E. S. (1988). *Linking auditing and metaevaluation: Enhancing quality in applied inquiry.* Beverly Hills, CA: Sage.

Seaberg, J. R. (1988). Child Well-Being Scales: A critique. *Social Work Research and Abstracts 24*(3), 9–15.

Seelig, W. R., Goldman-Hall, B. J., & Jerrell, J. M. (1992). In-home treatment of families with seriously disturbed adolescents in crisis. *Family Process 31*, 135–149.

Seelig, W. R., & Pecora, P. J. (under review). The changing world of services to children and families. In *Leading child welfare agencies into the 21st century* (tentative title). Washington, DC: Child Welfare League of America.

Select Committee on Children, Youth, & Families. (1990). *No place to call home: Discarded children in America.* Washington, DC: Author, U.S. House of Representatives, Report No. 101–395.

Silverman, D. (1985). *Qualitative methodology, & sociology.* Brookfield, VT: Gower.

Simeonsson, R. J., Bailey, D. B., Huntington, G. S., & Brandon, L. (1991). Scaling and attainment of goals in family-focused early intervention. *Community Mental Health Journal 27*, 77–83.

Skrtic, T. M. (1985). Doing naturalistic research into educational organizations. Pp. 185–220 in *Organizational theory and inquiry: The paradigm revolution*, edited by Y. S. Lincoln. Beverly Hills, CA: Sage.

Smith, M. J. (1990). *Program evaluation in human services.* New York: Springer.

Smith, M. L. (1987). Publishing qualitative research. *American Educational Research Journal 24*, 173–183.

Solis, M. L., & Abidin, R. R. (1991). The Spanish version Parenting Stress Index:A psychometric study. *Journal of Clinical Child Psychology 20*, 372–378.

Sonnichsen, S. E. (1994). Family factors related to parental involvement in children's mental health services: Exploratory analysis of the perceptions of parents and families (part of the Ft. Bragg Managed Care Evaluation). Presented at the 6th Annual Research Conference: A System of Care for Children's Mental Health, Tampa FL.

Soulé, C. R., Massarene, K., & Abate, K. (1993). Clinician-support worker teams in family preservation: Are two heads better than one? Pp. 39–55 in *Advancing Family Preservation Practice*, edited by E. S. Morton & R. K. Grigsby. Newbury Park, CA: Sage.

Spaid, W. M., Fraser, M. W., & Lewis, R. E. (1991). Changes in family functioning: Is participation in intensive family preservation services correlated with changes in attitudes or behavior? Pp. 131–148 in *Families in crisis: Findings from the family-based intensive treatment project*, edited by M. W. Fraser, P. J. Pecora, & D. A. Haapala. Hawthorne, NY: Aldine de Gruyter.

Sparrow, S., Balla, D., & Cicchetti, D. (1984). *Vineland adaptive behavior scales.* Circle Pines, MN: American Guidance Service.

Spencer, B. D., & Wiley, D. E. (1981). The sense and nonsense of school effectiveness. *Journal of Policy Analysis and Management 1*(1), 43–52.

Spradley, J. (1979). *The ethnographic interview.* New York: Holt, Rinehart, & Winston.

Spradley, J. (1980). *Participant observation.* New York: Holt, Rinehart, & Winston.

Stack, C. (1974). *All our kin: Strategies for survival in a black community.* New York: Harper & Row.

Stein, T. J. (1985). Projects to prevent out-of-home placement. *Children and Youth Services Review 7*(2/3), 109–122.

Stein, T. J., Gambrill, E. D., & Wiltse, K. T. (1978). Children in foster homes: Achieving continuity of care. New York: Praeger.

Stein, T. J., & Rzepnicki, T. L. (1983). *Decisionmaking at child welfare intake: A handbook for practitioners.* Washington, DC: Child Welfare League of America.

Stein, T. J., & Rzepnicki, T. L. (1984). *Decisionmaking in child welfare services: Intake and planning.* Boston, MA: Kluwer-Nijhoff.

Stewart, D. W., & Shamdasani, P. N. (1990). *Focus groups: Theory and practice.* Newbury Park, CA: Sage.

Stouthamer-Loeber, M., Loeber, R., Farrington, D., Zhang, Q., van Kammen, W., & Maguin, E. (1993). The double edge of protective and risk factors for delinquency: Interrelations and developmental patterns. *Development and Psychopathology 5*, 683–701.

Strauss, A., & Corbin, J. (1990). *Basics of qualitative research: Grounded theory procedures and techniques.* Newbury Park, CA: Sage.

Streeter, C. L., & Franklin, C. (1992). Defining and measuring social support: Guidelines for social work practitioners. *Research on Social Work Practice 2*(1), 81–98.

Szapocznik, J., Kurtines, W. M., Foote, F. H., Perez-Vidal, A., & Hervis, O. (1983). Conjoint versus family therapy: Some evidence for the effectiveness of conducting family therapy through one person. *Journal of Consulting and Clinical Psychology 51*, 889–899.

Szykula, S. A., & Fleischman, M. J. (1985). Reducing out-of-home placements of abused children: Two controlled field studies. *Child Abuse and Neglect 9*(2), 277–283.

Tardy, C. (1985). Social support measurement. *American Journal of Community Psychology 13*(2), 187–202.

Tatara, T. (1992). National child substitute care flow data for FY91 and current trends in the state child substitute care populations. *VCIS Research Notes 7*. Washington, DC: Voluntary Cooperative Information System, American Public Welfare Association.

Tatara, T. (1993). U.S. child substitute care flow data for FY '92 and current trends in the state child substitute care populations. *VCIS Research Notes 9* (August). Washington DC: Voluntary Cooperative Information System, American Public Welfare Association.

Tertinger, D. A., Greene, B. F., & Lutzker, J. R. (1984). Home safety: Development and validation of one component of an ecobehavioral treatment program for abused and neglected children. *Journal of Applied Behavior Analysis 17*, 150–174.

Testa, M. F. (1992). Conditions of risk for substitute care. *Children and Youth Services Review 14*, 27–36.

Theiman, A. A., & Dall, P. W. (1992a). Family preservation services: Problems of measurement and assessment of risk. *Family Relations 41*, 186–191.

Theiman, A. A., & Dall, P. W. (1992b). Iowa's family preservation program: FY 1991 evaluation. *Prevention Report* (Fall), 14–15.

Theiman, A. A., Fuqua, R., & Linnan, K. (1990). *Iowa family preservation three year pilot project: Final evaluation report.* Ames: Iowa State University, Child Welfare Research and Training Project.

Thomasson, E., Berkovitz, T., Minor, S., Cassle, G., McCord, D., & Milner, J. S. (1981). Evaluation of a family life education program for rural "high risk" families. *Journal of Community Psychology 9*, 246–249.

Thompson, M. (1980). *Benefit-cost analysis for program evaluation.* Beverly Hills, CA: Sage.

Thyer, B. (1993). Promoting evaluation research in the field of family preservation. Pp. 131–149 in *Advancing Family Preservation Practice*, edited by E. S. Morton & R. K. Grigsby. Newbury Park, CA: Sage.

Touliatos, J., Perlmutter, B. F., Straus, M. A., eds. (1990). *Handbook of family measurement techniques.* Newbury Park, CA: Sage.

Tracy, E. M. (1990). Identifying social support resources of at-risk families. *Social Work 35*(3), 252–258.

Tracy, E. M. (1991). Defining the target population for intensive family preservation services: Some conceptual issues. Pp. 138–158 in *Family preservation services: Research and evaluation*, edited by K. Wells & D. E. Biegel. Newbury Park, CA: Sage.

Tracy, E. M., & Abell, N. (1994). Social network map: Some further refinements on administration. *Social Work Research 18*(1), 56–60.

Tracy, E. M., Catalano, R. F., Whittaker, J. K., & Fine, D. (1990). Reliability of social network data. *Social Work Research and Abstracts 26*(2), 33–35.

Tracy, E. M., & Whittaker, J. K. (1987). The evidence base for social support interventions in child and family practice: Emerging issues for research and practice. *Child and Youth Services Review 9*, 249–270.

Tracy, E. M., & Whittaker, J. K. (1990). The social network map: Assessing social support in clinical practice. *Families in Society 71*(8), 461–470.

Tracy, E. M., Whittaker, J. K., Pugh, A., Kapp, S., & Overstreet, E. (in press). Network characteristics of primary caregivers in family preservation services: An exploratory study. *Families in Society.*

Truax, C. B., & Carkhuff, R. R. (1967). *Toward effective counseling and psychotherapy*. Chicago: Aldine.

U.S. House of Representatives, Select Committee on Children, Youth, and Families. (1990). *No place to call home: Discarded children in America*. Washington, DC: Author.

University Associates. (1993, March). *Evaluation of Michigan's Families First program: Summary report*. Lansing, MI: Author.

Usher, C. L. (1993). Building capacity for self-evaluation in family and children's services reform efforts. Paper presented at the annual meeting of the American Evaluation Association, Dallas, Texas, November.

Usher, C. L., Gibbs, D. A., & Wildfire, J. B. (forthcoming). A framework for planning, implementing, and evaluating child welfare reforms. *Child Welfare.*

Van Maanen, J., ed. (1983). *Qualitative methodology*. Beverly Hills, CA: Sage.

Van Maanen, J. (1988). *Tales of the field: On writing ethnography*. Chicago: University of Chicago Press.

Van Maanen, J., Dabbs, J. M., & Faulkner, R. R. (1982). *Varieties of qualitative research*. Beverly Hills, CA: Sage.

Vandenberg, J. (1993). Integration of individualized mental health services into the system of care for children and adolescents. *Administration and Policy in Mental Health 20*(4), 247–257.

VanGundy, A. B. (1988). *Techniques of structured problem solving*. New York: Van Nostrand Reinhold.

Visser, K. (1991). Original families first counties versus original non-families first counties. Unpublished memorandum, Michigan Department of Social Services, Lansing.

Vourlekis, B. (1990). The field's evaluation of proposed clinical indicators for social work service in the acute care hospital. *Health and Social Work 15*, 197–206.

Wahler, R. G. (1980). The insular mother: Her problems in parent-child treatment. *Journal of Applied Behavioral Analysis 13*, 207–219.

Wahler, R. G., & Afton, A. D. (1980). Attentional processes in insular and non-insular families. *Child Behavior Therapy 13*, 207–219.

Wahler, R. G., & Dumas, J. E. (1989). Attentional problems in dysfunctional mother-child interactions: An interbehavioral model. *Psychological Bulletin 105*(1), 116–130.

Wahler, R. G., Leske, G., & Rogers, E. S. (1979). The insular family: A deviance support system for oppositional children. Pp. 102–127 in *Behavioral systems for the developmentally disabled: School and family environments*, edited by L. A. Hammerlynck. New York: Brunner/Mazel.

Wald, M. S. (1988). Family preservation: Are we moving too fast? *Public Welfare* 46(3), 33–38, 46.

Wald, M. S., & Woolverton, M. (1990). Risk assessment: The emperors new clothes? *Child Welfare* 69(6), 483–512.

Walton, E. (1991). *The reunification of children with their families: A test of intensive family treatment following out-of-home placement.* Ph.D. thesis. University of Utah Graduate School of Social Work, Salt Lake City.

Walton, E., Fraser, M. W., Lewis, R. E., Pecora, P. J., & Walton, W. K. (1993). In-home family-focused reunification: An experimental study. *Child Welfare* 72(5), 473–487.

Walton, M. (1986). *The Deming management method.* New York: Perigee.

Weaver, S., general ed. (1984). *Testing Children, A reference guide for effective clinical and psychoeducational assessments.* Kansas City, KS: Test Corporation of America.

Webster-Stratton, C., Hollinsworth, T., & Kolpacoff, M. (1989). The long-term effectiveness and clinical significance of three cost-effective training programs for families with conduct-problem children. *Journal of Consulting and Clinical Psychology 57,* 550–553.

Wedeven, T., Pecora, P. J., Hurwitz, M., Howell, R., & Newell, D. (1994). *The Boise Division alumni survey—Summary report.* Seattle, WA: The Casey Family Program Headquarters.

Weisbrod, B. (1981). Benefit-cost analysis of a controlled experiment: Treating the mentally ill. *Journal of Human Resources 16(4),* 523–548.

Weiss, C. H. (1972a). *Evaluation research: Methods of assessing program effectiveness.* Englewood Cliffs NJ: Prentice-Hall.

Weiss, C. H. (1972b). The politicization of evaluation. Pp. 327–338 in *Evaluating action programs: Readings in social action and education,* edited by C. H. Weiss. Boston, MA: Allyn, & Bacon.

Weiss, C. H. (1978). *Improving the linkage between sound research and public policy. Knowledge and policy: The uncertain connection.* Washington, DC: National Academy of Sciences.

Weiss, C. H. (1987). The diffusion of social science research to policymakers: An overview. Pp. 63–85 in *Reforming the law: Impact of child development research,* edited by G. B. Melton. New York: Guilford.

Weiss, H. B. (1993). Home visits: Necessary but not sufficient. *Future of Children—Home Visiting 3*(3, Winter), 113–128.

Weiss, H. B., & Halpern, R. (1990). *Community-based family support and education programs: Something old or something new?* New York: National Center for Children in Poverty.

Weiss, H. B., & Jacobs, F. H., eds. (1988a). *Evaluating family programs.* Hawthorne, NY: Aldine de Gruyter.

Weiss, H. B., & Jacobs, F. H., eds. (1988b). *Home visiting.* Newbury Park, CA: Sage.

Weisz, J. R., Weiss, H. B., & Donenberg, G. R. (1992). The lab versus the clinic: Effects of child and adolescent psychotherapy. *American Psychologist 47(12),* 1578–1585.

Wells, K., & Biegel, D. E., eds. (1991). *Family preservation services: Research and evaluation.* Newbury Park, CA: Sage.

Wells, K., & Freer, R. (1994). Reading between the lines: The case for qualitative research in intensive family preservation services. *Children and Youth Review* 16(5), 323–378.

Wells, K., & Whittington, D. (1993). Child and family functioning after intensive preservation services. *Social Service Review* 67(1), 55–83.

Werner, E. (1990). Protective factors and individual resilience. Pp. 97–116 in *Handbook of early childhood intervention*, edited by S. Meisels & J. Shonkoff. Cambridge, MA: Cambridge University Press.

Werner, E., & Smith, R. (1992). *Overcoming the odds: High risk children from birth to adulthood*. Ithaca, NY: Cornell University Press.

Wheeler, C. E., Reuter, G., Struckman-Johnson, D., & Yuan, Y. T. (1992). *Evaluation of state of Connecticut intensive family preservation services: Phase V annual report*. Report prepared for Division of Family Support and Community Living, Department of Children and Youth Services, Hartford, CT. Sacramento, CA: Walter R. McDonald, & Associates.

White, K. R. (1988). Cost analyses in family support programs. In *Evaluating family programs*, edited by H. B. Weiss & F. H. Jacobs. Hawthorne, NY: Aldine de Gruyter.

Whittaker, J. K. (1991). The leadership challenge in family-based services: Policy, practice, and research. *Families in Society: Journal of Contemporary Human Services* 72(5), 294–300.

Whittaker, J. K., & Garbarino, J. A. (1983). *Social Support Networks*. Hawthorne, NY: Aldine de Gruyter.

Whittaker, J. K., Kinney, J. M., Tracy, E. M., & Booth, C. (1990). *Reaching high-risk families: Intensive family preservation in the human services*. Hawthorne, NY: Aldine de Gruyter.

Whittaker, J. K., & Maluccio, A. N. (1988). Understanding families in trouble in foster and residential care. In *Families in Trouble (Vol. 5): Variant family forms*, edited by F. Cox, C. Chilman, & E. Nunnally. Newbury Park, CA: Sage.

Whittaker, J. K., & Tracy, E. M. (1989). *Social treatment: An introduction to interpersonal helping in social work practice*, 2nd ed. Hawthorne, NY: Aldine de Gruyter.

Whittaker, J. K., Tracy, E. M., & Marckworth, M. (1989). *Family support project: Identifying informal support resources for high risk families*. Seattle: University of Washington, School of Social Work, and Washington, DC: Behavioral Sciences Institute, Federal Way.

Whittaker, J. K., Tracy, E. M., Overstreet, E., Mooradian, J., & Kapp, S. (1994). Intervention design for practice—Enhancing social supports for high risk youth and families. In *Intervention Research: Design and Development for Human Service*, edited by J. Rothman & E. J. Thompson. New York: Haworth.

Whyte, W. F. (1984). *Learning from the field*. Beverly Hills, CA: Sage.

Willems, D. M., & DeRubeis, R. (1981). *The effectiveness of intensive preventive services for families with abused, neglected or disturbed children*. Trenton: Bureau of Research, New Jersey Division of Youth and Family Services.

Wilson, W. J. (1987). *The truly disadvantaged*. Chicago: University of Chicago Press.

Wirt, R., Lachar, D., Klinedinst, J., & Seat, P. (1984). *Multidimensional description of child personality: A manual for the personality inventory for children*, revised ed. Los Angeles: Western Psychological Services.

Wolcott, H. F. (1990). *Writing up qualitative research*. Newbury Park, CA: Sage.

Wolfe, D. A. (1988). Child abuse and neglect. Pp. 627–669 in *Behavioral assessment of childhood disorders*, 2nd ed, edited by E. J. Mash & L. G. Terdal. New York: Guilford.

Wolfe, D. A., Edwards, B., Manion, L., & Koverloa, C. (1988). Early interventions for parents at risk of child abuse and neglect: A preliminary investigation. *Journal of Consulting and Clinical Psychology 56*, 40–47.

Wolfensberger, W. (1972). *Normalization*. New York: National Institute on Mental Retardation.

Wood, S., Barton, K., & Schroeder, C. (1988). In-home treatment of abusive families: Cost and replacement at one year. *Psychotherapy 25*(3), 409–414.

Wooden, K. (1976). *Weeping in the playtime of others*. New York: McGraw-Hill.

Wulczyn, F. H., & Goerge, R. M. (1992). Foster care in New York and Illinois: The challenge of rapid change. *Foster Care 66*(2), 278–294.

Yale Bush Center in Child Development and Social Policy, & Family Resource Coalition. (1983). *Programs to strengthen families: A resource guide*. Chicago: The Family Resource Coalition.

Yuan, Y. T., McDonald, W. R., Wheeler, C. E., Struckman-Johnson, D., & Rivest, M. (1990). *Evaluation of AB 1562 in-home care demonstration projects, Volume 1: Final report*. Sacramento, CA: Walter R. McDonald, & Associates.

Yuan, Y. T., & Struckman-Johnson, D. L. (1991). Placement outcomes for neglected children with prior placements in family preservation programs. Pp. 92–118 in *Family Preservation Services: Research and Evaluation*, edited by K. Wells & D. E. Biegel. Newbury Park, CA: Sage.

Zeller, N. (1987). A rhetoric for naturalistic inquiry. Unpublished Ph.D. dissertation, Indiana University, Bloomington.

Zerbe, R. O., Jr. (1992). *Recommendations for government discount rate policy*. Working paper 92–1, University of Washington, Graduate School of Public Affairs, Seattle.

Zerbe, R. O., Jr., & Dively, D. (1994). *Benefit cost analysis in theory and practice*. Scranton, PA: Harper Collins.

Zigler, E., & Black, K. (1989). America's family support movement: Strengths and limitations. *American Journal or Orthopsychiatry 59*, 6–20.

Zill, N., & Coiro, M. (1992). Assessing the condition of children, *Children and Youth Services Review 14*(1/2) 119–136.

Index

AAPI (Adult-Adolescent Parenting Inventory), 141, 145–147, 148
Abuse cases, 69
Accidental sampling, 53
Adoption Assistance and Child Welfare Act of 1980 (P.L.96-272), 273
Adult-Adolescent Parenting Inventory (AAPI), 141, 145–147, 148
Alternative-treatment control groups, 37
Attachment theory, 142
Attrition, 64, 223–225
Authenticity, 199–200
Availability sampling, 53
Aversive relationships, 160

Bayley Scales of Infant Development, 125
Beavers Family Systems Model of Family Functioning, 101–102
Benefit-cost analysis
  assumptions about services and, 26
  benefit-cost ratios, 189–190
  benefits attributed to program, 182–184
  comparison of benefits and costs, 188–189
  complexities of, 182
  costs of program, estimating, 186–187
  "discount" rate and, 182, 185–186
  distributional effects of program and, 187–188
  importance of, 179
  length of benefits and, 185
  overview, 181
  program efficiency evaluation and, 24, 26, 179, 185–190
  secondary effects of program and, 187
Bivariate analysis, 251

CAP (Child Abuse Potential Inventory), 147–148

Case-overflow comparison group design without random assignment, 39, 49
Case reports, 209–211
Case reviews, 69–73, 175, 238–239
Case screening, 39, 170–171
Case targeting, 7–8
Catalytic authenticity, 199
CD-ROM searches of literature, 27
Certification process, 50
Child Abuse Potential Inventory (CAP), 147–148
Child Behavior Checklist, 238
Child development research, 91–92, 118
Child functioning evaluation
  cautions regarding, 137
  challenges of, 117–118
  child most "at risk" and, 117
  cultural competence and, 126–128
  developmental perspective, 124–125
  different viewpoints and, 128–130
  domains of, 130, 135–136
  ecological perspective, 122–124
  family-based services evaluation and, 117–119, 126, 136–137
  outcomes of family and, 117, 136
  population served, 121–122
  purpose of, 119–120
  research instruments in, 118–119
  resilience, 125–126
  service versus risk, 120–121
  vulnerability, 125–126
Childhood Level of Living Scale (CLL), 107, 142, 148, 149–150
Child protective service (CPS), 169–170
Children's participation in research, 61, 63
Child welfare, 49, 67, 169, 273–274
Child Well-Being Scales (CWBS), 67, 106–107, 109, 142, 148
Class issue, 143, 145

Clinical Measurement Package, 106
Clinical service, 65
Clinical Services Checklist, 74, 78
Clinical significance, 14, 243–244,
    253–254
CLL (Child Level of Living Scale),
    107, 142, 148, 149–150
Cluster samples, 52
Coaching, 160
Coding systems, 70–71, 80
Computer-assisted data analysis tech-
    nologies, 209
Concrete service, 65–66
Confirmability, 198–199
Consent, informed, 60–61
Constructivist evaluation
    assumptions in, 193
    authenticity and, 199–200
    challenges of, 211–213
    confirmability and, 198–199
    credibility and, 197–198
    data analysis in, 206–208
    data collection in, 204–205
    data management in, 205–211
    dependability and, 198
    emergent evaluation method and,
        202–203
    expectations for, 195–200
    principles of, 200–201
    qualitative research questions for,
        194–195
    researcher and, 203–204
    situations for using, 201–202
    transferability and, 199
Control, 33, 41–42, 73
Control group studies, 14 (*See also*
    specific types)
Convenience sampling, 53
Cost-effectiveness analysis
    assumptions about services and,
        26
    program efficiency evaluation and,
        24, 26, 179, 181
    use of, 179
Counseling, 65
CPS (child protective service), 169–
    170
Credibility, 197–198
Cultural competence, 9, 126–128
CWBS (Child Well-Being Scales), 67,
    106–107, 109, 142, 148

Data
    baseline, 30–31
    missing, adjusting, 248
    organizing, 28
    overload, 206
    time series, 20–21
    univariate, 247–249
Data analysis
    case reports in, 209–211
    computer-assisted technologies,
        209
    in constructivist evaluation, 206–
        208
    data management and, 206–208
    error reduction in, 247–254
    family-focused measures and, 250
    in implementation evaluation, 227–
        229
    missing data in, adjusting, 248
    outliers in, 248–249
    scales/indices in, constructing,
        250–251
    significance of findings in, 252–254
    statistical analyses in, conducting,
        251–252
    transformations in, 249
    univariate data and, 247–249
    variables in, recoding, 249–250
Data analysis plan
    data coding/entry protocol, devel-
        oping, 247
    importance of, 241
    measures, specifying, 242–243
    overview, 242
    raw data examination/correction
        protocol, devising, 246–247
    significance, defining, 243–244
    statistical analysis, making plan
        for, 244–246
Data collection
    in constructivist evaluation, 204–
        205
    in defining problem, 27
    in implementation evaluation, 225–
        226
    interview, 204
    observation, 205
    participant-observation, 204–205
    on program, 94
    in research proposal, sample, 237–
        239

Data management in constructive evaluation, 205–211
DCS (Department of Children's Services), 217, 218–226
"Decay" rate, 185
Department of Children's Services (DCS), 217, 218–226
Dependability, 198
Descriptive analysis, 251
Design (*See* Evaluation design; Research design)
Directive guidance, 160
"Discount" rate, 182, 185–186
Dismantling design, 39–40
Disproportional stratified samples, 52
"Double recording," 219

Ecological model of parenting, 139
Educative authenticity, 199
Effect sizes, 14, 56–57, 237, 252–253
Efficiency assessment, 24, 26
Emergent evaluation method, 202–203
Empathetic friendship, 160
Enacted social support, 154, 158
Ethnicity issue, 143, 145
Evaluation design
    elements of, 24
    group, 31–33, 35–41
    single-system, 30–32
Evaluation domains, 18–20
Evaluation questions, 24–26
Experiment, 37
Experimental design studies, 73–74

FACES (Family Adaptability and Cohesion Evaluation Scales), 99–101, 102, 105–106
Factor analysis, 151, 160
Factorial design, 39–40, 74
FAD (Family Assessment Device), 104–106
FAF (Family Assessment Form), 110–111, 113, 148, 218, 219–220, 237–238
Fairness, 199
Family Adaptability and Cohesion Evaluation Scales (FACES), 99–101, 102, 105–106
Family Assessment Device (FAD), 104–106

Family Assessment Form (FAF), 110–111, 113, 148, 218, 219–220, 237–238
Family-Based Attitudes Scale, 85
Family-Based Intensive Treatment (FIT) Project, 74, 78
Family-based services (FBS) evaluation
    challenges of, 9–11, 14–15
    child functioning evaluation and, 117–119, 126, 136–137
    for clinical purposes, 94–96, 119
    differences of other program evaluations and, 23
    early, 1, 91
    for evaluation purposes, 96–98, 119
    family functioning evaluation and, 91–92
    government requirement for, 1
    implementation evaluation and, 215–216
    models and, 9–11
    multipurpose modular assessment instrument and, 114
    parent functioning evaluation and, 139, 141
    problems in, 1, 7
    program staff involvement in, 95
    promise of, 15–16
    purpose of, 11
    questions facing, 91
    real-world settings and, 215
    research design in, 11, 14
    sampling children/families and, 45
    scope of, 11
    social policy evaluation and, 277–278
    systems perspective for, 15
    variety of, 95–96
Family Beliefs Inventory, 141
Family Environment Scale (FES), 102–104, 105–106, 146, 147, 148, 156
Family-focused measures, 250
Family functioning evaluation
    benefits of, 113–114
    changes in family and, measuring, 30, 93–94, 150
    for clinical purposes, 94–96, 119
    domains of, 98–99
    for evaluation purposes, 96–98, 119

family-based services evaluation and, 91–92
outcome measurement and, 92–94
research instruments in, 99–107, 109–111, 113, 114
stability and, 30
Family Relationship Index (FRI), 155–156
Family Risk Scales, 109, 142, 148
Family Support Scale, 161
Family Systems Change Scale (FSCS), 67, 109
Family Therapist Rating Scale, 85
FBS (*See* Family-based services evaluation)
FES (Family Environment Scale), 102–104, 105–106, 146, 147, 148, 156
Field journals, 205
FIT (Family-Based Intensive Treatment) Project), 74, 78
Follow-up, 97–98, 220
Foster care, 17, 185
FRI (Family Relationship Index), 155–156
FSCS (Family Systems Change Scale), 67, 109

Gantt charting, 227
G.A.S. (Goal Attainment Scaling), 110
Gender issue, 143, 145
Goal Attainment Scaling (G.A.S.), 110
Group designs
case-overflow comparison group design without random assignment, 39, 49
common, 32–33
dismantling design, 39–40
elements of, essential, 32
factorial design, 39–40
matched-pairs comparison group design, 37–39
posttest-only control group design with random assignment, 36–37
pretest-posttest control group design with random assignment, 35–36
pretest-posttest single-group design, 33
selecting, guidelines for, 40–41

single-system designs versus, 31–32
time-series single-group design, 33, 35

HAPI (Home Accident Prevention Inventory), 142
Hazard rates, 173–174
Head Start programs, 91, 146
Home Accident Prevention Inventory (HAPI), 142
HOMEBUILDERS program, 74, 78, 81, 85, 172
HOME (Home Observation for Measurement of the Environment), 142
Home Observation for Measurement of the Environment (HOME), 142
Human subjects committee, 59–60
Human subjects (*See* Protections in research process)

IFR (Index of Family Relations), 106
IFS (intensive family services) programs, 73–74, 101, 102
Implementation
barriers to successful, 220
challenges of, 9–11, 14–15
conditions necessary for successful, 232–234
consistency and, 8–9
Implementation evaluation
attrition in, sample, 223–225
data analysis in, 227–229
data collection in, 225–226
family-based services evaluation and, 215–216
goals/objectives, agreement on, 216–219
impact of, 229–232
measurement choices and, 219–220
project management in, 227
research design in, 220–222
risk of imminent placement and, 216
sampling criteria in, 222–223
Index of Family Relations (IFR), 106
Information systems, data from, 239
Informed consent, 60–61
Institutional review board, 59–60, 63

Intensive family services (IFS) programs, 73–74, 101, 102
Interrupted time-series design, 33, 35
Interval characteristics, 245
Intervention evaluation
  case reviews, 69–73
  experimental design studies, 73–74
  measuring intervention and, problem of, 65
  research instruments in, 74, 78, 80
  single-case studies, 66–69
Interventions Checklist, 74
Interview, 204, 237–238
Inventory of Socially Supportive Behaviors (ISSB), 158
IQ scores, 91, 118–119
ISSB (Inventory of Socially Supportive Behaviors), 158

Literature, searching, 27

McMaster Model of Family Functioning, 104–105
Matched-pairs comparison group design, 37–39
Maternal Social Support Index, 160–161
Member checking, 198, 203
Milan model of systemic family therapy, 110
Milardo Social Support Inventory (SSI), 158, 160
Model drift, 8, 29
MST (multisystemic treatment), 100–101
Multisystemic treatment (MST), 100–101
Multivariate analysis, 251–252

Needs assessment, 24
Neglect cases, 71–72
Nominal characteristics, 245
Nonprobability sampling methods, 53–54, 64
No-treatment control groups, 37
Nurturing Programs, 146–147

Observation, 205
Ontological authenticity, 199
Ordinal characteristics, 245
Outcome measurement, 92–94

Outcome studies, 25–26
Outliers, 248–249
Overinclusion, 46

Parental Acceptance-Rejection Questionnaire, 152
Parental Disposition and Household Adequacy scales, 109
Parental Disposition Subscale of CWBS, 148–149
Parental Locus of Control Scale, 152
Parental permission, 61, 63
Parent functioning evaluation
  attachment theory and, 142
  class issue in, 143, 145
  description of methods, 143
  domains of, 141–143
  ecological model of parenting and, 139
  ethnicity issue in, 143, 145
  family-based services evaluation and, 139, 141
  family outcomes and, 139
  gender issue in, 143, 145
  parental functioning and, 139, 141
  research instruments in, 141–142, 145–152
  social learning theory and, 141
  social support and, 152–155
Parenting Stress Index (PSI), 148, 151–152
Parent Opinion Questionnaire, 141
Participant-observation, 204–205
Peer debriefing, 197–198
Perceived social support, 154, 155
Permission, parental, 61, 63
Personal logs, 206
Personal Network Matrix, 161
P-I-E-E-E-S mnemonic, 124–125
P.L. 96-272 (Adoption Assistance and Child Welfare Act of 1980, 273
Placement (See also Risk of imminent placement)
  case targeting and, 7–8
  days in, 173
  definitions of, 164–167
  environmental influences on, 167–170
  hazard rates and, 173–174
  organizational influences on, 167–170

quality of, 171
rates, 163–164, 167–170, 174–177
as "service failure" or success, 166–167
stability of, 171
time to, 173–174
Placement prevention
benefits of placement and, 163
placement rates and, 163–164, 167–170, 174–177
as restrictive measure, 171–173
screening cases for family-based services and, 170–171
Policy evaluation (*See* Social policy evaluation)
Posttest-only control group design with random assignment, 36–37
Power analysis, 14, 57, 237
PRAG (Professional Review Action Group), 175
Pretest-posttest control group design with random assignment, 35–36
Pretest-posttest single-group design, 33
"Principles of Policy-Research Connections," 265–266
Probability sampling methods, 32, 50–53, 64
Problem, defining, 27–29
Process questions, 25
Professional Review Action Group (PRAG), 175
Program
accountability, 217
aims of, traditional, 93
benefits attributed to, 182–184
components of, 18–20
consistency of, 8–9
costs, estimating, 186–187
criteria, for inclusion in family-based services, 47–48
data collection on, 94
distribution of benefits of, 187–188
impact, 18–19
length of benefit of, 185
management/structure, 18
model, 9–11
operations, 18
secondary effects of, 187
Program drift, 29

Program efficiency evaluation
benefit-cost analysis, 24, 26, 179, 185–190
cost-effective analysis, 24, 26, 179, 181
Program evaluation
control and, 41–42
designing, 24
differences of other program evaluations and, 23
domains of family functioning evaluation and, 98–99
group designs, 31–33, 35–41
multipurpose modular assessment instrument and, 114
qualitative, 26–29
quantitative, 26–29
questions for, 24–26
service model and, 29–30
single-system designs, 30–32
variation and, 42
Proportional stratified sampling, 52
Protections in research process
for children, 61, 63
human subjects committee, 59–60
informed consent, 60–61
institutional review board, 59–60, 63
need for, 57, 64
questions regarding, 59
research committee, 59–60
responsibilities in, 57, 59
PSI (Parenting Stress Index), 148, 151–152
Public policy context, 18
Purposive sampling, 54

QI (quality improvement), 81, 84
Qualitative evaluation, 26
assumptions on, underlying, 192–194
challenges of, 211–213
questions appropriate for constructivist evaluation and, 194–195
rationale for, 191–192
Quality assurance, 81, 84
Quality Enhancement Systems and Training Program (QUEST), 81
Quality improvement (QI), 81, 84
Quantitative evaluation, 26
Quasi-experiment, 37

QUEST (Quality Enhancement Systems and Training Program), 81
Quota sampling, 54

Random assignment, 32, 35–39, 73, 220–222, 237
Randomized control groups, 49
Random sampling, 32
Ratio, 245
Recoding variables, 249–250
Reconstructed/retrospective baseline single-system designs, 30–31
Referrals, 39, 220–221
Reflexive control, 33
"Relaxation" criterion, 50
Reports (*See* Case reports; Research reports)
Research committee, 59–60
Research design, 11, 14, 220–222
Research instruments (*See also* specific names)
  in child functioning evaluation, 118–119
  in family functioning evaluation, 99–107, 109–111, 113, 114
  in intervention evaluation, 74, 78, 80
  in parent functioning evaluation, 141–142, 145–152
  researcher as, 203–204
  in research proposal, sample, 237
  in service evaluation, 74, 78, 80
  in social support evaluation, 155–158, 160–161
  standardized, 93, 118
  in worker performance evaluation, 85
Research proposal, sample
  data collection, 237–239
  overview, 235
  research instruments, 237
  research methodology, 236
  research questions, 235–236
  sampling, 236–237
Research reports
  Discussion Section of, 257
  Executive Summary section of, 256
  Introduction Section of, 256–257
  Methods Section of, 257
  overview, 254–257
  Results Section of, 257

style of, 257
Title Section of, 256
writing skill and, 254
Resilience of child, 125–126
Risk assessment, 120–121
Risk of imminent placement
  case targeting and, 7
  criteria of, need for, 64, 171
  implementation evaluation and, 216
  question of, 48–50
  sampling criteria and, 222
  service evaluation and, 171–172
  single-system designs and, 30

Sample size, 14, 54–57, 64, 237
Sampling children/families
  decisions about, 45–46
  family-based services evaluation and, 45
  nonprobability sampling methods and, 53–54, 64
  probability sampling methods and, 32, 50–53, 64
  sample size and, 54–57, 64
  targeting family-based services and, 46–50, 64
Sampling error, 55–56, 64
Scales/indices, constructing, 250–251
Screening cases, 39, 170–171
Self-Report Family Inventory (SFI), 101–102, 105–106
Sensitivity, 46
Service
  benefit-cost analysis and assumptions about, 26
  checklists, 74, 78, 80
  clinical, 65
  components of, 18–20
  concrete, 65–66
  consistency of, 8–9, 29–30
  control and, 41–42
  cost-effectiveness analysis and assumptions about, 26
  cultural competence and, 9
  model, 29–30
  standardization among different, lack of, 89
  targeting, 7–8
  variation and, 42

Service evaluation
  challenges of, 85, 89
  quality assurance/improvement in,
    81, 84
  research instruments in, 74, 78, 80
  risk of imminent placement and,
    171–172
  worker performance evaluation
    and, 84–85
SFI (Self-Report Family Inventory),
  101–102, 105–106
Shadow price, 179, 184
Signed-cause single-system designs, 31
Significance, 14, 243–244, 252–254,
  269–270
Simple random samples, 51
Single-case studies, 66–69
Single-system designs (SSD), 30–32
Single-system time-series design, 31
SNM (Social Network Map), 157
Snowball sampling, 54
Social climate, 102
Social embeddedness, 154, 157
Social learning theory, 141
Social Network Map (SNM), 157
Social policy evaluation
  conceptual framework, 261–263
  critical tests and, 267
  definition of social policy and, 264–
    265
  expectations of program evaluation
    and, 263
  family-based services evaluation
    and, 277–278
  issues in, 263–265
  legislation and, 273–274
  limitations in approaches to, 266–
    269
  politics and, 268
  "Principles of Policy-Research Con-
    nections" and, 265–266
  recommendations of, 270–271
  significance of findings of, 269–270
  time frames/lags and, 271–273
  value judgments and, 268

Social support evaluation
  forms of social support and, 154
  importance of, 162
  parenting and, 152–155
  research instruments in, 155–158,
    160–161
  selecting aspects in, 154–155
Specificity, 46
SSD (single-system designs), 30–32
SSI (Milardo Social Support Inventory), 158, 160
Statistical analysis, 244–246, 251–252
Statistical significance, 14, 243
Systematic sampling, 51–52
Systems evaluation
  changes in, measuring, 20–21
  components of service/program
    and, 17, 21
  foster care and, 17
  outcome studies and, 26
  policy context of, 18–20
  program context of, 18–20
Systems perspective, 15

Tactical authenticity, 200
Targeting, 7–8, 46–50, 64
Teacher interview, data from, 239
Time-recording systems, 80
Time-series single-group design, 33,
  35
Time-to-placement, 173–174
Transactional model, 118
Transferability, 199
Transformation, 249

Underinclusion, 46–47
Univariate analysis, 247–249

Variables, recoding, 249–250
Variation, 42
Vulnerability of child, 125–126

Worker performance evaluation, 84–
  85, 238